Understanding Knowledge

Michael Huemer

Text copyright ©2022 Michael Huemer, all rights reserved.
Cover photo: Washington Square Park, New York, ©2019 Michael Huemer, CC BY 4.0. Back cover photo: Barn Owl by Sheribeari, CC BY-ND 2.0.

ISBN: 979-8359316699

Brief Contents

Preface	xv
PART I: GENERAL ISSUES ABOUT KNOWLEDGE & JUSTIFICATION	1
1. Introduction	2
2. What Is Knowledge?	11
3. More Logical and Semantic Debates	38
4. The Structure of Knowledge	56
5. Grounds of Foundational Justification	81
6. Meta-Knowledge	101
7. Taxonomy and Paradigms of Knowledge	116
PART II: SOURCES OF KNOWLEDGE	130
8. Perception & Skepticism	131
9. Theories of Perception	150
10. Pure Reason	168
11. Memory	193
12. Induction	201
13. Testimony	239
PART III: AREAS OF KNOWLEDGE	250
14. Scientific Knowledge	251
15. Moral Knowledge	274
16. Religious Knowledge	303
PART IV: APPLIED EPISTEMOLOGY	323
17. Irrationality	324
18. Critical Thinking and Trust in Experts	341
19. Peer Disagreement	357
Afterword	382
Glossary	384

Full Contents

Preface	xv
Why Read This Book?	xv
About the Author	xv
My Approach in Writing This	xvi
Vocabulary Words	xvii
Recycled Philosophy?	xvii
Acknowledgements	xvii
PART I: GENERAL ISSUES ABOUT KNOWLEDGE & JUSTIFICATION	1
1. Introduction	2
1.1. What Is Epistemology?	2
1.2. Why Is Epistemology the King of All Fields?	2
1.2.1. Moore's Paradox	2
1.2.2. Epistemological Problems	4
1.3. Conceptual Background	5
1.3.1. Propositions	5
1.3.2. The Forms of Propositions	6
1.3.3. Arguments	7
1.4. Some Symbols	9
1.5. Conclusion	9
2. What Is Knowledge?	11
2.1. The Project of Analyzing "Knowledge"	11
2.2. The Traditional Analysis	12
2.3. About "Justification"	14
2.3.1. The General Concept of Justification	14
2.3.2. Epistemic vs. Non-Epistemic Reasons	14
2.3.3. Doxastic vs. Propositional Justification	15
2.4. Gettier's Refutation	16
2.5. Seven More Failed Analyses	17
2.5.1. No False Lemmas	17
2.5.2. Reliabilism	19
2.5.3. Proper Function	20
2.5.4. Sensitivity & Tracking	21
2.5.5. Safety	23
2.5.6. Relevant Alternatives	24

2.5.7. Defeasibility	26
2.6. Lessons from the Failure of Analysis	30
2.6.1. The Failure of Analysis	30
2.6.2. A Lockean Theory of Concepts	31
2.6.3. A Wittgensteinian View of Concepts	32
2.6.4. Lessons for Philosophy	35
2.7. Conclusion	36
3. More Logical and Semantic Debates	38
3.1. Contextualism	38
3.1.1. Motivating Contextualism	38
3.1.2. Clarifications	40
3.1.3. Assessment	41
3.2. The Closure Principle	43
3.2.1. The Closure Principle	43
3.2.2. Analyses of "Knowledge" that Reject Closure	44
3.2.3. A Counter-example to Closure?	45
3.2.4. Of Zebras and Mules	46
3.2.5. What About Justification?	48
3.3. Internalism vs. Externalism	49
3.3.1. Defining Internalism & Externalism	49
3.3.2. Why Externalism?	51
3.3.3. Why Internalism?	52
3.3.4. A Compromise Position	54
3.4. Conclusion	54
4. The Structure of Knowledge	56
4.1. Four Knowledge Structures	56
4.2. Infinitism	59
4.2.1. The Infinitist Theory of Justification	59
4.2.2. How to Continue the Series?	59
4.2.3. The Finite Mind Objection	60
4.2.4. Potential vs. Actual Reasons	61
4.3. Coherentism	61
4.3.1. The Coherence Theory of Justification	61
4.3.2. The Alternate-Coherent-Systems Objection	63
4.3.3. Coherence Justification Requires Foundations	64
4.4. Skepticism	67
4.4.1. The Skeptical View	67
4.4.2. Self-Refutation	69
4.4.3. The Moorean Response	70
4.5. Foundationalism	72

4.5.1. The Foundationalist Conception of Justification	72
4.5.2. Why Believe Foundationalism?	74
4.5.3. The Arbitrariness Objection	75
4.5.4. The Meta-Justification Objection	76
4.6. Conclusion	79
5. Grounds of Foundational Justification	81
5.1. The Acquaintance Theory	81
5.1.1. The Theory	81
5.1.2. The Sellarsian Dilemma	83
5.1.3. Explaining Justified Errors	85
5.2. Phenomenal Conservatism	88
5.2.1. The Phenomenal Conservative View	88
5.2.2. PC Is a Good Theory	89
5.2.3. The Self-Defeat Argument	90
5.2.4. Crazy Appearances	91
5.2.5. Tainted Sources	93
5.2.6. The Problem of Easy Knowledge	95
5.3. Qualified Appearance Theories	97
5.4. Foundherentism	98
5.5. Conclusion	99
6. Meta-Knowledge	101
6.1. The KK Thesis	101
6.2. An Argument for Global Justification Skepticism	101
6.2.1. The Skeptic's Argument	101
6.2.2. Don't Be an Annoying Skeptic	103
6.2.3. The Skeptic's False Premise	104
6.2.4. Natural Faculties vs. the 8-Ball	105
6.3. How to Know You Are Reliable	106
6.3.1. The Meta-Coherence Norm	106
6.3.2. Epistemic Circularity	108
6.3.3. Track Record Arguments	109
6.3.4. What's Wrong with Track Record Arguments	110
6.3.5. Benign Epistemically Circular Arguments	111
6.4. Justified Theories of Justification	112
6.5. Conclusion	114
7. Taxonomy and Paradigms of Knowledge	116
7.1. A Traditional Taxonomy	116
7.1.1. Inferential vs. Non-inferential Knowledge	116
7.1.2. Empirical vs. A Priori Knowledge	117
7.1.3. Four Cognitive Faculties	118

7.2. Traditional Paradigms of Knowledge	118
7.3. Some Hard-to-Classify Cases	120
7.3.1. Recognition	120
7.3.2. Categorization	121
7.3.3. Judgment	122
7.3.4. What Makes a Good Taxonomy?	123
7.4. Noticing, Judging, and Calculating	125
7.5. Top-Down Versus Bottom-Up Cognition	126
7.6. Conclusion	128

PART II: SOURCES OF KNOWLEDGE — 130

8. Perception & Skepticism — 131

8.1. The Foundation of External-World Knowledge	131
8.2. Skeptical Scenarios	132
8.2.1. The Dream Argument	132
8.2.2. The Brain-in-a-Vat Argument	134
8.2.3. The Deceiving God Argument	135
8.2.4. Certainty, Justification, and Craziness	135
8.3. Responses to Skepticism	136
8.3.1. The Relevant Alternatives Response	136
8.3.2. The Contextualist Response	138
8.3.3. Semantic Externalism	139
8.3.4. BIVH Is a Bad Theory	143
8.3.5. Direct Realism	146
8.4. Conclusion	148

9. Theories of Perception — 150

9.1. Four Theories About Perception & Perceptual Knowledge	150
9.2. Explaining Direct Realism	152
9.2.1. Awareness	152
9.2.2. Direct vs. Indirect Awareness	152
9.2.3. How Perception Is Direct Awareness	153
9.2.4. A More Extreme Direct Realism: Disjunctivism	154
9.3. Objections to Direct Realism	155
9.3.1. Perspectival Variation	155
9.3.2. Illusion	157
9.3.3. Hallucination, Part 1: Against Disjunctivism	158
9.3.4. Hallucination, Part 2: For Awareness of Mental Objects	159
9.3.5. Hallucination, Part 3: About Foundational Justification	160
9.3.6. The Time Gap	161
9.3.7. Double Vision	161
9.4. Objections to Indirect Realism	162

9.4.1. Spatial Properties	162
9.4.2. Indeterminacy	163
9.4.3. The Conditions for Awareness	164
9.4.4. The Knowledge Problem	165
9.5. Conclusion	166
10. Pure Reason	168
10.1. Analytic A Priori Knowledge	168
10.1.1. A Priori vs. Empirical	168
10.1.2. Analytic vs. Synthetic	168
10.2. Traditional Empiricism	170
10.2.1. The Empiricist Creed	170
10.2.2. The Argument for Empiricism	170
10.2.3. Is the Empiricist's Argument Self-Defeating?	171
10.2.4. Is Empiricism Self-Defeating in General?	171
10.3. (Il)logical Positivism	172
10.3.1. The Positivist Creed	172
10.3.2. Motivations for Positivism	174
10.3.3. Objections	176
10.4. Quine's Radical Empiricism	177
10.4.1. Quine's View	177
10.4.2. Objections	178
10.5. Rationalism	179
10.5.1. The Rationalist Creed	179
10.5.2. Examples of Synthetic A Priori Knowledge	180
10.5.3. The Case for A Prioricity	181
10.5.4. But How Can That Be??	182
10.6. Kantianism	184
10.6.1. The Two-Page Summary	184
10.6.2. The Glasses Analogy	187
10.6.3. Primary and Secondary Qualities	187
10.6.4. Another Analogy	189
10.6.5. Weird Things about Kant	189
10.6.6. Objections	190
10.7. Conclusion	191
11. Memory	193
11.1. The Puzzle of Forgotten Evidence	193
11.2. Four Theories of Memory Justification	194
11.2.1. The Inferential Theory	194
11.2.2. The Foundational Theory	195
11.2.3. The Preservation Theory	196

11.2.4. The Dualistic Theory	197
11.3 Conclusion	199
12. Induction	**201**
12.1. The Problem of Induction	201
12.1.1. Background Concepts	201
12.1.2. Hume's Skepticism	202
12.1.3. Comment	204
12.2. Weak Responses	205
12.2.1. "Hume Misuses 'Reason'"	205
12.2.2. "The Skeptic Begs the Question"	206
12.2.3. "Induction Is Basic"	206
12.2.4. The Pragmatic Defense	207
12.2.5. Appeal to the Synthetic A Priori	209
12.3. Basics of Probability	210
12.3.1. A Smart Idea	210
12.3.2. The Laws of Probability	210
12.3.3. What Is Probability?	212
12.4. Proportional Syllogism and the Law of Large Numbers	215
12.4.1. Background: Proportional Syllogism	215
12.4.2. Background: Populations, Samples, and Representativeness	215
12.4.3. The Argument for Induction	216
12.4.4. The Key Premise	217
12.5. Subjective Bayesianism	218
12.5.1. The Subjective Bayesian Creed	218
12.5.2. Why Obey Probability?	219
12.5.3. Conditionalization	220
12.5.4. Bayes' Theorem	221
12.5.5. Subjectivist Induction	223
12.5.6. Objection	224
12.6. Objective Bayesianism	225
12.6.1. The Objective Bayesian Creed	225
12.6.2. Wherefore Indifference?	226
12.6.3. Inconsistencies in the PI	227
12.6.4. Defenses of the PI	228
12.6.5. The Problem of the PI Is the Problem of Induction	229
12.7. Inference to the Best Explanation	230
12.7.1. The IBE Theory of Induction	230
12.7.2. Alternative Explanations	232
12.8. The Grue Puzzle	234
12.8.1. Goodman's New Color	234

12.8.2. The Puzzle	235
12.8.3. What's Wrong with Grue?	236
12.9. Conclusion	237
13. Testimony	**239**
13.1. The Centrality of Testimony	239
13.2. The Inductive Account	240
13.3. The Default of Credulity	241
13.3.1. Natural Inclination to Believe	242
13.3.2. Intelligible Presentation as True	243
13.3.3. The Principle of Charity in Interpretation	244
13.4. Coherence	246
13.5. Conclusion	248
PART III: AREAS OF KNOWLEDGE	**250**
14. Scientific Knowledge	**251**
14.1. Confirmation Puzzles	251
14.1.1. The Idea of Confirmation Theory	251
14.1.2. Does Everything Confirm Everything?	251
14.1.3. The Ravens Paradox	252
14.1.4. Bayesian Analysis	253
14.2. Falsifiability	254
14.2.1. The Idea of Falsificationism	254
14.2.2. The Origin of Falsificationism	254
14.2.3. A Bayesian Account of the Virtue of Falsifiability	255
14.3. Simplicity	256
14.3.1. Occam's Razor and the Burden of Proof	256
14.3.2. Why Accept Occam's Razor?	257
14.3.3. What Shouldn't We Multiply?	259
14.3.4. Seven Weak Defenses of Simplicity	259
14.3.5. The Likelihood Account	263
14.3.6. Philosophical Applications	264
14.4. Realism & Skepticism	264
14.4.1. The Underdetermination Problem	265
14.4.2. Scientific Anti-Realism	267
14.4.3. A Realist Interpretation	267
14.4.4. The Skeptical Induction	269
14.5. Why Isn't Everyone a Bayesian?	271
14.5.1. The Problem of Old Evidence	271
14.5.2. The Probability of the Laws	271
14.5.3. The Problem of Priors	272
14.6. Conclusion	273

15. Moral Knowledge — 274
15.1. Background — 274
- 15.1.1. Evaluation vs. Description — 274
- 15.1.2. Species of Evaluation — 274
- 15.1.3. Questions About Moral Knowledge — 275
15.2. Skepticism — 276
- 15.2.1. Expressivism — 276
- 15.2.2. Nihilism — 277
- 15.2.3. Mere Skepticism — 277
15.3. The Is/Ought Gap — 278
- 15.3.1. The Traditional Doctrine — 278
- 15.3.2. The Open Question Argument — 279
- 15.3.3. Cute Philosopher Tricks — 279
15.4. Moral Explanations — 281
- 15.4.1. The Basic Explanationist Idea — 281
- 15.4.2. Objection #1: Presupposing Values — 282
- 15.4.3. Objection #2: Redundancy — 282
- 15.4.4. Objection #3: Alternative Value Systems — 283
15.5. Testimony — 284
15.6. Emotion and Desire — 285
- 15.6.1. Evaluative Statements Express Emotions — 285
- 15.6.2. Emotions Make Evaluative Statements True — 286
- 15.6.3. Evaluative Judgments Cause Emotions — 287
- 15.6.4. Emotions Represent Evaluative Facts — 288
- 15.6.5. Emotions Bias Evaluative Judgments — 289
15.7. Ethical Intuition — 289
- 15.7.1. The Intuitionist View — 289
- 15.7.2. What Is an Intuition? — 289
- 15.7.3. Some Ethical Intuitions — 291
- 15.7.4. How Intuitions Justify — 292
- 15.7.5. "Intuitions Cannot Be Checked" — 292
- 15.7.6. Disagreement, Part 1: Hypothetical Disagreements — 293
- 15.7.7. Disagreement, Part 2: The Fallibility of Intuition — 294
- 15.7.8. Disagreement, Part 3: The Unreliability of Intuition — 294
- 15.7.9. Cultural Biases — 296
15.8. The Relevance of Evolution — 296
- 15.8.1. Background: Evolutionary Psychology — 296
- 15.8.2. The Skeptical View — 297
- 15.8.3. The Byproduct View — 298
15.9. The Role of Empathy — 300
15.10. Conclusion — 301

16. Religious Knowledge — 303
16.1. Faith vs. Evidence — 303
16.1.1. Epistemic Evidentialism — 303
16.1.2. Moral Evidentialism — 305
16.1.3. Fideism — 307
16.2. Religious Testimony — 309
16.3. Foundational Theism — 311
16.3.1. The Sensus Divinitatis — 311
16.3.2. A Non-theistic Interpretation — 312
16.4. Religious Experience — 314
16.4.1. Prima Facie Justification by Religious Experience — 314
16.4.2. Freud & Marx — 315
16.4.3. Neurological Explanations — 316
16.4.4. The Problem of Conflicting Experiences — 317
16.4.5. Agent-Relative Justification — 318
16.4.6. Reconciling Religious Traditions — 319
16.5. Philosophical Arguments — 320
16.6. Conclusion — 321

PART IV: APPLIED EPISTEMOLOGY — 323

17. Irrationality — 324
17.1. The Disagreement Puzzle — 324
17.2. The Case for Irrationality — 325
17.2.1. Difficulty of Issues — 325
17.2.2. Ignorance — 326
17.2.3. Divergent Values — 327
17.3. The Theory of Rational Irrationality — 328
17.3.1. Rational Ignorance — 328
17.3.2. From Ignorance to Irrationality — 329
17.3.3. What Are We Irrational About? — 330
17.3.4. Non-Epistemic Belief Preferences — 331
17.3.5. Doxastic Control — 332
17.3.6. Automatic Bias — 333
17.4. Becoming Rational — 334
17.4.1. Turning the Magnifying Glass on Ourselves — 334
17.4.2. Identify Your Biases — 335
17.4.3. Diversify Your Sources — 336
17.4.4. Consider Objections — 336
17.4.5. Avoid Speculative, Subjective, and Anecdotal Arguments — 337
17.4.6. Have Productive Discourse — 338
17.5. Conclusion — 339

18. Critical Thinking and Trust in Experts	341
18.1. The Issue of Critical Thinking vs. Trust	341
18.2. The Case for Deference	342
18.2.1. The Reliability Argument	342
18.2.2. The Coherence Argument	343
18.2.3. Objections	344
18.3. The Case Against Science	345
18.3.1. A Common Scientific Method	345
18.3.2. The Replication Crisis	346
18.3.3. Why Science Goes Wrong	347
18.4. The Case Against Political Experts	349
18.5. The Case Against Philosophy	351
18.6. Conclusions	352
18.6.1. In Praise of Withholding	352
18.6.2. When to Believe the Science	353
18.6.3. Some Political Biases to Avoid	354
18.6.4. What to Believe About Philosophy	355
19. Peer Disagreement	357
19.1. Peer Disagreement Scenarios	357
19.2. The Case for Equal Weight	359
19.2.1. The Obvious Motivation	359
19.2.2. More Examples	360
19.2.3. Don't Use First-Order Evidence to Assess Reliability	361
19.2.4. The Self-Defeat Objection to Equal Weight	362
19.3. The Case for Steadfastness	363
19.3.1. Non-Dogmatic Steadfastness	363
19.3.2. Examples of Steadfastness	363
19.3.3. Ineffable Evidence	364
19.3.4. Agent-Centered Evidence	365
19.3.5. The Importance of Self-Trust	366
19.3.6. The Common Humanity Objection	366
19.4. The Case for Right Reasons	368
19.4.1. The Right Reasons View	368
19.4.2. Is the Right Reasons View Analytic?	369
19.4.3. Examples	369
19.4.4. The Restaurant Check Objection	370
19.5. The Case for Total Evidence	371
19.5.1. The Total Evidence View	371
19.5.2. Accommodating the Examples	372
19.5.3. Weighing Evidence, Part 1: Downgrading Reliability	372

    19.5.4. Weighing Evidence, Part 2: Varying Confidence   374
    19.5.5. Identifying Peers   375
  19.6. Why Is There So Much Disagreement Anyway?   377
    19.6.1. The Disagreement Puzzle   377
    19.6.2. Gestalt Perceptions   377
    19.6.3. Finding the Right Gestalt   379
  19.7. Conclusion   379

Afterword   382

Glossary   384

Preface

Why Read This Book?

This is an introduction to the field of epistemology, which studies philosophical questions about knowledge, rational belief, and stuff like that. There are a fair number of other introductory epistemology books, but this one is better than all of them, so you should buy this one. Here's what is great about this book:

i. *The writing.* It is written in a clear, simple style. It should be easier to read and won't put you to sleep as fast as other epistemology books. (Admittedly, I am less skilled than most epistemologists at curing insomnia.)
ii. *The subject matter.* Epistemology is super-important, because it reflects on what makes beliefs justified and how we can know things in general, which is of central import for all other inquiry, whether in philosophy or in other fields. It's also fun to think about how you know you're not a brain in a vat.
iii. *The price.* Most epistemology books, from traditional publishers, are $30–$60 (even for e-books!). The ones that are intended as textbooks are especially expensive. By self-publishing this one, I can keep the price reasonable. I can also write in a more friendly and less turgid style, which traditional publishers wouldn't like.
iv. *The author.* I'm smart, I know a lot, and I'm not confused—which means you can probably learn some interesting things from this book without running into too many confusing nonsense passages.

About the Author

I've heard that it's rude to brag about oneself. On the other hand, you might legitimately want to know who I am before deciding whether to buy a textbook by me. So here is some information to show why I'm a good person to write this book:

I got my BA in philosophy from UC Berkeley. I got my PhD in philosophy from Rutgers University, which was then the #3 philosophy department in the U.S. (they later moved up to #2).[1] I am a tenured full professor at the University of Colorado at Boulder, where I have taught philosophy for over 20 years. As of this writing, I have published more than 70 academic articles in various fields, including more than 30 in epistemology. I've published articles in all 5 of the top 5 philosophy journals. (In philosophy, by the way, the good journals reject 90–95% of submissions.)

I have written eight and a half books (one is co-authored) before this one and edited a ninth, including two epistemology books. See the Afterword for abstracts.

My Approach in Writing This

That's enough about me. Now here are some comments about my approach in writing this:

1. I have included chapters on the most important and interesting topics in epistemology. Some topics are included because students like them (like brain-in-a-vat skepticism); others are included because I think that it's particularly important for your intellectual health to avoid confusion about them.
2. I give a basic presentation of each issue, including what I consider the most important and interesting arguments that can be explained reasonably briefly. (In each case, there are many more complicated and nuanced views and arguments to be found in the academic literature.) When you read these arguments, don't just memorize them and move on, as students sometimes do. Spend some time thinking about why you do or don't agree with them.
3. All of these are issues that people disagree about. In each case, my presentation aims to be (and I think is in fact) *objective*, but not *neutral*. That is:
   a. I give each view a fair hearing, presenting its case as strongly as I can (given space constraints), in terms that I think are faithful to its proponents' intellectual motivations. I do not select evidence, distort people's words, or use any other tricks to try to skew the assessment of any of the philosophical theories.
   b. I do *not*, however, promise a *neutral* presentation—one that just reports other people's ideas without evaluation (which I would find incredibly

---

[1] See the Philosophical Gourmet Report, http://www.philosophicalgourmet.com/. This is the most widely used set of rankings in philosophy.

boring). I am going to tell you what I think, and I am going to defend it with logical arguments that try to show you why that view is right.

If you don't like that, this isn't the book for you. Go get another book, like maybe my anthology.[2]

Vocabulary Words

Periodically in the text, you'll see an expression in bold, such as **epistemology**. This indicates an important philosophical vocabulary word, which will appear in the glossary at the back of the book.

Recycled Philosophy?

Some of the text in this book has appeared before, in my general introduction to philosophy, *Knowledge, Reality, and Value*. I'm totally reusing the epistemology chapters from that book, with some amendments and modifications. There is, of course, much more epistemology in this book.

Acknowledgements

I would like to thank Ross Levatter, Ari Armstrong, and Jun Lin Zeng for their helpful comments on the manuscript, which helped to correct numerous mistakes and shortcomings. I'd also like to thank Iskra Fileva for general awesomeness, God for not being a deceiver, and the evil genius for not existing. Naturally, none of these beings are to blame for any errors that remain. Any such errors are most likely *your* fault. Yes, you, the reader. Because you're dreaming, and you dreamed up this book with errors in it! Why did you do that? Next time, dream a perfect book.

---

[2] *Epistemology: Contemporary Readings* (2000).

Part I: General Issues About Knowledge & Justification

1. Introduction

In this chapter, I'm going to tell you what epistemology is and why you should study it. I'll also give you some conceptual and terminological background.

1.1. What Is Epistemology?

Epistemology, a.k.a. "the theory of knowledge", studies the nature of knowledge, whether and how we know what we think we know, whether and how our beliefs are justified, and stuff like that. (The word comes from the Greek root *episteme*, meaning "knowledge".)

Examples: What is the definition of "know"? How do we know that we can trust the five senses? How do we know what is right and wrong? Are all beliefs justified by observation, or are some things justified independent of observation? We'll address those questions (and so much more!) in this book.

We'll talk about the meaning of "know" in the next chapter. But right now, I want to clarify that when epistemologists talk about knowledge, we are generally talking about *propositional knowledge*, which is the state of knowing something to be the case, or knowing a fact—for example, knowing that it is raining, or knowing that 257 is prime.

There are other uses of "know"—e.g., you could be said to know a person or a place (as in, "I know Spongebob" or "I don't know Westeros very well"), or to know how to do something (as in, "I know how to ride a manatee"). Epistemologists generally are *not* talking about those things when we ask about the nature of "knowledge".

1.2. Why Is Epistemology the King of All Fields?

1.2.1. Moore's Paradox

I'm going to start with a little puzzle that G.E. Moore famously discussed.

> **Interlude: G.E. Moore**
> George Edward Moore (known as "G.E. Moore" due to Britishness) was a twentieth-century British philosopher. He is known for his disarmingly simple

> appeals to common sense (like the time he tried to refute external-world skepticism by showing people his hands), his staunch defense of ethical intuitionism, his tediously long discussions of word meanings, his repetitive belaboring of simple points, and his general opposition to philosophical skepticism. Also, he's known for Moore's Paradox, to be explained presently. Moore's Paradox was so named by Wittgenstein, who thought that the discovery of this "paradox" was Moore's greatest contribution to philosophy.

Imagine that you ask me what the weather is like outside, and I reply:

It is raining, but I don't think that it is raining.

There would be something badly wrong with my answer, right? It seems like a nonsensical thing to say, which is why you've probably never actually heard anyone say something like that. But what exactly is wrong with the statement?

In particular, would my statement be *contradictory*? Many people, on first hearing the sentence, answer "Yes". But they are wrong. A contradictory sentence is one that would not be true in any possible circumstance. Yet my answer above *could* be true. There is a possible circumstance in which it is raining outside and at the same time I fail to believe that it is.

You can perhaps see the point more clearly by noticing that there would be nothing wrong with *someone else* saying, "It is raining, but Mike Huemer doesn't think that it is." That person could even be completely correct in saying that. But the person who says that is asserting the same proposition that I assert when *I* say, "It is raining but I don't think that it is." The same proposition cannot be both contradictory and non-contradictory. So it must simply be non-contradictory, regardless of who asserts it.

Sentences like "*p* but I don't believe that *p*" and "*p* but I believe that not-*p*" are called "Moore-paradoxical sentences".[3] So here's the puzzle: What exactly is wrong with Moore-paradoxical sentences, and why do they *sound* contradictory even though they are not?[4]

Here is G.E. Moore's answer to the puzzle: Whenever you make an assertion, you are *implying* that you know the proposition that you assert. If you don't know it, you shouldn't be saying it. (*Note*: You're not *saying* that you know the thing in question; you're merely *implying* it. Sort of like how if I say, "Have you stopped harassing manatees?", I haven't actually said that you have harassed manatees in the past, but I definitely implied it.) So if you say that it is raining, you are implying that you know that it is raining. However, for you

---

[3] We also include as "Moore-paradoxical" such statements as "*p* but I don't know whether *p*", "*p* but I have no reason to think that", etc.

[4] I think it is this puzzle (rather than the Moore-paradoxical sentence itself) that Wittgenstein intended to name "Moore's Paradox".

to *know* that it is raining, you have to at least *think* that it is raining. Therefore, when you say, "It is raining but I do not think that it is raining", the second half of the sentence contradicts what the first half implies. The "it is raining" part implies that you know it's raining, while the "I do not think that it is raining" part entails that you do *not* know it's raining.

Questions you might raise:

1. Is it really true that asserting *p* always implies that one *knows* that *p*? What if you think *p* is probably true, but you're not sure; are you then barred from saying anything?

    Answer: No; what you do in that case is make a weaker statement, such as, "I *think* that *p*, but I'm not sure" or "*p* is *probably* true" or "*p seems to me* to be the case". And notice that all of these are actually asserting things that (plausibly) you *do* know: You may not know that *p* is true, but you can at least know that *you think* that *p*, or that *p* is *probably* true, or that *p seems to you* to be true. So all this is consistent with Moore's claim.

2. Why say that asserting *p* implies that you *know* that *p*, rather than just that asserting *p* implies that you *believe* that *p*? The latter would suffice to solve the original puzzle.

    Answer: Because sentences like "It's raining but I don't know whether it's raining" sound nonsensical in the same way as "It's raining but I don't believe that it's raining."

Let's say G.E. Moore is right.[5] Great, we explained a minor puzzle about a weird sentence that no one ever uses. So what? Well, the puzzle is interesting because the solution includes a striking general thesis about statements: *All statements are implied knowledge claims.*

I put that in italics because it's interesting and I'm making a big deal about it. Any time anyone says anything—whether in philosophy, or science, or ordinary life, or religion, or any other intellectual context—they are implicitly claiming to have knowledge of that whereof they speak. Epistemology is interesting because it studies the nature of this thing, knowledge, that everyone is constantly (implicitly) laying claim to. In that sense, the field of epistemology studies the conditions for *any* claim in any field to be apt. That makes epistemology of sweeping, fundamental importance for all intellectual inquiry.

1.2.2. Epistemological Problems

Here's another thing about why you should study epistemology. You may not be in a position to know this yet, but I'm just going to tell you this: There are

---

[5] For more on the solution to the puzzle, see my paper, "Moore's Paradox and the Norm of Belief" in *Themes from G.E. Moore* (2007).

a lot of very hard problems in epistemology. These problems call into question a huge portion of our putative knowledge. It is easy to construct arguments for the conclusion that we know none or almost none of the things we normally take ourselves to know. And these aren't just silly fallacies, but arguments whose premises are almost certainly going to seem obvious to you, and whose conclusions are almost certainly going to seem to you to follow from those premises. Trained philosophers have trouble rebutting these arguments, and there is in fact no consensus on what's wrong with them. And what this means is that most of us have some beliefs or intuitions about the nature of knowledge that are *inconsistent* with a huge portion of our normal judgments about what we know.

That is a very interesting and intellectually troubling situation. It suggests that something has gone very wrong in most people's understanding of knowledge—which, given the general importance of knowledge (as just discussed above), has the potential to mess up our thinking about all sorts of other matters.

My claim is not that in general, one must first have sound epistemological views in order to think clearly and cogently in other areas. My claim is that having *unsound* epistemological views can easily screw up your thinking in other areas—and that a great many people are in fact attracted to unsound epistemological views, which they have not carefully examined. That's why you should study epistemology.

1.3. Conceptual Background

Here are some notes about some important concepts that you should already know about if you've already taken some philosophy courses. But if you haven't, then you probably don't know them.

1.3.1. Propositions

Propositions are things that can be true or false—but wait, I need to distinguish three sorts of things that can be true or false.

i. *Sentences*. Sentences are sequences of words like what you're looking at right now. Not *all* sentences can be true or false; e.g., questions or commands cannot be. Only assertive sentences, or proposition-expressing sentences, can be true or false. For instance, "It is raining" is true or false; "Is it raining?" and "Make it rain!" are not.
ii. *Beliefs*. Beliefs are a kind of mental state, a state of thinking something to be the case. They are typically expressed using assertive sentences. They need not actually be expressed, though; you could just think silently to

yourself that it is raining. The thought must be either true or false. This contrasts with, e.g., emotions, desires, or sensations, which are neither true nor false.
iii. *Propositions.* **Propositions** are the sort of things that beliefs and statements are *about*. When you have a belief, there is something that you believe to be the case; when you make an assertion, there is something you are asserting to be the case. That thing is a "proposition". Propositions are sometimes thought of as ways the world could be (possible states of affairs), or ranges of possibilities.

A proposition should not be confused with a belief, since the proposition is the thing *that* one believes, the thing one's mental state is about, not the mental state itself. When you believe a proposition, that proposition is called the **content** of your belief. By the way, people can have different attitudes to the same proposition: One person may *believe* that we will colonize Mars, while another merely *hopes* that we will, a third *doubts* that we will, a fourth *is glad* that we will, and so on.

A proposition also should not be confused with a *sentence* or phrase in a particular language. The proposition is not the *phrase* "that we will colonize Mars"; it is the thing that that phrase *refers to*. (Compare: The Eiffel Tower is not to be confused with the *expression* "the Eiffel Tower"; the Tower is *the referent* of that expression.) The sentences "We will colonize Mars" and "Nous allons coloniser Mars" have something in common. (The second one is the French translation of the first.) They are obviously not *the same sentence*, but they do say the same thing—that is, they express *the same proposition*.

1.3.2. *The Forms of Propositions*

Propositions have structures—that is, they have different kinds of components, which can be connected to each other in different ways. The structure is often referred to as the "form" of the proposition.

The simplest kind of proposition has a simple subject-predicate form. That is, there is a thing the proposition is about (the "**subject**"), and there is a way that thing is said to be, or a property that is ascribed to the thing (the "**predicate**"). Example: [Donald is angry]. *Note:* I often use square brackets like that, to refer to propositions.[6] This proposition is about Donald, and the way he is said to be (the property ascribed to him) is *angry*.[7] So Donald is the

---

[6] More precisely, this is my convention: If you take a sentence that normally asserts a proposition and enclose it in square brackets, the whole expression becomes a singular term denoting the proposition that the original sentence normally asserts.

[7] All my hypothetical examples are purely fictional, and any resemblance to any actual persons, living or dead, is entirely coincidental.

subject, and the property of being angry is the predicate. Notice that neither of these things by itself is a proposition.

Some propositions are compound, meaning that they have other propositions as components. Example: [If Donald is angry, then he is dangerous]. In this case, there are two simple propositions, [Donald is angry] and [Donald is dangerous], which are combined using an "if-then". Sentences or propositions like this (using "if … then") are known as "**conditionals**". The "if" part (in this case, [Donald is angry]) is known as the "**antecedent**" of the conditional. The "then" part (in this case, [Donald is dangerous]) is known as the "**consequent**" of the conditional.

Another type of compound proposition is a **conjunction** (an "and" statement), for example, [Donald is angry and dangerous]. The two parts are called the "**conjuncts**". In this case, the first conjunct is [Donald is angry], and the second conjunct is [Donald is dangerous].

Another type is a **disjunction** (an "or" statement). The two parts are called **disjuncts**. So in the disjunction [Jesus is a liar, a lunatic, or the Lord], there are three disjuncts. The first disjunct is [Jesus is a liar], the second disjunct is [Jesus is a lunatic], and the third disjunct is [Jesus is the Lord].

We also sometimes talk about **negations**, which are propositions that deny another proposition. For instance, [Jesus is not a liar] is a negation; specifically, it is *the negation of* [Jesus is a liar].

1.3.3. Arguments

An **argument** is a series of statements, some of which are supposed to provide reasons for others, where the whole series is meant to justify a particular conclusion. (We also sometimes speak of an argument as the series of *propositions* expressed by such statements.) These are the different parts of an argument:

i. *Premises:* The **premises** of an argument are the statements that are used to support the other statements. We reason *from* the premises. Premises are usually chosen to be things that are widely accepted or would seem obvious to most people. (If not, then you may need further arguments to support the premises.)
ii. *Conclusion:* The **conclusion** of an argument is the statement that the argument is meant to justify. We reason *to* the conclusion. The conclusion is usually something that is initially controversial or non-obvious. (Otherwise, we would not need the argument.)
iii. *Intermediary steps:* Sometimes an argument has intermediary steps. These are steps in between the premises and the conclusion that help you to see how the premises support the conclusion.

Now here are some characteristics an argument can have:

i. *Valid or invalid:* An argument is said to be **valid** (or "deductively valid" or "logically valid") when the premises entail the conclusion; that is, *it would be impossible (in the sense of* contradictory*) for all the premises to be true and the conclusion to be false.*

   Note: This is not the ordinary English usage of "valid"; this is a special, technical usage among philosophers. Virtually all philosophers use the word this way, so you have to learn it. In this sense, "validity" does not require the premises of the argument to be correct, or reasonable, or even consistent. The only thing that is required is that it not be possible that the premises all be true *and* the conclusion be false.

   Example: "Socrates is a fish. All fish live on Mars. Therefore, Socrates lives on Mars." That's valid, because it could not be that Socrates is a fish, and all fish live on Mars, *and* that Socrates doesn't live on Mars.

ii. *Sound or unsound:* An argument is said to be **sound** when it is valid (in the sense given above) *and* all of its premises are true. (In this case, of course, the conclusion must also be true—you can see that if you understood the definition of "valid".) An argument is unsound whenever it is invalid *or* has a false premise. This is also a technical usage, not the ordinary English usage, and again, philosophers take the stated definition perfectly strictly and literally. Example: "The sky is blue. If the sky is blue, then it isn't green. Therefore, the sky isn't green." That's sound.

iii. *Circular or non-circular:* We say that an argument is **circular** or **begs the question** when the premises contain the conclusion, or they contain a statement that is so *similar* to the conclusion that you couldn't believe the premises without already believing the conclusion, or they contain a statement whose justification *depends upon* the justification of the conclusion. Example: "God exists; therefore, God exists."

   Here is a more realistic example: "Everything the Bible says is true, since the Bible is the word of God. And we know the Bible is the word of God because the Bible *says* that the Bible is the word of God."

   By the way, the phrase "beg the question" *does not mean* "to *raise* the question"! It means "to give a circular argument". It fills me with a burning rage when I see people abuse the phrase "beg the question", so don't do that.[8]

The above categories are used for assessing arguments, especially for discussing what might be wrong with a given argument. If you have a deductive argument, then the argument needs to be valid, sound, and non-circular. If it is invalid, or

---

[8] Really? No, not really. I'm exaggerating my annoyance for comedic effect.

has a false premise, or begs the question, then it's a bad argument. (It's also bad if we merely lack justification for believing one of the premises. But we don't have a separate term for that.)

1.4. Some Symbols

The following symbols are commonly used in epistemology (and philosophy generally).

Symbol	Meaning
S	Commonly used to stand for any person or conscious being ("S" for "subject"; a "subject" is just a conscious being).
$p, q, r, \ldots$	Stands for some proposition. You can use any letter. Capital letters are also sometimes used. p, q, and r are epistemologists' favorites. Example: We might say, "S knows that p only if S believes that p." (A subject knows a proposition only if they believe that proposition.)
$\sim p$	It's not the case that p. Often read "not-p".
$(p \lor q)$	Read "p or q". Note that the "or" is normally read inclusively, so this means "p or q or both."
$(p \ \& \ q)$	p and q.
$(p \to q)$	If p then q.
$\therefore$	Read "therefore". This is often placed before the conclusion of an argument.

Example: Consider the argument, "Either Skeezix or Ted ate the goldfish. Ted didn't do it. Therefore, Skeezix did it." This can be symbolized like so:

$(s \lor t)$
$\sim t$
$\therefore s$

That's a valid inference.

1.5. Conclusion

Epistemology studies philosophical questions about knowledge and justified belief. Knowledge is interesting and important because whenever you assert anything, you are implying that you *know* that thing (this is shown by the absurdity of asserting "p but I don't know whether p"). Also, there are lots of very hard puzzles that arise in epistemology, which show that a lot of us must be pretty confused about knowledge. That's a big thing to be confused about.

To understand what follows, you should know these terms: *proposition*, *content* (of a belief), *subject* (of a mental state), *subject* (of a proposition), *predicate*, *conditional*, *antecedent*, *consequent*, *conjunction*, *conjunct*, *disjunction*, *disjunct*, *negation*, *argument*, *premise*, *conclusion*, *valid*, *sound*, *begging the question*.

2. What Is Knowledge?

In this chapter, we will try and fail to define "knowledge".

2.1. The Project of Analyzing "Knowledge"

What does it mean to "know" something? A lot of people have tried to answer this, and it's a lot harder than it sounds. I'd like you to put up with some complexities in the next three sections, so that we can get to some interesting lessons at the end.

The goal here is to define "know"—that is, to correctly analyze the current use of the word "know" in English. To correctly analyze a word, you have to give a set of conditions that correctly classifies things in all possible circumstances. So if someone gives a definition of "know", it is considered legitimate to raise any conceivable scenario in which someone could be said to "know" or "fail to know" something, and the analysis has to correctly tell us whether the person in the scenario counts as knowing. In assessing this, we appeal to linguistic intuitions—that is, if normal English speakers would (when fully informed) call something "knowledge", then your analysis should classify it as knowledge; if not, then not.

> **Aside: Analysis & Analytic Philosophy**
> Since the early 20th century, there's been a style of philosophy known as **analytic philosophy**. Analytic philosophers emphasize clarity and logical argumentation (like this book!). At its inception, analytic philosophy was also largely devoted to analyzing the meanings of words. (They had a bad theory according to which this was the central job of philosophers.) Since then, "analytic philosophers" have drifted away from that emphasis, but there's still a good deal of attention paid to word meanings.
> This might seem unimportant to you—who cares about semantics? Why not just stipulate how *you* intend to use a word, and forget about the standard English usage? There are three reasons for not doing that. First, this causes

confusion for other people who are familiar with the ordinary English use of the word.

Second, ordinary usage usually serves important functions. Human beings, over the millennia, have found certain ways of grouping and distinguishing objects (that is, certain **conceptual schemes**) to be useful and interesting. These useful conceptual schemes are embodied in our language. Current usage reflects, in a way, the accumulated wisdom of many past generations.

Third, it is actually almost impossible to escape from the conceptual scheme that you've learned from your linguistic community. If you use a common word, such as "know", it is almost impossible to not be influenced in your thoughts by the actual usage of that word in your speech community. People who try to come up with new concepts usually just confuse themselves; they sometimes use the word in the new way they invented, but then slip back into using it in the normal way that others in their speech community use it. (That's particularly a risk if the new usage is *close to* the standard usage, so that the two are easily confused.)

So, all of that is to defend analytic philosophers' interest in the current, actual usage of "know" in our language.

The main contrast to analytic philosophy is a style of philosophy known as **continental philosophy**, mainly practiced in France and Germany, which puts less emphasis on clear expression and logical argumentation. But we won't talk about that here.

2.2. The Traditional Analysis

Here is a traditional definition, which I guess a lot of people used to accept: Knowledge is justified, true belief.[9] That is:

S knows that p if and only if:
  i. S at least believes that p,
  ii. p is true, and
  iii. S is justified in believing that p.

To illustrate: I had a roommate in graduate school who was a devout Christian. He once said to me, "Mike, don't you know that God loves you?" I told him no, I don't know that, for three reasons: because that's not true, and I have no good reason to believe it, and I don't in fact believe it.

---

[9] I put this in this cagey way because I can't find a lot of people asserting this definition in print. Gettier, in his famous refutation of the definition ("Is Justified True Belief Knowledge?"), cites Plato, Chisholm, and Ayer. But I don't think Plato or Ayer held the view. Still, other epistemologists say that it was widely held, so I guess it was. The definition, however, went out of style before I was born.

A word about each of the three conditions. About condition (*i*): Naturally, you can't know something to be the case if you don't even believe that it is. Almost all epistemologists regard knowledge as a species of belief. But some people think that "belief" is too weak and that knowledge is something better and stronger than belief. I have inserted the "at least" qualifier (which is not found in the most common formulation) to accommodate this: You have to believe that *p*, or possibly do something stronger and better than believing it. (*Note:* The negation of "*S at least* believes that *p*" is "*S does not even* believe that *p*.")

About condition (*ii*): You can't know something to be the case if it isn't the case. In case that's not obvious enough, here is a short argument: Knowing *that p* entails knowing *whether p*; knowing whether *p* entails being right about whether *p*; therefore, knowing that *p* entails being right about whether *p*. Similar points can be made in various cases using the notion of knowing *when* or *where* something is, knowing *why* something is the case, knowing *what* something is, and so on. Example: If John knows that cows have 4 stomachs, then John knows how many stomachs cows have. If John knows how many stomachs cows have, then John has the correct answer about the number of stomachs they have. Therefore, if John knows that cows have 4 stomachs, then he has to be correct in believing that.

Sometimes, people say things that seemingly conflict with (*ii*), such as: "Back in the Middle Ages, everyone knew that the Sun orbited the Earth." This sort of statement can be explained as something called *imaginative projection*. This is where you describe a situation *from the standpoint* of another person, pretending that you hold their views. When you say, "People in the Middle Ages knew that the Sun orbited the Earth", what this really means is: "People in the Middle Ages would have described themselves as 'knowing' that the Sun went around the Earth." They didn't genuinely know it, though.

By the way, those first two conditions are uncontroversial in epistemology. Some people reject condition (*iii*), and some people add other conditions, but virtually no one rejects (*i*) or (*ii*).

(*i*) and (*ii*) are only necessary conditions for knowledge. You can see that they are not *sufficient* for knowledge because of cases like the following:

> *Lucky Gambler:* Lucky has gone down to the racetrack to bet on horses. He knows nothing about the horses or their riders, but when he sees the name "Seabiscuit", he has a good feeling about that name, which causes him to assume that Seabiscuit will win. He bets lots of money on it. As chance would have it, Seabiscuit does in fact win the race. "I knew it!" the gambler declares.

Did Lucky really *know* that Seabiscuit would win? I hope you agree that he did not.

Why not? Because he just made a lucky guess. Among epistemologists, it is widely accepted that, if you are to count as knowing something, it cannot be a matter of *luck* that you are right about that thing. However, this statement isn't clear and precise enough for philosophers; we want to know what it means for your correctness to not be "a matter of luck".

That's where the third condition on knowledge comes in. Maybe Lucky's problem is that he had *no justification* for thinking Seabiscuit would win. He just liked the name, but that is not evidentially relevant. That's why he didn't count as "knowing".

2.3. About "Justification"

2.3.1. The General Concept of Justification

Epistemologists talk *a lot* about the "justification" for beliefs (perhaps even more than we talk about knowledge), so I should say more about this concept before we go on.

Some synonyms: A justified belief is one that is *reasonable*, one that it *makes sense* to hold, one that is *likely to be true* given the believer's evidence. Another way to phrase the idea is that the "justified" beliefs are the ones that a rational person who was seeking to attain truth and avoid error would adopt. Believing justified (and only justified) propositions constitutes the rational pursuit of truth and avoidance of error.

In most cases, the justified beliefs are the ones that are supported by adequate *evidence* or *reasons*. (Later, we'll talk about exceptions to that; see chs. 4–5.)

2.3.2. Epistemic vs. Non-Epistemic Reasons

There are different kinds of "reasons" that a person may have, for different things. The kind of reasons that you have to *perform an action* are known as **practical reasons**. Practical reasons divide into prudential reasons (reasons that appeal to self-interest), moral reasons, and perhaps more. We can also speak of an action being "prudentially justified" or "morally justified" when it has sufficient reasons of the relevant kind in its favor. But I mention practical reasons/justification only to contrast it with the other kind of reasons/justification.

The kind of reasons that you have to *believe a proposition* are known as **epistemic reasons**, and a belief is said to be **epistemically justified** when there are sufficient epistemic reasons in its favor. (Again, we'll later discuss the possibility of justification in the absence of reasons.) Epistemic reasons are the kind of reasons that render a belief likely to be true.

It's possible, by the way, to have practical reasons for trying to get yourself to believe something—e.g., maybe believing in life after death would make you happier, so you have a prudential reason for trying to adopt that belief. That's not an epistemic reason, because that's not the kind of reason that renders the belief actually likely to be true.

2.3.3. Doxastic vs. Propositional Justification

Epistemologists have a weirdly-named distinction between **propositional justification** and **doxastic justification**. Basically, the distinction is between a situation in which you *have available* good enough reasons to believe some proposition, and a situation in which you actually have a justified belief. Here's an example:

> *The Irrational Evolutionist:* Bryan knows all about the scientific evidence for the Theory of Evolution (the fossil record, the patterns of morphological and genetic similarities among species, etc.), which is extremely compelling. But Bryan doesn't care about any of that evidence. He rejects evolution because he doesn't like the idea of having ancestors who were monkeys. Then one day, Bryan consults his tarot card reader, who informs him, based on a tarot reading (which is not good evidence at all!), that the Theory of Evolution is true. Then Bryan finally accepts Evolution.

In this case, is Bryan's belief justified?

This case motivates a distinction. We should say that Bryan *has justification for* the Theory of Evolution, since he knows all the scientific evidence that supports it. Epistemologists say he has "propositional justification" for the theory, or even that his belief "is propositionally justified". At the same time, Bryan's actual belief is unjustified because he does not hold the belief for the right reasons. Epistemologists say he lacks "doxastic justification", or that his belief is "doxastically unjustified". ("Doxastic" means "pertaining to belief", from the Greek word *doxa*, meaning "belief".)

It is generally held that, for a belief to be (doxastically) justified, you need two things to happen: (a) You have to have *propositional justification* for the content of the belief (the thing that you believe), and (b) your belief must actually be *based on* the thing that provides that propositional justification. In the above example, the scientific evidence constitutes propositional justification for the Theory of Evolution. To have doxastic justification, Bryan would need, in addition, to actually base his belief in Evolution on that scientific evidence.

2.4. Gettier's Refutation

In 1963, Edmund Gettier published a short article that became famous among epistemologists. The article refuted the "justified true belief" (**JTB**) analysis of knowledge, showing that conditions (*i*)–(*iii*) above (§2.2) are not *sufficient* for knowledge. (Gettier doesn't dispute that they are *necessary* for knowledge, though.) Here's an example from the article:

> *Jones and Brown:* You have extremely good reason to believe that Jones owns a Ford automobile. You decide to start inferring other things from this. You have no idea where Brown is, but you randomly pick a city, say, Barcelona, and you think to yourself: "Jones owns a Ford, *or* Brown is in Barcelona." That's justified, because the first disjunct is justified, and you only need one disjunct for the sentence to be true. Later, it turns out that Jones actually didn't own a Ford (he sold it just that morning), but coincidentally, Brown *was* in Barcelona. Q: Did you know [Jones owns a Ford or Brown is in Barcelona]?

Intuitively, no. But you satisfied the JTB definition: You had a belief, it was true, and it was justified. Therefore, justified, true belief doesn't suffice for knowledge.

(*Note:* You *do not think that Brown is in Barcelona* in this example. So please don't talk about this example and complain that the person is unjustified in thinking that Brown is in Barcelona. Don't confuse [Jones owns a Ford, *or* Brown is in Barcelona] with [Brown is in Barcelona]!)

Gettier's argument uses three assumptions: He assumes (*i*) that if you're justified in believing something, and you correctly deduce a logical consequence of that, then you're justified in believing that consequence too;[10] (*ii*) that you can be justified in believing a false proposition; and (*iii*) that you can validly infer a true conclusion from a false premise (you can be right about something for the wrong reason). Given these principles, you can construct Gettier examples.

Many students hate the Jones and Brown example, because the proposition it has you believing is so strange. People don't make up random disjunctions like that. So here is a less annoying example:[11]

> *Stopped Clock:* You look at a clock to see what time it is. The clock reads 3:00, so you reasonably conclude that it's 3:00. Unbeknownst to you, that clock

---

[10] This is sometimes called "the **closure principle**".
[11] Due to Bertrand Russell, though he failed to note that it refutes the JTB analysis.

> is stopped. However, coincidentally, it happens to be 3:00 at the time that you look at it (even a stopped clock is right twice a day).

Here, you had a justified, true belief, but we would not say that you *knew* that it was 3:00.

2.5. Seven More Failed Analyses

Philosophers have tried to improve the definition of knowledge. Some add other conditions onto JTB; others try replacing the justification condition with something else. Other philosophers then come up with new counter-examples to the improved definitions. Then people try to repair the definitions by adding more complications; then more counter-examples appear; and so on.

2.5.1. No False Lemmas

Here's the first thing you should think of (but you probably didn't): Just add a fourth condition that stipulates away the sort of cases Gettier raised. Gettier raised examples in which you infer a correct conclusion from a false (but justified) belief. E.g., you infer "Jones owns a Ford or Brown is in Barcelona" from the justified but false belief "Jones owns a Ford." So just add a condition onto the definition of knowledge that says something like:

iv. No false beliefs are used in S's reasoning leading to p.

By the way, this does not require p to be based on reasoning; if p is not based on reasoning at all, then condition (*iv*) is automatically satisfied. What is required is simply that it *not* be the case that S reasoned to p from one or more false beliefs. This condition is also known as being "**fully grounded**", or having "**no false lemmas**". (*Note 1:* Please don't confuse "fully grounded" with "fully justified"! To be fully grounded is to fail to be based on any false propositions; this is neither necessary nor sufficient for justification. *Note 2:* A "lemma" is an intermediary proposition that is used in deriving a theorem.)

That takes care of the Jones and Brown example: The belief in that case violates condition (*iv*), so it doesn't count as knowledge. So the improved definition gets the right answer. Likewise, in the Stopped Clock case, we could say that the belief "It is 3:00" is partly based on the false belief that the clock is working.

But now, here's a new counter-example:

> *Phony Barn Country:* Henry is driving through Phony Barn Country, a region where (unbeknownst to Henry), there are many barn facades facing the road, which look exactly like real barns when viewed from the road, but they have nothing behind the facade. There is exactly one real barn in this

> region, which looks just like all the facades from the road. Henry drives through, thinking, as he looks at each of the barnlike objects around him, "There's a barn." Each time, Henry is wrong, except for the one time he happens to be looking at the real barn.

Obviously, when he looks at the fake barns, he lacks knowledge—he doesn't know they are real barns (since they aren't), and he doesn't know they are fake barns (since he doesn't believe they are). But what about the one real barn in the area—does he *know* that that one is real?

You're supposed to have the intuition that Henry does *not* know. He's correct that time, but just by chance. The no-false-lemmas principle doesn't help with this case, since the belief that that object is a barn does not seem to be inferred from anything that's false. If it is inferred from anything, it is inferred from the visible features of the object (its shape, size, distribution of colors), perhaps together with some background beliefs about what barns normally look like when viewed from the front—but those beliefs are all *true*. So Henry satisfies all four proposed conditions for knowledge. There must be some other condition on knowledge that he is missing.

Here's another counter-example that some people find more convincing.

> *Holographic Vase:* Henry comes into a room and sees a perfect holographic projection of a vase. The projection is so good that Henry believes there is a real vase there. Oddly enough, someone has put a real vase, looking exactly like the holographic projection, in the same location. So Henry is correct that there is a real vase there, though it is the holographic projection that is causing his experience, and if the real vase were removed, things would look exactly the same.

Does Henry *know* that there is a (real) vase there? Intuitively, he does not, though he has a justified, true belief, which he did not infer from any false beliefs.

The above examples show that conditions (*i*)-(*iv*) are not sufficient for knowledge. For a long time, epistemologists assumed that they are at least *necessary* for knowledge. But here's an example that seems to show that condition (*iv*) isn't even necessary:

> *Border Rally:* Sue hears on the news that the President is speaking to supporters in Utah today. She correctly infers that the President is *not* attending today's NATO talks in France, since he is in Utah. Unbeknownst to Sue, the President's rally is located at the border of Nevada and Utah, and (though the audience is in Utah) at the time Sue makes the above inference,

> the President happens to be standing just on the Nevada side of the border.[12]

In this case, it seems that Sue knows the President isn't in France, even though she inferred this from a false belief (that the President was in Utah). So you can have knowledge based partly on a false belief.

2.5.2. Reliabilism

According to one influential view ("**reliabilism**"), knowledge is true belief that is produced by a reliable belief-forming process, where a reliable process is one that would generally produce a high ratio of true to false beliefs. Some people regard the reliability condition as simply *explaining* the notion of justification; others would view it as a *replacement* for the justification condition on knowledge. Let's not worry about that, though.

The biggest problem for reliabilism: How do we specify "the process" by which a belief was formed? There are more and less general ways to do this, and you can get the same belief being "reliably" or "unreliably" formed depending on how you describe the process. (This is known as the **generality problem**.)

Take the Jones and Brown case: If the belief-forming method is (as you might expect) something like "deduction starting from a justified belief", then that's a reliable process.[13] So in that case, we have a counter-example to reliabilism—the same counter-example that refuted the JTB definition. If the belief-forming method is instead described as "deduction starting from a false belief", then it's unreliable, so we get to say that the Jones & Brown case *isn't* a case of knowledge.

For another example, take Phony Barn Country. If Henry's belief-forming process is described as "visual perception", that's highly reliable. But if it is described as "looking at barnlike objects in Phony Barn Country", that's unreliable.

It's not clear what general, principled way we have to describe "the process" by which a belief was formed. Without such a principled way, you can get pretty much any belief to count as either reliable or unreliable.

---

[12] From Ted Warfield, "Knowledge from Falsehood", *Philosophical Perspectives* (2005).
[13] Or, to be a little more detailed: Valid deduction is a *conditionally reliable* process (it's reliable when given reliable starting beliefs). Furthermore, we can stipulate that the initial belief [Jones owns a Ford] was formed reliably (however you want to characterize reliability, as long as you don't require *100%* reliability). So according to a standard form of reliabilism (ala Alvin Goldman), the belief [Jones owns a Ford or Brown is in Barcelona] counts as reliably formed.

Another objection is that reliabilism allows people to count as "knowing" things that, from their own internal point of view, are not even reasonable to believe. For example:

> *Reliable Wishing:* Don believes that he is going to become King of the Earth. He has no evidence or argument for this whatsoever. He believes it through pure wishful thinking: He likes the idea of being King of Earth, so he tricks himself into believing it. Unbeknownst to Don, there is a powerful demon who likes Don's irrationality, and this demon has decided that whenever Don forms an irrational, wishful belief, the demon will make it come true. The demon thus orchestrates a sequence of bizarre events over the next two decades that wind up making Don the King of Earth. Q: Did Don *know* that he was going to become King of Earth?

In this case, Don's belief was true and formed by a reliable (for him) method. (Of course, wishful thinking is not reliable in general. But it is reliable for Don, due to the demon.) But it does not seem right to say that he *knew* that he was going to become King.

2.5.3. Proper Function

Another analysis:

S knows that p if and only if:
  i. S believes that p,
  ii. p is true,
  iii. The belief that p was formed by one or more properly functioning cognitive faculties,
  iv. Those faculties were designed to produce true beliefs,
  v. S is in the environment for which those faculties were designed, and
  vi. These faculties are reliable in that environment.

Note: The notions of "design" and "proper function" could be explained in terms of a divine creator, or they could be explained in terms of evolution (evolutionary psychologists often speak of how evolution designed various aspects of us to serve certain functions—of course, this is a sort of metaphorical use of "design").

Notice that this analysis is similar to Reliabilism, except that the **Proper Function** analysis avoids the problem with cases like Reliable Wishing. Don doesn't have knowledge, because he didn't form his belief by a properly functioning faculty that was designed for producing true beliefs. It's not clear, in fact, that Don was using a *faculty* at all; in any case, certainly there is no human faculty that was designed to produce true belief via wishful thinking. So the Proper Function theory works for this case.

Problem: The analysis falls prey to the original Gettier example. When you form the belief [Jones owns a Ford or Brown is in Barcelona], you do so by inferring it from [Jones owns a Ford]. There is no reason to think any of your cognitive faculties are malfunctioning here (you made a valid deduction, after all), or that they weren't designed for getting true beliefs, or that they were designed for some other environment, or that they're not reliable. So the analysis incorrectly rules this a case of knowledge.

2.5.4. Sensitivity & Tracking

Intuitively, knowledge should "track the truth"—i.e., when you know, you should be forming beliefs in a way that would get you to p if p were true, and get you to something else if something else were true. This leads to the **tracking analysis** of knowledge:

S knows that p if and only if:
  i. S believes that p,
  ii. p is true,
  iii. If p were false, then S would not believe that p.
  iv. If p were true, then S would believe that p.[14]

Condition (*iii*) is sometimes called the **sensitivity** condition (knowledge must be "sensitive" to the truth). (*iii*) is commonly understood among philosophers to mean something like the following: "Take a possible situation as similar to the way things actually are as possible, except that p is false in that situation. In that situation, S does not believe that p." Philosophers sometimes refer to possible scenarios that are similar to the actual situation as "**nearby possible worlds**", so we could also explain (*iii*) as: "In the nearest possible worlds in which p is false, S doesn't believe p." (There's a similar interpretation of (*iv*), but I'm not going to discuss condition (*iv*) because it won't matter to the problems we discuss below.[15])

This accounts for the Gettier example (Jones and Brown). According to condition (*iii*), you know [Jones owns a Ford or Brown is in Barcelona] only if:

---

[14] This is from Robert Nozick, in his *Philosophical Explanations* (1981). Slight complication: Nozick later modifies the antecedent of (*iii*) to something like: "P were false *and* you used the same method to form a belief about p as the one you actually used". A similar clause belongs in (*iv*).

[15] You might think (*iv*) is redundant with (*i*) and (*ii*). But in Nozick's interpretation, (*iv*) requires that you continue to have a true belief, not just in the actual world, but in a sufficient range of worlds similar to the actual world in which p remains true.

> If [Jones owns a Ford or Brown is in Barcelona] were false, then you would not believe [Jones owns a Ford or Brown is in Barcelona].

That condition is *not* satisfied. Rather, if [Jones owns a Ford or Brown is in Barcelona] were false, it would be false because Brown was somewhere else while everything else in the example was the same. Since your belief had nothing to do with Brown and was solely based on your belief about Jones, you *would* still believe [Jones owns a Ford or Brown is in Barcelona]. That's why you don't count as knowing [Jones owns a Ford or Brown is in Barcelona].

The tracking account has other problems, though. The theory implies, for instance, that you can never know that a belief of yours is not mistaken. Let's say you believe p, and you think that you're not mistaken in believing p. To *know* that you're not mistaken, you must satisfy the following condition:

> If [you are not mistaken in believing p] were false, then you would not believe [you are not mistaken in believing p].

This is equivalent to:

> If you *were* mistaken in believing p, then you would not believe you weren't mistaken.

But you never satisfy that condition: If you were mistaken in believing p (whatever p is) you would still think you weren't mistaken, since, by definition, you would believe that p was the case. You can't (coherently) think something is the case and also think that thing is mistaken. (Note: "Being mistaken in believing p" means believing p when p is in fact false.) So the tracking account implies that you don't know you're not mistaken in believing p. This is a problem, since it seems that we often know we're not mistaken about particular things, e.g., I know I'm not mistaken in thinking rocks exist.

Here is another interesting implication of the sensitivity condition, which you may or may not find problematic: It's impossible to know that you're not a **brain in a vat** (**BIV**). This refers to the following hypothetical:

> *Brain-in-a-vat Scenario:* Scientists are keeping a brain alive in a vat of nutrients, with lots of tiny wires attached to the brain to stimulate it. (*Note:* In normal people, all sensory experiences are proximately caused by electrical signals from our nerve endings to our brains.) The scientists have figured out how to give the brain exactly the right pattern of electrical stimulation to create a perfect simulation, for the brain, of living a normal life. The brain thus thinks that it is a normal person with a body, living in the real world.

Fortunately, you are not in fact a brain in a vat. (Amazon and Barnes & Noble don't fulfil orders from brains in vats, so I know none of my readers are

BIVs.) But, even though you (I assume) correctly believe that you're not a BIV, and even though *I* know that you're not a BIV, *you* still can't know that you're not a brain in a vat, according to condition (*iii*). That's because if you *were* a brain in a vat, you would still think that you *weren't* one. You'd think that because all your experience would be the same as it is now.

Some people find that problematic. However, others think that's a correct implication, and even that it's an *advantage* of the theory that it explains why you can't know you're not a BIV. That's Robert Nozick's view.

Okay. But now here's an implication that is more clearly problematic: Nozick's theory implies that you can know a conjunction without knowing one of the conjuncts. For instance, I now know [I'm not a brain in a vat *and* I'm in Denver]. I satisfy condition (*iii*) because: If [I'm not a brain in a vat and I'm in Denver] were false, it would be false because I was in another city, most likely Boulder. (Again, we look at the situation *most similar* to the actual world that makes the antecedent hold. In this case, a situation in which I'm not in Denver but am still a normal human is closer to the actual world than a situation in which I'm a brain in a vat.) In that situation, I would know I was in that other city, so I would not believe [I'm not a brain in a vat and I'm in Denver]. However, according to the sensitivity condition, as we've seen, I *can't* know [I'm not a brain in a vat]. Hence, I can know (p & q) but not know p. That seems wrong.

2.5.5. Safety

Maybe we should replace the sensitivity condition with a similar but distinct condition, like so:

S knows that p if and only if:
  i. S believes that p,
  ii. p is true, and
  iii. If S believed that p, p would be true.[16]

Condition (*iii*) is known as the **safety** condition (knowledge must be "safe" from error). Among epistemologists, (*iii*) is understood as meaning that S could not easily have been mistaken in believing that p; in other words, in all the nearby possible worlds in which S still believes that p, p is true.

This accounts for the Gettier case: In that case, Brown could easily have been in another city while you still believed [Jones owns a Ford or Brown is in Barcelona]. So your belief is not safe, so it isn't knowledge.

---

[16] This derives from Ernest Sosa, "How to Defeat Opposition to Moore" (*Philosophical Perspectives*, 1999). Sosa only gives (*iii*) as a necessary condition for knowledge, though; he doesn't say what the full, necessary-and-sufficient conditions would be.

The safety account also avoids the problems with the sensitivity condition above. On this view, you *can* know things like [I'm not mistaken in believing *p*]. You just need it to be the case that there aren't any nearby possible worlds in which you believe that you aren't mistaken in believing *p* and yet you are mistaken in believing *p*. This is probably always the case when you (intuitively) know *p*. You can also know things like [I'm not a brain in a vat]. That's because all the *nearby* possibilities in which you think you're not a brain in a vat are possibilities in which you're a normal human. The worlds in which you're actually a brain in a vat are much farther from actuality, so they don't prevent your belief from being safe.

As you might be starting to suspect by now, this analysis also has counter-examples:

> *Halloween Party:* There's a Halloween Party at Andy's house. Andy is giving everyone correct directions to the party. However, he doesn't want Donald Trump to come, so if Trump asks where the party is, he plans to give the same directions, but then move the party somewhere else. You, not knowing about this, are thinking about wearing your incredibly realistic Donald Trump costume when you go to Andy to ask for directions. You *almost* do it, and if you did it, Andy would have been fooled and would have moved the party. But you don't, and so you get the directions and the party continues in that location as planned.[17]

In this case, intuitively, you know where the party will be after Andy tells you. However, your belief is not safe, because there is a nearby possibility in which you would have been wrong. In the nearby possible world where you wore the Trump costume, you'd have the same belief about where the party was going to be, but that belief would have been false.

2.5.6. Relevant Alternatives

The **relevant alternatives** theory is designed to explain why you count as knowing all sorts of stuff about the world around you (where you live, what a giraffe looks like, what's the capital of France, etc.), even though (as many people think) you can't prove that you're not a brain in a vat. The theory is something like this:

S knows that *p* if and only if:
 i. *S* believes that *p*,
 ii. *p* is true, and

---

[17] From Juan Comesaña, "Unsafe Knowledge" (*Synthese*, 2005). I made minor modifications to the example, including adding Trump to it for amusement.

iii. *S*'s evidence rules out all the relevant alternatives to *p*.

An alternative to *p* is just a possibility that is incompatible with *p*. Evidence "rules out" an alternative provided that the evidence is logically incompatible with the alternative.[18] Fortunately, however, in order to know that *p*, you do not need to rule out *every* alternative. You only have to rule out *some* of the alternatives, the "relevant" ones.

What are the relevant alternatives? Generally, people say that the relevant alternatives are ones that could easily have been the case. For example, if the technology for putting brains in vats actually exists, and someone was considering envatting you after you were born but decided against it, then the Brain in a Vat Scenario is a relevant alternative for you. But if there is no such technology available, then there never was a real chance for you to have been a BIV, and so the BIV hypothesis is irrelevant, and thus you *don't* need to rule it out in order to know stuff about the external world.

Notice that what makes an alternative relevant to a person's knowledge is not a matter of whether the person *knows* or *has evidence* that the alternative could easily have been true. What matters is whether the alternative *in fact* could have easily been true. Example:

> *Gadwall Duck:* Fred sees a bird that looks like a Gadwall Duck in a pond (a species that Fred is very familiar with). He correctly believes that it is a Gadwall. However, he has no evidence to prove that it isn't some other species that happens to look exactly like a Gadwall. Fred isn't aware of and has no thoughts about any such other species.[19]

Does Fred know that the bird is a Gadwall? Intuitively, that depends on whether there actually *is* another species that looks just like a Gadwall. If there is, and if that other bird could easily have been in the pond, then Fred doesn't *know* that he's seeing a Gadwall. But if there *in fact* is no such species (while everything going on in Fred's mind is the same), then he *does* know.

Now, what's the counter-example to this account? Here's one:

> *Math Guess:* S wants to know what the millionth digit of pi is, but he doesn't want to look it up. So he just guesses. He guesses that the digit is "5", never bothers to check on this, and dogmatically ignores any other possibility.

---

[18] Fred Dretske says that the evidence against the alternative has to be strong enough for you to *know* that the alternative is false. I've avoided this formulation to avoid circularity. David Lewis ("Elusive Knowledge", *Australasian Journal of Philosophy*) takes a strong reading of ruling out, as in the text above.

[19] From Fred Dretske, "The Pragmatic Dimension of Knowledge" (*Philosophical Studies*, 1981).

> As it happens, S's guess is correct. Furthermore, since the exact decimal expansion of pi is mathematically necessary, that digit could never have been anything other than "5".

Does S *know* that the millionth digit is "5"? Intuitively, no. But on the relevant alternatives theory, all other digits ("0"–"4" and "6"–"9") would be *irrelevant* alternatives, since none of them could really have been the millionth digit. So we'd have to say that S can count as *knowing* that the digit is "5" without doing anything to rule out any of the alternatives.

The same point applies to any sufficiently robust truth (one that could not easily have been false), including beliefs about the laws of nature and other important features of the world—the alternatives must be deemed "irrelevant" on the relevant-alternatives theory. Thus, someone who guesses correctly can, on this theory, just dismiss the alternatives and thence count as "knowing" that his guess is correct. This results from the fact that relevance is supposed to be a matter of what alternatives are "really possible".

Why not modify the account of relevance? Why not say that all logically possible alternatives are relevant? Or that an alternative is irrelevant only when you *have reason to think* that it is not really possible? Because either of those things would defeat a *central point* of the relevant alternatives theory, which is to enable us to ignore things like the Brain-in-a-Vat Scenario *without* having to give arguments against it.

2.5.7. Defeasibility

Let's conclude with the most sophisticated and most nearly adequate analysis of knowledge, the defeasibility analysis. The **defeasibility theory** states:

S knows that *p* if and only if:
  i.   S believes that *p*,
  ii. *p* is true,
  iii. S is justified in believing that *p*, and
  iv. There are no genuine defeaters for S's justification for *p*.

To explain: In this context, a **defeater** for S's justification for *p* is defined to be *a true proposition that, when added to S's beliefs, would make S no longer justified in believing p*.[20]

---

[20] Annoyingly, there are two uses of "defeater" in epistemology. One is as I just said. The other use is this: A defeater for *p* is a proposition that you believe or have justification for believing, which gives you grounds for doubting *p*. Note that it doesn't have to be true; also, it *actually* undermines your justification (it's not merely that it *would* undermine your justification *if* you believed it).

This theory easily explains all the examples that we've discussed so far. In the Jones and Brown case, there is the defeater, [Jones does *not* own a Ford]. It's *true* in the example that Jones doesn't own a Ford, and if you believed that Jones doesn't own a Ford, then you would no longer be justified in believing [Jones owns a Ford or Brown is in Barcelona], since your only reason for believing [Jones owns a Ford or Brown is in Barcelona] was that you thought Jones owned a Ford. That explains why the person in the example does not know [Jones owns a Ford or Brown is in Barcelona].

Now I'll just list the defeaters in other cases we've discussed where people lack knowledge:

Example	Defeater
Stopped Clock	The clock is stopped.
Phony Barn Country	Most of the barnlike objects around here are not real barns.
Holographic Vase	There is a holographic projection of a vase there.
Reliable Wishing	(Doesn't need a defeater since justification condition is violated.)
Gadwall Duck (if the alternative species actually exists)	There is another species that looks just like a Gadwall Duck.

I'll leave it to you to think those through.

Interlude: A Bad Objection to Defeasibility and Some Other Analyses

Here's something students sometimes ask: "But how could I *know* whether there are any defeaters for my belief?" I think this is intended as a sort of objection to the defeasibility theory, but the question/objection rests on two misunderstandings. (People often have the same misunderstandings when they hear about reliabilism and some other analyses.)

The first misunderstanding is to think that the analysis is intended to *help you decide*, in an individual case, whether *you know* some particular proposition. That's not what we're doing here. We're just trying to explain *what it means* to say that someone knows something. Whether and how you can know that you know something is a separate question.

Second, students often assume that it would be impossible to know whether there are defeaters, and thus that, even if you knew p, you could never know that you knew it. But that's not true. You can know that there are no defeaters for p, as long as (*i*) you believe that there are no defeaters for p, (*ii*) there are no defeaters for p, (*iii*) you're justified in believing that there are no defeaters for p, and (*iv*) there are no defeaters for the proposition [there are no defeaters for p]. There's no reason why all those conditions couldn't hold.

So do we finally have a correct analysis? Well, before you get too excited, I have two more examples:

> *Tom Grabit:* You're sitting in the library one day, when you see Tom Grabit, whom you know well, grab a book and hide it in his coat before sneaking out of the library. You conclude that Tom Grabit stole that book. Unbeknownst to you, Tom has an identical twin brother, John Grabit, who is a kleptomaniac. If you'd seen John, you would have mistaken him for Tom. However, it was really Tom that you saw.

Comment: In this case, it seems that you *don't* know that Tom stole the book, because it *could* have been John, and your evidence can't distinguish Tom from John, so you're only right by luck. The defeasibility theory handles this case: The defeater is [Tom has a kleptomaniac identical twin]. But now here's a different variation:

> *Deluded Mrs. Grabit:* Things are as in the above case, except that Tom *doesn't* have a twin; however, his crazy mother has been going around *saying* that Tom has an identical twin who is a kleptomaniac. You are unaware that Mrs. Grabit has been saying this, and also unaware that she's crazy.

Comment: In this case, it seems that you *do* still know that Tom stole the book. You don't need evidence capable of distinguishing Tom from a hypothetical twin, given that in reality there is no twin.

Deluded Mrs. Grabit poses a problem for the defeasibility theory. [Mrs. Grabit says that Tom has a kleptomaniac identical twin] is a defeater. It's true (although it's false that Tom *has* the twin, it's *true* that his mother *says* that he has one), and if you believed that Mrs. Grabit says Tom has a kleptomaniac identical twin, then you wouldn't be justified in believing that Tom stole the book. That is of course because you would justifiedly suspect that it was the twin who stole the book. So it looks like the defeasibility theory would (incorrectly) rule this *not* a case of knowledge.

So now we have to refine the definition of knowledge. Defeasibility theorists like to distinguish "misleading" defeaters from "genuine" defeaters (where "genuine" just means "non-misleading"). They then say that knowledge requires that there be no **genuine defeaters**, but it doesn't require that there be no **misleading defeaters**. [Mrs. Grabit says that Tom has a kleptomaniac identical twin] is said to be a misleading defeater when Tom doesn't actually have a twin.

How should we define misleading defeaters? There are several possible approaches; I'll just mention three. Bear in mind that we want it to turn out that there is a *genuine* defeater in the Tom Grabit case with the actual twin, but only a *misleading* defeater in the Deluded Mrs. Grabit case. Now here are three suggestions:

a. A misleading defeater is one for which there exists a restorer, where a restorer is another true proposition such that, if you added it to your beliefs after adding the defeater, you would get back your justification for believing *p*.

   Example: In Deluded Mrs. Grabit, the restorer is [Mrs. Grabit is deluded in thinking she has two sons].

   Problem: In the Tom Grabit case with the actual twin, there is also a restorer: [It was not the twin that you saw].

b. A misleading defeater is one that would defeat your justification by supporting something false, as, for example, [Mrs. Grabit says Tom has an identical twin] supports the false claim [Tom has an identical twin].

   Problem: Then the original Tom Grabit case would also have a misleading defeater, because [Tom has a kleptomaniac identical twin] defeats by supporting the false proposition that it was the twin whom you saw.[21]

c. A defeater for *p* is genuine if the subject's justification for *p* depends on the subject's being justified in denying that defeater. A defeater for *p* is misleading if the subject's justification for *p* does *not* depend on the subject's being justified in denying that defeater.

   Example: In the Jones and Brown case, there is the defeater [Jones does not own a Ford]. This is genuine because your justification for believing [Jones owns a Ford or Brown is in Barcelona] depends upon your being justified in denying [Jones does not own a Ford] (i.e., in believing Jones owns a Ford).

   But in Deluded Mrs. Grabit, your justification for believing [Tom stole the book] does not depend upon your being justified in denying [Mrs. Grabit says that Tom has an identical twin]. So this is a case of a misleading defeater.

   Problem: We could also say, with about equal plausibility, that in Tom Grabit (with the actual twin), your justification for believing [Tom stole the book] does not depend upon your being justified in denying [Tom has

---

[21] Klein (who is the source of this account of misleading defeaters) says that [Tom has an identical twin] only supports that it *might* have been the twin that you saw, not that it *was* the twin. Response: [Tom has an identical twin] lowers the probability that you saw Tom by raising the probability that you saw the twin; that's how it defeats [Tom stole the book]. Similarly, [Mrs. Grabit says Tom has a twin] lowers the probability that you saw Tom by raising the probability that Tom has a twin and that you saw that twin, and that's how it defeats [Tom stole the book]. So these cases seem parallel to me.

an identical twin]. So this would be (incorrectly) ruled a misleading defeater.

2.6. Lessons from the Failure of Analysis

2.6.1. The Failure of Analysis

There are many more attempts to analyze knowledge, and also some more complications that people have added to the ones I listed above. I've just given you a few examples so that you can see what the discussion of the meaning of "know" is like.

That discussion has been going on since Gettier published his paper in 1963. One book that appeared twenty years later surveyed the discussion up to that point.[22] It listed 98 different hypothetical examples that had been used to test the dozens of different analyses offered up to that point. To this day, there is no consensus on the proper analysis of "knowledge". Indeed, for every analysis, there are counter-examples that most epistemologists would agree refute the analysis.

Isn't that weird? Philosophers are not dumb people (usually), and they understand the word "know" as well as anyone. A fair number of them have been working on this project, and they've been at it for about 60 years as of this writing. And all they're trying to do is correctly describe how we use the word "know". You'd think they would have done it by now. Why can't we just introspect, notice what we mean by "know", and write it down?

Epistemology is not unique in this respect. Philosophers have tried to analyze many other concepts, such as those expressed by "good", "justice", "cause", "time", and "if". Philosophers have tried to define things for as long as there have been philosophers, but they tried especially hard in the twentieth century because there was a popular school of thought at the time according to which analyzing concepts was the central job of philosophers. But none of our attempts has succeeded. Ever.

Caveat: Some philosophers would dispute that; some claim to have correctly analyzed one or more important concepts. So here is a more cautious statement: No philosophical analysis that has ever been given has been generally accepted as correct among philosophers. "Knowledge" isn't special; it is merely the most striking example of the failure of analysis, because philosophers tried extra hard with this particular word.

---

[22] Robert Shope's *The Analysis of Knowing* (1983).

2.6.2. A Lockean Theory of Concepts

Why did we think that defining "knowledge" would be tractable? Here is one reason you might think of:

1. We understand the word "know".
2. Understanding a word is knowing its definition.
3. Therefore, we know the definition of "know".

So it should be a simple matter to state that definition. Here is another reason you might have:

1. Concepts are introspectively observable mental items.
2. Most concepts are constructed out of other concepts.
3. Introspection is pretty reliable.
4. Therefore, for most concepts, we should be able to see how the concept is constructed from other concepts.

A definition would then simply describe how the given concept is constructed from other concepts.

> **Interlude: John Locke**
> John Locke was a major philosopher of the 1600s. He's best known for his political works, like his *Letter Concerning Toleration* (which defends religious tolerance) and his *Second Treatise of Government* (which kind of provided the philosophical basis for the American Revolution). But he also wrote a really important work of epistemology, the *Essay Concerning Human Understanding*. It's a very long and repetitive book that spends a lot of time talking about where concepts come from and how we know all kinds of things. He makes a big deal about denying that we have innate ideas and trying to show that all our concepts derive from sensory experience.

The above two arguments embody an understanding of words and concepts that is pretty natural at first glance.[23] It's what you would probably think if no one told you otherwise. To illustrate, take the concept TRIANGLE (it's common to use all caps to denote a concept). This concept is constructed from the concepts THREE, STRAIGHT LINE, CLOSED, etc. If one possesses the concept TRIANGLE, one can directly reflect on the concept and see that it contains these other concepts, arranged in a certain way. One can then simply describe one's concept by saying: "A triangle is a closed, plane figure bounded by three straight lines." Furthermore, if you *don't* know one of these things

---

[23] This is basically John Locke's view of words and concepts. He also thought that we got our basic concepts from sensory experiences, but I won't discuss that view here.

about triangles—for instance, you don't know that they have to be *closed* (so you think they might allow gaps in the perimeter), then you don't understand the concept TRIANGLE.

Similarly, provided that one understands KNOWLEDGE, one ought to be able to introspectively examine this concept, and (unless it is among the few *simple* concepts that aren't formed from any other concepts) one should be able to see what other concepts it is composed of and how those concepts are combined to form the concept KNOWLEDGE.

Granted, our minds are not always transparent to us. Sometimes we confuse one thought or feeling with another, sometimes we deceive ourselves about our own motivations, sometimes we fail to notice subtle mental states, and sometimes we have unconscious mental states that we are entirely unaware of. All that has been known for a long time. But none of those phenomena should make it extremely difficult to analyze typical concepts. It's not as if our understanding of the concept KNOWLEDGE is completely unconscious (is it?), or we're trying to deceive ourselves about it, or we're not noticing it. Epistemologists have attended very deliberately to this concept, and epistemologists are not generally very confused people. So it shouldn't be *that* hard to describe the concept.

2.6.3. *A Wittgensteinian View of Concepts*

The Lockean theory of concepts implies that linguistic analysis should be tractable: We should be able to state many correct definitions, without too much trouble. The experience of philosophy, however, is the opposite: After the most strenuous efforts over a period of decades (if not centuries), we've managed to produce approximately zero correct definitions.

Qualification: Not *all* words are indefinable. Most *mathematical* expressions can be correctly defined ("triangle", "prime number", "derivative", etc.). Also, of course it is possible to create a technical term and give it a stipulative definition, as scientists sometimes do. There may even be a very small number of terms from ordinary life that have definitions—for instance, a "grandfather" is a father of a father. But there are, at most, *very few* definable concepts, and probably none that are philosophically interesting (in the way that "justice", "knowledge", "causation", and so on are philosophically interesting).

Anyway, the inference seems unavoidable: The Lockean theory of concepts is wrong. In its place, I would advance a broadly Wittgensteinian view of concepts.[24]

---

[24] I discuss this more in "The Failure of Analysis and the Nature of Concepts" in *The Palgrave Handbook of Philosophical Methods* (2015).

> **Interlude: Ludwig Wittgenstein**
> Ludwig Wittgenstein was a famous philosopher from the early 20th-century who wrote a lot of very confusing stuff about language, logic, and the mind. I think what I have to say about concepts is like some stuff that Wittgenstein said, but I don't actually care how well it matches Wittgenstein's views. I also don't care, by the way, whether the "Lockean theory" matches Locke's views. You have to add in caveats like this whenever you mention a major philosophical figure, because there are always people who have devoted their lives to studying that figure and who, if you let them, will give you all sorts of arguments that the famous philosopher has been completely misunderstood and never really said any of the things they're famous for saying.

There are three things wrong with the Lockean view. First, understanding a word (except in rare cases) is not a matter of knowing a definition. Understanding a word is a matter of having the appropriate *dispositions* to use the word—being disposed to apply the word to the things that it applies to, and not apply it to the things it doesn't apply to. Accordingly, the way that we learn words is hardly ever by being given a verbal description of the word's meaning. We learn almost all of our words by observing others using the words in context. We then attempt to *imitate* others' usage—to apply the word in circumstances that seem to us similar to those in which we have previously observed others using the word. Each time we hear the word used, that slightly influences our dispositions. You understand a given word to the extent that you can successfully imitate the accepted usage.

Second, because concepts are *dispositional* mental states, most features of a given concept are not directly introspectively observable. Our main access to the implications of a concept comes, not through directly reflecting on the concept, but through *activating* the dispositions that constitute our understanding. When we confront a particular situation (whether in reality or in our imagination), we find ourselves inclined to describe that situation in a particular way, using particular words. That reveals the contours of the concepts expressed by those words. This, by the way, explains the common method of testing definitions by consulting our linguistic intuitions regarding specific scenarios. If the way we applied concepts were by applying a pre-given definition, then this methodology would be backwards; we would reject judgments about cases that conflict with our pre-given definitions, rather than the other way around. (E.g., philosophers would have just insisted that the Gettier case *is* a case of knowledge since it fit the traditional definition.)

Third, concepts are typically *not* constructed out of other concepts. The way we acquire the great majority of our concepts is by learning new *words*, i.e., being exposed to a word sufficiently that we ourselves gradually become disposed to apply that word in a similar range of conditions to those in which it is generally applied by other people. There is in this nothing that resembles combining and rearranging simple concepts to form compound ones.

What does all this imply for the project of defining words like "knowledge"? In order to successfully define a word (by the lights of contemporary philosophers), one would have to find a way of combining *other* terms in such a way as to pick out exactly the same range of cases. There is no reason for thinking that this should generally be possible.

You could think about it like this: Think of an abstract space, the "quality space", in which the dimensions are different characteristics that things could have to different degrees. The exact characteristics of an object determine its "location" in that space. And you could think of concepts as drawing lines around regions in the quality space, where the things inside the lines fall under the concept. Each concept corresponds to a particular region with a particular shape. The boundaries can also be fuzzy, which is an extra complication (that is, there can be cases in which a concept only *sort of* applies, also known as "borderline cases").

Note that you can generalize this idea: You can imagine a quality space for actions, states of affairs, properties, or whatever we may have concepts of. You can also imagine adding dimensions for *relationships* that things bear to other things. So the spatial metaphor can be applied to concepts quite generally.

Now, what factors affect the contours of a concept? Again, most concepts correspond to specific words in a natural language; my concept of knowledge is, more or less, just my concept of that which the word "knowledge" applies to. Thus, the concept's contours are shaped by the pattern of usage of the word in our language. That usage pattern is affected by all sorts of messy factors. It's affected by the predilections of the people using the language, what they care about, what they find interesting. It's also affected by the distribution of things in the outside world. For instance, we have the concept CAT because we keep seeing objects in which certain characteristics tend to cluster together. If there were a lot fewer cats, the word might fall into disuse or change its meaning. If there were many objects that were intermediate between cats and dogs on various dimensions, then we'd probably have different concepts—perhaps we'd have one concept covering those objects together with cats and dogs. We decide how to divide up the world based partly on what classification schemes enable efficient transmission of information, given background experience that most people in our linguistic community have.

Meanings also drift over time. You can tell this because most words in our language originated from words in other languages with very different meanings. For instance, the word "happiness" derives from the Norse *hap*, meaning chance. "Phenomenon" derives from the Greek *phainomenon*, meaning appearance. "Virtue" comes from the Latin root *vir*, meaning man. The uses of these words drifted quite a ways over time, and our current words are probably still in flux, on their way to some other set of meanings that people in 10,000 years will have. There is no one directing this process; each word's meaning just drifts in unsystematic ways according to the needs and interests of all the various individuals using the language.

All of this is to explain why the particular "shapes" of our concepts (the contours of the regions in the quality space that they include) are normally complex, fuzzy, and unique. There is no reason at all to expect a nice, neat set of conceptual relations, whereby you could take a concept and restate it using some different set of concepts. There is nothing in our language or in the world that requires there to be, for any given concept, some other collection of concepts that happen to match the exact boundaries of the given concept. There is no need for the boundary drawn by one concept to exactly coincide, for any distance, with the boundary of another concept.

That is why most concepts are undefinable. In order to define a concept, you have to find some way of combining other concepts (using something like set union and intersection operations) so as to exactly reproduce the unique contours of the original concept.

2.6.4. Lessons for Philosophy

Now you can see why I like to teach some of the literature on the analysis of "knowledge" to epistemology students. They don't end up learning the correct definition of "know", but they might end up learning that there isn't one and that we don't need one. If I just asserted those things at the outset, you probably wouldn't have believed me, nor should you have. You have to go through some of the attempts to define knowledge and see what's wrong with them, in order to understand what I'm talking about when I say that philosophers can't define anything.

This is no counsel of despair. The same theory that explains why we haven't produced any good definitions also explains why it was a mistake to want them. We thought, for instance, that we needed a definition of "know" in order to understand the concept and to apply it in particular circumstances. But that isn't how one learns a concept, nor how one applies it once learned. We learn a concept through exposure to examples of its *usage* in our speech community, and we apply it by imitating that usage. Indeed, even if philosophers were to one day finally articulate a correct definition of "knowledge", free of counter-examples, this definition would doubtless be so complex and abstract that telling it to someone who didn't already understand the word would do more to confuse them than to clarify the meaning of "knowledge" for them.

In contemporary intellectual discussions, it's often thought to be a mark of rigor and rationality to insist that we "define our terms". Now you know why I reject that. You should *not* define your terms, nor should you ask other people to define theirs. Doing so is actually more of a source of confusion than clarity, because the definitions people supply almost never match what they actually mean. There is also a risk of being drawn into endless and pointless debates about definitions.

To be clear, this concerns the ordinary senses of words that appear in ordinary language. I'm saying that if someone is using words in their ordinary English senses, you should not ask for, nor attempt to give, definitions of them. Technical terms are another matter. Naturally, if someone introduces a new term, or proposes to use a term in a different sense from the ordinary sense, they still need to explain what it means.

Also, this is not to say anything against trying to *clarify* ordinary terms, e.g., by distinguishing them from similar words that they might be confused with, by mentioning some of the important logical connections between terms, and by discussing what is important or useful about a given term. You can do all that without claiming to provide necessary and sufficient conditions for the application of the term across all possible worlds.

2.7. Conclusion

The traditional definition says that knowledge is justified, true belief. This was refuted by Gettier's examples in which a person has a justified but false premise and justifiedly infers a *true* conclusion from that premise. This gives the person a justified, true conclusion which isn't knowledge. A more intuitive example is that in which one looks at a stopped clock that just happens to be right.

In the wake of Gettier, epistemologists offered many new analyses of "knowledge". One account says you need a justified, true belief with no false beliefs in its evidential ancestry. Another says you need a true belief formed by a reliable mechanism. Another says you need a true belief formed by a properly-functioning, reliable, truth-oriented faculty operating in the environment it was designed for. Another says that you need a belief that is sensitive to the truth, in the sense that if the proposition were true, one would believe it, and if it were false, one would not believe it. Another says that you need a belief that is safe, in the sense that its content would be true in all the nearby possible worlds in which you believe it. Another says that you need a true belief with justification good enough for ruling out all the relevant alternatives, where alternative possibilities that aren't objectively, physically possible in the situation count as irrelevant. And another says that you need a justified, true belief with no genuine defeaters, where defeaters are true propositions that, if added to your beliefs, would result in your initial belief no longer being justified.

All of these theories and more have been subjected to pretty convincing counter-examples. Thus, no one knows how to define "knowledge". Some people claim to, but no analysis is generally accepted.

Interestingly, the same fate has befallen every other word or concept that philosophers have tried to define. And of course, no one else has done any better at defining concepts to the satisfaction of philosophers, with the exception of mathematical concepts and perhaps a handful of others.

This is all very surprising and distressing if you hold a Lockean theory of concepts, whereby concepts are introspectively accessible states, most concepts are composed of other concepts, and understanding a concept is knowing a definition which describes how the concept is composed.

The extreme difficulty of defining most concepts suggests that the Lockean theory of concepts is wrong. An alternative, Wittgensteinian view of concepts holds that in most cases, understanding a concept consists of possessing the right set of dispositions to apply or not apply a certain word in one's language. One acquires these dispositions through observing the usage of the word in one's linguistic community and striving to imitate that usage. These dispositions are often extremely complex and messy, subject to many different influences, and they tend to drift unpredictably over time. As a result, there is no reason to expect different concepts to be related to each other in the simple, systematic ways required by definitions.

Indefinability of words is perfectly normal and does not pose a problem, since understanding is not constituted by knowledge of definitions. The best way to convey a word's meaning is through examples.

3. More Logical and Semantic Debates

In this chapter, I'm going to address a few logical and semantic debates about knowledge and justification in contemporary epistemology. Most students find these pretty boring, but I have to talk about them because other epistemologists go on about them a lot.

3.1. Contextualism

3.1.1. Motivating Contextualism

Contextualism is an idea about the meaning of "know", but it isn't an actual *analysis* of knowledge (like the theories in §2.5), i.e., it doesn't tell you exactly what "know" means. **Contextualism** says that the meaning of "know" *changes* depending on the conversational context; more specifically, the standards for knowledge go up or down in different contexts.

To explain what I mean, let me start with an example involving another word whose meaning changes depending on context, the word "here":

> *Dennett Is Here:* I'm at the annual meeting of the American Philosophical Association, and I'm looking for Daniel Dennett at the reception. (I want to poke him and see if he feels anything, you see.[25]) I don't know what he looks like, so I go to the table for people from his school, and I say, "Is Daniel Dennett here?"
>
> Two weeks later, I am visiting Humboldt State University in Kansas, when one of the philosophers says to me, "Did you know that we've just hired

---

[25] This is funny because Dennett denies that people have experiences with an intrinsic, qualitative feel. See his article "Quining Qualia" or his book *Consciousness Explained* (1991).

> Daniel Dennett?" I say, incredulously, "Daniel Dennett is *here?*"[26]

Notice how the meaning of "here" changes. The first time I use it, "here" means roughly "at this table". The second time, it means roughly "at this university". The location changes (since I'm in different places when I say "here"), and the *size* of the area referred to also changes (in the second case, a much larger range of physical locations is allowed for Dennett to count as being "here").

Well, contextualists think there is a similar phenomenon with the word "know": Its meaning becomes more or less strict, depending on the context in which the word appears. Here are two more cases to illustrate this:

> *Car Check:* Somebody asks me if I know whether my car is working, because if it's not, he can sell me a new car. "Sure," I answer, "I know my car is working because I drove it last week, and it was fine."
>
> *Spaceship Check:* I am the chief safety officer for the first manned mission to Mars. The spaceship is scheduled to be launched tomorrow, and I am responsible for making sure all systems are working. If anything goes wrong, there's a good chance that the rocket will explode shortly after launch, or that crucial systems will shut down in outer space millions of miles from Earth, leaving the astronauts stranded. My boss, Elon Musk, comes up to me and asks, "Hey Mike, do you know if the spaceship is working?" "Sure," I reply, "I know it's working because I looked at it last week, and it was fine."

To be clear, I want you to assume that in both cases, I've taken the same amount of care, and I have the same amount of evidence that the machine in question is in working order, so the probability of my being correct is the same in both cases. Also assume that both the car and the spaceship are in fact working. Was I correct to claim knowledge in these cases?

You're supposed to have the intuition that in the first case, it's perfectly fine (and correct) for me to say "I know my car is working", but in the second case, it's very much *not* fine (and not correct) for me to say "I know the spaceship is working." In the Spaceship case, the *standards* for "knowing" are higher than they are in the Car case, because the stakes are higher. That is, I have to do *more*, I have to gather more evidence and rule out more possibilities, in order to count as "knowing" that the spaceship is working, because the consequences of being wrong are so much worse.

---

[26] This is purely fictional. I have never tried to poke Daniel Dennett, and there is no Humboldt State University in Kansas (there is one in California, though).

3.1.2. Clarifications

Some points of clarification about contextualism. Contextualism is a theory about what's going on when someone says that someone knows a proposition. E.g., suppose Jasmine says, "Randall knows that honey badgers are mean."[27] So Jasmine has attributed knowledge to Randall. In this case, we say Jasmine is the *attributor* of knowledge, and Randall is the (alleged) *subject* of knowledge. The subject is the person who has or lacks knowledge; the attributor is the person who *says* that someone has or lacks knowledge.

Now, everyone agrees that facts about the *subject* (or **"subject factors"**, as we say) can affect whether a knowledge attribution is correct. E.g., facts about Randall's situation, obviously, affect whether it's correct to say "Randall knows that honey badgers are mean." Whether Randall believes that honey badgers are mean, why he believes this, what evidence (if any) he has for doubting this—those are all *subject factors*, which everyone agrees are relevant.

What's unusual about contextualism is that it says that **attributor factors** (features of the attributor's situation) can affect whether a knowledge attribution is correct. E.g., facts about *Jasmine's* situation when she says "Randall knows that honey badgers are mean" affect whether Jasmine's statement is true.

What attributor factors might affect this? Well, as suggested above, it matters *how important* the proposition in question is to the attributor. If it's super-important whether p is true, then the standards for a person to count as "knowing" p are going to be extra high (as in Spaceship Check). If it doesn't much matter, then there will be low standards (as in Car Check).

Here's another thing that matters: What other possibilities have been discussed or thought about in the particular context in which someone attributes knowledge to someone. Let's say that, when Jasmine makes the remark about Randall and the badgers, it's just a normal conversation in which people are talking about whether honey badgers tend to be mean or nice. Then, when Jasmine says "Randall knows that honey badgers are mean", this will mean that Randall has sufficient evidence to rule out the alternative that honey badgers are generally nice—for example, maybe he's observed several honey badgers and noted their behavior.

But now suppose, instead, that people have recently been discussing outlandish scenarios, such as the Brain in a Vat scenario (from §2.5.4), and treating them as serious possibilities. *In this context*, if Jasmine announces, "Randall knows that honey badgers are mean", she will be implying that

---

[27] For discussion, see Randall, "The Crazy Nastyass Honey Badger" (2011), https://youtu.be/4r7wHMg5Yjg.

Randall has evidence that can rule out the hypothesis that honey badgers are just an illusion created by the computer stimulating the BIV. In that sense, the standards for knowledge have gone up. In a *normal* conversation, you don't have to rule out things like the BIV scenario, but in certain conversations where that hypothesis is being discussed and taken seriously, you do.

You might be tempted to draw the lesson that discussing outlandish scenarios like the BIV scenario causes you to *lose knowledge* (in which case, maybe philosophy is bad for you!). But, if you're understanding contextualism properly, that is *not* what a contextualist should say. There is no sense of "knowledge" such that you first have knowledge and then lose it after discussing the BIV scenario. In the low-standards sense of "knowledge", you continue to have knowledge of the external world even after discussing the BIV hypothesis; in the high-standards sense of "knowledge", you never had knowledge of the external world. When you start seriously discussing BIVs, all that happens is that you shift from using a low-standards sense of "knowledge" to using a high-standards sense of the word. It doesn't cause you to lose anything.

Some people, on hearing about contextualism, are tempted to think that contextualism implies that knowledge can't be defined, and that perhaps this is why contextualism doesn't try to define "knowledge". But no, contextualism doesn't imply anything about whether knowledge can or can't be defined. Suppose that the meaning of "know" shifts depending on the conversational context. It doesn't follow from this that it's impossible to describe how that meaning shifts. So, *if* you could describe exactly how the meaning is determined by context, then there's no reason you couldn't define "know". Example: The word "now" changes its meaning depending on the time at which the word is uttered. But that doesn't mean you can't define "now". Rather, you can say something like, "'now' refers to the time at which the utterance in which the word appears is made", or something like that—that would be a perfectly good definition, which at the same time captures context sensitivity.[28]

3.1.3. Assessment

Is contextualism right? It has some plausibility, as we just saw (at least, *I* saw that; I hope you did too). However, I'm not sure that the word "know" really works as the contextualists say.

---

[28] The definition given in the text is not in fact *correct*, but that is irrelevant to my point, which is merely that it's possible to have a definition that recognizes context-sensitivity. The reason the definition of "now" given in the text is wrong is (among other things) that "now" sometimes refers to the time at which a message is *received* rather than the time at which it is created.

Start by thinking about a word that we know changes meaning with context: the word "here". Suppose I'm outside on a summer day, when the temperature is 90°F, and I say, "It's hot here." Then I walk inside my air-conditioned house and I say, "It's *not* hot *here*." You happen to be with me, and you say, "Aha, you're contradicting yourself, Mike! First you said 'It's hot here', then you said 'It's *not* hot here.' Which is it?"

Obviously, I can easily rebut the charge of inconsistency. I could reply: "I stand by both of my statements. Indeed, it's not hot here. This is entirely consistent with my earlier statement, because when I said, a minute ago, 'It's hot here', of course I didn't mean that it was hot *here*."

That's all fine, because the meaning of "here" has shifted to refer to the location inside the house; thus, when I say "…I didn't mean that it was hot *here*," I am saying that I didn't mean that it was hot inside the house. Normal English speakers would perfectly well understand this, and thus there is nothing odd or confusing about my saying "By 'it's hot here', I did not mean that it was hot *here*."

Okay, now suppose that "know" works similarly to "here", but instead of changing with the speaker's location, the meaning of "know" changes when someone mentions weird scenarios like the BIV scenario. In that case, we should be able to have a conversation like this:

You: What do you know about Mars?
Me: Hm… Well, I know that Mars is the fourth planet from the sun.
You: Ah, but what if you're a brain in a vat, and everything in your experience is illusory? Can you rule that out?
Me: Well, no… So I guess I don't know that Mars is the fourth planet from the sun.
You: Aha, you're contradicting yourself! First you said, "I know that Mars is the fourth planet from the sun"; now you say, "I don't know that Mars is the fourth planet from the sun." Which is it?
Me: I stand by both of my statements. Indeed, I don't know that Mars is the fourth planet from the sun. This is entirely consistent with my earlier statement, because when I said, a minute ago, "I know that Mars is the fourth planet from the sun", of course I didn't mean that I *knew* that Mars was the fourth planet from the sun.

Notice that the above dialogue is perfectly analogous to the earlier dialogue about the statement "It's hot here"—I just switched a statement using "here" for a statement using "know". If "know" changes its meaning, then that whole dialogue should be fine, just as the analogous dialogue using "here" is fine.

But the above dialogue is not fine. There is one part that sounds bizarre: my final declaration that by "I know that Mars is the fourth planet from the sun," I didn't mean that I knew that Mars was the fourth planet from the sun. If I say that, you would conclude that I must not have been using "know" correctly, i.e., I had to have been using it in some nonstandard sense. (Or you might think that I'm just lying, but let's leave that aside.)

This suggests that the word "know" *doesn't* work like "here"—we treat "know" as having a fixed meaning, in a way that we *don't* do for terms whose meaning uncontroversially shifts with context. Maybe this shows that contextualism is wrong. Alternately, maybe the meaning of "know" actually *does* shift, but we nevertheless, for some reason, have a convention of pretending that it doesn't shift.

3.2. The Closure Principle

3.2.1. *The Closure Principle*

The **Closure Principle** in epistemology is something like the following principle:

Closure (for Knowledge): If S knows that p, and p entails q, then S knows that q.

I said it's "something like" that, because there are a number of variations on that idea, all of which are considered versions of "the Closure Principle". E.g., maybe the principle should be stated in one of these ways:

- If S knows that p, and S knows that p entails q, then S knows that q.
- If S knows that p, and p entails q, then S is in a position to know that q.
- If S knows that p, and p entails q, and S correctly deduces q from p and believes q as a result of that deduction, then S knows that q.

Epistemologists don't fuss too much about exactly what is the best formulation (which is kind of odd, because they tend to be really fussy about the exact formulation of everything else, but anyway). There's a debate about whether "the Closure Principle" is true—that is, whether there is anything in this neighborhood that is true. (Obviously, the first formulation I gave makes Closure false, but the other three formulations are plausible, or at least not obviously false.)

By the way, you can also have a closure principle for *justification*, which would be something like this:

Closure for Justification: If S has justification for believing that p, and p entails q, then S has justification for believing that q.

(Again, there are variations on that idea that all count as versions of closure.) Usually, unless otherwise specified, "the Closure Principle" refers to Closure for Knowledge.

> *Aside:* Where did this terminology of "closure" come from? Well, in logic, there is an expression "closed under". A set is said to be *closed under* some operation when, for every item in the set, everything that results from applying that operation to that item is also in the set. Example: The set of integers is closed under the operation of adding 1 (in other words: If n is an integer, then $n+1$ is also an integer). Using this terminology, we could say "the set of known propositions is *closed under entailment*", and what this would mean is that if p is known, then anything entailed by p is also known.

3.2.2. Analyses of "Knowledge" that Reject Closure

Most people find it extremely intuitive that some version of Closure is correct; I take it that I don't have to explain that. But there are some epistemologists who dispute the Closure Principle, i.e., they think none of the above versions (or anything close to them) is correct.

By the way, if you think that rejecting Closure is contradictory, or that Closure (for knowledge) is trivial, then you're probably misunderstanding the principle. You might be confusing Closure for *knowledge* with Closure for *truth*. Of course, *truth* (or the set of true propositions) is closed under entailment, by definition. That just follows from the meaning of "entailment". But knowledge is something much *stronger* than truth. When you know p, and p entails q, obviously q must be *true*; however, it's not immediately obvious that there isn't some *other* condition on knowledge (besides truth) that you *might* not satisfy with respect to q.

Okay, so why do some people deny Closure? One reason is that there are particular analyses of knowledge that conflict with Closure. Of particular interest, if you endorse the Sensitivity condition (§2.5.4), then you have to reject Closure. This is because you could have a situation in which (*i*) if p were false, you wouldn't believe p, (*ii*) p entails q, but (*iii*) if q were false, then you *would* still believe q. Example: Let

p = [I have two hands.]
q = [I am *not* a Brain in a Vat.]

If I didn't have two hands, I would not think I had two hands. That's true because the nearest possible world in which I don't have two hands is one in which I somehow lost one of my hands, but everything else is normal, and in that situation, I would realize that I only had one hand. On the other hand, if I were a BIV, I would still think I *wasn't* one (as explained in §2.5.4). But notice that *p* entails *q* (having two hands is incompatible with being a brain in a vat). So the Sensitivity condition does not satisfy closure: Your belief that *p* can be sensitive, and *p* can entail *q*, while your belief that *q* is *not* sensitive. Since Sensitivity doesn't satisfy closure, that means that knowledge doesn't satisfy closure, *if* sensitivity is a condition on knowledge. In other words: You can know that you have two hands (per the tracking account of knowledge), but you cannot know that you're not a BIV, even though your having two hands entails that you're not a BIV.

The relevant alternatives account of knowledge (§2.5.6) also rejects Closure. In fact, rejecting Closure is kind of the main thing it does. The main point of the RA account is that there are some alternatives (the "irrelevant" ones) that you do not have to rule out in order to know something. So let's say that *p* is something you know, and A_i is an *irrelevant* alternative to *p*. By definition, that means that you can know that *p* without being able to rule out A_i. Since you can't rule out A_i, you cannot know $\sim A_i$. But note that *p* entails $\sim A_i$ (this is what is meant by *p* and A_i being "alternatives"—that they can't both be true). So we have a counter-example to Closure: You know *p*, *p* entails $\sim A_i$, yet you can't know $\sim A_i$.

My take on this: I am unconvinced; see the objections to sensitivity and relevant alternatives in §§2.5.4 and 2.5.6.

3.2.3. A Counter-example to Closure?

Some epistemologists claim to have found counter-examples to Closure that don't rest on any particular analysis of knowledge but that just directly appeal to our intuitions. Here's one:

> *Slightly Hard Calculation:* I perform a slightly difficult math problem, say, 16×23. I am highly reliable with such calculations, though of course not as reliable as a computer. I do the calculation by hand, get the answer 368, and check my calculation carefully enough that I can reasonably be said to know the answer. So, I know [16×23 = 368]. Now, notice that [16×23 = 368] entails [If my computer says that 16×23 *isn't* 368, then the computer is wrong]. Do I know that if the computer says 16×23 isn't 368, then the computer is wrong?[29]

Intuitively, no. The computer is more reliable than I am, and I know that. Therefore, what I should think is that *if* the computer disagrees with me, then

---

[29] I got this from Robert Audi (*Belief, Justification, and Knowledge*, 1988), except that I changed the calculation, and I switched Audi and his wife for me and my computer.

I'm probably wrong, not the computer. And therefore I surely do not *know* that if the computer disagrees with me the computer is wrong.

My take: I think this example turns on an ambiguity in "if-then" statements. Here's one way of interpreting a conditional: "If *A* then *B*" means "It's not the case that *A* is true and *B* false." (Conditionals so understood are known as "material conditionals". You probably learned this interpretation in your logic class. It's equivalent to (~*A* ∨ *B*), but the way I put it is slightly less counter-intuitive.) If we interpret the conditional in the example in this way, then I think I *do* know the conditional. I.e., I know that it's not the case that the computer will say 16×23 isn't 368 and not be wrong. Of course, the main way that I know this is that I am almost certain that the computer will not in fact say that 16×23 isn't 368 (which is enough for the conditional to be true).

Why does the example seem plausible at first? I think the reason is that there is another way of interpreting conditionals. On this other interpretation, "If *A* then *B*" means something like this: "My current evidence, conjoined with the supposition that *A*, supports the conclusion that *B*". (I'm sure that's not exactly right, but I don't care. That's enough to give you the general idea.) On *this* interpretation, I do not know the conditional to be true, because the conditional is in fact false. If someone had my current basic evidence, plus the knowledge that my computer says that 16×23 isn't 368, that person *should not* conclude that the computer is wrong.

But also notice that, on this interpretation of the conditional, the conditional *does not follow* from the proposition [16×23 = 368]. That is: Even if 16×23 = 368, it does not follow that my current evidence, conjoined with the supposition that the computer says 16×23 isn't 368, would support the conclusion that the computer is wrong.

3.2.4. *Of Zebras and Mules*

Here's another putative counter-example to the Closure Principle.

> *Zebra in the Zoo:* Fred takes his kid to the zoo, where they see some black-and-white striped, equine-looking animals in an enclosure labelled "Zebras". The kid asks Fred what those animals are. "Those are zebras," Fred replies. Then the kid asks, "Do you know that they aren't mules that the zoo authorities have cleverly disguised as zebras by painting them black and white?"[30]

---

[30] I got this from Fred Dretske ("Epistemic Operators," *Journal of Philosophy*, 1970).

Intuitively, Fred knows that the animals in the pen are zebras. He knows this because he can see that they are horse-shaped animals, a little smaller than horses, with black and white stripes, located in a pen marked "zebras". All of this is excellent evidence that the creatures he is dealing with are zebras. However, none of that evidence shows that they aren't cleverly disguised mules, since cleverly disguised mules would have all those same characteristics. So he doesn't know that they aren't cleverly disguised mules. But notice that being zebras *entails* not being cleverly disguised mules.

So we have a counter-example to the Closure Principle: Fred knows that the animals are zebras, the fact that they are zebras entails that they are not cleverly disguised mules, but he does not know that they aren't cleverly disguised mules. Or so Fred might claim.

My take: I find this example dubious. Let's extend the dialogue from the example a little bit:

Kid: What are those?
Fred: Those are Zebras.
Kid: Do you know that they aren't cleverly disguised mules?
Fred: No, I don't.
Kid: So you don't know what kind of animals they are after all?
Fred: No, I *do* know they're zebras. It's just that for all I know they're disguised mules instead.

I submit that the conclusion to this dialogue is nonsensical. Yet that's just what Fred should say, *if* this is really a sound counter-example to the Closure Principle. (By the way, I think another way of phrasing Fred's last claim would be this: "Those animals might be cleverly disguised mules, but they're definitely zebras.") Since that sounds crazy, I don't find this a compelling counter-example to Closure.

Here's a further argument against Fred's position:

1. If Fred knows those animals are zebras, then he knows what kind of animals those are.
2. If Fred knows what kind of animals those are, then he knows whether they are mules.
3. Therefore, if Fred knows those animals are zebras, then he knows whether they are mules.

But, you might ask, what is the right diagnosis of the example? *Does* Fred know that the animals are zebras? Does he know they aren't cleverly disguised mules? I'm not going to discuss that at length now, but we'll discuss very closely related questions in the chapter on external-world skepticism later. I'm inclined to say that Fred knows the animals are zebras and also knows they're not cleverly disguised mules (though *the evidence* for these two propositions isn't the same).

3.2.5. *What About Justification?*

All that was about Closure for Knowledge. What about Closure for Justification? If you have adequate justification for p, and p entails q, do you necessarily have adequate justification for q?

The two alleged counter-examples above (Slightly Hard Calculation and Zebra in the Zoo) could equally be given as counter-examples to Closure for Justification, and I would again find them unconvincing, for essentially similar reasons to those given above.

There is also an argument for Closure for Justification that doesn't apply to knowledge. If p entails q, then the probability of q must be greater than or equal to the probability of p. That's an uncontroversial theorem of probability theory. Now, if we think that beliefs are justified whenever they are sufficiently likely to be true (which is a plausible view of justification), then whenever p passes the necessary threshold for justification, everything that p entails must also pass that threshold, since it is *at least* as likely to be true as p is.

That argument is debatable, though. It *could* be that the threshold probability needed for a proposition to count as "justified" varies depending on the proposition. So it could be that p is justified, q is more probable than p, and yet q isn't justified because a higher level of probability is needed for q to count as justified than for p. Why might q have a higher threshold? Well, perhaps "justification" is context sensitive in the way that contextualists suggest for "knowledge" (§3.1).

I think that might be the case. But I still think there's an important closure principle related to justification. It's this:

> *Closure for Degrees of Justification:* If p entails q, then the *degree* of justification that one has available for q is greater than or equal to the degree of justification that one has for p.

I accept that because of the point about probabilities (the probability of q will have to be at least as high as the probability of p). Notice that this is compatible with *denying* the following:

> *Closure for Qualitative Justification:* If one has adequate justification to believe p, and p entails q, then one has adequate justification for q.

Because, again, even if q has at least as much justification as p, q might need a higher level to count as "adequate".

I'm not going to tell you whether Closure for Qualitative Justification is true, because I don't know myself. But I think Closure for Degrees of

Justification is true, and I think that for most purposes, that's really what matters. (E.g., when we talk about arguments for skepticism later, I think all we need is Closure for Degrees.)

3.3. Internalism vs. Externalism

3.3.1. Defining Internalism & Externalism

Internalism vs. externalism is a huge debate in contemporary epistemology. Epistemologists love going on about it for some reason.

> **Aside:**
> Philosophers just love the words "internalism" and "externalism". You can tell that because there are about a bazillion uses of those words in philosophy. E.g., there's a debate between *semantic* internalism and externalism in philosophy of language; then there's a debate between *reasons* internalism and externalism in moral psychology; and then there's the debate between *epistemological* internalism and externalism. Each of these debates has different formulations. There is also an "internalism vs. externalism" debate in aesthetics, and another one in philosophy of sport. All of these are *completely different* debates, with essentially no connection to each other. I'm telling you this partly so that, if you hear about "internalism" and "externalism" in some other context, you won't mistakenly assume that it's connected to the stuff we're talking about here. If a philosopher mentions "internalism", you have to ask what sense of "internalism" he's talking about.

It's tricky to say exactly what the debate is, because part of what epistemologists like to go on about is how to define "internalism" and "externalism". But basically, internalists believe (a) that knowledge requires justification (you know that *p* only *if* you're justified in believing *p*), and (b) justification is internal. (More on "internal justification" below.) Externalists believe one of two things: An externalist might think either (a) that knowledge does not require justification at all, or (b) that knowledge requires justification, but justification need not be internal.

Now, about the notion of internality. There are two ways people characterize it. One is that something is "internal" to you if it is entirely determined by the state of your own mind. The other characterization is that something is internal to you if you have introspective access to it (i.e., you could be aware of it by self-reflection). These two notions are very similar, but they're not *the same* because you *could* have some mental states that are introspectively inaccessible to you. These states would then be "internal" in the first sense but not the second.

So putting all that together, there are two formulations of internalism:

Internal-state internalism: (a) To know that *p*, one must have adequate justification for *p*, and (b) this justification is solely a matter of one's own mental states.

Access internalism: (a) To know that *p*, one must have adequate justification for *p*, and (b) this justification is solely a matter of one's introspectively accessible states.

What do I mean by "solely a matter of"? Well, what the internalists are saying is that whether a person counts as "justified in believing *p*" must be determined by what's going on in their own mind (or by stuff that is introspectively accessible to them). Stuff that's going on outside your mind (or that you don't have access to) can't be directly relevant to your justification for believing anything. (Why did I insert "directly" there? Well, stuff going on outside your mind could *affect* your internal states, and it could thus *indirectly* affect what you're justified in believing. But it never *directly* affects your justification for anything, i.e., without affecting your mental states.)

In other words: If two people have the same stuff going on in their minds (or the same introspectively accessible states), then they are justified in believing exactly the same propositions to exactly the same degree, regardless of what else is going on in the world around them. That's what is meant by saying justification is "internal".

Exercise for the reader: Which views that we discussed earlier support externalism, and which support internalism? (Look especially at section 2.5.) You can go look back and reflect for a few minutes. I'll wait here.

. . .

Okay, are you done? Here's the answer. Reliabilism, the Proper Function analysis, the Sensitivity/Tracking analysis, and the Safety analysis are all externalist views of knowledge.[31] That's because none of them specify justification as a requirement for knowledge.

The No-False-Lemmas and Defeasibility analyses are compatible with internalism. They don't *entail* internalism, because (as formulated in §2.5) neither specifies whether justification must be internal or external. So one could have an internalist or externalist version of each of those views.

The Relevant Alternatives theory is a little tricky. It requires a person to have justification for *p* in order to know *p*, in the sense that the person must

---

[31] As formulated in §2.4. Of course, you could convert any of these into internalist theories by *appending* a condition that requires internal justification in order for one to know *p*.

have evidence that rules out the relevant alternatives. However, a person does not need any evidence against the *irrelevant* alternatives. And which alternatives are "relevant" depends on external factors. Therefore, the *adequacy* of your justification for a belief (whether the justification is good enough or not) can depend on external factors. There could be two people with the same introspectible mental states, who believe a proposition for the same reasons, and those reasons could be good enough for the first person to count as "knowing" but not good enough for the second person, because the relevant alternatives differ between the two believers, due to purely external factors. For this reason, I classify the Relevant Alternatives theory as externalist.[32]

3.3.2. Why Externalism?

Why would anyone believe externalism?

I think the main reason is that when you start thinking about a lot of typical, mundane examples of (what we normally call) knowledge, it's hard to see what the subject's internal justification is, and it can easily seem as if we're ascribing knowledge simply because the subject is a reliable detector of certain facts.

Example: You throw a tennis ball to your dog. The dog catches the ball in the air. It seems obvious that the dog knew the tennis ball was coming, and he knew, with pretty good precision, where the ball was. The dog knows this because he *sees* the ball. (Contrast the case where the dog catches the ball reliably, despite being blindfolded. We would wonder, "How did he know where it was?"—but we would not question *that* he knew where it was.) What is the dog's internal justification for believing the ball is there? It's not as though the dog went through some kind of argument in its mind. The dog could not supply any *reasons* for thinking that the ball was where it appeared to be. (And not just because the dog can't talk—a typical dog, I take it, wouldn't even be able to silently reason about the reliability of the senses in its own mind.)

Come to think of it, even *you* might not be able to supply any presentable justifications for most of the things that you know. For example, you know that multiplication is commutative, right ($a \times b = b \times a$)? Can you prove that? Most people cannot. You might be tempted to say that you don't need a proof; some experts told you that it's true, and you trust them. That might be enough justification, if you could identify the person or people who taught you that principle, and then cite some compelling evidence showing that those

---

[32] It's not externalist merely because there is *some* external condition on knowledge. *Every* analysis of knowledge includes some external condition. Rather, it's that the RA theory makes *the adequacy of a justification* depend on external factors.

individuals are highly reliable about mathematical principles. Most people can't do that either. For my part, I have no idea who first told me that multiplication is commutative, and whoever it was, I'm sure I never tried to verify that person's reliability. I think multiple other people told me about commutativity since then, and I can't remember those people either, nor did I check the reliability of any of them.

It goes that way for a lot of things. How do you know that there are eight planets in the solar system? Did you search the sky with powerful telescopes, counting the planets? Did you at least verify the reliability of whoever told you that there were eight planets?

The point is that there is an awful lot of stuff that we normally say that people (and animals) *know*, for which the knower doesn't seem to have an internal justification to speak of. Maybe it's enough that the person gets it right, and reliably so. Maybe something like that is all we mean by "knowing".

Don't respond with "But how does the person or animal know that they're reliably right?" *They don't have to*; that's the externalist's point. From an external point of view, we say that someone knows something when we see that person getting it right reliably (or something like that); it's not required that the person also have evidence or even beliefs about their own reliability (or anything like that). They don't have to know that they know (cf. §6.1).

3.3.3. Why Internalism?

Many people have the strong intuition that you can't claim to know *p* if, from your own point of view, there's no justification for thinking that *p* is true. If you form such unjustified beliefs, and you turn out to be right, it seems that you would only be right by luck—which, as is widely agreed, is incompatible with your really having *knowledge* (see §2.2).

In response to the argument of §3.3.2, some people (the skeptics) would say that we simply don't know as much as we normally think we know. E.g., maybe I *don't* know that there are eight planets in the solar system, since my reason for believing it (some people whom I can't remember and whose reliability I never checked on told me) is so lame.

Most epistemologists don't like that sort of response, though; we like to avoid skepticism and hold onto our ordinary knowledge as much as possible. So instead, it's more common to argue that internal justification is not that hard to come by. For instance, maybe for a belief to be internally justified, it's enough that the belief seems true to you and you have no specific reasons for doubting it (see ch. 5). Or maybe your beliefs can be justified simply because they all support each other (see §4.3). Notice how both of these suggestions satisfy the internality condition: On these views, your justification would be solely a matter of your internal mental states.

Suppose we agree that knowledge requires justification. Why think that justification must be *internal*? I myself find this highly intuitive (so much so that externalist views of "justification" strike me as using a completely different sense of the word "justification" that has been bizarrely invented by the externalists). But there's more to say than just a direct appeal to linguistic intuition.

One of the main arguments for adopting an internalist view of justification is the "new evil demon argument". Imagine that there was a powerful demon capable of planting any sort of image or experience in someone's mind. This demon likes deceiving people. He has created a disembodied soul, which the demon deceives into thinking that it (the soul) is a normal, embodied person. In this hypothetical story, in fact, let's suppose that the soul has experiences qualitatively exactly like the experiences that you are actually having. The disembodied soul would have a belief system just like yours, it would think that it was living a normal life in the physical world, etc., and yet almost all of its beliefs would be false.

Now, I know what you're thinking, and no, I am *not* raising this hypothetical in order to question whether you actually have any knowledge of the world around you. Set that question aside (I know it's hard, but do it!). I'm raising the hypothetical in order to ask: What would the soul (the demon's victim) be *justified* in believing? Or: If it was a rational soul, what would it believe? (Note: If you don't like the idea of a disembodied soul, you can instead imagine a brain in a vat, and ask the analogous questions about it.)

There's a certain sense in which the soul *should* believe that it is a normal person living in the physical world. When it has the experience of seeming to see a cat on a mat, it should think that there is a cat on a mat. This belief would be *mistaken* but nevertheless entirely *reasonable*, given what the soul has to go on. Indeed, if the soul believed (what is actually true) that it was a disembodied soul being deceived by an evil demon, it would be *insane*. Just as insane as *you* would be if you thought that right now.

At least, that is the intuition that most people have about this scenario. But if we take an externalist conception of justification—for instance, if we say that a belief is justified when and only when it is formed by a reliable method—then it looks like we'd have to say that the soul is *unjustified* in its beliefs about the world around it. (Nearly all of its belief-forming methods are unreliable, thanks to the demon.)

So that is supposed to show that justification does not require reliability. In fact, the case seems to show (assuming you agree that the demon-victim has justified beliefs) that justification does not require anything beyond what is going on in one's own mind.

3.3.4. *A Compromise Position*

Maybe internalism and externalism are both right, in a sense. Some people think there are two kinds of knowledge, or two concepts of knowledge, one externalist and one internalist.[33] The externalist kind of knowledge, sometimes called "animal knowledge", is the one we commonly ascribe to animals and children. Animal knowledge requires reliability but does not require internal justification or knowledge of one's own reliability.

The internalist kind of knowledge, sometimes called "reflective knowledge", is a higher grade of knowledge that requires one to be able to justify one's belief on reflection. This is the sort of knowledge that philosophers have traditionally sought after.

My take: I find this distinction pretty plausible. However, I don't think that we should spend much more time on this, because it's just a semantic issue. More generally, I don't want to spend more time on debates about the meaning of "knowledge". I think there is at least *a sense* of "knowledge" such that knowing requires having justification, but if you don't agree with that, I don't think this much matters.

I also assume that justification is internal, because I just can't really see any externalist notion (e.g., "reliability") as being about what I call justification. If you think I'm misusing the word "justified", I don't think that much matters either.

3.4. Conclusion

Epistemologists like to debate semantic and logical questions about "knowledge". One debate concerns contextualism, the view that the standards for someone to count as "knowing" something shift up or down depending on features of the conversational context. These features include how important it is to be right and what other possibilities have been mentioned in the conversation. This view has plausibility but entails that some weird statements should be okay, such as "When I said 'I know that p', I didn't mean that I *knew* that p" (said after a change in context has occurred).

Another debate concerns the closure principle for knowledge, which says something like: If S knows p, and p entails q, then S is in a position to know q. Some accounts of knowledge conflict with this, such as the sensitivity

---

[33] Ernest Sosa discusses this in *Reflective Knowledge* (2009), ch. 7, although he formulates the distinction differently.

condition and the relevant alternatives theory. However, these accounts are open to independent objections. There are also some alleged counter-examples to the closure principle, but they're dubious. One example turns on an ambiguity in "if-then" statements. Another example suggests that one could sensibly claim to know that some animals are zebras while also conceding that for all one knows, they are disguised mules.

A particularly big debate in epistemology is that between internalists and externalists. Internalists think that knowing requires having internal justification for one's belief, a kind of justification that depends entirely on one's own mental states or on what is introspectively accessible to oneself. Externalists deny this.

Externalism can be motivated by thinking about many cases of ordinary knowledge in which people or animals are unable to supply justifications for their beliefs. Internalism can be motivated by thinking about skeptical scenarios like the evil demon or the brain in a vat: Most people have the intuition that people in those scenarios are justified in believing the same things that normal people justifiedly believe. This shows that justification is a function of what is going on in one's own mind.

Perhaps the most plausible position is that there simply are two notions of knowledge, one of them externalist ("animal knowledge") and one of them internalist ("reflective knowledge").

4. The Structure of Knowledge

In this chapter, we talk about the overall structure that a series of reasons leading to knowledge might have.

4.1. Four Knowledge Structures

Suppose you know p. I might ask you *how* you know it. Usually, the answer to that will cite a *reason* that you have for believing p: You know p on the basis of q, where q is something else that you know that supports p.[34] In that case, I could go on to ask, "And how do you know q?" If you cite a reason for q, say, r, then I could go on to ask "How do you know r?" And so on.

If I keep asking "How do you know that?", how does this process ultimately end? There are four logical possibilities:

i. *Infinite regress:* The process never ends, because you have an infinite series of distinct reasons, such that you can keep supplying new reasons forever.
ii. *Circularity:* At some point, you repeat a reason that was offered earlier. E.g., you know p on the basis of q, which you know on the basis of r, which you know on the basis of p.
iii. *Foundations:* At some point, you reach a proposition that you know in some way not based on reasons. (Alternately: You reach a proposition that is known on the basis of one or more reasons, but the reasons are not themselves known. But hardly anyone likes this idea, so I'll ignore it henceforth.)
iv. *Ignorance:* The process never even starts, because you don't actually know anything and don't have any reasons for anything.

---

[34] In the case where more than one proposition combines to support p, just think of q as the conjunction of all the propositions that jointly support p.

I depict these four possibilities in figure 1 below.

The same basic issue could be raised without using the word "know"; we could just ask about justified belief, or about reasons for belief. Thus, even if you don't agree that knowledge requires justification (perhaps you're an externalist, as discussed in §3.3), you can still wonder about the structure of

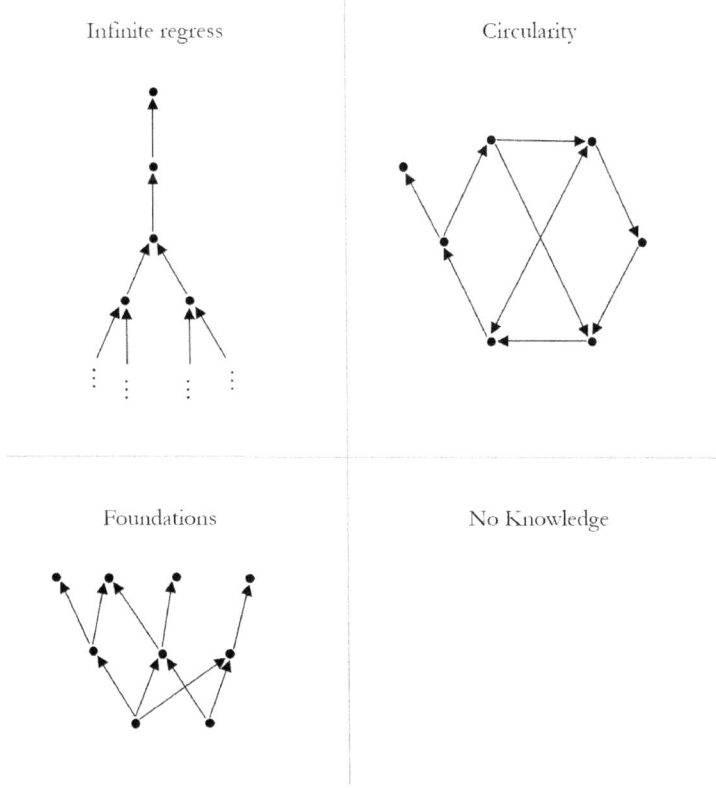

Figure 1: Four structures of knowledge

our justified beliefs, or the structure of a typical series of reasons, and there would be these four logical possibilities.

By the way, this division into four logical possibilities is not something specific to the logic of *reasons for belief*. There is an analogous four-way division of possibilities whenever you have a relation that two things can stand in.[35] Take the relation of cause and effect: For any event, you can ask what caused

---

[35] Qualification: For some relations, you can have two or three of the four possibilities simultaneously. E.g., take the less-than relation defined on the non-negative real numbers. You can have an infinite series of numbers each less than the last (1, ½, ¼, …), *and* there is also a "foundational" element that is less than all other elements (0).

it, and then what caused that cause, and so on. If we ask about the overall structure of the series of causes, there are four logical possibilities: (*i*) an infinite series of causes, (*ii*) circular causation, (*iii*) one or more *first* causes that started everything else, or (*iv*) no causation at all.

That issue (the structure of causes) is a big, famous issue in metaphysics. Here is a less famous issue: Given a person, you can ask who that person's mother is, and who is the mother's mother, and so on. What is the structure of the series of mothers? There are again four logical possibilities: (*i*) an infinite series of mothers, (*ii*) circular motherhood (some person is her own ancestor), (*iii*) a *first* mother (a mother who had no mother), or (*iv*) no mothers at all. I give that example just to illustrate that this four-way division of possibilities applies to any two-place relation.

Anyway, back to our question: What is the structure of the series of reasons for a typical item of knowledge? Traditionally, many people thought that the first three alternatives (infinite regress, circularity, foundations) are all problematic in one way or another. Also, the fourth possibility (no knowledge) was traditionally not even listed as a possible structure of the series of reasons. Thus, people say that we face a "trilemma" (a choice among three undesirable options) in accounting for the structure of reasons. Epistemologists usually call this "**Agrippa's Trilemma**", after the ancient skeptic who used the trilemma to argue that there was no knowledge.[36] (However, lay people who have read the Wikipedia entry on the topic call it "Munchausen's trilemma", because apparently this is the term used by some random German dude that no one other than the author of that Wikipedia entry has ever heard of.) (*Note:* For obvious reasons, it should really be called a *quadrilemma*, but I'm nevertheless going to continue calling it a trilemma.)

In the next four sections, I'll talk about what's problematic about each of the four possible structures of knowledge.

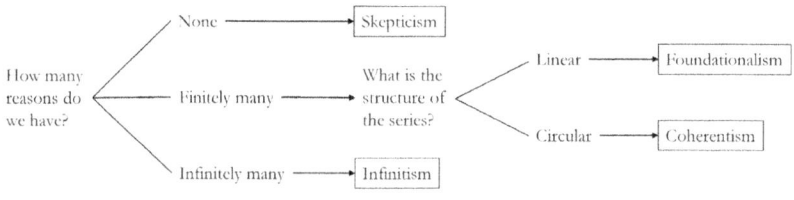

Figure 2: Arriving at four theories of the structure of knowledge

---

[36] See Sextus Empiricus, *Outlines of Pyrrhonism* (1990), which collects together a bunch of ancient skeptical arguments.

4.2. Infinitism

4.2.1. The Infinitist Theory of Justification

Most people don't feel the need for an argument against the infinite regress option. In most discussions of Agrippa's Trilemma, one just says, "Obviously, we can't have an infinite series of reasons" and then moves on. That's basically how things stood until the end of the 20th century, when Peter Klein (my old PhD advisor!) started defending a view called "infinitism". **Infinitism** holds that the key to justified belief is having an infinite, non-repeating chain of reasons standing behind each justified belief.

Wait, this isn't as ridiculous as it sounds! To see how it might be not-fully-ridiculous, you have to first distinguish between *actual infinities* and *potential infinities*. This is an old metaphysical distinction due to Aristotle. Basically, Aristotle thought that there could be things that have some kind of unlimited potential ("potential infinities"), but nothing could be actually infinite (larger than every finite number) at any given time. Illustration: There might be no limit to how many times you can walk around the block, but no matter what you do, you will never have walked around the block infinitely many times. It will always be some specific, finite number, but that number could be as large as you like. (Assume that you're immortal, and the block is also indestructible.) That's an illustration of potential infinity without actual infinity.

The important thing about infinitism is that it posits only a *potential* infinity, not an *actual* infinity. In other words, the infinitist (Peter Klein) doesn't think that for a belief to be justified, a person must have actually completed an infinitely long chain of reasoning. Rather, he thinks that for a belief to be justified, the believer must be *capable* of supplying a reason for the belief if the belief is challenged, and also capable of supplying a reason for that reason (in case the first reason is challenged), and so on, ad infinitum. So there should be *no limit* to how many reasons you could supply, but of course at any given time you will only have given a finite number of reasons.

If one of your beliefs comes under question, and you are able to find a satisfying reason for it, then the belief becomes a little bit more justified. If you can then find a reason for that reason, the original belief becomes more justified still. As the chain of reasons approaches an infinite chain, your justification approaches complete, maximal justification. But you never actually reach complete justification.

4.2.2. How to Continue the Series?

People have raised several objections to infinitism. One objection points to the sheer difficulty of continuing the series of reasons beyond the first few stages, for any ordinary belief. For instance, suppose that I have a headache. I form the belief [I am in pain]. What is my *reason* for believing that I'm in pain?

Even at this first stage, it seems difficult to answer that (it would be very odd to *reason* to the conclusion that one is in pain, wouldn't it?). When asked about this, Klein says something like: My reason is [I am good at recognizing pains]. I find this questionable, but let's say we accept that.[37] What's my reason for believing [I am good at recognizing pains]? Again, hard to say. Maybe I could say, "I've successfully recognized a lot of pains in the past"? Or, "Pains are inherently conscious states"? I don't know. Anyway, try to imagine continuing this series of reason-giving. If there is really an *infinite* series of reasons that could be given, it should be a cinch for Klein to just write down, say, the first 50 reasons in the series. Sadly, he has not done so, and neither has anyone else. In fact, no one seems to have ever written down more than a few stages, and it seems pretty clear that no one knows how to write down fifty. This casts doubt on the idea that we could really come up with infinitely many.

4.2.3. The Finite Mind Objection

A second objection appeals to the finitude of the human mind.[38] There is a limit to the degree of complexity and abstractness of a proposition that a human mind can comprehend. Some people are smarter than others and thus can grasp more complicated or more abstract propositions than others, but each individual has *some* limit. Furthermore, in order for a person to be capable of using a given proposition as a reason for one of their beliefs, the person must at least be capable of *grasping* the proposition. Therefore, there is a limit to the complexity and abstractness of the reasons that could be available to a given person. But, if you try to imagine an infinite series of propositions (*any* infinite series of propositions, never mind even trying to connect them to each other by evidential support relations), there does not seem to be any way of doing it without having the propositions getting more complex or more abstract as the series goes on. Thus, at some point, the propositions become incomprehensible to any given human being. As a result, it seems impossible that there should be an infinite series of propositions that a person is capable of citing as reasons for beliefs.

Klein says this isn't true because you can imagine an infinite collection of propositions that are all equally simple and easily graspable by a normal person. Consider a set of propositions of the form [*This* is red], where "This" refers to

---

[37] My problem is that "I'm good at recognizing pains" does not at all support "I am in pain." Lots of people who are good at recognizing pains are not in fact in pain right now.

[38] See my "Finite Minds" in *Themes from Klein: Knowledge, Scepticism, and Justification* (2019).

some specific object that one is pointing to. All you have to do is be pointing to a different object, and you get a different proposition. There is no limit to how many different objects you could point to, so there's no limit to how many propositions you can believe.

In response, I think that fails due to the limited capacity of human senses to discriminate among objects. There are only so many distinct things that a human being could actually *recognize* as distinct objects, because there are only so many properties we can observe, and objects that are too similar to each other in any given dimension will just look to us the same. I also think the propositions [This is red] and [*This* is red] are not meaningfully distinct if the person believing those propositions can't tell that the "This" refers to different things. What do I mean by "not meaningfully distinct"? Well, they couldn't serve different roles in reason-giving—i.e., you couldn't appropriately cite the one proposition as a reason in any context in which you could not cite the other, *given* that the two propositions are indistinguishable to you. And thus, we effectively have only finitely many propositions available as reasons.

4.2.4. Potential vs. Actual Reasons

A third concern is with the efficacy of merely potential reasons. It seems that, for a belief to be justified, it is not enough that one *could come up with* a reason for the belief, like some sort of ex post rationalization. Rather, a reason justifies a belief only if the believer actually holds the belief for that reason. But surely we can't have an infinite series of *actual* reasons behind any given belief. So it seems that we need some account of justification that works with finite reasons.

4.3. Coherentism

4.3.1. The Coherence Theory of Justification

The **Coherence Theory of Justification** (or "**coherentism**") holds that belief systems are justified by *internal coherence*. In other words, if you have a lot of beliefs that fit together really well, then that belief system is probably by and large correct.

What is meant by "coherence" or "fitting together"? Well, at minimum, your beliefs should be logically consistent with each other. But coherence (as coherentists use the term) goes beyond mere consistency. A coherent system of beliefs has many beliefs that support each other—either entailing each other or probabilistically supporting each other. It's also good if many of the things one believes can be *explained* by other things one believes and there are relatively few anomalies (things that you can't explain).

Why should we care about coherence? How does coherence help to justify a belief system? Well, the basic idea is that, if one's beliefs were generally unreliable, then it would be an amazing coincidence if a large, complicated set of them happened to fit together well.[39] To illustrate:

> *Crime Witnesses:* The police have received reports of a recent bank robbery, with several witnesses. They go to interview each of the witnesses separately (without giving the witnesses a chance to confer with each other); then they compare the witnesses' stories to each other. There are two ways the example can continue from here. Either:
> a. The witnesses might tell stories that fit together well—in some places, their testimonies directly support each other; in other places, what one witness reports just seems to make sense given things that other witnesses have reported. E.g., two witnesses report the same license plate number for the getaway car; one witness reports that it was a dark colored car, another that the car was black; etc. Or:
> b. The witnesses might tell incoherent stories—some of them outright contradict each other, while others simply assert things that are highly unlikely or difficult to understand given what other witnesses have asserted. E.g., one witness says the robbers were armed with rifles, another that they carried only pillows.

In version (a), the police would reasonably conclude that the witnesses were more or less correctly describing a real crime. Why? Because unless the robbery happened roughly the way the witnesses describe, it would be too much of a coincidence that the witnesses' testimonies would happen to fit together so well. Notice, by the way, that the detectives could draw this conclusion even if they knew nothing about these witnesses and thus had no prior opinion about whether the witnesses would be trustworthy or how trustworthy they might be. This seems to show that the *coherence* of the witnesses' testimonies *by itself* provides justification for believing the basic story that the witnesses are telling.

By contrast, in version (b), the police would conclude that they had very little idea what happened. If the testimonies were sufficiently incoherent, the cops might even doubt whether any robbery had occurred at all.

This is supposed to be analogous to your belief system as a whole. You have a bunch of beliefs from different sources—e.g., your senses of vision, hearing, taste, touch, and smell; the testimony of various other people; memory; reasoning; and intuition. These sources are like the witnesses in the

---

[39] This was Laurence BonJour's argument in *The Structure of Empirical Knowledge* (1985), though he later gave up coherentism and wisely embraced foundationalism. That was a good day for philosophy.

example. The beliefs you form via these sources are like the witnesses' testimony. If your beliefs tend to fit together well, then you can conclude that you have a pretty good idea of basically what's going on in the world, just as the detectives in the above example (in version (a)) could conclude that they have a basic grasp of what happened during the bank robbery. And just as the detectives need not have any *prior* opinions about the witnesses' reliability, you need not have any prior opinions about the reliability of your cognitive faculties. The *coherence* of your various beliefs is enough to provide justification.

This doesn't mean that *all* your beliefs are justified, though, any more than *all* the witnesses' claims are necessarily credible. Suppose that, though the witnesses' stories are *generally* highly coherent, there is one witness who makes one claim that doesn't fit with what anyone else said—e.g., this one witness thinks that the robbers left in a helicopter, though no one else mentioned anything about this. In that case, you should probably reject that particular claim.

Similarly, if you have a particular belief that doesn't fit together with the rest of your belief system, that one belief is unjustified.

So, for a particular belief to be justified, you need two things: (*i*) That belief has to be supported by other beliefs in your belief system, and (*ii*) the belief system as a whole needs to be highly coherent.

4.3.2. The Alternate-Coherent-Systems Objection

What's wrong with Coherentism? One problem is that it is possible to find multiple, incompatible belief systems, each of which is internally coherent. Schizophrenics, for example, often construct elaborate delusional belief systems, where every piece fits together, and every item in the system seems designed to help defend the system and provide explanations for any possible counter-evidence. (The same sort of thing also happens to political ideologues and, to a lesser extent, philosophers in general.)

An appeal to coherence could not tell us *which* coherent belief system is correct. So, given that there is more than one coherent system, coherence alone can't establish any particular belief system as more likely than not to be correct.

In response, the coherentist's best move is to emphasize certain qualifications to the coherence theory. In particular, coherence only provides justification for trusting a belief system if the individual beliefs were formed *independently*, and they had some external source (i.e., you didn't just *decide* to come up with these beliefs). The problem with the schizophrenic is that his beliefs weren't independently formed. Rather, the schizophrenic specifically devised all these beliefs *in order* to make them fit together and to provide explanations for any apparent counter-evidence.[40] Thus, it isn't surprising that the beliefs fit together well, and we don't need to suppose that they are by and large true in order to explain their coherence.

Our ordinary beliefs, however, are not like that: We don't make them up to make them coherent. Most of our beliefs come from the five senses, and we believe whatever we seem to observe; we don't make up stuff to fit with our other beliefs, and we don't have control over whether, say, what we *hear* will match with what we *see*. That's why it is impressive when our beliefs turn out to fit together well.

4.3.3. Coherence Justification Requires Foundations

Another objection is that the justification provided by coherence is dependent on there being some *other* (presumably foundational) source of justification. This would be bad news for the Coherence Theory, because it is a central point of the theory to avoid appealing to foundations. That's kind of the theory's main motivation.

In what way does coherence justification depend on foundational justification? I can think of three ways. First, the argument for trusting coherent belief systems (based on the Crime Witnesses case, §4.3.1) depends on knowledge about *probability theory*. In the Crime Witnesses example (version (a)), the police conclude that the witnesses are basically telling the truth, in part because the police have an understanding of some principles of probability theory (e.g., that $P(A \& B) = P(A) \times P(B|A)$). This knowledge of probability could not itself be justified by appealing to coherence, since one has to first understand probability theory in order to understand the appeal to coherence. (Unless you want to use a blatantly and directly circular argument, which coherentists generally do not want to do, because they're trying to be at least minimally plausible, because they're not intellectual jerks.)

In reply, the coherentist might grant that you have to have some prior knowledge of probability, which the coherence theory doesn't explain. Instead, the coherentist might say, the coherence theory is only supposed to explain the justification for *empirical* beliefs (those based on observation), not mathematical beliefs.[41]

Another possible reply is that knowledge of probability theory is not actually needed by the believer. Principles of probability theory explain why a

---

[40] At least, that is what I think the coherentist would want to argue. It's not so straightforward to make this case, though. The schizophrenics would deny that they're just making stuff up to make a coherent story. They would say that they are simply inferring the best explanations for all the evidence that they see.
[41] This was BonJour's view during his coherentist phase.

person is justified in believing a coherent belief system, but the person does not have to know those principles at the start. It's enough that you form beliefs in a way that *in fact* makes them likely to be true; you don't have to *know that* you did that.[42]

Here's the second way in which you need some foundational justification: You need to have foundational knowledge *about your own beliefs*. Remember the Crime Witnesses case. In order for the police to use the coherence of the witness reports as a justification for believing the witnesses, the police must first know *the content of those reports*. That is, they have to know what the witnesses in fact said, and *this* knowledge could not be based on coherence.

Similarly, in order for you to use the coherence of your belief system as a justification for thinking that that belief system is correct, you must first know the facts about *what you believe*, and *this* knowledge could not be based on coherence. (Note: This may seem a little weird, because normally there is no question about whether you know your own beliefs. E.g., if you believe p, no one asks you how you know that you believe it. But that's not because you don't in fact know what you believe; it's because it's normally trivially easy to know what you believe, which of course could be because that knowledge is foundational.) If you know that you believe p, and that you believe q, and then you see that p and q cohere, then you can give this argument that probably p and q are approximately true (per §4.3.1). But you have to first know, in some other way, that you believe p and that you believe q.

Possible reply: Maybe you know that you believe p (etc.) also by coherence. It would just be a different appeal to coherence. E.g., *the belief that you believe p* coheres with some other beliefs you have about your own beliefs, and therefore this set of beliefs about your own beliefs is probably by and large correct. Okay. But now this requires you to know *that you believe that you believe p*. How do you know that? If we repeat the same style of explanation (appealing to coherence again in an analogous way), then we're embarked on an infinite regress.

Finally, the third way in which coherence justification requires foundational justification: Return to the Crime Witnesses example again. In order for the coherence of the witnesses' testimony to be evidence of their truthfulness, there must be *some initial credibility* that you assign to the witnesses. By that, I mean that you must start out at least thinking that each witness is better than a pure random guesser (they are more likely to make a true statement than a randomly chosen false one). There is a formal mathematical exposition of this point, but I won't bore you with it here.[43] The intuitive idea

---

[42] BonJour would hate this reply, though. He thinks that you *do* need to be in a position to know that your belief-forming method is highly likely to lead to true beliefs.

[43] See my "Probability and Coherence Justification", *Southern Journal of Philosophy* (1997).

is this: Suppose you have two people who are just random guessers. Then, if *p* were true, that *would not* make the two people more likely to agree on *p*. They would be just as likely to agree on any randomly chosen false proposition as to agree on the truth. Therefore, if they happen to agree on a bunch of stuff, that agreement *cannot be explained* by hypothesizing that the stuff they are agreeing on is true. It would make just as much sense to hypothesize that *p* is *false* as an explanation for why the two people agree on *p*.

Thus, in order to use the probabilistic argument given in §4.3.1, you have to *start out* assigning to the witnesses (or the belief sources) a greater credibility than a mere random guesser.

Now, that may not sound like much. But that is to assign the witnesses *some* degree of initial credibility. It means that if a single witness asserts *p*, you should then *raise* your degree of confidence that *p* is true, above what it was before the witness said *p*.

The analogous point is that if, say, one of your senses "tells you" *p*, you should become more confident of *p*. E.g., if you seem to see a cat on a mat, you should, just from that one observation, become *at least to some degree* more confident that there is really a cat on a mat. If you *don't* become more confident, that means you're treating your senses as like random guessers, which in turn means that even the coherence of multiple different seeming observations won't provide you with any justification at all for believing anything.

Again, this may not sound like much. But it is in fact a victory for foundationalism. Remember Agrippa's Trilemma. Coherentists are basically people who are trying to avoid the other horns of the trilemma—they're trying to avoid infinite regress, foundations, and skepticism. That is the *core motivation* for coherentism. And the arguments against foundations (see below, §4.4) apply just as well to having *a little bit* of foundational justification as they do to having a lot of foundational justification. So if you have to admit that there is some foundational justification in order to make your coherence justification work, you've kind of given up the game.

Let me put the problem another way. The story of the Crime Witnesses was supposed to show how coherence, by itself, can provide justification for beliefs. But it doesn't show that, because in that example, coherence can only provide justification for the detectives' beliefs about the crime if the detectives already have some justification for beliefs about (a) the laws of probability, (b) what the witnesses said, and even (c) the reliability of each witness. So the best we could say is that the coherentist fails to motivate her view that coherence alone can be a source of justification.

4.4. Skepticism

4.4.1. The Skeptical View

Skepticism in epistemology is the view that we don't know, or aren't justified in believing, a lot of the things we ordinarily take ourselves to know or be justified in believing. There are more and less extreme forms of skepticism. Some skeptics claim that we don't know anything about the world outside our own minds (that's "**external world skepticism**"); others that we don't know anything whatsoever, not even the truth of skepticism itself (that's "**global skepticism**"). Also, some skeptics claim that we lack knowledge merely because our beliefs are not *absolutely certain* (that's "certainty skepticism"); others make the more extreme claim that we don't even have *any justification* for our beliefs (that's "justification skepticism").

The kind of skepticism I'm interested in here is *global justification skepticism*, the thesis that we have no justification for believing anything whatsoever. This is the most radical and therefore, in a sense, the most *interesting* form of skepticism. It is also the form of skepticism that is suggested by Agrippa's Trilemma. Notice that the trilemma can be applied to the justification for *any* belief, not just, say, beliefs about the physical world. Notice also that it can be applied to *any* reason that one might provide for a belief, not just reasons that are claimed to be absolutely conclusive. If you claim to have *any reason at all*, even a tiny reason, to believe p, then one can ask what that reason is, and then, whatever it is, one can ask what reason there is for believing that reason … and we're off to the races.

So, some philosophers have thought that we can't have any justified beliefs, basically because the other three alternatives (infinite regress, circularity, and foundations) are all bad. The argument goes something like this:

1. A chain of reasons must have one of three structures:
   a. It's infinite.
   b. It's circular.
   c. It ends in one or more propositions for which there are no reasons.
2. You can't have an infinite series of reasons.
3. Circular reasoning can't generate justification.
4. A proposition for which there are no reasons is unjustified.
5. If a proposition is unjustified, then you can't justify anything else on the basis of it.
6. Therefore, no chain of reasons can provide justification for believing anything. (From 1–5.)
7. Therefore, no belief can be justified. (From 4, 6.)

Something close to this argument goes back to the ancient skeptics (especially Agrippa and Sextus Empiricus), and it is frequently rediscovered independently by undergraduate students and lay people. This is sometimes called **the regress argument** (but note that "the regress argument" can also be used to refer to an argument for foundationalism; see §4.5.2 below).

> **Aside: Disjunctive Syllogisms**
>
> The skeptical argument is a process-of-elimination argument, or, as the logicians say, a **"disjunctive syllogism"**. This is an extremely common form of argument in philosophy. Basically, you try to list all the possible views about some topic (or at least all the views worth considering), you reject all but one of those views, then you conclude that the last one must be true. This is, as a matter of fact, the main argumentative strategy for *each* of the four theories of justification (infinitism, coherentism, foundationalism, *and* skepticism): The partisans of all four views regard the *other* three views as unacceptable and therefore conclude that their own view must be correct.

We've already discussed the reasons for rejecting infinitism (§4.2), so I won't say more about that now.

Most people don't need any reason for rejecting circular reasoning. Imagine I announce that the world is going to end in the year 2100.[44] You ask me why I think that, and I reply, "Because the world is going to end in the year 2100." This doesn't seem good. Or suppose I say, "I think the world will end in 2100, because the Plutonians are going to launch a lethal nuclear strike against us in that year." When asked how I know about the Plutonians' plans, I say, "I think they're going to do that, because I think the world is going to end in 2100." Again, not good. And it doesn't seem to matter how big I make the circle (I could go through several more steps before circling back to the original claim, and it still doesn't seem okay). Anyway, we've already discussed the reasons for rejecting coherentism (§4.3), which is often regarded as a sophisticated way of embracing circular reasoning.

What about the reasons for rejecting foundations (premises 4–5)? We'll say more about that below (§4.5; I'm leaving foundationalism for last because I like to save the best for last). But basically, skeptics consider any belief that one lacks reasons for to be "arbitrary". They sometimes say that if such "arbitrary" beliefs are acceptable, then one could believe anything—e.g., I could just declare that there are purple unicorns living on Mars. There's no reason to

---

[44] This example is from Richard Fumerton in *Metaphysical and Epistemological Problems of Perception* (1985).

believe that, but if we're allowed to believe things without reasons, as the foundationalists claim, then that should be no problem.

Also, if you have no justification for believing q, then it seems that you can't use q to justify p. Suppose I announce that I have no reason to believe the Plutonians are going to attack in the year 2100; that's just a whimsical hunch I invented. Nevertheless, on the basis of this arbitrary speculation, I conclude that the world will end in 2100. This seems obviously unjustified.

4.4.2. Self-Refutation

The first thing that comes into most people's minds after hearing the thesis of global skepticism is that global skepticism is self-refuting. There are better and worse versions of this objection. Here's a bad version: "Global skeptics claim to know that we know nothing. But that's contradictory!" Reply: No, they don't. Global skeptics may be crazy, but they are not idiots. They say that we know nothing; they don't say that anyone *knows* that.

Slightly better version: "Okay, they don't explicitly say that we know global skepticism to be true. But they *imply* this. Because whenever you make an assertion, you are implying that you know the thing that you're asserting (see §1.2.1). That is why, e.g., if you say, 'Joe Schmoe is going to win the next election', it is totally appropriate for someone to ask, 'How do you know?' It's also why it's nonsensical to say, 'I don't know who is going to win the election, but it's going to be Joe Schmoe.'"

Reply on behalf of the skeptic: So maybe there is this rule of our language that you're not supposed to assert p unless you *know* p. Then the skeptic can be justly charged with violating the social conventions and misusing language. (He's only doing that, though, because our language provides no way of expressing his view without violating the rules. Language was invented by non-skeptics for use by non-skeptics.) Big deal, though. That doesn't show that the skeptic is substantively wrong about any philosophical point.

Counter-reply: "No, it's not just a linguistic convention that the skeptic is violating. There is an inherent norm of *rational thought*. That's why it seems nonsensical or irrational to think—even silently to oneself—such things as, 'Joe Schmoe is going to win the next election, but I don't know who is going to win.' It is likewise irrational to think, 'Global skepticism is true, but I don't know whether global skepticism is true.'"

That counter-reply seems pretty reasonable to me. Anyway, here is another version of the self-refutation charge: What exactly was supposed to be going on in section 4.4.1? The skeptic gave an *argument* for global skepticism. An argument is an attempt to justify a conclusion. That's really the main thing about arguments. (And by the way, if the skeptic *didn't* give any arguments, then we wouldn't be paying any attention to skepticism in the first place.) So, if the skeptic's argument is any *good*, it is a counter-example to its own conclusion. The argument is supposed to show that we can never justify any belief. But if the argument shows that, then we *can* justify at least one belief, because that very argument justifies the belief in skepticism. If, on the other hand, the skeptic's arguments are not good and don't show anything, then presumably we should disregard those arguments.

Finally, there is a general norm of rationality that one should not hold unjustified beliefs (the skeptic is relying on this norm to get us to give up our common sense beliefs). But since, again, the skeptical arguments claim that *no* belief is justified, this would mean that we should not believe either the premises or the conclusions of those arguments. So the arguments are self-defeating.

This objection to skepticism is so obvious that the (very few) skeptics in the world cannot have failed to notice it. Usually, their response is something along these lines: "Yep, that's right: Global skepticism itself is unjustified. I never said it was justified. I only said it was true."

It's hard to see how this is supposed to address the objection at all, though. It's really just granting the objection and then moving on as if granting the objection is the same as refuting it. The best I can figure is that the skeptics who say things like this are assuming that there is only one possible objection that someone might be making, and that would be to claim that skepticism is literally an explicit contradiction, i.e., a statement of the form "A & $\sim A$".

But that's not the objection. The objection is that skepticism is irrational for the reasons stated above; none of those reasons are rebutted by merely agreeing that skepticism is irrational.

4.4.3. *The Moorean Response*

The **Moorean response** to skepticism, also known as "the **G.E. Moore shift**", was pioneered by the twentieth-century British philosopher G.E. Moore.[45] It works for any skeptical argument. To illustrate, consider the following five propositions:

A. I know that I have two hands.
B. Knowledge must be supported by reasons.
C. Reasons must themselves be known.
D. No one can have an infinite series of reasons.
E. Circular reasoning cannot generate knowledge.

---

[45] For amusement, look up the song "The G.E. Moore Shift" by the 21st Century Monads (2010, http://youtu.be/lXdqieipJgs). It's about this.

Each of those propositions has some **initial plausibility**. That is, before hearing arguments for or against any of them, each of them (at least sort of) sounds correct. But they are jointly incompatible (they can't all be true). Therefore, we have to reject at least one of them.

The skeptic thinks we should reject (A) because it conflicts with (B)–(E). That is the point of the argument of §4.4.1. However, one could instead reject (B) on the grounds that it conflicts with (A), (C), (D), and (E), or reject (C) on the grounds that it conflicts with (A), (B), (D), and (E), etc. To be consistent, we could reject *any* of the five propositions, in order to retain the other four. We have to think about which of these five logically consistent options is most reasonable.

Plausibility comes in degrees: Among propositions that are initially plausible, some are *more* plausible (they are more obvious, or more strongly seem correct) than others. So, if you have an inconsistent set of propositions that each seem plausible, you should reject whichever proposition has the *lowest initial plausibility*. Surely you shouldn't reject something that's *more* plausible, in order to maintain a belief that is *less* plausible; that would be unreasonable.

Now, it is just *extremely* initially plausible (it seems totally obvious to almost everyone) that a person in normal conditions can know that they have hands. It is not *as* obvious, say, that knowledge must always be supported by reasons. In fact, if I had to choose, I'd say proposition (A) is the *most* initially plausible of the five propositions. So the skeptic's approach is actually the *least* reasonable option: The skeptic is rejecting the most initially plausible proposition out of the inconsistent set, rather than the least initially plausible one.

As I say, the Moorean response can be applied to pretty much any skeptical argument. When you look at skeptical arguments, you see the same thing with all or nearly all of them: The skeptic keeps asking us to reject the *most* initially plausible proposition out of the inconsistent set. Prior to considering skeptical arguments, such propositions as "I know I have hands", "I know how much two plus two is", and "I know I exist" are pretty much *maximally* initially plausible—you can't find anything that more strongly seems correct. Yet those are the sort of propositions that skeptics want us to reject. Meanwhile, the skeptics' premises generally include abstract, theoretical assumptions that are much less obvious. In the case of the Regress Argument, these include the assumptions that knowledge always requires reasons, that circular reasoning is always illegitimate, and that infinite series of reasons are impossible. Plausible as each of these may be, they are not as obvious as the proposition that I know I exist. Certainly "I know I exist" would not be the least plausible proposition in this set.

* * *

Now, even though global skepticism is self-defeating and implausible, it is still an interesting topic of discussion, and more needs to be said about it. The reason we (that is, most epistemologists) are interested in skepticism is not that we think we have to figure out whether skepticism is true. It's obviously false. (*Pace* the handful of skeptics out there.) The reason we're interested in it is that there are some initially plausible premises, each of which is accepted by many, which lead to this unacceptable conclusion. So the problem is to figure out exactly what went wrong. Which premise is false, and why? That should shed some light on the nature of knowledge and rationality.

4.5. Foundationalism

4.5.1. *The Foundationalist Conception of Justification*

Okay, now we come to the dominant view of justification in the history of philosophy: **foundationalism**. Foundationalists believe two things:

i. Some beliefs are justified in a way that does not depend on reasons, i.e., does not depend on their being supported by other beliefs. These are known as **foundational beliefs**, and their justification is known as **foundational justification**. (Also, propositions that we have foundational justification for are known as "foundational propositions".)
ii. All *other* justified beliefs ultimately depend upon the foundational beliefs for their justification. Everything must be built up from the foundations.

Now I have to make two clarifications, because people get confused about these things all the time. First clarification: A foundational belief is not defined as a belief that *does not have* or *cannot have* any reasons supporting it. It is defined as a belief that does not *need* reasons, in order to be (to some degree) justified. So it is logically possible for a belief to have foundational justification *and* be supported by reasons. If that sounds confusing to you, here is an analogy: In order to run for President, you *do not need* to have held public office before. Notice how that is completely different from saying that people who run for President *cannot* have held public office before, which would be ridiculous.

Second clarification: A foundational belief does not need reasons in order to be justified; it does not follow from this that one cannot have reasons *against* the belief. Reasons for doubting a belief are sometimes called "**defeaters**", and a belief that can have defeaters is said to be "defeasible". So to restate the point: There is no reason why a foundational belief can't be defeasible. Students and lay people often just *assume* that foundational beliefs have to be absolutely certain and incapable of being doubted or revised, but hardly any foundationalist philosophers think that. Unfortunately, even after I say this, some people still continue to think that foundational beliefs can't be revised. I've never been able to figure out why, except that I guess they just didn't understand the definition of "foundational". So if you're tempted to make this mistake, maybe review the definition of "foundational" above, and note how it doesn't say anything about the belief being unrevisable, or absolutely certain, or anything like that.

Now, about defeaters: There are two kinds of defeaters, **rebutting defeaters** and **undercutting defeaters**. A rebutting defeater for p is something that directly supports $\sim p$. An undercutting defeater for p is something that suggests that your means of arriving at the belief that p is unreliable (this need not provide any evidence against p). Example: Rick says that p. Then Morty says p is false. Summer has no opinion about p itself, but she says that Rick is unreliable and his word should not be trusted. In this situation, Morty has provided a *rebutting* defeater for p, while Summer provided an *undercutting* defeater. All epistemologists, whether or not they endorse foundationalism, accept the possibility of both rebutting and undercutting defeaters for propositions that are initially justified. That is to say, if you start out with a justified belief, you can later acquire evidence that the belief is false, or evidence that the belief was formed in an unreliable way, and this can make the belief no longer justified.

By the way, "foundational" is a technical term, which just means what I said above (that stuff about not needing reasons to be justified). That is really *all* it means. If you have some *other* associations with the word because of how it sounds, or because of what you infer from the metaphor of the foundation of a building, or anything like that, get rid of them. The word isn't defined by a metaphor or other vague associations.

Now, what are these foundational beliefs? Well, there's some disagreement on that among foundationalists. Nevertheless, some examples are widely accepted. The belief that one exists is typically viewed as foundational (thank you, Descartes); also, propositions describing one's own present, conscious mental states, such as [I am in pain now]; also, simple necessary truths, such as [2 is greater than 1]. The great majority of foundationalists would accept all those examples. But there is controversy about other examples. *Some* foundationalists (the direct realists) would add that propositions about the physical world are also foundational, when one observes them to be the case (e.g., [There is a round, red thing in front of me now]). But others (the indirect realists) would insist that claims about the external world must always be supported by reasons.

4.5.2. Why Believe Foundationalism?

One common motivation for foundationalism is known as **the regress argument** (not to be confused with the regress argument for skepticism). Basically, the argument is that none of the other views (skepticism, coherentism, infinitism) is plausible, so foundationalism must be true. (Compare that to the argument of §4.4.1.) This is called "the regress argument" because traditionally, people emphasized the idea that you needed foundational beliefs to avoid an infinite regress of reasons. It's more accurate, though, to say you need foundations in order to avoid having *either* an infinite regress *or* circular reasoning *or* a complete lack of justified beliefs. The regress argument for foundationalism goes back at least to Aristotle,[46] and it is commonly rediscovered independently by undergraduate students and lay people.

Here's the other motivation for foundationalism: Just think of some examples. When you think about the paradigm examples of putatively foundational propositions, it just seems that you can know those things directly; you don't have to infer them from something else. Example:

> *Arthritis Pain:* I go to the doctor. "Doctor," I say, "I think I have arthritis." The doctor asks, "Why do you believe you have arthritis?" I give my reason: "Because I'm feeling a pain in my wrist." The doctor then responds, "And why do you believe that you're feeling pain?"

The doctor's first question is a completely reasonable one to ask; I need a reason to think I have arthritis. But his second question is simply bizarre. If someone actually asked me why I think I'm in pain, I'm not sure how I should respond. I would probably assume that either I'd misunderstood the question or the person was making some weird joke. If you asked an ordinary person this sort of question, they would probably either confusedly ask, "What do you mean?", or indignantly insist, "I know I'm in pain!", or just rephrase the initial claim, like "Because it hurts!" They wouldn't start citing evidence for their being in pain.

On its face, then, it seems that there are things that one doesn't need reasons for believing. Granted, perhaps there are not very many of them—*most* claims that a person makes, they need a reason for. We only need there to be at least *some* claims that don't require reasons.

Suppose you disagree: You think that *all* beliefs require reasons. In that case, on pain of contradiction, you'd need a reason for thinking that; you couldn't just claim that it's self-evident. In my experience, it's extremely common for people to *assume* that all beliefs require reasons, but extremely rare

---

[46] *Posterior Analytics* I.2–3.

for them to offer any *reason* for believing that (other than blatantly circular reasons, as in §4.5.3). "Beliefs require reasons" may be a plausible generalization when you think about it purely abstractly (probably because *most* beliefs really do require reasons). But if you focus on certain specific beliefs, such as the belief that one is in pain or the belief that A=A, the generalization just doesn't seem plausible at all *as applied to these cases*.

This is worth remarking on, by the way, because this sort of thing is very common in philosophy. Some generalization sounds plausible when stated purely in the abstract, before you start thinking about all the cases that it subsumes. But then when you start thinking about specific cases, the generalization seems obviously false as applied to certain particular cases. When that happens, some philosophers stick to their initial intuition formed when thinking in the abstract. They may contort themselves trying to avoid the implications for particular cases, or they may just embrace all the counter-intuitive consequences.

Other philosophers, the rational ones, reject the generalization and move on.

4.5.3. The Arbitrariness Objection

The dominant objection to foundationalism is that putatively foundational beliefs are *arbitrary*. The argument seems to be this:

1. If one lacks reasons for believing p, then p is arbitrary.
2. Arbitrary propositions are not justified. Therefore,
3. If one lacks reasons for p, then p is unjustified.

This is an extremely common argument among both professional and amateur skeptics. (Usually, it's not stated that explicitly, but the use of the specific word "arbitrary" is very common.) I, however, find it extremely lame.

What does the anti-foundationalist mean by "arbitrary"? People rarely try to explain that, but I can think of three interpretations:

First interpretation: "Arbitrary" means "unjustified". In this case, premise (1) just means: "If one lacks reasons for believing p, then p is unjustified." Notice that that is just the conclusion, (3). So the argument is blatantly circular. You can't include your conclusion as one of your premises.

Second interpretation: "Arbitrary" means "not supported by reasons". In this case, premise (2) means: "Propositions not supported by reasons are not justified." Once again, that's just a paraphrase of the conclusion, (3), so the argument is blatantly circular.

On either of these first two interpretations, the critic of foundationalism is really just *assuming*, without any reason, that all beliefs require reasons. (Which is pretty much just assuming the negation of foundationalism.) This is, by their own lights, arbitrary.

Third interpretation: "Arbitrary" means roughly, "Not distinguishable in any relevant way from any randomly chosen proposition." In this interpretation, the argument assumes that not just any randomly chosen proposition is justified (which everyone agrees with), and it further assumes that foundationalists can't cite any way in which putatively foundational propositions differ from any randomly chosen proposition.

The third interpretation is the only one I can think of whereby the critic of foundationalism is not blatantly begging the question. Instead, the critic is merely making a false assumption—the assumption that all beliefs that aren't supported by reasons are relevantly alike, so that there is nothing to distinguish a "foundational" belief from a belief in any randomly chosen proposition. The critic would say, for instance, that if we may believe things that we lack reasons for, then I can just decide to believe that purple unicorns live on Mars. Why can't I just declare that to be "foundational"?

In response, there are a variety of forms of foundationalism, which give different accounts of which propositions are foundational. To illustrate, consider René Descartes' view: The foundational propositions are the propositions that correctly describe one's present, conscious mental states. E.g., if you're presently in pain (which I assume is a conscious state), then you can have foundational knowledge that you're in pain. Perhaps also, simple necessary truths that one fully understands count as foundational, like "1+1=2". That is a very traditional foundationalist view, and it obviously does not allow [Purple unicorns live on Mars] to count as foundational.

By the way, I'm not saying that is *the correct* view. There are other and better foundationalist views (as we'll discuss later). That is just to illustrate the general point that the foundationalist theories people have actually held are not subject to the charge of arbitrariness. None of them endorse just any randomly chosen belief.

4.5.4. The Meta-Justification Objection

Let's try for a more sophisticated objection.[47] As we just said, no foundationalist thinks that *just any* proposition can be foundationally justified; that would be a dumb, crazy view. Every foundationalist thinks that there is *some characteristic* or set of characteristics that foundational beliefs have that differentiates them from merely arbitrary, unjustified beliefs. (And the characteristic is not just that of "being justified"; rather, it is some descriptive

---

[47] I base this one on BonJour's *The Structure of Empirical Knowledge* (1985), §2.3.

property that *explains why* the beliefs are justified.) The characteristic might be that of being a belief that correctly reports one's present, conscious mental state; or a belief correctly describing something one is directly acquainted with; or a belief that was formed by a reliable mechanism; etc.

There's no general agreement on what the key characteristic(s) is or are. It doesn't matter, though; just let "F" stand for whatever property foundational beliefs have that explains why they count as justified and differentiates them from randomly chosen, unjustified beliefs.

Question: Should the person who has the foundational belief *be aware* of this feature F? Well, it's a little hard to see how the presence of F would render a belief justified, if the person has no idea that the belief actually has F. So it's plausible to assume that the person must be aware of F.

Second question: Should F be a feature that makes a belief *likely to be true*, or can it be something that has nothing to do with the probability of being correct? Intuitively, it seems that beliefs with F should be likely to be true, in virtue of having F. Otherwise, we've kind of lost sight of the point of the concept of justification—justification is supposed to help us get to the truth.

Third question: Should the believer be aware that feature F makes a belief likely to be true? Again, intuitively, it seems that the answer is "Yes." If the person can't see this, then it's unclear how the presence of F would make it rational *for that individual* to hold the belief in question.

But now it looks like the believer does, after all, have available a *reason* for their belief. The reason would be this argument:

1. This belief has feature F.
2. Beliefs with F are likely to be true.
3. Therefore, probably, this belief is true.

(That argument is referred to as a "**meta-justification**". Basically, this means that, rather than directly arguing for the proposition that the belief is about, the argument deploys premises about the belief itself. Beliefs that are about other beliefs are called "**meta-beliefs**".) That seems to undermine the claim that the belief is *foundational*, doesn't it?

But wait. Remember in section 4.5.1, when I pedantically noted that foundational beliefs are defined as beliefs that *do not need* reasons, not as beliefs that *cannot have* reasons? We could deploy that point now. We could say the belief is still foundational, even though there is a reason for it available.

That isn't terribly persuasive, though, because the way we arrived at the meta-justification was by asking about what would have to be the case for feature F to render a belief justified. What we said was that the availability of premises (1) and (2) above is *a necessary condition* on F's providing justification for the belief in question, and therefore a necessary condition (given the circumstances) for the belief to be justified. It's not just an optional extra.

To continue the anti-foundationalist argument, it now looks like we actually *don't* have a foundational belief. If, starting from the assumption that some belief is foundational, you can argue that that very belief *isn't* foundational, then it must be that *there are no foundational beliefs*. So, that's the objection to foundationalism.

What is wrong with that objection? I think there are a couple of expressions that have to be clarified to see the problem. First, what does it mean to say a belief is "likely to be true"? There are a number of different interpretations of probability, which I won't bore you with now (I'll bore you in chapter 12). I'll just say that in my view, probabilities are essentially *degrees of available justification*.[48] So when you say something is "probable", what you're saying is basically that the thing is justified given your current evidence (or: more justified than its negation).

Second point of clarification: What does it mean to be "aware of" something? I think this is pretty close to a synonym for knowledge—you're aware of a belief's having feature F, roughly, if you *know* that the belief has F.[49] Furthermore, I assume that knowledge requires justification.

With that understood, let's restate what the meta-justification objection is saying. The objection claims that, in order for the presence of feature F to render a belief justified, the subject has to *be aware* that the belief has F and that beliefs with F are *likely to be true*. This means, roughly: In order for the presence of feature F to render a belief justified, the subject has to *know* that the belief has F and that beliefs with F are *justified*. Since knowledge requires justification, this entails: In order for the presence of feature F to render a belief justified, the subject has to *be justified in believing* that the belief has F and that beliefs with F are *justified*. And that is very close to the following claim: In order for a belief to be justified, the subject has to be justified in believing that it is justified.

I think this premise is what epistemologists call a **level confusion**—a confusion between the conditions for knowing p and the conditions for knowing that one knows p, or between the conditions for having a justified belief and the conditions for being justified in believing that one has a justified belief.

For belief B to be justified, it is necessary that B in fact *be* likely to be true (because *being justified* and *being likely to be true* are the same thing). But it is not

---

[48] I'm not saying that no other interpretations of probability are sound. I'm saying that the "degrees of justification" interpretation is the one that is relevant in this context.
[49] I added "roughly" because I don't think "to be aware" is an exact synonym for "to know". But I think the slight semantic difference isn't important here.

necessary that one *be justified in believing* that B is likely to be true. That's only required if you want to be justified in believing that you're justified in holding B. Of course, it is also not required that you *know that* B is likely to be true—that is only required if you want to *know that* B is justified. In general, when a person knows that *p*, it is not necessary that they know that they know that *p* (which would generate an infinite regress; see §6.1). Similarly, when a person is justified in believing that *p*, it is not necessary that they be justified in believing that they are justified in believing that *p*.

So I think the meta-justification objection relies on false premises. It is not necessary that one be aware that one's belief has feature F, nor need one be aware that beliefs with F are likely to be true.

4.6. Conclusion

In sum, there are four possible structures for a series of reasons: It could be infinite, it could be circular, it could have one or more starting points, or it could be completely empty. These four structures are advanced, respectively, by infinitism, coherentism, foundationalism, and skepticism.

Infinitism holds that a belief is justified only if the subject is able to cite a reason for it, and a reason for the reason, and so on, though the subject need not have *actually* gone through these reasons. This faces the problems (*i*) that it is difficult to see how to continue any series of reasons for even, say, the first fifty stages; (*ii*) that human minds are finite and therefore can't have infinitely many reasons available; and (*iii*) that it's not clear why merely being able to cite a reason would make a belief actually justified, if the belief wasn't actually based on that reason.

Coherentism holds that coherent belief systems, which contain many mutually supporting beliefs, are likely to be generally accurate since unreliable information sources are unlikely to happen to produce information that all fits together. Thus, a given belief is justified when it is supported by a highly coherent belief system. This view faces the problems (*i*) that there can be many different, incompatible belief systems that are all internally coherent and (*ii*) that the justification provided by coherence can't work on its own, without some foundational justification, since one must first have justification for beliefs about probability, beliefs about the content of one's belief system, and some kind of belief to the effect that one's information sources are at least more reliable than chance.

Skepticism (i.e., global justification skepticism) holds that no beliefs are justified and there are no reasons to believe anything. This faces the problem that it is self-defeating and maximally implausible.

Finally, foundationalism holds that some beliefs need no reasons to be justified (e.g., that one exists, that one is in pain, that $A=A$), and that all other beliefs are justified on the basis of these "foundational" beliefs. This view faces the alleged problem that the foundations are "arbitrary". However, examination of the meaning of "arbitrary" reveals that the objection either begs the question by *assuming* that there cannot be foundational justification, or else falsely assumes that foundationalists have no account of what differentiates foundational beliefs from randomly chosen, unjustified beliefs.

Another objection holds that, whatever feature makes a belief foundationally justified, the subject must be aware of that feature and aware that it renders beliefs that have it highly probable, and therefore the subject must actually have a reason available for the belief. Once we understand the notions of probability and awareness, however, this objection amounts to claiming that in order for a belief to be justified, one must be justified in believing that it is justified. This principle is false and leads to an infinite regress.

So foundationalism is the best account of the structure of knowledge.

5. Grounds of Foundational Justification

In this chapter, we'll talk about the source of foundational justification. E.g., it is commonly said that [I exist] is foundational, yet [Purple unicorns live on Mars] is not. Why?

I'm going to discuss two main theories about this: the *Acquaintance Theory* and the theory of *Phenomenal Conservatism*.

5.1. The Acquaintance Theory

5.1.1. The Theory

The Acquaintance Theory of foundational justification says that there is a kind of direct awareness that you can have, known as "acquaintance". Acquaintance can't really be defined apart from what I just said, but it is a relation that you can stand in to an object that enables you to directly know about the object, without the need of any reasoning.

Bertrand Russell was the best known acquaintance theorist.[50] Russell drew a distinction between *knowledge of truths* and *knowledge of things*. Knowledge of truths is the kind of knowledge we've been talking about all along in this book (a.k.a., "propositional knowledge"). Knowledge of things is the kind of knowledge you're talking about when you say stuff like "I know Paris pretty well", "I know John Smith", or even "I know this apple."

Note: Russell had a pretty minimal notion of "knowing" a thing. You just have to be aware of the thing in some way. When you have knowledge of a thing, that enables you, at a bare minimum, to *refer to* or to *think about* that thing, but you really don't have to know much about it. Nevertheless, Russell had the idea of basing our knowledge of *truths* on knowledge of *things*.

---

[50] See his *The Problems of Philosophy* (1912). For a more recent acquaintance theorist, see Richard Fumerton, *Metaepistemology and Skepticism* (1995).

> **Interlude: Bertrand Russell**
>
> Bertrand Russell was a British analytic philosopher, perhaps the most important analytic philosopher of the twentieth century. He co-authored (with Alfred North Whitehead) a very important book that nobody reads anymore called *Principia Mathematica* (that's Latin for *Principles of Mathematics*), which tried to derive mathematics starting purely from the truths of logic and set theory. (That was a big project that some early analytic philosophers were into. You see, Russell had earlier ruined Gottlob Frege's system that tried to do the same thing; he ruined it by coming up with Russell's Paradox. So it was on him to come up with a new system.) Russell & Whitehead's mathematical system was itself later ruined by Kurt Gödel.
>
> Russell also wrote a famous history of Western philosophy that a lot of people find entertaining; he wrote a lot of stuff about epistemology; he wrote some pretty interesting essays, such as "Why I Am Not a Christian"; and boatloads of other books. In 1950, he won the Nobel Prize in Literature for his social/political writings.
>
> Russell also had Ludwig Wittgenstein as a doctoral student, for which he deserves our deepest sympathy.

Russell further distinguished two kinds of knowledge of things: **knowledge by description** and **knowledge by acquaintance**. When you have knowledge by description, that means that you're able to refer to the thing by virtue of grasping some description that uniquely applies to that object. For example, I can right now talk about the tallest man in the world. I know at least some truths about him, e.g., I know that he is more than four feet tall. But I can only think about that person (whom I have never met, never seen a picture of, don't even know the name of, etc.) in an indirect way. I can think about this person only by using this description, "tallest man in the world". This is indirect, because my thoughts about the person depend upon my prior grasp of the taller-than relation, the property of being a man, the world, and the relation of being *in* something. So I have to first know all those things.

Now notice that not all awareness of things can be by description, since that would generate an infinite regress, since knowledge by description is always indirect. So there must be some *direct* way of being aware of something. This is what Russell calls "acquaintance". When you're acquainted with something, you are able to refer to or think about the thing directly, without having to use a description and hence without needing prior awareness of anything else. When you are aware of something in this direct way, Russell held, that puts you in a position to know at least some truths about that thing, without the need for any reasoning.

What are we acquainted with? Acquaintance theorists (including Russell and others) say that we are acquainted with (facts about) our own present, conscious mental states. If I'm in pain, then I am acquainted with that particular mental state, and with exactly how it feels to me. That enables me to immediately know, without any reasoning, that I am in pain and that the pain feels the particular way that it does. Likewise, I'm acquainted with my sensory experiences, emotions, thoughts, memories, desires, and any other conscious mental states you can think of (but not purely unconscious states).

What about physical objects? *Most* acquaintance theorists (including Russell) would deny that we are ever acquainted with anything physical. Suppose you see an octopus in a tank. They would say that you are not acquainted with the actual octopus; rather, you are acquainted with *your visual experience* of an octopus. This visual experience is something going on in your own mind, which you assume to be *caused by* a physical octopus. Your awareness of the physical object is by *description*. You can refer to the physical octopus using a description, something like "the physical object causing this visual experience"—that's what you really mean by "the octopus".

Russell (and probably most acquaintance theorists) also thought that a person could be acquainted with certain abstract objects, such as the number 2, or the property of squareness. Note that this does not mean that abstract objects causally interact with us, that you could bump into the number 2 on the street, or anything crazy like that. Again, being acquainted with something just means that you are aware of it in a direct way that doesn't require you to rely on awareness of any other things. Also note that he isn't saying you are acquainted with *all* abstract objects. You are only acquainted with *some*. There are others that you're only aware of by description (e.g., the one-millionth prime number), and lots more that you aren't aware of at all.

Due to our acquaintance with our own minds and with abstract objects, Russell thought that we had foundational knowledge of truths about our own present, conscious mental states as well as simple necessary truths such as [2 > 1], [No object can be both completely red and completely blue], and [All squares have four sides].

5.1.2. The Sellarsian Dilemma

The acquaintance theory is a pretty good theory. It just has one or two problems. I'm going to start with a (pseudo-)problem that's sometimes called the Sellarsian dilemma (after Wilfred Sellars, who made a big deal about it).[51]

---

[51] See Sellars' very confusing paper, "Empiricism and the Philosophy of Mind". Or, if you prefer something clear, see BonJour's discussion in *The Structure of Empirical*

First, some terminology. A mental state is said to have **propositional content** when it represents something (some proposition) to be the case. What it represents to be the case is called the "content" of the state. The paradigm example is beliefs: When you have a belief, there is a proposition that you believe to be the case. E.g., you might believe *that it is snowing*, or *that 11 is a prime number*, or *that you are 40 years old*. Those phrases in italics all express propositional contents that your beliefs would have. On the other hand, not all mental states have propositional content. Suppose that you have a headache. The sensation of pain does not seem to represent anything to be the case.

Now, let's say you are directly aware of x. Let's think about this state of *awareness*. Does it have propositional content, or not? If the state *has* propositional content, then (one might argue) it follows that you need some sort of justification for that content, since it *could* be false. Therefore, this awareness can't produce *foundational* justification. So the acquaintance theory would fail.

On the other hand, suppose that the state of direct awareness *does not* have propositional content. In that case, it wouldn't make sense to ask for justification for the awareness state. But it would also be mysterious how the state of awareness could render a *belief* justified. Beliefs, again, *have* propositional content, and it is that propositional content that needs to be justified. If you have some mental state that doesn't represent anything to be the case, how could that mental state make you justified in believing some proposition?

Now, I'm not an advocate of the acquaintance theory, but I don't find this objection telling. (By the way, the objection can also be applied to any other theory that appeals to experiences to justify foundational beliefs.) I think an acquaintance theorist can grasp either horn of the putative dilemma without being gored.

On the one hand, one could claim that states of acquaintance have propositional content but deny that this means one needs a *reason* for that content. Claiming that one must have a reason for the content, I think, just begs the question in this context, since the foundationalist's core claim is that one *doesn't* need such a reason. The fact that the content could be false (if that's true) doesn't entail that it needs a justification. Anyway, many acquaintance theorists would say that the content *cannot* be false. E.g., if you are directly acquainted with a pain right now, it cannot be false that you're in pain.

Alternately, the acquaintance theorist could say that states of acquaintance *don't* have propositional content, but that they nevertheless guarantee the truth

---

Knowledge (ch. 4). I call this a pseudo-problem because I don't think it is actually a significant problem.

of certain propositions and thus make one justified in believing those propositions. Suppose that I'm directly aware of a pain. Maybe this state of awareness doesn't have a *proposition* as its content (it doesn't represent some proposition as true); maybe it just has PAIN as its content (it simply represents pain). In spite of its having this non-propositional content, this state still guarantees certain propositions. Notably, whenever anyone has a state like this, it is guaranteed that that person is in pain. Thus, you're justified in believing [I am in pain].

By the way, the way I just described that seemed to suggest that you have two separate mental states—a pain and the awareness of that pain. But this need not be the case; these need not be separate states. Some philosophers believe, plausibly, that conscious mental states are self-representing, i.e., the awareness of the state is built into the state itself. So when you have a conscious pain, the pain and the awareness of the pain are the same state.

5.1.3. Explaining Justified Errors

Now here's a problem that I think is more pressing. It seems that, for any type of justified belief that a person can have, it is *possible* to have a justified belief of that kind and yet be mistaken. This is obvious for perceptual beliefs, where you could have a hallucination without having any clues suggesting that it's a hallucination.

Admittedly, the point is less obvious for some other sorts of beliefs: How can you have a false belief about your present, conscious mental states? Or about a simple necessary truth like [1+2=3]?

I think it really is possible to be mistaken about these sorts of things. In the case of conscious mental states, I think a person could mistake one mental state for a similar but distinct mental state. E.g., a person could think that they are feeling indignation, when instead they are feeling envy. Or a person could think that they have 75% confidence in some proposition, when actually their confidence level is 78%.

In the case of simple, necessary truths, we actually have a great example that Bertrand Russell should appreciate. At the beginning of the 20th century, set theory was still in an early stage of development. In its initial development, one of the key axioms was the Comprehension Axiom (now called "the **Naïve Comprehension Axiom**"), which basically says that if you have a well-formed predicate, then there should be a set of all and only the things that satisfy the predicate. Example: There's a predicate "is red", so there is a set of all the red things. This set contains everything that's red and nothing that isn't red.

That principle has seemed *self-evident* to most people who first consider it, including some very clever mathematicians and logicians. If it doesn't seem totally obvious to you, you probably either didn't understand it, or you just don't believe in sets. Gottlob Frege used this axiom in developing his own logical/mathematical system.

It is now known, however, that the Comprehension Axiom is false (all mathematicians and logicians now agree with this). The proof is due to Bertrand Russell, which is why I said Russell should appreciate this example. Russell's refutation of the Comprehension Axiom goes like this: Just consider the predicate "is not a member of itself". The axiom tells us that there is a set of all and only the things that satisfy that predicate, i.e., a set of all things that are not members of themselves. About this set: *Is it a member of itself?* Well, if you think it through, this set has to be a member of itself if and only if it is *not* a member of itself. This is a contradiction, so there just can't be such a set. (This is known as **Russell's Paradox**.)

Interlude: Formal Description of Russell's Paradox

Technically, the Naïve Comprehension Axiom is not a single axiom but an axiom *schema*:

$$(\exists x)(\forall y)(y \in x \leftrightarrow \varphi(x))$$

The fact that this is an "axiom schema" means that you're allowed to replace "$\varphi(x)$" in the above with any well-formed formula that contains x as a free variable, and treat the result as an axiom. To generate Russell's paradox, we replace "$\varphi(x)$" with "$x \notin x$". If you've taken formal logic, the following will make sense to you; otherwise, it won't:

1. $(\exists x)(\forall y)(y \in x \leftrightarrow x \notin x)$ Axiom.
2. $(\forall y)(y \in r \leftrightarrow r \notin r)$ 1; Existential Instantiation
3. $r \in r \leftrightarrow r \notin r$ 2; Universal Instantiation

Step (3) is a contradiction (it takes a few more steps to get it explicitly in the form (p & ~p), but they're trivial). So the supposed axiom must be false.

This isn't a chapter about set theory, so don't worry about what the right version of set theory is or how we avoid paradoxes. I'm just using this example to illustrate the following point: You can have something that *seems* just like a self-evident axiom, and it can still be false. Furthermore, in terms of the acquaintance theory: You can have a state that *seems* just like being acquainted with a simple, necessary truth, and yet you can still be wrong. (Of course, it no longer seems that way after you learn about Russell's Paradox. But *before* you learn about Russell's Paradox, the Comprehension Axiom seems just like a necessary truth that you're "acquainted" with.)

I know what you're thinking now. You're thinking I'm making some kind of irritating skeptical point, like, "Aha, so we can never really know if an axiom is true!" No. That's totally not my point at all.

Here is my point:

1. Before learning about Russell's Paradox, people had the same sort of justification for believing the Comprehension Axiom that we normally have for believing simple, necessary truths.
2. In the case of the Comprehension Axiom, that justification did not consist in anyone's being acquainted with a fact that made the axiom true.
3. Therefore, the justification we normally have for believing simple, necessary truths does not consist in our being acquainted with the facts that make them true.[52]

Premise 1 is intuitive. Mathematicians and logicians at the time had no reason for thinking that the Naïve Comprehension Axiom was any different from any of the other seemingly self-evident axioms of mathematics. It seemed to them just as obvious, and they seemed to know it in the same way. Thus, it seems that they were justified in believing the Naïve Comprehension Axiom, and in the same way that they are normally justified in believing mathematical axioms. If someone at the time had refused to accept the Comprehension Axiom, they could not have given any good reason for this (since, again, they did not know about the paradox generated by the axiom); they would just have been unreasonable.

Premise 2 follows from the concept of acquaintance. By definition, it is impossible to be acquainted with something that does not exist. (Acquaintance theorists agree with this; indeed, they insist on it.) In the case of the Comprehension Axiom, there *was no* fact that made it true, since it isn't true. So no one could have been acquainted with such a fact, so no such acquaintance could have explained the justification for believing the Comprehension Axiom.

Step 3 follows from steps 1 and 2. So acquaintance is not the explanation for why we are justified in believing simple, necessary truths. A similar argument can be given regarding introspective beliefs, if you accept the possibility of justified, introspective errors (I leave it to you to work out how that goes).

---

[52] Ironically, this argument is inspired by Richard Fumerton's argument against direct realism in his *Metaphysical and Epistemological Problems of Perception* (78ff.). I have modified it to be an argument against the acquaintance theory as an account of a priori justification. This is ironic because Fumerton is a prominent proponent of the acquaintance theory.

5.2. Phenomenal Conservatism

5.2.1. *The Phenomenal Conservative View*

What gives us foundational justification, if not acquaintance? The above example suggests an answer. I said that, when mathematicians thought about the Comprehension Axiom, it seemed to them just as obvious as other mathematical axioms, and they had no reason for doubting it since they didn't know about the paradox. So maybe that's what makes a belief justified: its *seeming* true, while one has no reason for doubting it. A couple of decades ago, I coined the name "**Phenomenal Conservatism**" for this view:

PC If it seems to S that p, and S has no reason for doubting this appearance, then S thereby has some degree of justification for believing p.[53]

("Phenomenal" comes from the Greek word *phainómenon*, which means "appearance". The above principle is sort of about preserving appearances; hence the name "phenomenal conservatism".)

To clarify, I take it that there is a particular type of mental state, known as an **appearance** or **seeming** state, which we report when we say things like, "It seems to me that p" or "It appears to me that p". This state is distinct from *belief*, since it is possible to doubt or deny what seems to you to be the case. However, appearances *normally* cause beliefs (when something seems true to you, you normally believe it).

There are several species of appearances, including:

a. *Sensory experiences:* These are experiences in which something looks, feels, tastes, sounds, or smells a certain way. (Includes normal perceptions as well as illusions and hallucinations.)
b. *Memory experiences:* These are experiences in which you seem to remember an event that you experienced, or a fact that you previously learned.
c. *Introspective appearances:* These are experiences in which you seem to be in some particular, conscious mental state. (In this case and only this case, the seeming may be the same as the thing it represents. E.g., it's plausible that *seeming to be in pain* is the same as *being in pain*.)
d. *Intuitions:* These are experiences in which a proposition just seems correct to you when you reflect on it intellectually, without going through an argument for it.

Examples: It seems to me that there is a table in front of me (sensory experience), that I ate a tomato today (memory experience), that I am happy

---

[53] See my *Skepticism and the Veil of Perception* (2001), ch. 5, and my paper "Compassionate Phenomenal Conservatism" (*Philosophy & Phenomenological Research*, 2007).

(introspective appearance), and that nothing can be completely red and also completely blue (intuition).

So, on the phenomenal conservative view, all of the above kinds of experiences give you justification for believing whatever the experience represents to be the case, in the absence of grounds for doubt. E.g., if it looks to you as if there is a cat on a mat, then you're justified in believing there is a cat on a mat (in the absence of grounds for doubt). If you intuit that the shortest path between two points is a line, then you're justified in believing that (in the absence of grounds for doubt). Etc.

PC does not hold that all appearances are in fact true. There are such things as illusions, hallucinations, false memories, and so on. Nevertheless, according to PC, the rational *presumption* is that things are the way they appear, unless and until you have specific grounds for doubting that. These grounds would themselves have to come from *other* appearances. For instance, if you submerge a stick halfway in water, the stick will *look* bent (visual appearance). But if you *feel* the stick, you can feel that it is straight (tactile appearance). Since you consider the tactile appearance more trustworthy, you reject the initial visual appearance. You should not, however, reject an appearance for no reason; there must be some other appearance that shows the first appearance to be defective.

Most appearances are **defeasible**—i.e., you could acquire reasons for distrusting them, which would make it rational to stop believing what initially appeared to be the case. Notice that this doesn't stop this justification from being foundational (see §4.5.1). Another name for justification that is foundational but defeasible is "**prima facie justification**". When we say that appearances confer prima facie justification, this just means that *if* there are no reasons for doubting the accuracy or reliability of an appearance, a believer should accept the appearance as accurate.

There may, however, be *some* appearances that are indefeasible. E.g., the appearance that you are in pain, when you are in severe pain, seems to be indefeasible.

5.2.2. PC Is a Good Theory

Why believe PC? First, PC is intuitive. Say you want to form true beliefs and avoid false ones. Then it makes sense, on its face, that you would believe propositions that seem true to you, at least when you have no reasons to the contrary. And this (it is plausible to think) is what justification is about: Justified beliefs are beliefs that make sense to hold from the standpoint of the goal of attaining truth and avoiding error.

PC is a good epistemological theory because it provides a simple, unified explanation for all or nearly all of the things we initially (before encountering skeptical arguments and such) thought were justified. It accounts for our knowledge of the external world, our knowledge of mathematics and other abstract truths, our knowledge of moral truths, our knowledge of the past, and so on. These are all things that philosophers have had a hard time accounting for, and it is *very* hard to find a theory that gives us *all* of them. At the same time, PC is not overly permissive or dogmatic, because it allows appearances to be defeated when they conflict with other appearances. The theory seems to accord well with how we form beliefs when we are seeking the truth and also with how we evaluate other people's beliefs.

5.2.3. The Self-Defeat Argument

I'm going to tell you my favorite argument for PC. Most other philosophers hate it,[54] but I think it's a great argument. I claim that alternative theories to PC are self-defeating.

Think about how you actually form beliefs when you're pursuing the truth. You do it based on what *seems true* to you. Now, there are some cases where beliefs are based on something else. For instance, there are cases of wishful thinking, where someone's belief is based on a *desire*; you believe *p* because you *want* it to be true. But those are not the cases where you're seeking the truth, and cases like that are generally agreed to be unjustified beliefs. So we can ignore things like wishful thinking, taking a leap of faith, or other ways of forming unjustified beliefs. With that understood, your beliefs are based on what seems right to you.

You might think: "No, sometimes my beliefs are based on *reasoning*, and reasoning can often lead to conclusions that initially seem wrong." But that's not really an exception to my claim. Because when you go through an argument, you're still relying on appearances. Take the basic, starting premises of the argument—by stipulation, we're talking about premises that you did not reach by way of argument. (There must be some such, else you would have an infinite regress.) To the extent that you find an argument persuasive, those premises *seem* correct to you. Each of the steps in the argument must also seem

---

[54] "Hate" is a bit strong, but the argument has attracted several criticisms; see, e.g., Moti Mizrahi's "Phenomenal Conservatism, Justification, and Self-defeat", Ali Hasan's "Phenomenal Conservatism, Classical Foundationalism, and Internalist Justification", Clayton Littlejohn's "Defeating Phenomenal Conservatism", Michael DePaul's "Phenomenal Conservatism and Self-Defeat", and John DePoe's "Defeating the Self-Defeat Argument for Phenomenal Conservativism".

to you to be supported by the preceding steps. If you don't experience these appearances, then the argument won't do anything for you. So when you rely on arguments, you are still, in fact, relying on appearances.

Notice that all this is true of *epistemological* beliefs just as much as any other. For instance, beliefs about the source of justification, including beliefs about PC itself, are based on appearances. The people who accept PC are those to whom it seems right. The people who *reject* PC do so because it doesn't seem right to them, or because it seems to them to conflict with something else that seems right to them.

Now, in general, a belief is justified only if the thing it is based on is a source of justification (§2.3.3). So if you think that appearances are not a source of justification, then you have a problem: Since that belief itself is based on what seems right to you, you should conclude that your own belief is unjustified. That's the self-defeat problem.

If you want to avoid self-defeat, you should agree that some appearances (including the ones you're relying on right now) confer justification. If you agree with that, it is very plausible that the appearances that confer justification are the ones that you don't have any reasons to doubt—which is what PC says.

You might try adding other restrictions. Suppose, e.g., that you said that only abstract, intellectual intuitions confer justification, and sensory experiences do not. (External world skeptics might say that.) You could claim that this view itself is an intuition, not something based on sensory experience, so it avoids self-defeat. It is, however, pretty arbitrary. If you accept one species of appearances, why not accept all? There is no obvious principled rationale for discriminating.

5.2.4. Crazy Appearances

Some critics of Phenomenal Conservatism appeal to examples in which a person has an appearance that, intuitively, they should not trust. Consider:

> *Tree Intuition:* You look at a particular walnut tree, and it occurs to you, for no apparent reason, that that tree was planted on April 24, 1914. You have no idea why it seems that way to you, nor any account of how you could reliably detect the planting date of a tree, but it just *seems* to you that that is when the tree was planted. Are you justified in believing the tree was planted on April 24, 1914?[55]
>
> *Terrorist Intuition:* Osama is sitting in his cave one day, when it strikes him that there is a God, that this God wants him to kill infidels, and that he (Osama)

---

[55] This example is from Peter Markie in "The Mystery of Direct Perceptual Justification" (*Philosophical Studies*, 2005).

> should do God's will. Osama does not have a religious experience, though, and he doesn't know why things seem to him this way, but those things just seem to him to be the case. Is Osama justified in believing that he should kill infidels?[56]

Intuitively, the answer to both questions above is "No"; neither person is justified. Yet both have undefeated appearances; hence, PC must be false. The second example raises frightening practical issues—if Osama *is* justified in his beliefs, then it looks like he's also going to be justified in actually killing some infidels.

I don't myself find these examples persuasive. I want to make three points about them.

First, I find these examples bizarre and unimaginable, and I don't think we should rest much weight on putative intuitions about bizarre, unimaginable (or difficult-to-imagine) scenarios. Remember that an *appearance* is not simply a *belief*, nor is it a groundless disposition to believe something. An appearance is supposed to be a type of *experience*, one that would naturally incline a person to believe the content of that experience, e.g., sensory experiences, memories, or intuitions. I can't imagine an experience of a tree just seeming to have been planted on April 24, 1914; I have no idea what such an experience would be like, if it is even possible.

Regarding the second example, I can perhaps imagine an experience of seeming to perceive God (at any rate, I know some people *have* such experiences), but I can't imagine having an experience of there seeming to be a God *without* having a religious experience; I'm not even sure what that means. (The part about not having any religious experience is taken from Michael Tooley's description of the example. For discussion of religious experience, see §16.4 below.) So suppose we instead just imagine that Osama has a religious experience in which he seems to be in the presence of God, and God tells Osama to kill the infidels. This makes the example more realistic. (In the real world, there are no people who claim to just intuit that they should kill infidels; there are, however, people who claim that God spoke to them and told them to do stuff.)

The second point I want to make is that it would be pretty hard for anyone to not have any grounds for doubt in either of the above two scenarios. In Tree Intuition, the subject would have to have no inkling that there was anything odd about having an intuition about the specific planting date of a tree, no doubts and no reasons for doubt about the reliability of such intuitions. In

---

[56] This is based on an example of Michael Tooley's in "Michael Huemer and the Principle of Phenomenal Conservatism" in *Seemings and Justification* (2013).

Terrorist Intuition, Osama would have to have no belief, and no reason to believe, that murder was wrong, no reason to doubt the reliability of his religious experience, and no reason to doubt that God exists. Thus, he'd have to not know about things like the problem of evil; the many other people who have religious experiences that they claim support different, incompatible religions; and the many other people who believe (on the basis of various other appearances) that terrorist attacks are wrong. So we have to stipulate all that. But I think at this point, we are being asked to imagine such a bizarrely counterfactual scenario, suspending so much of our familiar knowledge and experience, that we can't put much weight on any intuitions we might have about this case. Our intuitions are calibrated to normal cases, and a normal person would have plenty of reason for doubting the intuitions in the above cases.

A third observation, specifically about the Terrorist Intuition case, is that when a person is deciding on high-stakes actions, such as actions that might kill other people, they acquire an obligation to do extra investigation and to be especially careful before drawing conclusions. This is because the level of justification one needs before one may act on a belief increases when the potential cost of being wrong increases. Thus, though Osama might have *some* degree of justification for believing that he should kill infidels, he would be obligated to make extra efforts to verify his belief before acting on it, given the high stakes. Needless to say, actual terrorists in the real world are highly irrational and make almost no effort to verify their beliefs.

Having said all that, I think that if we can imagine a case in which someone really has the appearances described in the above two cases, and the person really has none of the background knowledge that would cast doubt on these appearances for normal people, then that person *would*, in fact, have some degree of justification for believing the content of those appearances.

5.2.5. *Tainted Sources*

Another type of objection rests on cases in which a person's appearances are caused by unreliable or irrational mental states.

> *Pastafarian Belief:* I irrationally adopt the belief that the Earth was created by the Flying Spaghetti Monster (FSM). (Just imagine the belief to be formed in some way that you consider clearly irrational—maybe pure wishful thinking, or maybe I adopt the belief to annoy my parents, etc.) And suppose that my having this belief *causes* it to just seem to me plausible that there is a Flying Spaghetti Monster. At the same time, I have no particular

> reasons for doubting the FSM's reality. Q: Do I now have (at least some) *justification* for this belief?

If we accept PC, it seems, we would have to say that my belief in the FSM, which was *initially* completely unjustified, suddenly *becomes justified* merely because I have an appearance *caused by that very belief.* Yet this seems wrong.

In response, there are two possible variants of this case. In the first version of the case, I am aware of how I came to have the belief and the appearance about the Flying Spaghetti Monster. In this case, I have grounds for doubt about the reliability of the belief and the appearance, because appearances based on irrationally adopted beliefs are not in general reliable. Because I have these grounds for doubt, PC does not imply that I have justification for believing in the FSM.

In the second version of the case, I somehow don't know where the belief and the appearance came from. Suppose that I have long since forgotten that I ever adopted belief in the FSM by wishful thinking (or whatever irrational method I in fact used). I am also unaware that my intuition that there is an FSM was caused by my earlier belief. In this case, the example is just like those of §5.2.4, and I would say similar things here to what I said about those. It is, again, very difficult to imagine what it would be like for it to just *seem* that there is a Flying Spaghetti Monster, unless one has some sort of religious experience in which one seems to be in the FSM's presence, or something like that. It would also be pretty weird for a person, even after having such an experience, to have no grounds for doubting its veracity.

Nevertheless, if someone has an experience of seeming awareness of a Flying Spaghetti Monster, and they have no grounds for doubting its veracity, then I think the person would indeed have some justification for believing in an FSM. I don't think that's an absurd or otherwise problematic implication.

What might be wrong with the FSM experience? You might say that the person has no positive grounds for thinking that the FSM experience is reliable. (This is compatible with their having no grounds for *doubting* its reliability either—one might have no evidence one way or the other.) But this, I think, is not really different from ordinary perceptual experiences. It's not like you first construct a proof that the five senses are reliable before you form perceptual beliefs; you just start out trusting your senses, until you have a reason not to. So I don't see how my apparent awareness of a Flying Spaghetti Monster would be relevantly different, if I had such an experience.

Of course, the FSM (I assume) does not really exist. So the apparent awareness of him would be hallucinatory. But that wouldn't stop me from having *some justification* for believing what this hallucination represents to be the case. Compare: Suppose that as I'm walking down the street, I have a completely realistic hallucination of a squirrel on the sidewalk. I would be *justified* (though mistaken) in believing there was a squirrel there. That's like the person who has a false experience of a Flying Spaghetti Monster.

5.2.6. The Problem of Easy Knowledge

Here's an example that is said to pose a problem for PC:

> *Red Table:* You're looking at a table, which looks red, and so you believe that it is red. Then someone comes along and tells you that that table is actually white, but there's a red light illuminating it, and that's why it looks red. (Assume that a white table illuminated by red light would really look just like a red table.) Because you can't see the light source, you're unable to verify whether there is really a red light shining. You respond: "No, you're wrong, because I can see that the table is *red*. Since it is red, it cannot be a white table illuminated by red light."[57]

Intuitively, your imagined response here is unreasonable; it seems something like circular reasoning.

Yet, on a Phenomenal Conservative view, a case could be made that the response is fine and not circular at all. Since the table *seems* to be red, you have foundational justification for believing that it is red. From this, it logically follows that it is not a white table illuminated by red lights. Even when someone comes and *tells* you that it is a white table illuminated by red lights, you should not necessarily believe them. After all, as is widely recognized, first-hand observation is typically a stronger form of evidence than testimony from another person. (If you *see* x, this is much better than merely hearing someone *tell* you x exists.) Thus, after hearing the other person assert that it's a white table illuminated by red lights, you should still think that it's probably red.

If that seems wrong to us, we might want to avoid this conclusion by denying Phenomenal Conservatism and hence denying that you have foundational justification to believe that the table is red.

In response, I think this example is really an example of a larger problem, a problem about *undercutting defeaters*, which arises regardless of your theory of the sources of justification. Recall that there are two kinds of defeaters, rebutting defeaters (which provide evidence against *p*), and undercutting defeaters (which merely provide evidence that your way of forming the belief that *p* was unreliable) (see §4.5.1).

---

[57] Based on Stewart Cohen, "Basic Knowledge and the Problem of Easy Knowledge" (*Philosophy & Phenomenological Research*, 2002).

Now suppose that you have an initially justified belief that *p*. It doesn't matter how *p* is justified—let it be justified according to whatever is your favorite theory of justification. And suppose that *U* is an undercutting defeater for *p*. (Pretty much everyone agrees that there can be undercutting defeaters for initially justified beliefs, so there's nothing controversial here so far.) Now imagine you get some evidence for *U*. You respond by using *p itself* as evidence against *U*. That seems problematic. For some reason—even though we *stipulated* that *p* was initially justified—it seems wrong to use *p* to reject an undercutting defeater for *p*. (In fact, this seems problematic whether or not you have any positive evidence for *U*.)

What would be an example of this? Well, just take the Red Table example above, but assume that the belief that the table is red is justified for some reason other than the truth of Phenomenal Conservatism. Just take your favorite alternative theory of justification; pretty much every theory of justification is going to have an account of how people can be justified in believing things like this. E.g., maybe the belief is justified because it was formed by a reliable method, or because it's supported by an internally coherent belief system, or because it provides the best explanation for a visual experience that you're directly acquainted with. *Whatever* the source of justification is, it still seems wrong for you to say, "The table is red. Therefore, it isn't a white table illuminated by red lights."

So I think this example isn't specifically a problem for PC or foundationalism. If it's a problem, it's a problem for everyone. What the example seems to show is that there is a special epistemological principle that *you can't use p to refute an undercutting defeater for p*. In the Red Table case, [the table is illuminated by red light] is an undercutting defeater for [the table is red], so you can't use [the table is red] to refute [the table is illuminated by red light]. Since you have an undercutting defeater for [the table is red] and no way of countering that defeater, you have to give up the belief that the table is red.

Note: The defeater in the example was stated as "The table is white but illuminated by red lights." This is really two propositions. [The table is white] would be a rebutting defeater, and *by itself* that proposition could be rejected simply on the basis that the table is red. However, [The table is illuminated by red lights] is an undercutting defeater, since color perception is unreliable in such unusual lighting conditions. Again, what is going on in this example isn't something special about Phenomenal Conservatism or foundationalism. Anyone with any theory of justification is presumably going to have to say something like this.

5.3. Qualified Appearance Theories

Some philosophers hold that appearances provide justification for belief, but *only* when one has grounds for believing that one's appearances in a particular area are reliable. E.g., color appearances provide justification for beliefs about the colors of things, *provided* that you have reason to think your color vision is reliable.

These philosophers have an explanation of what goes wrong in cases like Tree Intuition and Terrorist Intuition (§5.2.4). In Tree Intuition, the problem is that the person has no evidence for thinking that they can reliably recognize the dates on which trees were planted. In Terrorist Intuition, the person has no evidence that their religious experiences are reliable.

This sounds reasonable at first glance. The main problem with this kind of view: How would you ever gather evidence that your appearances are reliable? Either you have some *other* source of knowledge that doesn't itself rely on appearances, or you would have to rely on appearances to tell you that your appearances are reliable.

The problem with the first option is that, well, there just aren't any plausible candidates for knowledge sources that don't rely on appearances. All our knowledge (and justified belief) comes from perception, introspection, memory, intuition, or reasoning. And all of those belief-forming mechanisms rely on appearances. (You can have non-appearance-based beliefs, such as beliefs based on wishful thinking or blind faith, but these are not plausible candidates for justified beliefs.)

So you'd have to rely on appearances to tell you that your appearances are reliable. The problem with this is that you're going to run into either an infinite regress or circularity (similar to the problem discussed in ch. 4).

Typically, defenders of qualified appearance theories appeal to the value of *coherence* (see §4.3) as a source of justification, but they think coherence *alone* isn't enough to provide justification for belief. Rather, a belief has to be supported by appearances *and* the belief has to cohere with one's other beliefs and appearances, in order for the belief to be justified.

My main problem with this is that *if* appearances by themselves don't provide any justification for believing anything, then I don't see how coherence will make any difference. It doesn't matter if a belief coheres with a bunch of other things that are all *completely unjustified*.

Probably the best view in this vicinity is that appearances provide a small amount of justification, which is insufficient by itself for having a "justified belief", but coherence among many appearances augments the justification to the point where one can have a justified belief. (I assume that, for a belief to count as "justified", it must pass some threshold level of justification.) This brings me to the next major idea I wanted to talk about …

5.4. Foundherentism

As I say, I don't think that beliefs that start out with *no justification at all* can become justified (to any degree) merely because they support each other. However, if p by itself is just a little bit justified, and q by itself is a little bit justified, and p and q support each other, then each of them can add to the justification of the other. If you have a large collection of beliefs, each of which is a little bit justified on its own, then the mutual support relations among these beliefs can produce a high overall degree of justification. So the whole belief system could wind up being strongly justified, if it is highly coherent.

This view of how justification works is sometimes called **foundherentism** (because it combines elements of foundationalism and coherentism), or **weak foundationalism** (because it only posits a weak degree of foundational justification). (To have a complete theory of justification, foundherentism must be combined with a specific view of the source of the small amount of foundational justification. E.g., it could be combined with phenomenal conservatism, or some other theory.)

I think this view is generally reasonable, and probably many beliefs are justified in the foundherentist way. I don't think *all* beliefs are like that, though. For instance, I don't think I need to appeal to coherence to justify [I exist]. I think my foundational justification for believing that is enough, by itself, for me to count as having a justified belief, and indeed *knowledge*, that I exist.

Perhaps foundherentists would accept this point. If so, then I think "foundherentism" is really not a distinct theory of justification; foundherentism is just foundationalism. Standard, middle-of-the-road foundationalists do not, in fact, insist that all foundational beliefs have to have some *really high* degree of justification, nor do they deny that coherence can strengthen your beliefs' justification. They're not dummies. Pretty much any normal foundationalist is going to agree that some beliefs could have a small degree of foundational justification, and that mutual support among such beliefs could strengthen their justification.

Given Phenomenal Conservatism, for example, it's easy to see why some beliefs might have only a small degree of foundational justification. Appearances come in varying strengths: Some propositions seem extremely obvious, while others seem only kind of obvious, and still others seem merely somewhat plausible. It's natural to think that this results in varying amounts of justification.

5.5. Conclusion

We've considered four versions of foundationalism. The first and most traditional version was the Acquaintance Theory, which holds that we are directly aware of certain things (especially our own mental states and certain abstract objects), and that this enables us to have foundational knowledge about those things. This theory supposedly faces a dilemma: If states of direct awareness have propositional content, then they need to be justified; if they don't, then they can't justify beliefs. However, neither horn of that dilemma is particularly compelling. A more serious problem is how to explain cases in which a person *seems* to themselves to be directly acquainted with some fact, but they are mistaken. In at least some such cases, the person is, intuitively, *justified* in believing what they seemingly perceive to be the case, yet this cannot be explained by acquaintance, since one cannot be acquainted with a non-existent fact.

The second theory we considered was Phenomenal Conservatism, which holds that we have some degree of foundational justification for believing whatever *seems* to us to be the case, unless and until we have grounds for doubting it. This theory explains all or most of the things that we intuitively consider justified. Alternative views are, I claim, self-defeating because they are themselves based on the way things seem to the people who hold those views; hence, if appearances don't provide any justification for belief, not even in the absence of defeaters, then the belief in an alternative theory of justification is itself unjustified.

Phenomenal Conservatism faces objections based on crazy appearances that, intuitively, don't seem to provide justification for belief; appearances that are caused by irrational or unreliable beliefs; and cases in which one uses a belief to reject an undercutting defeater for that very belief. I, of course, didn't find any of those objections compelling.

A third theory is a variant on phenomenal conservatism in which we stipulate that a person must have evidence that their appearances are reliable in order to be justified in forming beliefs based on those appearances. The main problem with this is that there is no way of acquiring such evidence without relying on appearances; hence, one either has an infinite regress or one must use circular reasoning.

A fourth theory is foundherentism, which holds that we have some small degree of foundational justification for certain beliefs, but we must rely on coherence among these beliefs to augment that justification to the level required to count as having a "justified belief". One objection to this is that at least *some* beliefs appear to have enough foundational justification that they don't need to rely on coherence, e.g., the belief that I exist, or the belief that I am in pain (when I am in fact having a severe, conscious pain). If foundherentists accept this point, then their view just becomes standard foundationalism. Which is fine, but then we don't need a weird new name for the view.

6. Meta-Knowledge

In this chapter, we'll discuss **meta-knowledge**, or **second-order knowledge**, which is knowledge about one's own knowledge. I'm using the term here to include knowledge of the reliability of one's own belief-forming methods, knowledge of the justification of one's own beliefs, and stuff like that. Meta-knowledge poses deep, longstanding puzzles for epistemology.

6.1. The KK Thesis

Let's start with an easy issue. The **KK Thesis** is the thesis that if you know that p, then you know that you know that p. This strikes many people as intuitive. However, it must be false since it generates an infinite regress—it would follow that you also know that you know that you know that p, and then that you know that you know that you know that you know that p, and so on. It's not plausible that you have all those items of knowledge.

For example, I know that Cheetos are tasty, but I don't know the following:

> [I know that Cheetos are tasty.]

I don't think I *know* the above proposition, since I can't even grasp it. So the KK Thesis is false. Similarly for the JJ thesis ("if you're justified in believing p then you're justified in believing that you're justified in believing p").

6.2. An Argument for Global Justification Skepticism

6.2.1. The Skeptic's Argument

We've already encountered one form of skepticism in section 4.4 above. But there are many more; skepticism is a recurring theme in philosophy, especially in epistemology. (Among academic researchers, only philosophers seriously debate whether their subject matter even exists.) Here, I'll explain a second argument for global justification skepticism, the view that there is no justification for any belief.

When we acquire our putative knowledge, we do so using one or more **cognitive faculties**. These are faculties that are supposed to give us knowledge, such as vision, hearing, taste, touch, smell, memory, introspection, reasoning, and intuition. Maybe you have other things you'd like to add to that list, or maybe you'd like to remove some of the items on it. Let's not worry too much about the proper list of cognitive faculties; that's not going to matter for our purposes.

Now, here is something that seems like a plausible requirement for knowledge: Since all your putative knowledge comes from one or more of these faculties, it seems that you should first verify that your faculties are reliable, before you rely on them. If you don't know whether your faculties are reliable, then you can't really know whether any of the beliefs that you form using them are correct.

Here is an analogy. I have a toy called a Magic 8-Ball (I bought it for my epistemology classes; it helps me grade papers). It looks like a large, plastic 8-ball, and it's meant to be used like this: You hold the 8-Ball in your hand, ask it a yes/no question, then turn it over. An answer floats up to a window in the bottom. Possible answers include, "Yes, definitely", "My sources say no", "Outlook good", and so on. Now suppose I were forming lots of beliefs using the Magic 8-Ball. It seems that this would *not* be a way of acquiring knowledge. I wouldn't actually *know* any of the 8-Ball beliefs to be true, because I have no reason to believe that the 8-Ball is a reliable source of information. I have to first verify the 8-Ball's reliability, *then* I can use it to find out other things.

Furthermore, if I wanted to verify the 8-Ball's reliability, I obviously cannot simply ask the 8-Ball. That would be like circular reasoning. I need an independent source of information to check on the 8-Ball. And of course I must already know that *other* source to be reliable.

You can see where this is going. Just as with the Magic 8-Ball, in order for me to know anything using any cognitive faculty, I must first verify that that faculty is reliable. And I can't use a faculty to verify its own reliability; I must have an independent source. But I don't have an infinite series of faculties, and I can't rely on circular reasoning (e.g., using two faculties to "verify" each other's reliability). So it looks like I'm screwed. (That's a very sophisticated technical term in epistemology; in more colloquial terms, it looks like I can't gain any knowledge.)

Variant on the argument
Some people don't like talk of "faculties". If you prefer, you can phrase the argument in terms of *methods of forming beliefs* (which I guess is broader—e.g.,

> "asking the 8-Ball" counts as a method of forming a belief). You can also speak in terms of justification (which is really what we're concerned with) rather than knowledge. So the argument would be that you need justification for thinking a belief-forming method is reliable before you can justifiably rely on it. But you can't have an infinite series of methods, nor may you rely on circular reasoning, so you're screwed.

Take, for example, the five senses. How do we know we can trust them? I could try taking an eye exam to see if my vision is good. But to collect the results of the exam, I would have to either use my vision (to read the results) or use my hearing (to hear the doctor telling me the results). These things only work if I already know I can trust my senses.

Or take the faculty of memory. How do I know that memory is reliable? Here's one argument: In the past, I have often seemed to remember things and then later verified those things. E.g., I seem to remember where I live, I go to that location, and I find an apartment just like the one I was expecting. This sort of thing has happened over and over again. That tends to confirm that my memory is generally reliable. The only problem is that my knowledge that things like that have happened comes to me by the very faculty whose reliability is in question: I *remember* that I've previously tested my memory and found it by and large reliable. So this looks circular.

Even more troublingly, suppose we ask how we know that *reason* is reliable. We could try constructing an argument to show that reason is reliable. But if we did that, we would be using reason to verify reason's reliability. There is no way around this. So once again, it seems that there is no way for us to know anything. Here is a summary of the argument:

1. All putative knowledge is formed using some belief-forming method. (Premise.)
2. In order to know *p*, one must first know that one's method of forming the belief that *p* is reliable. (Premise.)
3. One cannot have an infinite regress of belief-forming methods. (Premise.)
4. One cannot rely on circularity in verifying the reliability of belief-forming methods. (Premise.)
5. Therefore, one can never know anything. (From 1–4.)

Again, you can substitute "justified belief" for "knowledge" in the above, and get the conclusion that no one can be justified in believing anything.

6.2.2. Don't Be an Annoying Skeptic

Skeptics are annoying. No matter what you say, they say, "How do you KNOW that?", and they won't accept any answer. A skeptic never says, "Oh, I get it.

Thanks!" Moreover, the skeptical argument that we just discussed is subject to the same two general problems we raised in sections 4.4.2 and 4.4.3. First, it is self-refuting since, if correct, it would be a counter-example to itself. It purports to justify the claim that nothing can be justified.

Second, a Moorean response applies to the skeptical argument. The argument asks us to reject propositions that are *more* initially plausible (e.g., [I know I exist]) on the basis of propositions that are *less* initially plausible (e.g., [To know that *p*, one must first know that one's method of forming the belief that *p* is reliable]).

So, here as elsewhere, we proceed on the assumption that skepticism is false. Our task in what follows is not to *persuade skeptics*, which is likely impossible. (And by the way, one's task in philosophy in general is almost never to persuade people who have a completely opposite starting position—that's almost always impossible. One's task is usually either to persuade *undecided, open-minded* people, or simply to *explain* an idea to other people.) Our task in what follows is to explain what went wrong in the reasoning of the preceding section.

6.2.3. *The Skeptic's False Premise*

The skeptical argument as formulated above (§6.2.1) has four premises. Which one is false? The answer is premise 2:

2. In order to know *p*, one must first know that one's method of forming the belief that *p* is reliable.

Why think that this is the false premise? First, notice that premise 2 is pretty much a straight-out denial of foundationalism. *Any* premise of the form, "In order to know anything, one must first know *x*" is a rejection of foundationalism, since, if one has *foundational* knowledge of *p*, then *by definition* one does not need to first know anything else to know *p*. So if we think foundationalism is at all plausible, we can't reasonably start by assuming premise 2.

But maybe you don't like foundationalism. In spite of what I've said on its behalf (chs. 4–5), not everyone accepts it. But even if you have some other view of the structure of knowledge, you should still reject premise 2, because premise 2 is conceptually confused.

Why do I say that? If there is knowledge at all, there must be some way of acquiring it. And it should at least be *possible* for the way that you acquire a belief to also be a way that you acquire *knowledge* of the thing that you believe. So suppose *M* is a belief-forming method that (on at least one occasion) produces knowledge. It doesn't matter what this method is; it can be anything you like. It could include any inferences you like, including inferences about the reliability of other methods. It could rely on the coherence of a belief system, or somehow having an infinite series of reasons, or whatever.

Now, imagine someone saying that before one can know things using M, one must first verify that M is reliable. Notice that that is tantamount to saying that M is *not actually* a method of acquiring knowledge after all—that to acquire knowledge, one must rather follow method M', which consists of first verifying that M is reliable, then finding out what conclusion M produces and accepting that conclusion. On this view, M *by itself* cannot produce knowledge.

This is confused. It cannot be that M is not really a method of acquiring knowledge, because we *stipulated* that it was a method of acquiring knowledge. (By the way, if Premise 2 is correct, method M' wouldn't work either, because you'd have to first verify that M' was reliable, etc.)

Of course, there can be methods of acquiring knowledge that involve verifying the reliability of other information sources. But it cannot be that all methods of acquiring knowledge involve verifying the reliability of those same methods.

6.2.4. Natural Faculties vs. the 8-Ball

When setting out the skeptic's argument, I tried to make Premise 2 plausible using the example of the Magic 8-Ball. If I'm forming beliefs using the 8-Ball, it seems that I need to first verify the 8-Ball's reliability. Is this true? If so, why would I *not* need to verify the reliability of some *other* methods? What methods do I not need to thus verify, and why are they different from the 8-Ball method?

These are good questions. The answers depend on your theory of justified belief. Whatever theory you have, there is going to be a straightforward way of answering the above questions.

Take the case of Phenomenal Conservatism. On this theory, if you form a belief based on your appearances (in the absence of defeaters), then you have a (to some degree) justified belief. You do not need to first verify that this way of forming beliefs is reliable (nor do you have to do *anything else at all*), because you've already satisfied what this theory identifies as a sufficient condition for foundational justification.

Why are 8-Ball beliefs (beliefs formed as a result of trusting the Magic 8-Ball) different? Because Magic 8-Ball beliefs *do not* satisfy the theory's sufficient condition for foundational justification. The presence of the word "yes" in the window of the 8-Ball does not constitute a *seeming* that the proposition recently asked about is true. Rather, the 8-Ball user *infers* a particular answer to his question from the belief that a particular expression is appearing in the 8-Ball's window. This inference is not valid or cogent unless one includes an implicit premise along the lines of "What the 8-Ball says tends to be true."

That's just one example. *Any* decent general theory of justification is going to say something analogous. Suppose your theory of justification says, "A belief is justified as long as it satisfies condition *C*." Then as long as a belief satisfies *C*, it's justified; one need not *add* anything to condition *C* (such as a condition that the believer has first verified that beliefs that satisfy *C* are reliable). Furthermore, if you have a halfway decent theory, 8-Ball beliefs are simply not going to be justified according to the theory; i.e., they won't on their own satisfy *C*. So that will explain why the 8-Ball beliefs require some further argument to back them up.

What the skeptic has done is to overgeneralize. *Some* possible belief sources fail on their own to justify a belief. About these sources, one needs evidence that they are reliable information sources. The skeptic mistakenly generalizes from here to the conclusion that *all* information sources are just like these non-justification-conferring sources.

This diagnosis can be supported by contrasting our intuitions about the 8-Ball with our intuitions about other examples. Consider two more cases:

> *A=A:* Ann thinks about the proposition [*A=A*]. Upon fully and correctly understanding that proposition, she finds it self-evident and thus accepts it. She does not, however, first verify that seemingly self-evident truths are in general reliable.
>
> *Squirrel in the Tree:* Fido the dog sees a squirrel in a tree (this is of great interest to him). Fido does not, however, have an argument to show that vision is reliable, or that the senses in general are reliable.

Unlike the 8-Ball case, in these cases there is no common sense intuition that the subjects lack knowledge. Intuitively, Ann knows that *A=A*, and Fido knows that there's a squirrel in the tree. This suggests that the skeptic's Premise 2 results from overgeneralizing in the manner I have described.

6.3. How to Know You Are Reliable

6.3.1. *The Meta-Coherence Norm*

Okay, let's say the above is correct: To know something using your natural cognitive faculties (observation, reason, etc.), you don't *need* to first know that your faculties are reliable. That's a good thing, because most people and animals do not even think about whether their faculties are reliable. You see something, and you believe that thing exists; you don't first think to yourself, "Wait, are my senses reliable?"

Nevertheless, it is always *possible* for a smart, self-aware person to ask that question. Especially if they've studied philosophy. *If* you ask yourself that question, how should you answer it?

It would certainly be a problem if, on reflection, you decided that your senses were *not* reliable sources of information. If you came to that conclusion, then it seems that you would be rationally compelled to give up your beliefs about the external world. At that point, you would lack knowledge of the external world (even if you were mistaken in thinking your senses were unreliable). So, although knowledge does not require *believing* that your faculties *are reliable*, it *does* require *not* believing that they are *un*reliable.

Now, what if, rather than thinking your senses are unreliable, you merely *suspend judgment* on the question, so that you neither believe nor disbelieve that they are reliable? To be clear, this is different from merely failing to think about the question. You explicitly think about whether your senses are reliable, and you say to yourself, "I dunno. Maybe they're reliable, maybe not."

This also seems like a problem. At that point, it seems that you can't just go on believing all the things about the external world that your senses tell you. There would be something incoherent about that. It's not a contradiction, but it would be an incoherence in the sense that your ordinary beliefs about the world would not fit together with your attitude about the *source* of those beliefs.

This leads to what I call the Meta-Coherence Norm (I made up that term; it's not widely used). The Meta-Coherence Norm is the principle that if you believe p, and you reflect on whether your method of forming the belief that p is reliable, you have to conclude that it *is*; otherwise, you have to give up the belief that p.[58]

That seems pretty plausible to me. (I don't have any argument beyond the above appeal to intuition, though.) If that's right, that makes it all the more important to ask: How can we know (or at least justifiably believe) that our cognitive faculties are reliable? Notice that nothing we've said up till now answers that. And of particular interest, how can we avoid either an infinite regress or some kind of circularity in trying to confirm that our faculties are reliable?

The short answer is: We have to rely on a kind of circularity. But it's a benign kind. Maybe.

---

[58] See my "The Puzzle of Metacoherence" in *Philosophy & Phenomenological Research* (2011). There, however, the principle is stronger: I say that if you believe p, then you're committed, on reflection, to thinking that you *know p* (which entails that your belief-forming method was reliable, among other things).

6.3.2. Epistemic Circularity

Epistemologists like to distinguish two kinds of "circularity" in reasoning: *premise circularity* and *epistemic circularity*.[59] **Premise circularity** is the error an argument commits when one of the premises of the argument is identical with the conclusion, or a paraphrase of the conclusion, or depends for its justification on the conclusion. Almost everyone agrees that this is bad and not a way of acquiring knowledge.

Epistemic circularity occurs when an argument's conclusion endorses a certain cognitive faculty or belief-forming method (as reliable, or a good source of justification, or something like that), and one or more premises of the argument were formed using that same faculty or method.

We saw a few examples in §6.2.1 above. All the examples of using your cognitive faculties to verify that those faculties are reliable were examples of *epistemic* circularity, not premise circularity. E.g., if I take a vision test, then read the results of the test using my eyes, and conclude that my vision is reliable, that's epistemic circularity (I used vision to find out that vision is reliable). Why is that not *premise* circularity? Because when one forms ordinary beliefs using vision, one need not and does not infer those beliefs from the premise "Vision is reliable." E.g., when you see an orange, you just immediately believe that the orange is real; you don't (and don't need to) first form the belief "Vision is reliable" (see §6.2.3). So the conclusion of the argument is not among the premises.

Similarly, the case where you rely on memory in concluding that your memory is reliable (because you've often correctly remembered stuff in the past) is a case of epistemic circularity, not premise circularity. And similarly for the case of constructing an argument that reason is reliable (if you can think of such an argument).

Some philosophers think that epistemic circularity is *sometimes* okay. (No one thinks that it is *always* okay, though.) Why do they think that? For one thing, it seems that we know, or at least have some justification to believe, that our faculties are generally reliable, and there just doesn't seem to be any way that we could know this without some kind of epistemic circularity. So it must be that epistemic circularity is sometimes okay.

What's the theoretical explanation for why epistemic circularity would be okay? Assume that belief-forming method M (by itself) is a legitimate source of justification, so that if I form a belief using M, this belief is justified without

---

[59] A third kind of circularity is **rule circularity**. This occurs when an argument's conclusion endorses a rule of inference which the argument itself follows. E.g., "The sky is blue; if the sky is blue, then modus ponens is valid; therefore, modus ponens is valid."

my first verifying that M is reliable. In that case, it seems that I should be able to infer further conclusions from that belief, as long as they are logically supported by it. So if one of these beliefs supports the conclusion that method M is reliable, then I should conclude that M is reliable. In a sense, this isn't *really* circular, since, by hypothesis, I did not need to assume that M is reliable at the start (per the arguments of §§6.2.3–6.2.4).

If this still seems fishy to you, you're in good company; many epistemologists find it fishy. We're going to discuss some reasons why presently.

6.3.3. Track Record Arguments

One prominent *species* of epistemic circularity is known as a **track-record argument**. This is an argument in which you use some cognitive faculty to form a series of beliefs, note in each case that the beliefs were formed by that method, conclude in each case that the method gave you a true belief, and then inductively generalize to the conclusion that the method is reliable. For example, let's say you look at a series of color samples, and you think to yourself:

1. Sample #1 is red. (Arrived at using your color vision.)
2. Sample #1 looks red to me. (Arrived at by introspection.)
3. Sample #2 is teal.
4. Sample #2 looks teal to me.
5. Sample #3 is mauve.
6. Sample #3 looks mauve to me.
… (Repeat for many more samples.)
C. Therefore, in general, things look to me the color that they are. (From above steps, by induction.) I.e., my color vision is reliable.

What do we think of this type of argument?

It definitely doesn't sound good. Some philosophers consider this sort of reasoning "pathetically circular"[60] (though, again, there is no *premise* circularity; the conclusion does not appear in the premises). Some think that this shows that epistemic circularity in general is bad.

Other philosophers claim that track record arguments are okay, despite how lame they sound. Then they try to explain why the arguments *sound* bad. One explanation is that the argument wouldn't *persuade* someone who initially *doubted* the conclusion, since such a person would be equally skeptical of premises 1, 3, and so on. Likewise, if you have some *reason* for doubting the conclusion (a defeater, as we say), the track record argument cannot put that

---

[60] Richard Fumerton, *Metaepistemology and Skepticism* (1995), 177.

doubt to rest. However, notice that all that is compatible with saying that if you *don't* initially doubt the conclusion, nor have any reason to doubt it, then the argument could be fine.

Opponents of track record arguments find those explanations weak. Intuitively, track record arguments seem bad, even when you're not trying to persuade anyone else, and even when you don't have any particular reasons for doubting the conclusion. You could just be thinking the track record argument to yourself, without ever having doubted the reliability of your faculties and without having any particular reason for such doubt, and it still seems like there's something irrational about this way of justifying a belief.

6.3.4. What's Wrong with Track Record Arguments

Okay, now I'm going to tell you what's wrong with track record arguments. What's wrong is that the method of reasoning automatically delivers the result that your cognitive faculties are reliable. E.g., no matter what objects you see, and no matter how reliable your color vision is or isn't, if you use a track record argument to "test" your color vision, you always get the result "my color vision is reliable". You can tell ahead of time that this is true. So, e.g., you don't need to actually *look* at Sample #1, since you know that whatever it looks like, you're going to say that it both is a certain color and looks that color.

What's bad about this? Well, it means that the *probability* that your color vision is reliable, given that you can construct a track record argument, is exactly the same as the initial probability that your color vision is reliable. Looking at the color samples and going through the argument should not change your degree of confidence that your color vision is reliable. And that means that the track record argument does not in fact support its conclusion.

Suppose, for example, that you initially estimate that your color vision is 90% reliable. (Let's say that means that 90% of the time, it gives you the true colors of things; 10% of the time, you see a random color that's not the actual color of the object you're looking at. For simplicity, assume that your introspective beliefs, about how each object *looks to you*, are guaranteed to be correct.) Then when you go through the track record argument, you should be only 90% confident of each of the odd-numbered premises (the premises stating the actual colors of things). Overall, then, you should estimate that about 90% of the odd-numbered premises are correct. Then when you draw your inductive conclusion about the reliability of your color vision, you obviously cannot infer that it's more than 90% reliable.

Or consider another variant of the case. Suppose that you're 75% confident that your color vision is *completely* reliable, but you think there's a 25% chance that it's completely unreliable. Then when you construct the track record argument, you should think that there's a 75% chance that all the odd-numbered premises are true, and a 25% chance that they're all false. You obviously cannot, from this position, justify *increasing* your confidence that your color vision is reliable above 75%.

So the track record argument doesn't do anything. It's not just that it doesn't provide reasons suitable for convincing someone who *doubts or denies* its conclusion; it's that, *no matter what* your starting attitude is about the reliability of your color vision, the argument gives you no reason to change that attitude.

6.3.5. Benign Epistemically Circular Arguments

This doesn't mean that *no* epistemically circular arguments are any good. It's possible to have an epistemically circular argument in which the structure of the argument *allows* for more than one conclusion to be supported by the evidence.

For example, suppose I want to test the reliability of my hearing. I listen to some sounds in the environment, then I ask other people if they hear the same sounds. If they say yes, that tends to support the reliability of my hearing. I also ask other people to describe other sounds that they hear in the environment. If I also hear those sounds, then, again, that supports that my hearing is reliable.

Of course, I have to use my *hearing* to know what the other people are telling me. So that's an example of "epistemic circularity", as we've defined the term. But it's not like the track record argument, because in *this* case, it *is* possible for the method to lead to a negative conclusion: I *could* hear the other people saying, "No, I don't hear the sound you're talking about." Or I could hear other people telling me, "I hear a bell ringing" while I myself do not hear a bell. If those things happened, I'd have to lower my estimate of how reliable my hearing is. By the same token, then, if those things *don't* happen, and in fact I hear other people confirming that they hear the same sounds in the environment that I do, then I should *increase* my estimate of how reliable my hearing is.

Here's another example. I want to test the reliability of my memory. So I think of some events that I witnessed with other people, and I ask the other people how they remember the events. If the other people describe pretty much the same stuff that I remember, then I conclude that my memory is at least reasonably reliable. I do this a number of times, with different remembered events. Each time, I *remember* what the result of the experiment was, i.e., I remember whether other people confirmed the things that I myself seemed to remember. After I've successfully confirmed that other people tend to remember more or less what I remember when we have observed the same event, I conclude that my memory is reliable. This is, again, epistemically circular according to our above definition. But again, it's not a useless procedure like the track record argument. If my memory was in fact unreliable, then I *could* very well remember other people frequently contradicting my own memories. I could, e.g., remember riding a purple lion with my wife last Saturday, and also remember my wife saying that that did not happen. If I had collections of memories like that, I'd have to lower my credence in the reliability of my memory. Conversely, if stuff like that *doesn't* happen, I should *increase* my confidence in my memory.

So those are examples of benign epistemic circularity.

Now, you might say that I'm actually relying on a distinct belief-forming method, the method of "coherence reasoning" (the kind of reasoning wherein you conclude that a belief-forming method is probably reliable because it gives coherent results; see §4.3.1). You might then say that we now need an explanation of how I can know that coherence reasoning is reliable.

I would respond, basically, by appealing to the laws of probability, which follow from a certain set of simple, self-evident axioms. You might then say that I need an explanation for how I know that my *reasoning* is reliable, as well as how I know that *believing seemingly self-evident axioms* is reliable.

From this point, I don't think that I should continue this regress further. I should not, for example, try to deploy coherence reasoning again (which I think would be the bad kind of epistemic circularity). When we get to questioning reasoning or self-evident axioms, I think I should say the reliability of both reason and intuitions about self-evident axioms is itself foundational; I need no argument for the reliability of those things. I would take the same view about introspective awareness of one's present, conscious mental states.

6.4. Justified Theories of Justification

Here's another question that seems to invite circular answers: How can we justify a theory of justification? Or, perhaps better: Suppose we are justified in believing a certain theory of justification. How might we account for *how* we are justified in believing this theory?

We could appeal to the theory itself. But that seems kind of circular. Let's say that Joe has the following theory of justification:

> *Joe's Theory of Justification:* S is justified in believing p if and only if S hears Joe say that p.

We ask Joe what his justification is for that theory. Joe replies: "I say the theory is true. So now you and I are justified in believing it." Surely this is no good.

Similarly, suppose someone asks me why I think I'm justified in believing Phenomenal Conservatism (PC). I could respond by saying that PC seems right to me and I don't have sufficient reason for doubting it. A skeptic might then accuse me of a kind of vicious circularity, since I appealed to PC in explaining how PC is justified. Is this a problem?

I don't think it is. To see why, let T be the *correct, complete* theory of justification. Maybe we don't yet know what T is; maybe epistemologists will discover it in the distant future. It seems that it should at least be possible for someone to discover it. So, after some brilliant epistemologist discovers T (and comes to know that it's the correct theory), some annoying skeptic asks the epistemologist to explain how he's justified in believing T.

Now, there are three ways the epistemologist could respond:

a. He could *use T itself* to explain his justification for believing T, i.e., he could say that his belief in T satisfies the conditions that T itself gives for a justified belief.
b. He could give some *other* reason why his belief in T is justified.
c. He could concede that T isn't justified, or that he doesn't know whether or how it is justified, or something like that.

Option (c) doesn't seem good. Again, it seems that the correct theory of justification should not be in principle unknowable, so we should be able to stipulate a scenario in which someone discovers it. That person should not be debarred from explaining how he knows it.

Option (b) definitely isn't cool either. If the epistemologist cites some other reason why his belief in T is justified, that means he is conceding that T *isn't* the complete and correct theory of justification after all. By definition, if it's the complete and correct theory, then it must explain why *any* justified belief is justified (including belief in the theory itself). But we stipulated that T *is* the complete and correct theory.

So it seems that the epistemologist should choose (a). What this shows is that the (putative) circularity involved in using an epistemological theory to explain why that theory is justified is not a problem *per se*. It can't be a problem *per se*, because that is exactly what you would do *if you had the correct theory*.

What, then, is wrong with Joe's using his theory of justification to explain why we're all justified in believing that theory? Well, the only problem is that Joe's theory just is not in fact the correct theory. Since it's not the correct theory of justification, the fact that some proposition satisfies that theory doesn't mean the proposition is justified. So in particular, the fact that Joe's theory satisfies itself doesn't mean that Joe's theory is justified.

At this point, you might wonder about how two epistemologists with conflicting theories could possibly resolve their disagreement. Assuming each theory is self-supporting (justified by its own lights), the two epistemologists could each claim that their own theory is justified since it is in fact true, and that the other person's theory is unjustified since it is in fact false.

This sort of situation could in theory generate an unresolvable conflict. I don't think that will happen, though. In practice, people (both philosophers and smart lay people) share a wide range of intuitions about which particular beliefs are justified and unjustified, as well as dispositions to reason in particular ways. Philosophers with incorrect epistemological theories are (I hope) not people with fundamentally different implicit belief-forming norms and practices, but rather people who have thought of different ways of systematizing their common norms and practices. People can be induced to give up incorrect theories when they come to see that those theories do not in fact correspond to their implicit belief-forming norms.

6.5. Conclusion

Meta-knowledge is knowledge about one's own knowledge, including knowledge about the reliability of one's belief-forming methods or the legitimacy of one's justification sources. Many people are tempted to think (mistakenly) that knowledge requires meta-knowledge. But knowing something cannot in general entail knowing that one knows it, since that leads to an infinite regress.

Knowing something also does not in general require first knowing that one's belief-forming method is reliable. That idea would rule out *any* belief-forming method from (by itself) producing knowledge, since, however one formed a belief, one would still have to supplement this with some other procedure to verify that the original procedure was reliable. That would of course lead to an infinite regress.

There remains, however, a plausible norm according to which, *if* one reflects on whether a given belief was formed in a reliable way, one must think that it was; otherwise, one should give up the belief. This raises the question of how one can know one's fundamental belief-forming methods (especially the use of the five senses, memory, introspection, intuition, and reasoning) to be reliable. There seems to be no way of doing this without epistemic circularity, i.e., using your cognitive faculties to verify their own reliability.

Epistemologists debate about whether epistemic circularity is ever acceptable. At least some kinds are bad, especially "track record arguments". Bad forms of epistemic circularity are those in which the method of reasoning automatically delivers the result "my faculties are reliable" no matter what. However, there are benign forms of epistemic circularity in which the method of reasoning *could* show one's faculties to be unreliable if they were unreliable, even though the method uses those same faculties. This is essentially because unreliable faculties do not tend to give coherent answers. So one can use benign epistemically circular arguments to show that sensory perception and memory are generally reliable. In the case of reason, introspection, and intuition, it's probably best to just posit a foundational principle that those are reliable.

Finally, there is the question of how a theory of justification can be justified. The answer is that the correct theory of justification must be justified by satisfying itself—that is, the theory is justified if and only if it satisfies the conditions that the theory itself cites as sufficient for justification. That must by definition be true of the correct theory. Of course, the same does not hold for incorrect theories.

7. Taxonomy and Paradigms of Knowledge

How can we best classify the different kinds of knowledge? Epistemologists rarely spend time discussing this, but there is a fairly standard taxonomy. I'm going to describe it, criticize it, then propose another possible classification.

7.1. A Traditional Taxonomy

7.1.1. Inferential vs. Non-inferential Knowledge

Traditionally, we divide knowledge into inferential and non-inferential knowledge.

Inferential knowledge is knowledge that is justified on the basis of one or more other beliefs. The paradigm would be knowing a mathematical theorem by proving it from a set of axioms. In that case, you have knowledge based on *deductive* inference. There is also knowledge based on *inductive* inference. For instance, say you meet a bunch of rabbits in different circumstances, notice that they are all furry, and this is how you come to know that all rabbits are furry. Your knowledge that all rabbits are furry is inferential because you inferred it from the premise that this particular rabbit is furry, and that other one is furry, and so on. As a result, if your premises were unjustified, then your conclusion would be unjustified. Also, if (enough of) your premises were *false* (whether or not they're justified), then your conclusion (even if true) would not constitute knowledge (this is the lesson of the Gettier examples of §2.4).

Non-inferential knowledge (also called **foundational knowledge**) is knowledge that is *not* justified on the basis of any other beliefs. (Of course, this assumes foundationalism, which is okay since all sensible people are foundationalists.) Good examples of non-inferential knowledge would be the knowledge that you are in pain (when you are) and the knowledge that 1+1=2. Some cases are controversial, e.g., it's controversial whether knowledge about things you perceive with the five senses is foundational or inferential (see ch. 9).

7.1.2. Empirical vs. A Priori Knowledge

We also traditionally divide knowledge into empirical (or "a posteriori") knowledge and a priori knowledge. (*Note:* The expression "a priori" is *one word*. There is no word "priori" by itself. There is only "a priori", which is an *adjective* applying to beliefs, items of knowledge, and ways of justifying a belief. I have to mention this because some students seem to think that there is a noun "priori".)

Empirical knowledge (sometimes called "a posteriori knowledge") is knowledge that is justified (directly or indirectly) by observation. That includes observation by the five senses; it is also usually taken to include introspective "observation", i.e., the direct awareness of your own conscious mental states. Good examples of empirical knowledge would be your knowledge that you're in pain (when you are), your knowledge that there is a cat on the refrigerator (when you see this), and our knowledge that humans evolved by natural selection.

A priori knowledge is knowledge that is justified *not* on the basis of observation. This could include innate knowledge (Plato believed in this, but few philosophers today do) or knowledge acquired by some non-observational faculty. Good examples would be the knowledge that 2+3=5, the knowledge that all grandsons are male, and the knowledge that nothing can be entirely red and also entirely blue.

Now here's another thing I have to clarify because I know some of you readers are already making this mistake: The distinction between "empirical" and "a priori" knowledge is *not* about how you *acquire concepts*. So don't say that some item of knowledge is empirical because you *acquired the concepts* through observation. For example, don't say that "all grandsons are male" is empirical because we acquire the concepts "grandson" and "male" through experience. That's not what we're talking about. (John Locke and David Hume were obsessed with how people acquired concepts, but contemporary epistemologists hardly ever talk about that.) What we're talking about is what is the *justification* or *evidence* for a given item of knowledge. "All grandsons are male" is considered to be known a priori because you don't have to *justify* it by citing observations that you've made of grandsons (or of anything else). (You just have to understand the meaning of "grandson".)

The above distinctions yield four possible kinds of knowledge: (*i*) foundational empirical knowledge, (*ii*) inferential empirical knowledge, (*iii*) foundational a priori knowledge, and (*iv*) inferential a priori knowledge. All four of these exist; see examples below.[61]

7.1.3. Four Cognitive Faculties

Our "cognitive faculties" are general, knowledge-gathering capacities that we have. There are at least four that epistemologists traditionally recognize: (*i*) sensory perception (including sight, hearing, taste, touch, and smell), (*ii*) introspection (the capacity for awareness of your own mental states), (*iii*) memory, and (*iv*) reason (a.k.a. "the understanding" or "the intellect"). The last one (reason) is the faculty that enables us to make inferences. Some (sensible and wise) epistemologists also say that this same faculty enables us to recognize certain self-evident truths, such as "the shortest path between any two points is a straight line", "if A is better than B and B is better than C, then A is better than C", and "nothing can be red all over and also blue all over" (see ch. 10). The capacity for recognizing these self-evident truths is sometimes called "**intuition**", and the mental state you're in when you see such a self-evident truth is often called "an intuition". So I could say that I have the intuition that $1+1=2$, or that my intuition tells me $1+1=2$. Please note that most contemporary philosophers consider intuition to be a *part* or *aspect* of the faculty of reason, not an *alternative* to reason.

Perception and introspection both count as types of observation, so the faculties of perception and introspection both produce foundational, empirical knowledge. Reason, when applied to the material provided by perception and introspection, produces inferential, empirical knowledge. Reason also (according to sensible and wise epistemologists) produces some foundational, a priori knowledge through intuition. When we reason from those intuitions, we obtain inferential, a priori knowledge.

7.2. Traditional Paradigms of Knowledge

A "paradigm" of a category is something that is an excellent example of that category. A sparrow is a paradigm bird, the Empire State Building is a paradigm skyscraper, etc. So the paradigms of knowledge would be excellent examples of knowledge. It's useful to have some paradigms in front of us, partly just to make sure you understand all the above kinds of knowledge, and partly because it's easier to address philosophical questions about knowledge by thinking about specific examples. On the Wittgensteinian theory of concepts introduced earlier (§2.6), we form the concept of knowledge in the first place by grouping

---

[61] Again, I'm assuming foundationalism because I'm sensible.

together cases that strike us as similar, and we can identify the contours of the concept by reflecting on particular examples.

So here's a good example: Say you have a ripe tomato in front of you. It's nearby, directly in your line of sight, well-lit, unobstructed, and there is nothing wrong with your eyes or your brain. In this case, you would know by direct observation that there is a red, round thing in front of you. That's a traditional paradigm of *foundational, empirical knowledge.*

For a different kind of example, think about a scientist's knowledge that water is H_2O. The scientist does an experiment in which he sticks a negative and a positive electrode, both connected to a battery, into a sample of water. Bubbles of gas start forming at both electrodes, and the quantity of water starts decreasing. On further testing, the gas coming from the electrodes turns out to be hydrogen and oxygen. Measurements show that the total mass of gas produced equals the quantity of water that was lost. The scientist infers that water is composed of hydrogen and oxygen. (This is a real experiment that can be done. There's also an experiment in which you can burn hydrogen and oxygen and create water.) That's a paradigm of *inferential, empirical knowledge.*

Here's another sort of example that has influenced many thinkers throughout history: You're reading Euclid's *Elements*, when you come upon the proof that the interior angles of any triangle add up to 180°. When you read Euclid's axioms, you see that they are self-evidently true (this is *foundational, a priori knowledge*). When you go through the proof, you acquire *inferential, a priori knowledge* that the angles of a triangle sum to 180°.

> **Interlude: Euclid's *Elements***
> Euclid's *Elements* is among the most influential books in history. In it, the ancient Greek mathematician Euclid presented proofs of many theorems in geometry and number theory that had been discovered as of the time he lived (around 300 B.C.). Many generations of students since then have been taught geometry through Euclid. If you learned geometry in high school, you can thank/curse Euclid for most of the content of that class.
>
> Euclid starts out with some definitions (e.g., "an *obtuse* angle is an angle greater than a right angle"), postulates (e.g., "one can draw a straight line between any two points"), and axioms (e.g., "things that are equal to the same thing are equal to each other"). The postulates and axioms are generally self-evident and in no need of justification. (*Note:* The things he calls "postulates" are specific to geometry, whereas the "axioms" are more general truths of mathematics and logic. But this distinction does not matter, and most people just use "axiom" for both.) From the starting definitions, postulates, and axioms, Euclid proceeds to systematically enumerate and prove 468 different theorems.

> Many thinkers since Euclid have been deeply intellectually impressed by the beautifully systematic and rigorous edifice of knowledge set forth in the *Elements*. Many view the book as an ideal example of human knowledge, and some have set out to produce similar systems for other subjects. For instance, Spinoza (the famous 17th-century Dutch philosopher) tried to produce a similar system of knowledge of metaphysics, with definitions, axioms, and theorems in the style of Euclid.

The above are the sorts of examples that philosophers often give when thinking about the nature of knowledge and the different kinds of knowledge that we have.

7.3. Some Hard-to-Classify Cases

7.3.1. Recognition

Let me give you a different sort of example from the ones that are usually discussed by epistemologists. Say I'm getting a phone call, and I don't know whom it's from. I pick up, say "Hello", and the voice on the other end says, "Hey." As soon as I hear the voice, I recognize it: It is my friend Sue calling. She doesn't have to *say* who it is or give any other identifying information; I just recognize the voice.

Now suppose you ask me: "*How do you know* that it's Sue?" I would say: I know because it *sounds* like Sue. "And how exactly does Sue sound? What properties does her voice have that distinguishes it from all other voices?" Well, I don't have anything useful to tell you about that. I can't say exactly what properties of the voice pattern I'm responding to, and I certainly can't describe it in a way that would enable someone who hadn't heard it to recognize it. But I'm very familiar with Sue's voice, and so I know it when I hear it. That's really all I can tell you.

Now let's think about how this example fits into the taxonomy of knowledge. My recognitional knowledge that the voice I'm hearing is Sue's is empirical, not a priori, since it depends on my sense of hearing. But is it foundational or inferential?

It doesn't seem to be foundational, since the knowledge that *that's Sue* presumably depends upon my hearing certain properties of the voice, which are more directly perceived. (This is different from, say, seeing that something is red, since you can directly see that something is red; you don't have to perceive the redness *through* perceiving any other properties.) On the traditional view, the immediately observable properties of a sound would be things like pitch, loudness, and timbre, not "being made by Sue"—just as the immediately visible properties of an object are its color and shape, not things like "being a tomato". So it seems that this must be an example of inferential, empirical knowledge.

But that doesn't seem quite right either. I didn't really *infer* that the voice was Sue's. It's not as though I listed the properties of the voiceprint, cross-referenced them with previous samples of Sue's voice, then said to myself, "This voice has properties *A*, *B*, and *C*; only Sue's voice in the past has generally had *A*, *B*, and *C*; therefore, this is probably Sue."

You might want to say that perhaps I *unconsciously* or *implicitly* made this inference, rather than making a conscious, explicit inference. But this is still a bit odd. Normally, if someone is going to make an inference, the person must *believe* the premises of that inference and *see how* those premises support the conclusion. If we want to allow for unconscious or implicit inference, we might say that though one need not explicitly, consciously affirm the premises, the premises should at least be things that one *would* endorse *if* they were made explicit, and that one could then see how they supported the conclusion. In the present case, neither of these things is true. Suppose someone wrote down a precise and accurate description of the voiceprint, and I read and explicitly understood the description. If they asked me, "Hey, are these the properties of Sue's voice? And are these the properties of the voice you just heard?", I would have to say, "I don't know."

Now, you might say that, since people do in fact recognize voices, obviously there must be *some* mechanism in the brain that identifies the owner of a voice based on some (no doubt very complicated) set of properties of the voice. And I agree; there is some complicated neural processing that goes into voice recognition. But to say that *my brain* does some complicated *neural processing* is not to say that *I* make *an inference*. In order for something to count as an inference that *I make*, I think it must involve premises that I endorse, or at least would endorse if I thought about them, and for which I would see how they supported the conclusion.

My point is that this example doesn't fit the taxonomy comfortably. It is an ambiguous case, or on the borderline between inferential and non-inferential knowledge.

7.3.2. Categorization

Recognition of particular people or things, as in the above example, is one interesting kind of case. A related type of case is the recognition of a *type* of thing. When we look around us, we not only perceive particular objects and events; we automatically *classify* the things we observe as falling into various categories. We see this object *as a person*, that one *as a table*, and so on.

As in the case of recognizing an individual, this type of recognition occurs automatically, and one usually cannot fully describe its grounds. Check out this famous illustration, the "duck-rabbit" (figure 3).

You can see this picture as either a duck looking to the left or a rabbit looking to the right. You may be able to shift between them at will. Notice that these are two different *experiences* you can have, even though the colors and locations of the lines that you see on the page don't shift and even though your beliefs don't change either. You do, however, have to have some background knowledge and experience; a person who had no concept of a duck could not perceive the duck aspect of the image.

Figure 3: The duck-rabbit

This example illustrates that the human mind automatically classifies the things we observe according to the concepts we possess at the time, and that this classification is reflected in our experience, not simply our *beliefs*.

In this case, the object you're seeing is literally neither a duck nor a rabbit; it is just ink on the page. Hence, you don't know that it's a duck or a rabbit. But now take a case where you see a real duck. You immediately recognize it as such and hence *know* that it is a duck. What kind of knowledge is this?

There are similar issues here as in the previous case. Your classification of the duck obviously depends upon its shape and color properties, so it would be odd to call it foundational knowledge. At the same time, you didn't exactly *infer* that it was a duck, and you probably could not describe the characteristic visible qualities of ducks in sufficient detail to enable someone who hadn't seen one to recognize them and distinguish them from all other kinds of birds. So it would also be odd to call "that's a duck" inferential knowledge.

7.3.3. Judgment

Here is another interesting type of case. Say you're on the jury in a murder trial. Your task is to determine whether the evidence presented by the prosecution proves beyond a reasonable doubt that the defendant committed the crime. A lot of evidence is presented by both sides. Each side also tries to cast doubt on the other side's evidence, for example, suggesting that some witnesses might have a motivation to lie, or might not have seen events perfectly clearly, or might have imperfect memory. In the end, you have to weigh up all the evidence on both sides in your mind, form some sense of the overall weight of evidence for guilt, and decide whether it passes the "reasonable doubt" threshold. Needless to say, some people might be better at this than others, some might be more impartial than others, and different people might come to different conclusions.

Let's say that when you do this, you correctly and justifiedly come to the conclusion that the evidence *does* constitute proof beyond a reasonable doubt. Suppose, in fact (as might be the case), that you *know* that it does. What kind of knowledge is this?

Well, you have empirical knowledge of *what the evidence in the trial was*—you got that by observing the trial and remembering it. But *given* that the evidence was what it was, the knowledge that *that constitutes proof beyond a reasonable doubt* looks to be a priori; it is not itself based on some other evidence. (In other words, you know empirically that the evidence was a certain way, but you know a priori that *if* the evidence is that way, then there is proof beyond a reasonable doubt.)

Now, is your knowledge foundational or inferential? Well, the knowledge of [this set of evidence constitutes proof beyond a reasonable doubt] doesn't look much like the paradigms of foundational, a priori knowledge—it isn't a self-evident axiom. But it also doesn't look much like the paradigms of inferential knowledge. You look at the whole set of evidence and try to *weigh it* in your mind. This weighing isn't exactly going through a series of inferential steps. We *could* say that it's a one-step inference where the premises include all the details about the evidence and the conclusion is "the evidence constitutes proof beyond a reasonable doubt", but then we'd have to acknowledge that this does not follow any of the familiar inference rules that philosophers talk about, and that it is a very different type of inference from those usually discussed. Notice that it is neither a formal deductive inference, nor inductive, nor inference to the best explanation.[62]

7.3.4. What Makes a Good Taxonomy?

You might wonder: So what? Nearly all categories have borderline cases. There are things on the borderline between red and orange, between tall and non-tall, between an adult and an adolescent, etc. Usually, we just go ahead and use these categories anyway, without worrying about how to classify every case. If there is some particular purpose for which we need all cases to be definitively classified, then we can always stipulate a more precise definition. For instance,

---

[62] It is not inductive, since the conclusion is not a generalization from multiple particular cases. It also is not inference to the best explanation, since there is no premise stating that the conclusion is the best explanation for something.

for voting purposes, we need to definitively classify everyone as either an adult or not an adult; hence, we just stipulate a cutoff of 18 years of age. No problem.

But I want to point out how my examples differ from most borderline cases. Usually, borderline cases are *rare*, and that is important for the usefulness of our conceptual schemes. If you are classifying objects of some kind, you want a classification scheme that most objects fit comfortably, i.e., such that in most cases it is clear which of the categories the object falls into. E.g., most people fall comfortably into one of the categories, {adult, adolescent, child}. That scheme for classifying people would be less useful if most people were on the borderline between adolescent and adult, or between adolescent and child.

But *my* examples of borderline cases above *are not unusual.* An enormous range of human knowledge, perhaps most of it, is like those examples. As we navigate the world, we are *constantly* recognizing particular people and objects, classifying things into categories, and making judgments that weigh up complex sets of evidence. So the traditional taxonomy of knowledge has the shortcoming that an enormous range of actual knowledge doesn't comfortably fit into it. An enormous range of human knowledge fails to resemble the usual paradigms.

This doesn't mean the taxonomy is wrong. A classification scheme can't really be wrong; it can only be more or less useful. The traditional taxonomy is less useful than one might have hoped, because it was designed to fit a certain set of paradigms that do not in fact resemble a large class of actual cases of knowledge.

Operating with this taxonomy and these paradigms might also mislead people. When we try to formulate principles about the nature of knowledge, we tend to be guided by certain paradigms and by the examples that fit our conceptual scheme comfortably. Thus, there may be a tendency to think that all knowledge must have certain characteristics that those examples have. This might explain some of the felt force of arguments for skepticism. For instance, a budding skeptic might start out by thinking about the sort of examples given in section 7.2 above, decide in light of those paradigms that all knowledge must consist of direct observations, certain and self-evident axioms, or things deductively or inductively inferred from them. This skeptic might then notice that, say, the judgment [it is prima facie wrong to break your promises] doesn't fit any of those categories, whereupon the skeptic assumes that no one can know [it is prima facie wrong to break your promises]. In brief, the skeptic may think, the wrongness of promise-breaking doesn't resemble the theorems of Euclid, so it must not be real knowledge.

I suspect that something like that happens to many philosophy students. So it may be helpful to use a different set of paradigms, one that includes cases of recognitional knowledge, categorization, and judgment.

7.4. Noticing, Judging, and Calculating

Here is another way of classifying ways of knowing: We know things by noticing, judging, or calculating.

Noticing that *p* is something that typically occurs automatically, as when you see a tomato in front of you (in good viewing conditions) and you simply notice that there is a tomato. You can also notice things in an a priori way, e.g., when you think about it, you might notice that 3 is less than 7. In "noticing", something immediately seems to you to be the case, without the need to weigh any alternatives. This category includes exercises of our basic perceptual capacities as well as acquired perceptual abilities (like the ability to recognize a specific person's voice or the ability to perceive something as a duck) and intuition.

Judgment differs from noticing in that judgment involves weighing alternatives. It does not occur automatically but requires effort. One has the experience of *deliberating about* or *deciding* what to believe, rather than simply being presented with a fact. Judgment is usually based on a complex set of information, but one has no algorithm for going from that information to the conclusion. This kind of cognition may be specific to humans (and intelligent aliens, of course). Examples include weighing up the evidence in a trial to decide what verdict is warranted; evaluating the aesthetic merit of a piece of art based on its observable qualities; morally evaluating an action in light of the reasons for and against it and the set of surrounding circumstances; and evaluating the general plausibility of a philosophical theory.

"Calculation" is my term for a certain sort of inference—roughly, it's the sort of inference that a computer does. (This is a slightly technical use; I don't just mean doing math, and it's not limited to deductive inference but can include probabilistic reasoning.) Calculation is reasoning that doesn't demand exercises of judgment; at each stage, a certain step has to be accepted, with no need to weigh evidence or reasons for and against. Unlike noticing, calculation is volitional and effortful (one must decide to do it), but unlike judgment, there is no sense of *deciding* what to believe, apart from the decision to do the calculation.

By my read, much of the philosophical tradition, especially including the skeptics, has overemphasized calculation, underappreciated judgment, and underappreciated some forms of noticing. Importantly, we often know things—in perfectly ordinary, everyday cases that are not at all controversial—

without being in a position to *describe how* we know them. Sometimes, philosophy students are disturbed and puzzled by the inability to describe how particular things are known, but once you realize how completely normal that situation is, what you should *really* find weird is the cases in which we *can* describe how we know.

Apropos of this, some of the popular "paradigms" of knowledge are actually bizarre examples, in a certain sense. Mathematical proofs and scientific experiments are the *weird* cases, in the sense of being atypical instances of knowing, despite the enormous amount of attention that philosophers have given them. A normal human being can live an entire life without ever doing a single mathematical proof or scientific experiment—as many people in fact did throughout human history. Yet no normal person goes through life without doing such things as recognizing a friend's voice, or recognizing a familiar type of object, or judging a body of evidence. That is worth remembering when we want to theorize about the nature of knowledge.

7.5. Top-Down Versus Bottom-Up Cognition

When you see the sort of proofs in Euclid's *Elements*, it's very natural to have the reaction, "That is *real* knowledge." It is then natural to suppose that, to truly know any other subject matter, we must construct Euclid-style proofs— or at the very least, that we should strive to come as close to doing this as possible.

But the example of Euclid is highly misleading about how human knowledge works. Euclid's geometrical system is a *top down* system of knowledge: It starts from a small number of very general, abstract principles which are obvious and certain on their own; the rest of the system is then inferred from them by a series of calculations (in the sense of "calculation" explained in §7.4). And that is of course a genuine example of knowledge. But it is also, as I say, an extremely atypical kind of knowledge. Hardly any human knowledge works like a mathematical system.

Most human knowledge is *bottom up*. That is, one starts from a large number of cognitions about specific cases or particular individuals. When one has enough cases, one can start to see patterns and general rules. One then starts to formulate abstract principles based upon the cases. Once one has these abstract principles, one may then go on to use them to resolve certain difficult cases. Importantly, one can't skip the first step, that of gathering judgments about cases. If one tries to *start* from the abstract principles, there is almost a 100% chance of going wrong, often disastrously so. Human beings just are not that smart; we can't formulate the correct general principles of almost any subject without looking at examples. We're almost always going to commit oversights and confusions.

By the way, I have not adopted this point of view as an initial, a priori axiom. On the contrary, my natural inclinations are more in line with the top-down approach to knowledge-seeking. It is only through reflection on many examples of knowledge over the last few decades that I have eventually come to see this pattern—that most successful knowledge-seeking activities take a bottom-up approach.

That is part of what we learn from the history of natural science. Before modern science, there were many centuries during which the received scientific theories in different areas were things that we now know were absolutely and totally wrong. One of the reasons for this was that people started out by thinking abstractly about what seemed plausible in each area, rather than *looking and seeing* what was happening in particular cases. E.g., people thought that when you had a fever, this was because you had too much blood. This seemingly made sense, since blood is warm and since people look redder (from more blood in the skin) when they are warm than when they are cold. So the remedy for a fever was to drain blood from your body. To modern ears, that sounds stupid, but that's only because you already know something about the correct account, because someone else taught you. If you didn't already know anything, then the medieval account would probably strike you as plausible, as it struck many smart people before modern medicine was developed. Of course, the theory is 100% wrong—a fever has nothing whatever to do with having too much blood, and bleeding patients is *harmful*, not beneficial. What you have to do is gather a lot of data about particular cases before you start formulating theories about what causes or cures diseases.

Here's another illustration. Let's say that you have graduated college with a physics major. You know all the abstract physics theories that are relevant to explaining, say, how airplanes work—Newton's laws of motion, the conservation of energy, even the Navier-Stokes equations of fluid dynamics. Importantly, though, assume that you know *only general, abstract theory*. No one has taught you about any specific airplane designs, nor have you made any detailed observations of particular airplanes, nor have you talked to any airplane designers. Now let's say that, based solely on your knowledge of physics, you decide to design a new airplane. You draw up the design, pay some people to have it built, and then try finding some people to fly your new airplane for the first time. How do you think it would go?

Well, I am not getting in that airplane. It's probably going to crash, if it gets off the ground at all. I say that even though all kinds of airplanes regularly fly safely all over the world today, and even though I gave you by stipulation all the relevant modern *theoretical* knowledge that explains why those airplanes fly. The design of modern airplanes, cars, bridges, dishwashers, computers, and innumerable other things, is the product of *decades* of *experience*—of watching particular designs fail in different ways, figuring out what happened, then modifying the design and trying again. The first versions of anything suck. If you don't believe me, talk to any engineer.

Trying to produce a system of knowledge about some subject matter by reasoning from first principles, without relying on judgments about cases, is like trying to design a new airplane based on theoretical physics, without knowing details about any actual airplanes. Your system is almost certainly going to fail in some major way. If it's a philosophical system, though, there's a good chance that you won't recognize that it failed, because there won't be any decisive empirical test as there is in the case of an airplane, so when someone points out the problems with your theory, you can come up with rationalizations to keep holding on to it. That has happened to many, perhaps the vast majority of, philosophers throughout history.

So why did the top-down approach work so well for Euclid?

It didn't. The way that Euclid presents his system does not in fact reflect the way in which all that mathematical knowledge came about. The Greeks did not learn all those theorems by laying down a handful of simple axioms at the start and then systematically deducing their consequences. Human investigation of geometry began in Egypt around 3000 B.C., and for centuries the field consisted of a miscellaneous collection of principles and formulas, often devised for specific practical purposes in surveying, construction, and astronomy. The formulas were largely empirical, based on trial and error. As a result, they are often approximately but not exactly correct. One ancient document, for instance, gives the area of a circle as the square of eight ninths of the diameter (this is off by about 0.6%).[63] So that sort of thing went on for *2,700 years* before Euclid showed up in 300 B.C. and systematized what had been discovered. For perspective, the time between the start of geometry and the writing of Euclid's *Elements* is about 400 years longer than the time between Euclid and us. My point here being that even our knowledge of geometry doesn't work the way you would think from reading Euclid's *Elements*.

7.6. Conclusion

The traditional taxonomy divides knowledge into foundational empirical knowledge (which comes from sense perception and introspection), foundational a priori knowledge (which comes from intuition), inferential empirical knowledge (which results from applying reason to observations), and

---

[63] This is the Ahmes papyrus from Egypt circa 1500 B.C.

inferential a priori knowledge (which results from applying reason to intuitions). Traditional paradigms of knowing include things like seeing a red round thing right in front of you, doing a mathematical proof starting from self-evident axioms, and making an inference to the best explanation from a scientific experiment.

The tradition tends to overlook a wide range of ordinary cases, such as recognizing a friend's voice, automatically categorizing a familiar type of object, and making a judgment based on a complex body of information. These cases are hard to classify as they do not resemble the paradigms of either foundational or inferential knowledge. They also show that it is perfectly normal for individuals to know things without being able to describe how they know. The traditional taxonomy and paradigms have the potential to mislead people into thinking that cases that don't resemble the paradigms are weird and suspect.

An alternative set of paradigms would include cases of recognition, categorization, and judgment. An alternative taxonomy would divide ways of knowing into noticing, judging, and calculating. The tradition underemphasizes judgment and certain kinds of noticing.

Most human knowledge is bottom-up rather than top-down. The top-down approach is extremely unreliable in most areas. That is, rather than starting from general abstract principles and deducing implications, we need to start from many cognitions about particular cases before drawing generalizations.

Part II: Sources of Knowledge

8. Perception & Skepticism

In this chapter, we're going to discuss whether you can know things by observation.

8.1. The Foundation of External-World Knowledge

How do we know about the world around us? Short answer: by perception, i.e., by seeing, hearing, tasting, touching, or smelling things. I know the sun is yellow because I can see it. I know it's hot outside because I can feel the heat. I know someone is playing the piano because I can hear it.

Admittedly, not all physical phenomena that we know about can be perceived. For instance, we can't see, hear, taste, touch, or smell magnetic fields. But we know magnetic fields exist because they affect other things that we *can* see (for instance, pieces of iron). So our knowledge about stuff that we can't directly perceive still depends indirectly on perception.

Now for some philosophers' terminology: The stuff that exists outside your mind is known as "**the external world**". That includes tables, trees, planets, badgers, etc. It includes your own body as well as other people, including other people's minds (that is, other people's minds are external *to you*, though of course not external *to them*). The only thing that isn't external (to you) is your own mind, including your thoughts, feelings, sensations, memories, etc.

Also, some truths about the external world are **necessary** (they had to be as they are; they could not have been otherwise). For instance, it's necessary that all squares have four sides, that nothing is completely red and completely yellow at the same time, that the shortest path between two points is a straight line. These necessary truths can perhaps be known by just thinking about them. But we won't be concerned with that in this chapter. In this chapter, we want to talk about the **contingent** truths about the external world, the truths that are *not* necessary, the truths that could have been otherwise. For instance, [The sky is blue], [Cows have four legs], and [The population of India is larger than that of Peru]—these are all contingent facts about the external world. (Hereafter, I'll often drop the qualifier "contingent".)

So here is our starting question, stated more precisely: How do we know contingent truths about the external world? And the most basic answer, again, is that we know them on the basis of observation, using the five senses.[64]

8.2. Skeptical Scenarios

In this chapter, we discuss **external world skepticism**. External world skeptics think that we can't know (or justifiedly believe) any contingent truths about the external world (the world outside our own minds). So they would say that you don't know whether wallabies exist, whether there are any other people, whether you actually have a head, etc. (But these skeptics generally do *not* object to knowledge of necessary truths such as [2+2=4], [~(A & ~A)], and so on. Nor do they object to knowledge of one's own mind—e.g., you can know what thoughts, feelings, and sensations you are experiencing.)

Skeptics argue for their view using **skeptical scenarios**. These are possible situations in which everything would appear to you as it presently does, but your beliefs would be radically mistaken. Let's consider some skeptical scenarios …

8.2.1. The Dream Argument

Have you ever thought you were awake when you were actually dreaming? (If not, you're pretty weird. I'll assume you have.) In the dream, things might *seem* perfectly real to you, yet none of what you seem to see, hear, or otherwise perceive is real. Given that, how can you know that you're not dreaming *right now*?

If we're just thinking about normal dreams, of the sort that we all remember experiencing many times, there might be ways of telling that you're not dreaming. Maybe you could try pinching yourself; if you feel pain, then you're not dreaming. Or you could try to remember how you arrived at your present location; if you're awake, you should be able to remember roughly what you've done today, from the time you got up till you arrived at wherever you are. If you're dreaming, you won't be able to remember that.[65] Or you could pick up something written (like this book) and just try reading it—if you're dreaming, you won't be able to read the book, because your unconscious mind does not in fact have the information that's contained in a real book.

---

[64] There are actually more than five senses. E.g., besides sight, hearing, taste, touch, and smell, there is also proprioception (the sense of one's body position), equilibrioception (the sense of balance), interoception (the awareness of internal bodily states), etc. But for simplicity, I'll keep talking about perception as "the five senses".
[65] For more on this, watch the movie *Inception* (2010).

Those sorts of things are all well and good. But now consider the hypothesis that maybe *all* of your life that you currently remember has been one huge dream. What you think of as your past waking experiences were just part of the same really long dream, and what you think of as your past *dreams* were actually *dreams within a dream*. (Some people, by the way, have actually had dreams within dreams. I once had a dream in which I dreamt that I was dreaming *and that I woke up*. But in reality, I was still dreaming. Then I woke up for real … or so I think.) So, all the rules you've learned about how you can tell when you're dreaming are actually just rules for how to tell when you're having a dream *within* the larger dream, as opposed to merely being in the larger dream. Maybe, in the larger dream, you actually *can* experience pain—i.e., you can dream pain—and so on.

When you think about it, it seems impossible to refute this kind of hypothesis. Any evidence you cite, any experience you have, the skeptic can just explain as part of the dream.

This is all leading up to the following skeptical argument:

1. You can have knowledge of the external world only if you can know that you're not dreaming.
2. You can't know that you're not dreaming.
3. Therefore, you cannot have knowledge of the external world.

You might want to pause and think about that argument. Is it right? What might be wrong with it?

> **Interlude: René Descartes**
> Pretty much everyone who takes an introductory philosophy class has to learn about Descartes. He's sometimes called the founder of modern philosophy (where by "modern", we mean "the last 400 years". Seriously, that's how philosophers talk.) Here's what you need to know.
>
> He was a French philosopher of the 1600s. He invented analytic geometry; he said "I think; therefore, I am"; and he wrote a very famous and great book called *Meditations on First Philosophy* ("the *Meditations*", for those in the know), which philosophy professors commonly use to befuddle beginning college students.
>
> In the *Meditations*, he starts by trying to doubt everything. He entertains scenarios like "Maybe I'm dreaming", "Maybe God is deceiving me", and "Maybe my cognitive faculties are unreliable." He wants to find something that one cannot have any reason at all to doubt, so that he can build the rest of his belief system on that unshakable foundation. He first decides that nothing about the physical world is certain, given the skeptical scenarios. He then decides that his own existence, and the facts about his own present, conscious

mental states, are impossible to doubt. So they should be the foundation for the rest of his belief system. So far, so good.

He then tries to prove that God exists, starting just from his idea of God. (This is where most people think the *Meditations* goes off the rails. But the arguments are too long and weird to detail here.) Then he argues that since God is by definition a perfect being, God cannot be a deceiver. Therefore, God would not have given Descartes inherently unreliable faculties; so, as long as Descartes uses his faculties properly, he can trust them. And therefore, the physical world around him must really exist.

Most importantly, if you want to avoid sounding like a yokel: His last name is pronounced like "day-kart", not "DESS-karts" as some freshmen are wont to say.

8.2.2. The Brain-in-a-Vat Argument

Here's something else that could happen (maybe?). Let's say scientists in the year 3000 have perfected technology for keeping a brain alive, floating in a vat of liquid. They can also attach lots of tiny wires to the brain, so that they are able to feed the brain exactly the same pattern of electrical stimulation that a normal brain receives when it is in a normal human body, moving around the world. (Electrical signals from your nerve endings are in fact what cause your sensory experiences.) They can also attach sensors to the brain to detect how the brain thinks it is moving its body, so they can modify the brain's experience accordingly—e.g., the brain "sees" its arm go up when it tries to raise its arm, and so on. They have a sophisticated computer programmed to give the brain the exact pattern of stimulation to perfectly simulate a normal life in a normal body.

This is an odd scenario, but nothing about it seems impossible. As far as we know, this could in principle be done. And if so, the scientists could program, let's say, a simulation of an unremarkable life in the twenty-first century. They might even include in the simulation a funny bit where the brain has the experience of reading a silly story about a brain in a vat. The scientists have a good laugh when the brain thinks to itself, "That's silly; of course I'm not a brain in a vat."

So now, how do you know that *you* are not a brain in a vat right now? Again, it seems impossible to refute the scenario, because for any evidence that you try to cite, the skeptic can just explain that as part of the BIV (brain-in-a-vat) simulation. The logic of the skeptic's argument here is basically the same as that of the dream argument:

1. You can have knowledge of the external world only if you can know that you're not a BIV.

2. You can't know that you're not a BIV.
3. Therefore, you cannot have knowledge of the external world.

This is the most discussed argument for skepticism. Epistemologists have spent a lot of time trying to figure out what's wrong with it, since the conclusion seems pretty crazy to most of us. A small number of philosophers have endorsed the argument and become external-world skeptics.

8.2.3. The Deceiving God Argument

You can probably already guess how this one goes from the title. The skeptic asks you to consider the hypothesis that there might be an all-powerful being, like God, except that he wants to deceive you. This being can give you hallucinatory sensory experiences, false memories, and so on. There's no way of proving that there isn't such a being, because any evidence you cite could have just been produced by the deceiving god to trick you. You're then supposed to infer that you can't know anything about the external world, since everything you believe about the world *could* be a result of this being's deception.

8.2.4. Certainty, Justification, and Craziness

Note that the skeptic is not *completely* crazy. The skeptic isn't saying that any of these scenarios are actually *true* or even *likely*. That's not the issue. The issue isn't, e.g., whether there is in fact a desk in front of me now. The issue is whether *I know* that there is. Most skeptics say that the mere *possibility* that I'm dreaming, or that I'm a BIV, or that there's a deceiving god, means that I don't *know* that the table I see is real.

Now to be more precise. There are two kinds of external-world skeptic: **certainty skeptics**, and **justification skeptics**. The former say that you lack knowledge (of the external world) because it is not *absolutely certain* that your beliefs are true. The latter say that you lack knowledge because your beliefs are not even *justified* (not rational, not likely to be true).

Certainty skepticism is more common, but justification skepticism is much more interesting. It's interesting because if it turns out that our beliefs are not justified, then we should presumably change them. On the other hand, if our beliefs are merely uncertain but still justified, then we don't need to change anything important—we should keep holding our ordinary beliefs, keep using them to navigate the world and so on, but merely stop *calling* them "knowledge". Who cares about that?

Now, how would the argument for justification skepticism go? Pretty much the same as the arguments above.

1. Your beliefs about the external world are justified only if you have some justification for believing that you're not a BIV.
2. You have no justification for believing that you're not a BIV.
3. Therefore, your beliefs about the external world are not justified.

Premise 1 here still seems true, just as much as in the original BIV argument (I just substituted talk of justified belief for talk about knowledge).

Premise 2 still has a pretty obvious case for it. To have justification for denying that you're a BIV, it seems that you would need to have *at least some evidence* that you're not a BIV. But, as discussed above, it doesn't seem that you can have any such evidence. So it's not just that you can't be *absolutely certain* that you're not a BIV; it looks like you have *no reason at all* to believe that you're not a BIV.

Of course, you also have no evidence at all that you *are* a BIV. But the skeptic isn't claiming that you know you are a BIV, so there doesn't need to be any evidence that you are one. The skeptic is claiming that you *don't know whether* you are one or not. That's perfectly consistent with the fact that there is *no evidence either way*.

8.3. Responses to Skepticism

8.3.1. The Relevant Alternatives Response

Now I'm going to start telling you about things that philosophers have said to try to avoid skepticism. I find many of them unsatisfying, but that's par for the course when you're dealing with a big philosophical problem.

So here's the first response: The skeptic has misunderstood something about language, about how the word "know" is used in English. (This is the certainty skeptic we're talking about now.) To illustrate the idea, here is an analogy. Imagine that you work at a warehouse that stores merchandise. All the merchandise in the warehouse was supposed to be moved out this morning, and it was in fact moved out, which you observed. Now your boss calls you up on the phone and asks, "Hey, is the warehouse empty now?"

Clearly, the correct response is "Yes." You should not answer "No" on the grounds that there is still some dust on the floor, or a spider web in one of the corners, or light bulbs in the ceiling fixtures. You shouldn't do that, because those are obviously not the kind of things that the boss was concerned about. When he asked if the warehouse was empty, he meant "Has all the *merchandise* been moved out?", not "Is it a hard vacuum inside?" This example leads to the idea that "empty", in English, does not normally mean "having nothing whatsoever inside"; it means something like, "having nothing *of the relevant kind* inside", where the relevant kind is determined by the context of the conversation. (Cf. the contextualist view of §3.1.)

The skeptic is like the person who says the warehouse isn't empty because there's dust on the floor—except the skeptic is misunderstanding the word "know" rather than the word "empty". The skeptic thinks that to know a proposition, one must rule out every possible alternative whatsoever. In fact, though, this isn't how the word "know" works in English. To know something, in the standard English sense, it is only necessary to be able to rule out every *relevant* alternative. Or so the anti-skeptic would argue.

What are the relevant alternatives? Well, this is going to have something to do with what alternatives are close to reality, so that they really had a chance of being true, in some objective sense (per §2.5.6.) Let's not worry about the details of what determines "relevance". The important points are that the relevant alternatives are a proper subset of the logically possible alternatives, and that the skeptical scenarios are generally viewed (by relevant-alternative theorists) as being too remote or far-fetched to be relevant.

Recall this example from §2.5.6:

> *Gadwall Duck:* Fred sees a bird that looks like a Gadwall Duck in a pond (a species that Fred is very familiar with). He correctly believes that it is a Gadwall. However, he has no evidence to prove that it isn't some other species that happens to look exactly like a Gadwall. Fred isn't aware of, and has no thoughts about, any such other species.

Does Fred know that the bird is a Gadwall? Intuitively, if there actually *is* another species that looks just like a Gadwall, then that is a relevant alternative, and so Fred doesn't *know* that he's seeing a Gadwall. But if there *in fact* is no such species, then it's not a relevant alternative, so Fred doesn't need to rule it out to count as "knowing" that he's seeing a Gadwall.

Note that the relevant-alternatives (RA) theorist is not giving *an argument against* the skeptical scenarios. The RA theorist is saying that one *does not need* any argument against the skeptical scenarios in order to count as knowing stuff about the external world. (Compare: When I say the warehouse is empty, I'm not denying that there is dust on the floor. I'm saying that it was not necessary to remove the dust in order for the warehouse to count as "empty".)

* * *

Here is my take on the RA theory. I don't think it gives a correct analysis of "know" (see the counter-examples in §2.5.6). Nevertheless, the RA theorist has a fair point against the certainty skeptic: It's plausible that the certainty skeptic is misunderstanding the English word "know", assigning it an overly demanding meaning.

However, I don't find the dispute between the RA theorist and the certainty skeptic to be very *interesting*. It's not very interesting because it's semantic; they're just disagreeing about the use of the word "know".

The interesting debate would be with the justification skeptic. Against that skeptic, RA theory definitely fails. That's because the RA theory is all about how the word "know" works, but the justification skeptic's argument doesn't depend on that. The justification skeptic claims that our external-world beliefs are *unjustified*, which is bad enough.

Okay, what if we tried adopting a relevant-alternatives theory of *justification*? We could claim that a belief is justified as long as one has evidence against each of the relevant alternatives, and one need not have any evidence at all against the *irrelevant* alternatives, such as skeptical scenarios.

One *could* say that. I just don't think that is very plausible or helpful. I think that if a belief is to be justified, the belief must at least be very likely to be true. Now, if a belief is highly probable, then *any* alternative to it (whether "relevant" or not) must be highly *im*probable—that's just a theorem of probability. (If $P(A) > x$, and A entails $\sim B$, then $P(B) < (1 - x)$.) So, if our beliefs about the external world are justified, and they entail (as they do) that we're not brains in vats, then the probability of our being brains in vats must be very low.

But then, it seems that there must be some explanation of *why* the BIV scenario is very improbable given our current evidence. Whatever that explanation is, *that* would be the important and interesting response to give to the skeptic. We could then add that alternatives that are highly improbable are "irrelevant", but all the intellectual work would lie in showing that the skeptical scenarios are in fact highly improbable—and the RA theory wouldn't help us with that.

8.3.2. The Contextualist Response

This is another semantic response to skepticism, closely related to the RA theory.[66] Recall that contextualists think that the meaning of "know" shifts

---

[66] You may wonder: How is RA theory even different from contextualism? Well, you can have a non-contextualist version of RA theory. This would be a version where an alternative's *relevance* is determined entirely by *subject factors*. E.g., how far the alternative is from actuality is a subject factor. This version of the theory says the skeptic is simply wrong in thinking her scenarios are relevant.

But you could also have a contextualist version of RA theory; this would be a version where *attributor factors* affect relevance (e.g., which alternatives have been mentioned in the conversation). In this case, the skeptic's scenarios could be relevant

depending on the context in which the word is used (see §3.1). Basically, what the skeptic is doing with her skeptical scenarios is *raising the standards* for a person to count as "knowing". She raises the standards so high that indeed, no one counts as knowing anything about the external world.

This might seem like a concession to skepticism. However, note that it is still true that in the *ordinary* sense of the word "know" (the sense in use in normal everyday contexts), we know lots of things about the external world. When we stop talking about skepticism and have a more mundane conversation, the standards for "knowing" go back down, and we get to go on claiming to know where we live, what color the sky is, and so on.

Skeptics are not happy with this. They do not think they're raising the standards for "knowledge"; what they think is that the standards for knowledge are always very high, and we don't satisfy them, and thus our knowledge claims *in ordinary life* are *false*. The contextualist account is thus a skeptic-unfriendly diagnosis of what's going on.

* * *

My take on contextualism: There is some plausibility to it, though I'm not fully convinced of it (see §3.1.3). As in the case of RA theory, however, I don't find the contextualist response to skepticism super-interesting, because it is too semantic for my taste. It just raises a dispute about the use of a particular word, "know", and the response only applies to certainty skeptics who grant that the BIV scenario is highly improbable. Contextualism doesn't tell us how to respond to a justification skeptic, and it doesn't explain why the BIV hypothesis is unreasonable.

8.3.3. Semantic Externalism

Here's another idea. Maybe the BIV hypothesis has to be rejected because it's self-refuting.[67]

Why would it be self-refuting? Maybe because, in order for us to have the concepts required to entertain the BIV hypothesis, we would have to have had some contact with the real world, which the BIV hypothesis says we have never had. So if we were BIVs, we couldn't be thinking about whether we were BIVs. But the person who advances the BIV hypothesis presumably cannot think that we are not entertaining the very hypothesis that he is putting forward. So the hypothesis is self-undermining.

---

in some contexts. The original version of RA theory was non-contextualist, but many people think that a contextualist version is more plausible.
[67] See Hilary Putnam's *Reason, Truth and History* (1981), ch. 1.

Of course, all the work is going to be in showing that we couldn't have the concept of a BIV if we were BIVs. Why is that?

First, we need to think about a property that philosophers call **"intentionality"**. This is the property of representing something, of being "of" or "about" something. (*Note:* This is a technical use of the word "intentionality". It does *not* refer to the property of being *intended* by someone! Please don't confuse intentions in the ordinary English sense with intentionality.) Examples: Words, pictures, and ideas in the mind all refer to things. When you have a picture, it is a picture *of* something; when you have an idea, it is an idea *of* something or *about* something.

When you think about this phenomenon of intentionality, a good philosophical question is: What makes one thing be *about* another? I.e., under what conditions does *x* refer to *y*? Of particular interest to us here: What makes an idea in your mind refer to a particular thing or kind of thing in the external world?

Here is a partial answer (partial because it only gives a necessary condition, not a sufficient condition): In order for an idea, *x*, to refer to an external phenomenon, *y*, there has to be the right kind of causal connection between *x* and *y*. Example: You have certain visual sensations, such as the sensation of red. What this sensation represents is a certain range of wavelengths of light (or a disposition to reflect such wavelengths, or something like that). What makes your sensation count as being *of* that physical phenomenon? There is no intrinsic similarity between the sensation and the underlying physical phenomenon. The answer is: The sensation refers to that range of wavelengths of light because those are the wavelengths of light that normally *cause* you to have that sensation when you look at things.

Here is a famous thought experiment (that is, famous among philosophers, which is really not very famous overall):

> *Twin Earth:* Imagine there is another planet somewhere that is an almost exact duplicate of Earth. It has a molecule-for-molecule duplicate of every person on Earth, doing the same things that people here do, etc. There is just one difference between Twin Earth and our Earth: On our Earth, the rivers, lakes, clouds, and so on, are filled with the chemical H_2O. By contrast, on Twin Earth, the rivers, lakes, clouds, and so on are filled with a different chemical, which I will call XYZ. XYZ looks, tastes, feels, etc., just like H_2O. It's completely indistinguishable from H_2O to normal observation, though it has a different chemical formula. Now, assume that we're at a time before the chemical composition of water was discovered, say, the time of Isaac Newton. (Remember that people used to think that water was an element! The people on Twin Earth at that time also thought

> that their "water" was an element. The composition of water wasn't discovered until the 1800s.) Let's say Isaac Newton on Earth thinks to himself, "I want a cup of water." At the same time, Twin Isaac Newton on Twin Earth thinks to himself a corresponding thought, which he would also express by, "I want a cup of water." Question: What is our Isaac Newton referring to by his "water" thought? And what is Twin Isaac Newton referring to?

You're supposed to intuit that Newton is referring to H_2O (even though he does not *know* that this is what water is), because H_2O is in fact what fills the rivers, lakes, and so on around him. If someone gives him a glass filled with chemical XYZ, they would be tricking him (though he wouldn't know it): They'd be giving him something that looks like water but isn't real water.

At the same time, Twin Newton is referring to XYZ, not H_2O. If someone gives *Twin* Newton a glass filled with H_2O, they'll be tricking him.

Why does Newton's word "water" refer to H_2O, while Twin Newton's word "water" refers to XYZ? Because Newton's idea of water was formed by perceiving and interacting with rivers, lakes, etc., that were in fact made of H_2O. In brief, Newton's idea was *caused by* H_2O. Twin Newton's idea, on the other hand, was caused by interactions with XYZ. This is meant to show that the referents of your ideas are determined by what things you have actually perceived and interacted with, that caused you to form your ideas. This is known as the **causal theory of reference**.

The causal theory is an example of a **semantic externalist** theory, a theory on which the meanings of words or the contents of thoughts depend on things external to the speaker/thinker. Contrast **semantic internalism**, the view that meanings/contents are entirely determined by what's going on in one's own mind.

By the way, you may think the Twin Earth scenario is pretty silly (like many philosophical thought experiments). A perfect duplicate of Earth is ridiculously improbable, and obviously there is no compound like XYZ. But philosophers generally don't care how improbable our scenarios are. We don't even really care if they violate the laws of physics or chemistry.

Still, why posit such an outlandish scenario? Well, the purpose is basically to rule out alternative theories about intentionality. Assuming that you agree that our Newton is referring to H_2O, while Twin Newton is not, we have to find some *difference* between Newton and Twin Newton that could explain that. Since the two people are perfect duplicates of each other, with qualitatively indistinguishable experiences, the relevant difference *cannot be anything in their minds*, or even in their bodies.[68] If we didn't make Twin Newton a perfect duplicate of Newton, then someone could have said that they are referring to different things because maybe their thoughts are intrinsically different, or something else in them is different.

Anyway, back to the BIV argument. If you buy the causal theory of reference, what would happen if there was a brain that only ever lived in a vat, and only had experiences fed to it by the scientists? This brain has never perceived, nor interacted in any normal way with, *any* object in the real world. So none of the BIV's concepts can refer to real-world things. All of the BIV's concepts are going to refer to virtual objects, or perhaps states of the computer that stimulates the brain, since that is what causes the BIV's experiences. E.g., when the BIV thinks, "I want a glass of water", it is referring to a *virtual* glass of water. It can't be referring to a real glass of real water, since it has no experience with such.

If that's so, what would the brain mean if it thought to itself, "I wonder whether I am a brain in a vat?" What would "brain in a vat" refer to? It would have to refer to a *virtual* brain in a vat, not an actual brain in a vat. The BIV cannot think about actual brains in vats.

Now there are two ways of formulating the argument against the BIV scenario. First version:

1. I'm thinking about BIVs.
2. A BIV cannot think about BIVs.
3. Therefore, I'm not a BIV.

The skeptic who advanced the BIV scenario can't very well deny (1), since the central point of the skeptic's argument is to make you think about BIVs. This makes the skeptic's argument self-undermining.

Here's the second version:

1. If a BIV thinks to itself, "I'm a BIV", that thought is false.
   Explanation: By "BIV", it means a virtual BIV. But the BIV is not a virtual BIV; it's a real BIV. So the thought would be false.
2. If a non-BIV thinks to itself, "I'm a BIV", that thought is false.
3. So "I'm a BIV" is always false. (From 1, 2)
4. So I'm not a BIV. (From 3)

Notice that this response to skepticism does what the earlier responses avoided: It directly tries to show that you're not a BIV.

---

[68] Just ignore the fact that the human body contains water. We could have devised a thought experiment involving a substance that isn't actually found in the body.

* * *

My take: One obvious problem is that the above response only applies to *some* skeptical scenarios. It can't be the case that *all* of your experiences to date have been BIV experiences, since that would prevent you from having a concept that refers to actual BIVs. However, this does nothing to refute the hypothesis that you were kidnapped just *last night* and envatted—you could have formed the concept of a brain in a vat *before* being turned into one.

Possible response: True, but if my life before last night was normal, then I can use my knowledge of the world gained up to that point to argue that humans do not actually possess the technology for making BIVs.

Counter-reply on behalf of the skeptic: Maybe after they kidnapped and envatted you, the scientists also erased all your memories of all the news items you read reporting on how we actually *do* have the technology for creating BIVs. They would have done this to trick you into thinking that you couldn't be a BIV.

Another problem with the response to skepticism is that the BIV would still have many important false beliefs. When it sees a glass of water on a table, perhaps, the BIV is not deceived, because it thinks there is a virtual glass of water, and that is what there is. But when the BIV talks to other people (that is, it has virtual conversations with virtual people), the BIV will be thinking that these "other people" are conscious beings just like itself—that they have thoughts, feelings, and so on, like the thoughts, feelings, and so on that the BIV itself experiences. But that will be false; they're just computer simulations. And of course, a huge amount of what we care about has to do with other people's minds. The skeptic will claim that all of that is doubtful. And so semantic externalism doesn't do such a great job of saving our common sense beliefs.

8.3.4. BIVH Is a Bad Theory

When we started talking about responses to skepticism, you might have been hoping for an explanation of why the BIV Hypothesis is not a good theory for explaining our experiences, and why our ordinary, common sense beliefs are a better theory. At least, that's what *I* was hoping for when *I* first heard the BIV argument. Yet almost all responses by philosophers try to avoid that issue. Given the confidence with which we reject the BIV Hypothesis (many people find it laughable), we ought to be able to cite some extremely powerful considerations against it. The BIV Hypothesis should be a *terrible* theory, and our ordinary, common sense world view (the "**Real World Hypothesis**", as I will call it) should be *vastly* superior (or, as Keith DeRose once put it in conversation, the Real World theory should be kicking the BIV theory's ass).

So it's pretty odd that philosophers seem to have trouble citing anything that's wrong with the BIV Hypothesis as an explanation of our experience.

Sometimes, when you tell people (mostly students) about the BIV Hypothesis, they try claiming that the Real World Hypothesis should be preferred because it is "simpler". I can't figure out why people say that, though. It's obviously false. In the Real World Hypothesis, there are *lots* of separate entities involved in the explanation of our experiences—motorcycles, raccoons, trees, comets, clouds, buckets of paint, etc., etc. In the BIV Hypothesis, you only need the brain in its vat, the scientists, and the apparatus for stimulating the brain, to explain all experiences. Vastly simpler. Of course, there *may* be lots of other things in the world, but the BIV hypothesis makes no commitment regarding other things; it does not need to cite them to explain our experiences. If we just care about simplicity, then the BIV theory is *vastly better* than the Real World theory!

Here is something else you might have heard about judging theories: A good theory must be **falsifiable**. That means there has to be a way to test it, such that if the theory were false, it could be proved to be false. The BIV theory is unfalsifiable: Even if you're not a BIV, there is never any way to prove that.

For the skeptic, though, this is a feature, not a bug. The skeptic would say, "Yeah, I know it's unfalsifiable. That was my *point* in bringing it up! How is that problem for *me*?" So now we have to explain what is wrong with unfalsifiable theories.

The idea of falsifiability was most famously discussed by the philosopher of science Karl Popper. Popper's idea was that falsifiability is essential to scientific theories. So if you advance an unfalsifiable theory, then you cannot claim to be doing science. But so what? The skeptic will just say, "Yeah, I never claimed to be doing science. Again, how is this a problem for me?" We need a better answer than "You're not doing science."

A better answer can be found in probability theory. The way a theory gets to be probabilistically supported is, roughly, that the theory predicts some evidence that we should see in some circumstance, we create that circumstance, and the prediction comes true. More precisely, evidence supports a theory provided that the evidence would be *more likely* to occur if the theory were true than otherwise. The theories that we consider "falsifiable" are those that make relatively sharp predictions: That is, they give high probability to some observation that is much less likely on the alternative theories. If those observations occur, then the theory is supported; if they don't, then the theory is disconfirmed (rendered less probable). "Unfalsifiable" theories are ones that make weak predictions or no predictions—that is, they don't significantly alter the probabilities we would assign to different possible observations. They allow pretty much any observation to occur, and they don't predict any particular course of observations to be much more likely than any other. (On this account, "falsifiability" is a matter of degree. A theory is *more* falsifiable to the extent that it makes more and stronger predictions.)

Now there is a straightforward, probabilistic explanation of why falsifiability is important. (Popper, by the way, would *hate* this explanation. But it is nevertheless correct.) A highly falsifiable theory, by definition, is open to strong disconfirmation (lowering of its probability), in the event that its predictions turn out false—but, by the same token, the theory is open to strong *support* in the event that its predictions turn out *true*. By contrast, an unfalsifiable theory cannot be disconfirmed by evidence, but for the same reason, it cannot be *supported* by evidence either. (This is a pretty straightforward point in probability theory.)

Suppose that you have two theories to explain some phenomenon, with one being much more falsifiable than the other. Suppose also that the evidence turns out to be consistent with both theories (neither of them make any false predictions). Then the falsifiable theory is *supported* by that evidence, while the unfalsifiable theory remains unsupported. At the end of the day, then, the highly falsifiable theory is more worthy of belief. This will be true in proportion as it is more falsifiable than the other theory.

All of that can be translated into some probability equations, but I'm going to spare you that, since I think most readers don't like the equations so much.

Now, back to the BIV theory versus the Real World theory. The Real World theory, which holds that you are a normal human being interacting with the real world, does not fit equally well with every possible sequence of experiences. The Real World theory predicts (perhaps not with certainty, but with reasonably high probability) that you should be having a coherent sequence of experiences which admit of being interpreted as representing physical objects obeying consistent laws of nature. Roughly speaking, if you're living in the real world, stuff should fit together and make sense. The BIV theory, on the other hand, makes essentially no predictions about your experiences. On the BIV theory, you *might* have a coherent sequence of experiences, *if* the scientists decide to give you that. But you could equally well have *any logically possible* sequence of experiences, depending on what the scientists decide to give you. You could observe sudden, unexpected deviations from (what hitherto seemed to be) the laws of nature, you could observe random sequences of colors appearing in your visual field, you could observe things disappearing or turning into completely different kinds of things for no apparent reason, and of course you might observe random program glitches. In fact, the overwhelming majority of *possible* sequences of experience (like, more than 99.999999999999%) would be completely uninterpretable—they would just be random sequences of sensations, with no regularities.

> **Aside: An "Experimental" Illustration**
> Here's something I did one time. I programmed my computer to generate *random images*. I.e., it would assign a random color to each pixel in a 1000 × 1000 grid. I knew what the result would be, but I wrote and ran the program anyway, so I could tell people that I did this. I viewed a few hundred of the images generated. Every single one of them just looks like random static. None of them looks even slightly like a picture of anything. If you understand the mathematics, you'll see why I say that this is going to be true of a ridiculously high proportion of images. That illustrates the point that most possible sequences of experience are not like experiences of perceiving a real world.

Our actual evidence is consistent with both theories, since we actually have coherent sequences of experience. Since the Real World theory is falsifiable and the BIV theory is not, the Real World theory is supported by this evidence, while the BIV theory remains unsupported.

* * *

My take: That's all correct.[69] The BIV theory is a very bad theory.

8.3.5. *Direct Realism*

"**Realism**" in philosophy generally refers to a view that says that we know certain objective facts. There's "realism" about different things—e.g., "moral realism" says that there are objective *moral* facts, which we can know; realism in the philosophy of perception (or, realism about the external world) says that there are objective facts in the external world, which we can know. In this chapter, we're interested in realism in the philosophy of perception, so that will be what I mean by "realism".

Traditionally, there are two forms of realism: direct realism and indirect realism. It's easiest to explain **indirect realism** first. According to indirect realists, when we know stuff about the external world, that knowledge is always dependent upon our knowledge or awareness of something *in our own minds*. (Compare Descartes' idea that all knowledge must be built up from the knowledge of one's own existence and of the contents of one's own consciousness; see §8.2.1.) E.g., when you see an octopus, you are only directly aware of (and only directly *know* about) the image of the octopus in your mind. You have to infer that there's a real octopus causing that image.

The main alternative position is **direct realism**: Direct realists think that, during normal perception, we have direct awareness of, and foundational

---

[69] See my paper, "Serious Theories and Skeptical Theories: Why You Are Probably Not a Brian in a Vat" from *Philosophical Studies* (2016).

knowledge about, the external world. E.g., when you see an octopus, you are just aware of the octopus and have foundationally justified beliefs about it; you don't have to infer facts about the octopus from facts about an octopus image.

We're going to discuss both direct and indirect realism at greater length in chapter 9, so I won't elaborate any more now about what these views say and why people hold them. The point I want to talk about here is this: *If* you're a direct realist, then you have an escape from BIV-driven skepticism that is not available to the indirect realist. The skeptic's argument is really only an argument against indirect realists, not against direct realists. So now let me try to make out that point.

Indirect realists regard our beliefs about physical objects as something like theoretical posits—we start with knowledge of our own subjective experiences, and we have to justify belief in physical objects as the best explanation for those experiences. If you're doing that, then you have to be able to say why the belief in real, physical objects of the sort we take ourselves to be perceiving provides a *better explanation* than the theory that one is a brain in a vat, or that God is directly inducing experiences in our minds, or that we're having one really long dream, etc. The latter three theories (the skeptical scenarios) would seem to explain the evidence equally well, if "the evidence" is just facts about our own subjective experiences.

On the other hand, direct realists regard our perceptual beliefs as foundational: They do not need to be justified by any other beliefs. When you see an octopus, you're allowed to just start from the belief, "There's an octopus." You do not have to start from "Here is a mental image of an octopus." There is thus no need to prove that the Real World scenario is a better explanation for our experiences than the BIV scenario.

Another way to phrase the point: According to indirect realists, our evidence is our experiences; but according to *direct* realists, our evidence consists of certain observable *physical facts*. For instance, the fact that there is a purple, octopus-shaped object in front of you. Now, the BIV scenario is a competing explanation of *our experiences*, but it is not an explanation of the *physical facts* about the external world that we're observing. The BIV theory would explain, for example, the fact that you're having an octopus-representing mental image, but it does not even attempt to explain the fact that there is an octopus there. So if you regard our initial evidence as consisting of physical facts, then the BIV theory is a complete non-starter, as are all skeptical scenarios.

* * *

My take: Yep, this is also a good response to skepticism. I'm not going to defend direct realism right now, but we'll discuss it in the next chapter.

You might think direct realism offers a cheap response to skepticism. It's almost cheating. *Of course* you can avoid skepticism if you get to just posit that external-world beliefs are immediately justified. I don't think this is cheating, though, because I think direct realism is the view that most of us start with before we run into the skeptic, and I think that what skeptics are trying to do is to refute our common sense views. No one starts out just being a skeptic for no reason. What's interesting is when the skeptic has an *argument* that seems to force us to give up our ordinary beliefs. But what we've just seen is that the skeptic only really has an argument against indirect realists. If you start out as a *direct* realist, as I assume most normal people do, then the skeptic hasn't given you any reason to change your belief system.

8.4. Conclusion

External-world skeptics claim that you know no contingent facts about the external world because you can't rule out that you're dreaming, that there is a deceiving god, or that you are a brain in a vat. Indeed, it seems that you can have no evidence at all against such scenarios, and so no reason to reject them.

In response, some philosophers claim that skeptics misunderstand the meaning of "know" in English. Relevant Alternatives theorists say that knowledge doesn't require ruling out every logically possible alternative but only the "relevant" alternatives, which are something like the objectively possible alternatives. The BIV scenario isn't relevant, so we can know stuff about the world without ruling it out.

Contextualism claims that the standards for counting as "knowing" something go up or down depending on the conversational context. Skeptics create a weird conversational context in which we don't "know" anything about the external world, but in more ordinary contexts, we *do* count as "knowing" lots of things about the external world. The Contextualist and Relevant-Alternatives theories, however, only make semantic points and don't explain why it's unlikely that we are BIVs.

The Semantic Externalist response claims that in order to have an idea that refers to some type of thing, x, it is necessary to have interacted with x's in reality. Thus, if there were a brain in a vat, it could not have any ideas that refer to brains in vats. This means that the hypothesis that we are brains in vats is self-defeating. This works against the theory that you have always been a BIV; it does not, however, show that you could not have just been kidnaped and envatted last night.

Fortunately, there are at least two responses to the skeptic that are pretty good. One response points out that the BIV argument only works against indirect realists, who think that our initial evidence consists of facts about our own *experiences*. Direct realists hold that our starting evidence includes the actual physical facts that we observe. So the BIV scenario only *explains our evidence* on an indirect realist view; on the direct realist view, the BIV scenario doesn't even try to explain our evidence.

The other response works even for indirect realists. It argues that, due to its unfalsifiability, the BIV Hypothesis cannot be evidentially supported by our experiences. The Real World Hypothesis, however, can be and is supported, because it predicts a coherent course of experience, which is what we have.

9. Theories of Perception

In this chapter, we discuss direct realism, indirect realism, idealism, and skepticism. But mainly the first two.

9.1. Four Theories About Perception & Perceptual Knowledge

How, if at all, does perception put us in touch with the external world? There are four main views about this (see figure 4).

i. **Direct realism**: In normal perception, we are directly aware of the external world. Also, perception gives us foundational justification for some beliefs about the external world. This view is also called "**naïve realism**" (mainly by its opponents).
ii. **Indirect realism**: In perception, we are directly aware of something in our own minds, and we are only *indirectly* aware of the external world. Also, perception enables us to acquire (only) *inferential* justification for beliefs about the external world. Indirect realism is also sometimes called "**representationalism**", but that term is ambiguous, so we'll avoid it.
iii. **Idealism**: In perception, we are directly aware of something in our own minds, and there are no external, physical objects; all that exists are minds and ideas in the mind.
iv. **Skepticism**: We don't know whether there are any external objects. Perception gives us no reason for believing anything about the external world.

We already talked about skepticism (that is, external-world justification skepticism) in the last chapter, so I won't say more about it here. By the way, notice how skepticism and idealism differ: The skeptic thinks we *don't know whether* there are physical objects; the idealist thinks there definitely aren't any.

I'm also not going to say much about idealism in this chapter, because hardly anyone holds this view. It was most famously defended in Western

Figure 4: Four theories of perception

philosophy by Bishop George Berkeley (pronounced "BARK-lee") in the 1700s.[70] Berkeley thought that we were only aware of ideas in our own minds, and we had no reason for thinking that matter existed; in fact, he thought the very idea of matter, a non-mental substance existing independent of all minds, was absurd and could not possibly be correct. He thought that our perceptions were planted in our minds by God (a super-powerful mind), rather than being caused by physical objects.

Berkeley also started a now-venerable tradition of tricking people by misusing language. He claimed that he was not denying the existence of physical objects but was merely explaining their nature: that they are ideas in the mind.[71] Some students actually buy this and think this proves that Berkeley really wasn't denying the existence of physical objects. News flash: "Physical objects", in English, does not refer to ideas in someone's mind. If all you have are ideas in the mind, then you don't have any physical objects, in any normal sense of that term.

Samuel Johnson, a famous English writer of the 18th century, was once asked how he would refute Berkeley's theory. Johnson replied by kicking a rock and exclaiming, "I refute it thus!"

---

[70] And in case you're wondering, yes, UC Berkeley (where I went to college!) and the city of Berkeley are named after Bishop Berkeley (even though their names are pronounced differently).

[71] Actually, he didn't use the phrase "physical object". But he said he wasn't denying the existence of tables, trees, mountains, etc. You can apply the point in the text to these terms as well.

Despite Dr. Johnson's famous "refutation", idealism was a shockingly popular view in Western philosophy during the 19th century. Fortunately, it lost favor in the twentieth century due to its general craziness, and by now there are practically no idealists.

So we're going to focus on direct & indirect realism in what follows.

9.2. Explaining Direct Realism

9.2.1. Awareness

Before we talk about the arguments for direct and indirect realism, I want to clarify the issue between them. First, what is it to be *aware* of something? There's no generally accepted definition. Here, I'll just say my view (which I think is a not-very-unusual view). To be **aware** of something, you need to have an intentional mental state (see §8.3.3 on intentionality); there needs to be something that your mental state represents roughly correctly, at least in some important respects (this is the thing that you are aware *of*); and it must be non-accidental (not a matter of mere luck) that the mental state is roughly correct (see ch. 2, especially §2.2, on the notion of luck).

There are different species of awareness. Knowledge is one species of awareness, wherein the mental state is a *belief*, and the belief non-luckily corresponds to a *fact*. Perception is another species of awareness, wherein the mental state is a sensory experience, which correctly and non-luckily represents some objects, events, properties, or states of affairs in the external world. Other kinds of awareness include intuitions, memories, and concepts (but only when they non-accidentally correspond to reality).

Sensory experience, a.k.a. **perceptual experience**, is the type of mental state that you have during perception. You also have this kind of state when you are hallucinating or suffering an illusion; any experience that is qualitatively like the experiences you have during normal perception counts as a "sensory experience". Sensory experiences have intentional content, that is, there is a way that they represent the world to be. They also commonly have an intrinsic "qualitative feel" that can't be communicated to anyone who hasn't had the experience (e.g., there's an ineffable thing that it's like to smell basil, which you can only appreciate by having that experience).

9.2.2. Direct vs. Indirect Awareness

Now, what does it mean to be "directly" or "indirectly" aware of something?

Basically, to be **indirectly aware** of something is to be aware of it in a way that *depends upon your awareness of something else*. To be **directly aware** of something is to be aware of it in a way that does *not* depend upon your awareness of anything else. (Note: These are technical terms, and they mean what I just said. They don't mean anything else that you might be randomly thinking because you ignored my definition. I mention this because misunderstandings of "direct awareness" are incredibly common and generally result from ignoring the definition.)

To illustrate, let's say you look at a starfish. According to the Indirect Realists, what is happening is that the real, physical starfish reflects light to your eyes, then a bunch of electrical activity goes on in your brain, which does some information processing that you're not aware of, and then all this causes you to experience *an image of a starfish*, in your mind. The mental image is the thing you're really, directly aware of. Then you form the belief that there is a starfish in the outside world. Your belief about the physical starfish has to be justified on the basis of facts about the image in your mind. In that sense, your knowledge about the physical starfish is indirect. (Aside: Some indirect realists describe your mental state differently; some say you are aware of appearances, or sensory experiences, or "sense data", or something else like that. The key point is that what you're directly aware of is supposed to be something mind-dependent.) Indirect realism, by the way, is by far the majority opinion in the history of philosophy, among philosophers who address the issue at all.

Direct realists, by contrast, think you're aware of the starfish itself, and your awareness of the starfish does not depend upon your awareness of a mental image, or a collection of sensations, or any other mind-dependent phenomena. Note: Direct realists need not deny that sensations or other mental states are involved in perception. They just say that your awareness of the starfish *does not depend on your awareness of* any such mental states.

By the way, please don't confuse direct realism with any of the following completely dumb views: (*i*) that there are no causal processes going on between when an external event occurs and when we know of it, (*ii*) that our perceptions are always 100% accurate, (*iii*) that we're aware of external things in a way that somehow doesn't involve our having any experiences. People sometimes raise objections to "direct realism" that are only objections to one of the above views. No one (or almost no one), however, holds those ridiculous views, so I'm not going to discuss them, and you shouldn't either.

9.2.3. How Perception Is Direct Awareness

Now, why would someone say that perception is direct awareness of the external world?

Return to the case of the starfish. When you look at a starfish, you have a perceptual experience of a starfish (an experience of seemingly seeing a starfish). Under normal conditions, this experience roughly accurately represents the physical starfish in certain important respects. E.g., it looks to you as if the object has five arms, and the real starfish in fact has five arms. It also is not a matter of mere luck that you're accurately representing the starfish, because you have a reliable visual faculty that takes input from the world and produces corresponding experiences. Thus, on the above account of awareness, you count as being *aware of* the starfish.

Is this awareness direct or indirect? To be indirect, there must be some *other* thing that you are aware of, such that your awareness of the starfish depends on your awareness of that other thing. But there just isn't any such thing.[72] In particular, it's not the case that your awareness of the starfish depends upon your being aware of a mental image of a starfish. You don't have to first have an intentional mental state that represents *a mental image of a starfish*, before you can have the above-described awareness of the starfish. So your awareness of the starfish counts as direct.

So that's my version of direct realism, in brief. For more, see my book on the subject.[73]

9.2.4. A More Extreme Direct Realism: Disjunctivism

There are other, less sensible versions of direct realism. In particular, there is an extreme version which basically holds that during normal perception, you have a special kind of mental state that *entails* the existence of an external object; there's no way of separating the mental state from the physical object.[74] Thus, you could not have that experience without the external object existing.

Of course, these people know that there are such things as hallucinations. There can even be hallucinations that *seem* like normal perceptions, such that the person having the hallucination mistakenly thinks they are perceiving a real object. According to these extreme direct realists, such hallucinations are just a completely different kind of mental state. They may *seem* to the subject just like perceptions, but it doesn't logically follow from that that they in fact *are* the same type of mental state, or even that the hallucinations have anything in common with perceptual experiences. On this view, people who have hallucinations have a kind of error, not just about the external world, but about their own mental states.

---

[72] Unless you want to say something like: Your awareness of the starfish depends upon your awareness of the *facing surface* of the starfish, or the *pattern of colors* on that surface. But note that those things are both in the external world, so this is still compatible with direct realism.
[73] *Skepticism and the Veil of Perception* (2001), especially ch. 4.
[74] See John McDowell's incomprehensible book, *Mind and World* (1996).

This view is referred to as the **Disjunctive Conception of Experience**, or **Disjunctivism**, because it holds that the concept "sensory experience" (as introduced in §9.2.1) is a *disjunctive concept*.

This comes from the term "disjunction", which basically refers to an either-or statement or phrase. Basically, a disjunctive concept is one that covers two or more completely different things, like the concept "dog or planet", or the concept "symphony or smell". You have to use "or" to explain the concept, since there isn't any single characteristic that all the things falling under the concept have in common. Disjunctivists in the philosophy of perception claim that there is no state that hallucinations and perceptions have in common, so the concept of sensory experience (which covers both hallucinations and normal perceptions) is inherently disjunctive.

Anyway, you might be wondering why people would think this. Well, the view is meant to portray us as being in much closer *contact with reality* than other views of perception, which some people consider a good thing. Some disjunctivists may also be hoping to avoid external-world skepticism by denying that skeptical scenarios are possible, given our actual experiences. We'll discuss an argument against disjunctivism below (§9.3.3).

9.3. Objections to Direct Realism

Indirect realists have raised a dizzying array of objections to direct realism. Let's look at some of them and how direct realists should respond to them.

9.3.1. Perspectival Variation

Our first objection comes from the great skeptic/indirect-realist David Hume.[75] He imagines looking at a table, then backing away from it. What happens?

> The table which we see seems to diminish as we remove farther from it. But the real table, which exists independent of us, suffers no alteration. It was, therefore, nothing but its image which was present to the mind. These are the obvious dictates of reason, and no man who reflects ever doubted that the existences which we consider when we say *this house* and *that tree* are nothing but perceptions in the mind, and fleeting copies or representations of other existences which remain uniform and independent.[76]

---

[75] How could he be a skeptic *and* an indirect realist? Well, he says that he believes in external objects because one can't help believing in that; however, he denies that we have any good *reason* for this belief.

[76] Hume, *Enquiry Concerning Human Understanding* (1758), XII.1; emphasis Hume's;

Let's get this out of the way first: Hume's last sentence is ridiculously false. The English phrase "this house" does not refer to a perception in the mind; it refers to *a house*. E.g., if someone says, "This house was built in 2010", they do not mean that a *perception* was built in 2010. (Similarly for "that tree".) And obviously it's false that every person who reflects agrees with Hume. Nearly the opposite is the case. But I included that whole quote so you can see just how confident some indirect realists are.

> **Interlude: David Hume**
>
> David Hume was a Scottish philosopher of the 1700s who is among the most important figures in epistemology ever. He wrote the mammoth book *A Treatise of Human Nature*, which explains most of his philosophy, when he was practically a baby (i.e., between the ages of 23 and 26). It didn't do so well at the time (though it's now considered a classic of Western philosophy), so he wrote two short books, *An Enquiry Concerning Human Understanding* and *An Enquiry Concerning the Principles of Morals*, to re-explain his philosophy in briefer terms and get more social media likes.
>
> Hume's main thing was being an insane skeptic about everything. He was constantly claiming that various kinds of beliefs are irrational, like our beliefs about morality, beliefs about the external world, beliefs based on induction, and even beliefs based on deductive reasoning. Nevertheless, he was perfectly happy going on using those beliefs. His other main thing was being an empiricist, which we'll talk about in a later chapter.

Now let's address the main argument: When you move away from the table, it seems to get smaller, but the real, physical table does not get smaller. Does this prove that you're only really perceiving a mental image?

I don't think so. I have two problems with the argument. First, I think it's false that the table looks smaller. Rather, I think the table looks the same size but *farther away*. And the real table is indeed farther away. So there's no problem here.

Second, the argument is just deductively invalid.[77] Look at it again:

1. The table you see seems to get smaller.
2. The real table does not get smaller.

---

punctuation has been modernized. This argument is sometimes labelled "the argument from illusion", but that's a misnomer, since the phenomenon described in that passage isn't an illusion.

[77] In terms of Aristotelian logic, the argument has two middle terms: "diminish" and "seems to diminish". Thomas Reid pointed this out in his *Inquiry and Essays* (1983), 178–9. He also generally dunked on David Hume throughout.

3. Therefore, the table you see ≠ the real table.

Step 3 doesn't follow. It would be perfectly consistent to hold that the table you see is the real table, and that this one object *seems* to get smaller without *actually* getting smaller. Nothing about this situation forces us to introduce a second table or table-like entity.

The general phenomenon that Hume's example draws attention to is that of **perspectival variation**. This is the phenomenon where the appearances of things vary depending on *the observer's relation* to the objects, even when the objects remain *intrinsically* unchanged. In particular, our experiences change when we change our distance from an object, or the angle from which we view it, without the object itself changing. Does this show that we lack direct awareness of external objects?

Not really. You might think, plausibly enough, that this phenomenon shows that we do not directly perceive the *intrinsic* properties of physical objects. (Why? Because maybe a condition on a mental state's counting as awareness of some physical property is that the properties of the mental state co-vary with the physical property.) Or at least, this isn't *all* we perceive. Perspectival variation suggests that what we are aware of is, at least in part, our *relation* to the physical objects that we observe. For instance, maybe what you're directly, visually aware of is the *angular magnitude* of the table (the size of the angle that it subtends at the eye), rather than its linear width.

This is an interesting point. But note that this does not vindicate indirect realism. Indirect realism doesn't say that you're aware of relational properties of physical objects. Indirect realism says that you're aware of *a mental state* (or mental image, or something like that). And nothing about perspectival variation suggests that. The angular magnitude that a table subtends from the point in space where your eye is located is a *perfectly objective, physical fact*. It's not a mental fact. So if that's what we're visually aware of, that's still on the side of direct realism, not indirect realism.

9.3.2. Illusion

A brief terminological note: What's the difference between *illusion* and *hallucination*? In an **illusion**, there is a real object that you're perceiving, but you are misperceiving some of its properties (example: seeing a real stick but misperceiving its shape); in **hallucination**, there is no real object that you're perceiving (example: "seeing" a pink elephant when there is nothing at all like that in your environment). Both phenomena are sometimes thought to pose a problem for direct realism. Let's start with illusion.[78]

---

[78] Incidentally, there are two kinds of illusions: those that are mainly explained by

Suppose you submerge a stick halfway in a glass of water. The stick appears bent. But in reality, it is straight. Does this show that you don't directly perceive the real stick? We might argue:

1. When you look at the half-submerged stick, you see something that is bent.
2. The physical stick is not bent.
3. Therefore, when you look at the half-submerged stick, you see something other than the physical stick.

This other thing that you see must be a mental image or something like that, right?

Again, I remain unimpressed. I think (1) is false. When viewing a half-submerged stick, I think you see something that *looks* bent but *is* straight, not something that *is* bent. There is no need to posit some other stick or stick-like object that is really bent.

9.3.3. Hallucination, Part 1: Against Disjunctivism

Now let's turn to hallucinations. There are at least three different arguments from hallucination. The first one is a problem specifically for *disjunctivism*, the extreme form of direct realism discussed in §9.2.4.

Let's compare two possible cases. In one case, you see an orange cat on the kitchen counter, and everything is normal; the cat is there, causing your experience. In another case, imagine that you have the *exact same brain state* as in the first case, except that it isn't caused by a real cat, and there is no cat there. Rather, you're hallucinating due to having taken LSD, or mad scientists are stimulating your brain to create a simulation of seeing a cat, or whatever.

In the latter case, the hallucination, you have a sensory experience of a cat, which is a *purely internal mental state*. You're not directly aware of a cat, because there is no cat to be aware of.

Now, in general, if you reproduce the *proximate cause* of some effect (the last item in the causal sequence), you reproduce the effect; it doesn't matter if you also produce the earlier items in the causal sequence or not. In the case of the hallucination, you have a purely internal mental state proximately caused by a state of your brain. By stipulation, the same brain state occurs during normal perception. Therefore, the same effect—i.e., the same purely internal mental state—must also occur during normal perception.

---

something unusual in the external world (e.g., the straight stick that appears bent when half-submerged in water) and those that are mainly explained by quirks of how the brain processes information (e.g., the case where attaching arrows to the ends of a line makes it appear different lengths depending on the direction the arrows point).

My take on this: That's a good argument. That shows that disjunctivism is false.

9.3.4. Hallucination, Part 2: For Awareness of Mental Objects

Here's the second version of the argument from hallucination. Let's say you hallucinate an orange cat on the counter. Then you are aware of an orange, cat-shaped thing. But there is no relevant orange, cat-shaped thing in the physical world at this time.[79] Therefore, you must be aware of a non-physical thing that is orange and cat-shaped. What can this thing be? Presumably, it's a mental image.

Furthermore, this orange, cat-shaped, non-physical thing should also exist, and you should also be aware of it, during normal perception. (You can repeat the causal argument from §9.3.3 here.) Thus, in normal perception, you're aware of mental images.

My response: The first premise is false. In hallucinating an orange cat, a person is *not* aware of an orange, cat-shaped thing. A hallucination is not a state of awareness at all; it's more like pseudo-awareness, a state of merely seeming to be aware of something.

Why? Look at the account of awareness again (§9.2.1). In order to count as being *aware* of some thing, you have to have a mental state that at least roughly correctly represents that thing. In the case of the cat hallucination, there is no relevant object that your experience correctly represents, because there is no orange, cat-shaped thing present, or anything like that. So your mental state does not count as a state of awareness.

By the way, here's an analogy that might help, since philosophers will generally agree about this case: Suppose that Crazy Alex believes that vaccines cause autism. Of course, Crazy Alex is wrong (which shouldn't surprise us, given his name). Vaccines, in the real world, do not cause autism. Now, what is it that Alex *knows* by having this false belief? Imagine someone arguing as follows:

1'. Alex knows of something that causes autism.
2'. Real, physical vaccines don't cause autism.
3'. Therefore, Alex knows of some *other* thing that causes autism, like maybe a *mental* vaccine.

That reasoning is so mind-bogglingly confused that not even a nineteenth-century German philosopher would say that.[80] The obvious mistake is the

---

[79] Of course, there are orange cats *elsewhere in the world*, but none that you could plausibly be said to be aware of in this experience, so they're not relevant.
[80] Actually, the main reason a 19th-century German philosopher wouldn't say that is

assumption that Crazy Alex knows something via his false belief. Crazy Alex doesn't *know* anything relevant, and there is no reason to think that there is *anything* that satisfies the predicate of his false belief. There is therefore no need to posit some alternative, mind-dependent vaccine that really causes autism (which is a bizarre idea in itself).

That is analogous to the current version of the Argument from Hallucination. Knowledge is a form of awareness; perception is another form of awareness. The Argument from Hallucination is the application to *perception* of the logic used in the argument about Crazy Alex's *knowledge*. The Crazy Alex argument errs by assuming that when one has a false belief, there has to be some relevant thing that satisfies the predicate of that belief (e.g., something that *causes autism*). The Argument from Hallucination errs by assuming that when one suffers a hallucination, there must be some relevant thing that has the properties one seems to observe (e.g., something that *is orange and cat-shaped*). If you wouldn't be tempted by the Crazy Alex argument, you shouldn't accept the Argument from Hallucination either.

9.3.5. Hallucination, Part 3: About Foundational Justification

Finally, here's the third Argument from Hallucination. Again, assume you have a cat hallucination that is perfectly indistinguishable from a normal cat perception, and you have no reason to think you're hallucinating:

1. In the hallucination case, you have the same justification for believing that there is a cat there as you do when you normally perceive a cat.
2. In the hallucination case, your justification for believing that there is a cat there does not consist in your being directly aware of a cat.
3. Therefore, when you normally perceive a cat, your justification for believing that there is a cat there also does not consist in your being directly aware of a cat.[81]

Premise 1 is intuitive. Premise 2 is true because you can't be directly aware of a cat if there is no cat there. Conclusion 3 follows from 1 and 2. Of course, if this is right, then we can similarly argue that *none* of our perceptual beliefs are justified by direct awareness of external objects.

My response: That's correct. In normal perception, although we are directly aware of external objects, that is not the explanation of why our beliefs are justified. The explanation of why our beliefs are justified is that we have *appearances* in the absence of defeaters, as explained in §5.2. In the perfectly-

---

that it is too clear.
[81] This argument is from Richard Fumerton's *Metaphysical and Epistemological Problems of Perception*, 78ff.

realistic-hallucination case, you also have an undefeated appearance, so you have the same justification for belief.

9.3.6. The Time Gap

Say you look up at a particular star in the night sky. As you know, the other stars (besides our sun) are ridiculously far away. Let's say the particular star you are looking at is 1,000 light years away (which is nearby, in astronomical terms!). That means that it takes 1,000 years for light from that star to reach Earth.

And that means that actually, that star might not even exist anymore. The star could have ceased to exist up to a thousand years ago, and we'd still be receiving light from it. Things would look just the same on Earth.

Suppose that happened: Suppose that you're looking in the direction of a star that somehow ceased to exist 500 years ago (maybe it got destroyed by an extra powerful Death Star or something), but it was 1,000 light years away from Earth at the time. So people will continue to "see" that star for another 500 years. But since that star doesn't presently exist, what are you really seeing?

The indirect realist says: You're really seeing a mental image of the star. You can't be seeing the real star, since that doesn't exist anymore.

My response: You're seeing the star *as it was* 1,000 years ago. There's no need to posit some non-physical thing for you to be seeing.

By the way, the star is just an extreme case of something that is true of everything we see: Everything we see is at some distance from us, which means that there is some delay between when any event happens and when we see it. Usually, of course, the delay is negligible and unnoticeable (and most of the delay is usually due to the time it takes for your brain to process the signals). But this shows that in a sense, we're always looking into the past—usually the very near past, but occasionally, as when we look at the stars, we see into the distant past.

9.3.7. Double Vision

Have you ever seen double? If you're like most people, you probably answered "No." But you're mistaken; you probably see double every day, only you don't notice it.

Try this. Hold your finger in front of your face, in a place where you can easily see it. Now *focus* on something in the background (like the other side of the room), but *attend* to the finger. What you should notice is that it looks as if there are two blurry copies of your finger in your visual field, even though you know there is only one. Now, if instead you focus on the finger, all the objects in the background will appear double.

Thomas Reid says this shows that the objects in your visual field that are out of focus *regularly* appear double, but most people never notice this because we almost always attend to the thing that is in focus.

Anyway, this makes for another possible argument the indirect realist might advance:

1. When you focus on the background, you see two finger-shaped things.
2. There are not two finger-shaped physical objects at this time.
3. Therefore, you see something non-physical.

Again, once we get to step 3, we are supposed to infer that the non-physical thing we see is a mental image.

My take: This is the same sort of mistake as the argument from illusion and the argument from hallucination (version 2). It is false that you see two finger-shaped things. What is the case is that you see *one finger*, which *appears* to be in two places (but of course is *in fact* in only one place).

In sum, I think none of the phenomena we've discussed—perspectival variation, illusions, hallucinations, time delays in seeing things, or double vision—shows that anyone ever perceives anything non-physical.

9.4. Objections to Indirect Realism

9.4.1. *Spatial Properties*

Here's one of my arguments against indirect realism:

1. In normal perception, you are directly aware of things with spatial properties.
2. Only physical things have spatial properties.
3. Therefore, in normal perception, you are directly aware of physical things.

To explain premise 1: By "spatial properties", I mean shapes, sizes, locations, and spatial relations to other objects—i.e., the sort of properties had by things that are located in space. E.g., when you see a tomato, you're aware of a red, round thing in front of you. You are not aware of any shapeless, sizeless, locationless thing.

To explain premise 2: To have spatial properties, a thing has to be located in space. But only physical things are located in space. Purely mental, non-physical things aren't in space. It follows that in normal perception, you're aware of physical things.

Where would an indirect realist object to this? They would probably deny premise 2. They would say that there are non-physical things called "mental images", which can have sizes and shapes, and that's what we're directly aware of in perception.

If you say this, then I think you have to answer the following question: *Where* are these mental images? Since they have spatial properties, they must be in space. Since they're in space, they must have some definite locations in space. But there's no answer to this that makes the theory sound plausible.

E.g., suppose you say the mental objects are located where the distal object is (the physical object that causes your experience). In that case, when you look up at a star, a mental image appears *on the star*, trillions of miles away, instantaneously. This is bizarre on its face, in addition to the fact that it violates the theory of relativity (you'd be transmitting causal influence faster than the speed of light).

Or we could say that the mental objects appear literally *inside your head*. This invites the question of why, when brain surgeons open up someone's skull, they don't see little tables, people, apples, or whatever else the patient is seeing, inside the skull. Indirect realists would say that the little table images and such are only visible to the person whose images they are. But it still seems pretty silly to think that when you look at a table, a little table appears inside your skull.

Or we could say that the mental objects appear in their own, separate space. This also violates the theory of relativity, if you care about that, because in special relativity, space and time are connected; that is, there is a single, four-dimensional manifold, spacetime, not a separate space and time. So nothing could be in our *time* without being in our *space*.

The above answers are not *contradictory*, so one *could* say one of the above things. But I think that when you make the theory explicit, it just sounds naïve and implausible.

9.4.2. Indeterminacy

My second argument against indirect realism is the argument from indeterminacy. First, note that indirect realists generally hold that the mental images (or "sense data", or whatever term they prefer) that you're aware of have precisely the qualities that they appear to have. This is clear from the various arguments for indirect realism in the previous section—the arguments from perspectival variation, illusion, hallucination, time gaps, and double vision all posit mental objects that have exactly the properties we seem to observe. E.g., in the bent stick illusion (§9.3.2), where the half-submerged stick appears bent, you're supposed to think that we are aware of something that *is bent*.

My problem with this is that sometimes, appearances are *indeterminate*. Say you're looking at a road sign that's too far away to read. You can tell that it has writing on it, but you can't make out what the words are. That is, it appears to you that *there are words* on the sign, but there is no *specific* set of words that appear to you to be on the sign. You can't make out the shapes of the letters, which means that there are no *specific* shapes that appear to you to be on the sign.

That's an example of what I mean by "indeterminate appearances". You have indeterminate appearances when something appears to you to fall within some qualitative range, but there is no specific place within that range that it appears to fall. This is a generalization of the idea that a thing can appear to be (*A* or *B*), without appearing to be *A* and without appearing to be *B*. For example, you might be able to see that a particular letter on the sign is either an "R" or a "B" yet be unable to see which it is.

But while it is certainly possible for things to have indeterminate *appearances*, it is logically impossible for anything to have indeterminate *qualities*. (And here, it doesn't matter whether we are talking about a physical object, a mental object, or anything else. *Everything* has to obey the laws of logic.) That is, it is impossible for a thing to fall within some qualitative range without being at any particular point within that range. A thing cannot be (*A* or *B*) without being *A* and without being *B*. To return to the road sign example: While it's perfectly possible for the words to fail to *appear* any specific shape, it is impossible for the words to fail to *have* any specific shape. Similarly, an object cannot be colored in general without being any specific color; or be in space without being in any specific location; etc.[82]

It follows that the objects of awareness in perception cannot simply have exactly the qualities that they appear to have. They must be fully determinate, so they must have some qualities that they don't appear to have.

Now, why can't the indirect realist just accept this, and say that the mental items we're aware of have some properties beyond those they appear to us to have? One problem with this is that this abandons the central motivations for indirect realism—the indirect realist would have to renounce the arguments of section 9.3 above. Once you accept that, in perception, we're aware of something that need not be exactly as it appears, you might as well just admit that that thing is the actual physical object.

9.4.3. *The Conditions for Awareness*

I don't think indirect realism is a mere empirical mistake. I think it's a

---

[82] I'm sure about half of you are going to be saying now, "Wait, I heard that quantum mechanics refuted all that. Doesn't QM show that objects have indeterminate qualities whenever they're not being observed?" In response, that is indeed one of the interpretations of QM. But it's a really bad interpretation for precisely this reason—it's logically incoherent. For discussion of this and other interpretations of QM, I recommend David Albert's *Quantum Mechanics and Experience* (one of the world's best popular science books).

conceptual confusion. I think indirect realists confuse a *vehicle* of awareness with an *object* of awareness. In other words, they confuse that *by which* we are aware of things with that *of which* we are aware.[83]

When you perceive something, you have a certain kind of mental state, a perceptual experience. This is a state of the world's appearing to you to be a certain way. This experience is the means by which you are aware of something in the external world. The *object* of your awareness (the thing that you are aware *of*), is the thing that causes your experience and at least roughly satisfies its content (i.e., has the properties that you seem to observe the object to have), if there is some such thing. (Recall the account of awareness in §9.2.1 again.) The object of your awareness is not the experience itself, for the experience itself does not roughly satisfy its own content.

For example, when you look at a tomato, you have an experience of seeming to see a tomato, which appears red and round to you. The object of your awareness should be a (roughly) red and round thing. The *experience* of seeing the tomato is not red and round; *the tomato* is red and round. So the object of your awareness is not the experience of seeing the tomato; the object of your awareness is the tomato.

9.4.4. The Knowledge Problem

One final problem with indirect realism. This problem is about their theory of *justification*, rather than their theory of awareness. If we reject foundational justification for perceptual beliefs, it then becomes a problem to explain how we know anything about the external world. The standard indirect realist view is that we know about the external world by inference to the best explanation: We start with our sensory experiences, then we infer that there are physical objects of various kinds around us because that is the best explanation for what is causing all our experiences.

This might be a good inference; however, this is not how normal people form beliefs. I don't even think it's how philosophers form their beliefs. When you look at a tomato, you don't start by noting the characteristics of your experience, then entertain different hypotheses about what might have caused this experience, rule out alternatives like the brain-in-a-vat scenario or the dream hypothesis, and finally conclude that a physical tomato is the best explanation. You look at the tomato and immediately think there's a tomato there.

There's a widely-accepted principle in epistemology that, in order to *know* that p, you have to base your belief that p on something that provides adequate justification for p (see §2.3.3). This is known as the **basing condition** for

---

[83] Mortimer Adler made a big deal of this in his *Ten Philosophical Mistakes* (1985).

knowledge. If you get to the correct belief but for the wrong reasons, then you don't have knowledge. Even if good reasons for *p* were *available* to you, if you didn't actually base your belief on those reasons, then you don't have knowledge.

So, taking all this into account, the indirect realist is going to have a hard time explaining how anyone *knows* anything about the external world. It looks like the indirect realist is going to have to say that basically no one knows anything about the physical world, with the possible exception of some philosophers who have figured out the correct arguments for believing in external objects.

This is a bad result for indirect realists, who of course don't want to have to join the skeptics. No one wants to live in the skeptics' cave.

9.5. Conclusion

The two leading views about perception and perceptual knowledge are direct realism and indirect realism. Direct realists think that perception gives us direct awareness and foundational knowledge of the external world. Indirect realists think that we are only ever directly aware of things going on in our own minds, that our awareness of the external world is indirect, and our knowledge of the external world rests on an inference in which we posit external objects as the best explanation for what causes our sensory experiences.

The arguments for indirect realism sound persuasive at first but are not that great on reflection. The phenomena of perspectival variation, illusions, hallucinations, double vision, and the time delay between physical events and our experiences of them can all be accommodated by direct realists. Perspectival variation can be explained in terms of awareness of relational (but still physical) features of objects. Illusions can be understood as cases in which one is aware of a physical object, but the object is somewhat different from how it appears. Hallucinations can be understood as cases in which one only *seems* to be aware of an object, but one is not in fact aware of any object. Time delays show only that we sometimes perceive past things (but still physical, not mental things). And double vision is a case in which we are aware of one thing that falsely appears to be in two places.

Indirect realists have trouble explaining exactly where the mental things we're supposedly aware of are located. They also have trouble with the indeterminacy of our appearances, because no actual object can have indeterminate qualities. And they have trouble explaining how ordinary people count as knowing things about the external world, given that ordinary people do not in fact go through inferences to the best explanation before forming beliefs about physical objects.

Fundamentally, I claim that indirect realists are confused about the nature of awareness and its objects. Our experiences are the *means* by which we are aware of physical things; they aren't the *objects* of our awareness.

10. Pure Reason

In this chapter, we talk about whether and how we have knowledge independent of experience.

10.1. Analytic A Priori Knowledge

10.1.1. A Priori vs. Empirical

As we said earlier (§7.1.2), *empirical* knowledge (a.k.a. a posteriori knowledge) is knowledge whose justification depends on observations. *A priori* knowledge is knowledge that isn't empirical.

I emphasize again, in case you forgot, that *I am not talking about how you acquire concepts*. When I say, e.g., that [All purple unicorns are purple] is known a priori, I am not saying that you can acquire the concept "unicorn" or the concept "purple" without experience. I am only saying that you don't need to cite observations as *justification* or *evidence* for the statement. So don't say it's empirical because you acquired the concept "purple" by experience.

10.1.2. Analytic vs. Synthetic

Now, here's a major question of epistemology: Is all knowledge based on experience?

And here's the answer: No, it isn't. The great majority of philosophers (correctly) accept at least some examples of a priori knowledge, such as the following: I know a priori that 4 is less than 4,000, that all bachelors are unmarried, and that all purple unicorns are purple. (Note that the last one is true whether or not there *are* any purple unicorns. It just means there are no purple unicorns that aren't purple.) Those things are a priori in the sense that they do not depend for their justification on observations. I don't, for example, have to go out and look for purple unicorns in order to check whether they are purple or not. I don't have to check because purple unicorns are *by definition* purple, so I know without looking that there won't be any non-purple ones. No matter what observations I make, that won't change.

Those are examples of *analytic* statements. **Analytic** statements are statements that are, as we say, "true by definition". People sometimes say they are "true in virtue of the meanings of the words" used in the statement, or true in virtue of the relationships among the concepts used. Here's a more precise formulation, due to Frege: *A statement is analytic if it can be transformed into a logical truth by substituting synonymous expressions.*[84] Example: "All bachelors are unmarried" is analytic, since "bachelors" is synonymous with "unmarried men", so you can substitute the latter phrase for "bachelor", thus obtaining: "All unmarried men are unmarried." That is a logical truth, meaning that it can be derived just from the laws of logic. So the original statement, "All bachelors are unmarried", counts as analytic. Likewise, "All purple unicorns are purple" counts as analytic since it is already a logical truth.

> **Aside: The Laws of Logic**
> The laws of logic include things like the Law of Non-Contradiction, $\sim(A\ \&\ \sim A)$; the Law of Excluded Middle, $(A \vee \sim A)$; and the Law of Identity, $(x)\ x=x$. Those are the three most famous laws of logic. Notice that these things are all necessarily true, and you can see that each is true just in virtue of the *form* of the statement. That is, you don't need to know what A is; any statement of the form "$(A \vee \sim A)$" has to be true. Likewise, you don't need to know what x is in order to know that it's identical to itself. For purposes of defining analyticity, we count any sentence that is guaranteed to be true in virtue of its form as a "logical truth".[85]

The contrast to "analytic" is "synthetic". **Synthetic** statements are just those that are not analytic (and also not contradictory). For instance, "All bachelors are slobs" is synthetic because, even if all bachelors are in fact slobs, this slobbiness is not inherent in the definition of a bachelor.

It is widely agreed among philosophers that there is analytic a priori knowledge—i.e., one can know (the propositions expressed by) analytic sentences in a way that doesn't require justification by observations.

---

[84] In modern times, people tend to give broader, more subtle definitions, such as that analytic statements are statements for which one's willingness to accept them is a test of one's linguistic competence. I don't like this because it blurs the line between analyticity and a prioricity.

[85] Some more explanation: The *form* of a statement is sometimes glossed as the *logical structure* of the proposition. By stipulation, two sentences "have the same form" if you could get one statement from the other by replacing one or more non-logical expressions in the one statement with an expression having the same logical function—e.g., substituting one noun for another noun or one predicate for another predicate. But you can't swap logical expressions (like "or", "if", or "not"). For these purposes, the identity symbol ("=") counts as a logical expression; don't ask me why.

10.2. Traditional Empiricism

10.2.1. The Empiricist Creed

The real issue is with *synthetic* a priori knowledge: Is there any such thing? That is, are there any statements which, though not true by definition, can nevertheless be known to be true without relying on observational evidence?

Many philosophers, known as **empiricists**, have answered "no", mainly because they could not see *how* one could know a synthetic statement to be true without relying on observation. Empiricists think that any substantive knowledge about the world independent of one's concepts and language has to come from experience. Most empiricists think that *analytic* a priori knowledge is fine because it just consists of knowledge about how our concepts relate to each other, or about the meanings of our words. But *synthetic* statements are not made true by our concepts or the meanings of words, so they must be telling us something substantive about the world. So we need some kind of observation to verify any such statements.

10.2.2. The Argument for Empiricism

The above is only an articulation of the empiricist's intuition, not really an argument for it. Why think that substantive knowledge of the world requires experience? I know of one argument for this:

Recall that knowledge requires having a belief that is non-luckily true; that is, you have to get things right and it can't be just a matter of chance that you got things right (see §2.2). Truth is correspondence with reality, so, in order for you to know that p, it must be not a matter of luck that there is a correspondence between your belief and the facts. Now, it seems that there are two ways in which such a correspondence could fail to be due to chance: One way would be if the facts determine (or at least influence) what you believe; the other way would be if your mind somehow determines the facts.

The first case (where the facts affect your beliefs) is what happens in experience. In the absence of experience, there's no obvious way in which the facts could affect your beliefs.

The second case, where your mind determines the facts, is sort of what happens in analytic knowledge: We create some concepts in our minds, and the relationships among these concepts make the analytic truths true. E.g., all unicorns must have horns, not because of any facts in the external world, but simply because we made up the concept "unicorn" as that of a horse with a horn on its head.

So in the case of synthetic statements that are not supported by experience, it would seem that the facts don't influence our minds, nor do our minds influence the facts. So it could only be an accident if our beliefs corresponded to the facts. So, even if our beliefs were true, they wouldn't count as *knowledge*. So there's no synthetic, a priori knowledge.

10.2.3. Is the Empiricist's Argument Self-Defeating?

The preceding argument, if it succeeds, would give us knowledge: the knowledge that there is no synthetic, a priori knowledge. Interestingly, the argument itself seems to be a priori, as it does not appeal to any experience. The empiricists are not saying, for example, that they went out looking for items of knowledge and just found, every time, that the knowledge turned out to be either analytic or empirical. They're not generalizing from observations. Rather, they're saying that there could not in principle be any synthetic a priori knowledge.

Is this putative knowledge analytic or synthetic? The principle "There is no synthetic a priori knowledge" can be rephrased as "All a priori knowledge is analytic". So, is it analytic that all a priori knowledge is analytic? It doesn't seem to be. If you review the definitions of "a priori" and "analytic" above, the one does not seem to contain the other (we did not *define* a priori knowledge to be analytic).

You might try saying that the argument of §10.2.2 shows empiricism to be analytic, because the argument is based on the meaning of "know". But for this to work, it would have to be that *every* premise of the argument is analytic. It might be analytic that knowledge is non-luckily true belief. But it isn't analytic that there are only two ways for a correspondence between beliefs and facts to be non-lucky, nor is it analytic that facts can only determine our beliefs via observation (how would you derive either of those things from definitions?). Rather, both of those premises rely on intuition at best (at worst, they're just guesses). So it really seems as though empiricists are advancing empiricism itself as a synthetic, a priori truth.

10.2.4. Is Empiricism Self-Defeating in General?

Maybe I'm wrong about that; maybe the argument of section 10.2.2 somehow isn't self-defeating, or maybe the empiricist doesn't have to rely on that argument. But there is a more general argument that empiricism is self-defeating.

Empiricism is in part a normative epistemological thesis, a thesis about the justification for beliefs. Empiricists think that only experience can *justify* or provide *good reasons for* believing synthetic claims. Accordingly, one *shouldn't* believe synthetic claims that aren't supported by observations. (Above, I formulated empiricism as a claim about *knowledge* rather than justification, but empiricists think that we lack synthetic, a priori knowledge *because* synthetic claims can't be justified a priori.)

But observation never gives us normative information. Observation only tells us what *is*, not what *ought to be*. You can't see, hear, taste, touch, or smell justification. Normative propositions also can't be inferred from descriptive information alone—you can't figure out what ought to be solely on the basis of what is.[86] Therefore, empiricism itself cannot be justified on the basis of observation.

Furthermore, the normative claim of empiricism is obviously synthetic. That is, the claim that one *should not* believe synthetic propositions that aren't supported by observation, or that one *should not* rely on intuition, is not analytic. Again, you can't turn that into a logical truth by substituting synonymous expressions. Some philosophers think that one actually *should* rely on intuition, and this view (whether right or wrong) is not contradictory.

So the claim that *one shouldn't believe synthetic claims that aren't empirically supported* is itself a synthetic claim that isn't empirically supported. So it's self-defeating.

10.3. (Il)logical Positivism

10.3.1. The Positivist Creed

In the late 19th to mid-20th century, a philosophy known as "logical positivism" became popular in the English-speaking world. (At first it was just called "positivism"; then they decided to make it sound cooler by adding "logical" to the name. I, however, find the view highly illogical; hence the title of this section.)

Logical positivism is the conjunction of two theses: empiricism and **the verification criterion of meaning** (a.k.a. **verificationism**). I already explained empiricism above, so no need to say more about that now.

Verificationism holds, basically, that the meaning of a sentence is given by the conditions for verifying or refuting the sentence. Thus, if you have a sentence that could not in principle be tested, then the sentence is completely meaningless. And by "meaningless", they don't just mean that the sentence is pointless or uninteresting. They mean the sentence is literally without meaning—it does not say anything. More precisely, it lacks *cognitive* meaning (the kind of meaning whereby a sentence says some aspect of reality is some way); the sentence might still have *emotive* meaning, though (the kind of

---

[86] For more on this, see my *Ethical Intuitionism*, ch. 4.

meaning whereby a sentence expresses someone's feelings, e.g., "ouch!" or "hurray!").

Now, a few qualifications to make the theory not *too* easily refuted: First, by "verification", the positivists actually just mean having *some evidence* for the sentence. Their considered view is that the meaning of a sentence is determined by what counts as evidence for or against the sentence. This is important, since most empirical statements cannot be *conclusively* verified or refuted, yet they can be supported or undermined.

Second, you don't have to actually be in a position to test a statement in order for it to be meaningful. It just has to be *in principle possible*, in the broadest sense, for someone to have evidence for or against the statement. For example, "Aristotle had an odd number of hairs on his head at the time of his death" is not testable by us now, but in principle, someone *could have* had evidence supporting that (if, e.g., someone had counted his hairs when he died), so the sentence is meaningful.

Third, analytic statements and contradictory (or analytically false) statements are also meaningful. One way of getting this result is to claim that analytic statements count as "verified by" any possible experience, and contradictory statements count as "refuted by" any possible experience. That's a bit of a stretch, but whatever. Just accept that analytic and contradictory statements are meaningful on the positivist view.

One of the main things the positivists wanted to do was to reject metaphysics (of the sort that some Continental philosophers were doing at the time, as well as the metaphysics produced earlier by people like Leibniz and Spinoza). They didn't want to have to delve into people's metaphysical schemes to argue about them; they wanted to reject all metaphysics wholesale. They used the verification criterion to do this: Under the verification criterion of meaning, the entire field of metaphysics was deemed meaningless, since none of it could be tested by observations (and, per empiricism, intuition didn't count as a way of testing anything).

Another result was that, on most positivists' views, the entire field of ethics was meaningless. If you say, "Abortion is wrong", there is no way of testing that empirically, so it has no cognitive meaning. Instead, maybe it just has emotive meaning—maybe saying "Abortion is wrong" is sort of like saying "Boo on abortion!" It expresses your feelings, but it isn't either true or false because it doesn't describe any purported aspect of the world.

What about the rest of philosophy? Philosophers don't seem to be doing any experiments or otherwise gathering empirical evidence. Is all of philosophy meaningless? No, most positivists thought that philosophy was dedicated to producing analytic knowledge (which, again, counts as meaningful). For this reason, they thought the job of philosophers was mainly to analyze language.

What about mathematics, which the rationalists cite as a locus of synthetic a priori knowledge? The positivists generally view mathematics as analytic. And if some particular mathematical axioms aren't analytic, the positivists would say that they need to be empirically tested. For example, it used to be thought that Euclidean geometry was known a priori. But in the 20th century, physicists started using non-Euclidean geometry to describe our spacetime. This was supported by empirical evidence. Positivists would say that it is analytic and a priori that *given the axioms of Euclidean geometry*, all the Euclidean theorems are true; however, it is synthetic and empirical that the axioms of Euclidean geometry actually describe the space we live in.

10.3.2. Motivations for Positivism

You'd be surprised how popular positivism used to be. It had a big influence not only on philosophers but on scientists as well. Twentieth-century scientists appealed to positivist principles to justify major scientific theories. If you don't believe me, look up Einstein's book *Relativity*; then look at the Bohr-Einstein debate about quantum mechanics.

So there must have been some really persuasive arguments for the theory, right?

Actually, no. We talked about the motivation for empiricism above (§10.2.2), and it's not too bad. But it's hard to find any serious argument for the verification criterion of meaning. Usually, the positivists just assert the principle and then start deducing conclusions from it. Or they start out by saying that they're looking for a criterion of meaning that will rule out metaphysics as meaningless, then they explain how the verification criterion is good for this purpose. Given that many philosophers think metaphysics is perfectly meaningful and in fact are busy *doing* metaphysics, that's pretty lame.

If you ask an amateur positivist today (you have to ask an amateur because there are hardly any professional philosophers who are positivists anymore), they'll probably start giving examples of sentences that are obviously meaningless, then note that these sentences also can't be tested, then say that's evidence for the verification criterion. But obviously, everyone agrees that *if* a sentence is meaningless, it can't be tested. So the real issue has to be the converse: If a sentence can't be tested, does it follow that it's meaningless? It seems as if there are many counter-examples, such as all the statements of metaphysics and ethics (cf. §10.5.2 below). And you can't appeal to positivism to argue that those are really meaningless, since the question now is why we should accept positivism in the first place.

Here is my interpretation: Positivism is motivated by two things: scientism, and a confusion between knowledge and truth. Let's start with the first thing.

Scientism is, as one philosopher put it, "a sort of exaggerated respect for science—that is, for the physical and biological sciences—and a corresponding disparagement of all other areas of human intellectual endeavour. It hardly need be pointed out that scientism is the primary ideology of our age. It hardly need be pointed out that the illusions scientism engenders are so pervasive and so insidious that it is practically impossible to get anyone who is subject to them to consider the possibility that they might be illusions."[87]

The rise of scientism began in the Enlightenment, due to the great progress science had recently made. Victims of scientism wanted to say that *all* knowledge has to be like Science; anything that's not like Science is intellectually worthless. At this time, many philosophers thought (wrongly, in my opinion, but this is what they thought) that science is purely empirical knowledge. Therefore, they *wanted* to declare that all knowledge is empirical. They couldn't quite bring themselves to do that, since analytic knowledge was too obvious (plus, they didn't want to have to reject mathematics). So they declared that all *synthetic* knowledge must be empirical.

That was traditional empiricism. But then, in the 19th and early 20th centuries, philosophers started competing with each other to see who could be most extreme in their devotion to scientism. Just being a traditional empiricist was no longer enough; they wanted a more extreme way of rejecting all non-sciencey stuff. So instead of saying merely that the statements of metaphysics, ethics, and religion were *unjustified*, they took to declaring such statements *meaningless*. "Ha! It's not just that we don't know whether what you've said is true; you haven't even said anything!" If you want to be the most extreme science-worshipper, think how good it would feel to get to say that to non-sciencey people.

I think that is the core emotional motivation behind positivism—that's why people *wanted* to be positivists. And so they looked for ways of maintaining the view. But that wouldn't have been enough if there wasn't *some* sort of intellectual plausibility to the view, some way in which it could seem true to someone.

And here enters the other major factor I mentioned above: the confusion between knowledge and truth. TRUTH and KNOWLEDGE are clearly closely related concepts with substantial overlap, so it's not totally crazy that someone might confuse them. But they're definitely not the same thing, since there are many truths that we don't know—e.g., I don't know whether the number of atoms in the universe is *even* or *odd*, but one of those two alternatives must be true.

---

[87] Peter van Inwagen, *An Essay on Free Will* (1983), 215.

A plausible account of meaning (even among non-positivists) is that the meaning of a sentence is given by its truth-conditions: You understand a sentence when you know what would make it true or false. Now suppose you confuse knowledge with truth. You then come up with the idea that the meaning of a sentence is given by its *knowledge*-conditions, that is, the conditions under which one would come to *know* the sentence. That sounds a lot like "meaning is verification conditions".

10.3.3. Objections

Now for some more objections to logical positivism.

i. The first objection most people come up with is that verificationism is self-defeating. How can we verify the verification criterion? If we have no way of empirically testing it, then it must be meaningless, according to itself.

   In reply, the positivists would probably claim that the verification criterion is analytic, that "meaning" just *means* "verification conditions". Of course, that's false, but this objection doesn't *show* that it's false.

ii. A better objection is that, as suggested above, positivism rests on a confusion between truth and knowledge. Knowledge isn't the same as truth, so verification conditions aren't the same as truth conditions. Since it's more plausible to identify meaning with truth conditions, we should not identify meaning with verification conditions.

iii. There seem to be many counter-examples to the verification criterion—namely, all the statements of metaphysics and ethics. Of course, positivists disagree since they claim those statements are meaningless. But they have no argument for that other than appealing to the verification criterion, and it's not clear why we would accept the verification criterion in the first place, given that it has such implausible implications about these cases.

iv. Verificationism conflicts with the principle of the **compositionality of meaning**, the principle that the meaning of a sentence is determined by the meanings of its component parts and the structure of the sentence. There's no way of stopping someone from combining meaningful individual words in a structure that makes sense, in such a way that the resulting sentence can't be tested. E.g., suppose I say, "I have an invisible, inaudible, intangible, and otherwise undetectable turtle." Every word in that is clearly meaningful, and they are combined in a way that makes sense, so the sentence *should* count as meaningful (given compositionality of meaning). Yet it can't be tested, so the positivist would have to say it's meaningless. Since compositionality is more initially plausible than verificationism, we should reject verificationism.

v. Finally, *pace* the positivists, there seem to be many examples of synthetic, a priori knowledge. But I'll talk about that in §10.5 below, when we discuss the motivations for rationalism.

10.4. Quine's Radical Empiricism

10.4.1. Quine's View

Remember how I said that 20th-century philosophers were falling all over themselves trying to prove their extreme devotion to scientism? Well, one enterprising philosopher, Willard van Orman Quine, found a way to be even more extreme than the positivists: He decided to reject even *analytic* a priori knowledge.

This goes back to his famous annoying paper, "Two Dogmas of Empiricism" (1951), in which Quine denies that there is any clear distinction between analytic and synthetic statements. Because people have talked a lot about this article, I suppose I should tell you something about it so you won't be caught off guard if you encounter some crazy Quinean.

One thing Quine does is to mention difficult cases (or at least *one* difficult case) for the analytic/synthetic distinction: He says that he can't tell whether "All green things are extended" is analytic. (*Note:* "Extended" just means that a thing has a nonzero length in at least one spatial dimension.)

The other major thing Quine does is to attack attempts to define "analytic". Above, we characterized an analytic statement as one that can be transformed into a logical truth by substituting *synonymous* expressions. But Quine says he doesn't understand what *synonymy* is.

Of course, synonymous expressions are generally understood as those that have the same meaning. But Quine also says that he doesn't understand what a *meaning* is, and indeed that he does not believe in such things. (Not that he thinks all words are meaningless, but he does not think there is such an object as "a meaning".)

Quine was writing when positivism was popular, so many philosophers at the time would have said that A is synonymous with B if and only if the way that you would verify that A applies is the same as the way that you would verify that B applies. (E.g., the way to verify that someone is a "bachelor" is the same as the way to verify that he is an "unmarried man".) Quine doesn't like this because he thinks that individual statements *do not have* determinate verification conditions. Whether some piece of evidence counts as supporting some statement depends upon the rest of one's belief system; two people with different background beliefs could differ on whether E is evidence for or against H. So there aren't in general verification conditions for individual sentences, so you can't use that to explain meaning or synonymy. Instead, you can only empirically test a whole belief system (this view is known as **confirmation holism**).

Quine also disagrees that there are any statements that can never be disconfirmed (as most people say of analytic statements). He holds that any statement, even statements of logic, could be given up under some circumstances. The best I can do to make this seem plausible is to allude to quantum mechanics, which some people interpret as supporting a rejection of the law of excluded middle (e.g., there can be a particle that is definitely in a certain box, but neither in the left half nor the right half). So on Quine's view, everything is empirical.

10.4.2. Objections

Let's start with Quine's example, "All green things are extended": Is it a problem that it is unclear whether this is analytic or synthetic?

I think not. First, *most* concepts have difficult cases where it is unclear whether the concept applies; that hardly means that the concept is useless, confused, fails to pick out any aspect of reality, or anything like that. E.g., the existence of things on the borderline between red and orange doesn't mean that nothing is red.

Perhaps Quine would say that the analytic/synthetic distinction is supposed to be a qualitative, not quantitative distinction, so there shouldn't be any borderline cases. But this isn't so obvious; some ways of characterizing the distinction enable it to be a difference of degree. E.g., some would say that S is analytic provided that a disposition to accept S is a test of linguistic competence. There can be degrees of satisfying this condition.

Second, the case isn't really so hard anyway. Can you substitute synonymous expressions into the sentence "All green things are extended" and thereby turn it into a logical truth? I see no way of doing that. There is no verbal definition of "green", only an "ostensive definition", so to speak (the way one explains "green" is by pointing to examples of green things, not by giving a description of greenness). So there doesn't seem to be anything to substitute for "green". So it looks like the sentence is synthetic.

Now let's turn to Quine's attacks on proposed definitions of analyticity. "Analytic" is a philosopher's technical term, so Quine is certainly right to insist on an explanation of its meaning. But a perfectly reasonable explanation has been given using familiar English words. Quine's response is to claim not to understand one of the words in the explanation ("synonymy"). This word, too, can be explained using other familiar English words. But then Quine claims not to understand one of those words ("meaning").

This is really too much. Once a term has been explained in ordinary English words, we don't then have to define those ordinary English words, and then define the words in *those* definitions. There would be no difficulty showing any concept to be problematic if we impose demands like that (see §2.6). "Synonymous" is an ordinary English word, which is being used in its ordinary sense, so one should not pretend not to understand it. When someone explains that synonymous expressions are those with the same meaning, one should not then pretend not to understand "meaning".

Anyway, however it be defined, there certainly seems to be *some* distinction that philosophers are making when they talk about "analytic" and "synthetic" statements. If you give a list of "analytic" statements, almost everyone can see their similarity to each other, and anyone can continue the list with many more examples that they have not previously been told—"All sisters are siblings", "All octagons have eight sides", etc. I have never before seen the "octagons" statement used as an example of an analytic statement, yet I know that it counts as analytic, and any philosopher who accepts the analytic/synthetic distinction is going to agree on the classification of that statement. This shows that there is some difference between the things we call "analytic" and the things we call "synthetic". Hereafter, then, I'll assume that there are indeed such things as analytic and synthetic statements.

10.5. Rationalism

10.5.1. The Rationalist Creed

The main alternative to empiricism is **rationalism**. Rationalists think that it *is* possible to know substantive facts about the world in a way that doesn't rest on observation, and hence that there *is* synthetic a priori knowledge.

There are two versions of rationalism, which we could call the *nativist* and the *intuitionist* view. The **nativist** view is that the synthetic, a priori knowledge is *innate*, so it is somehow built into your mind from birth. This is Plato's view; see his dialogue, the *Meno*, in which he argues (or imagines Socrates arguing) that the soul had awareness of abstract objects before birth, which it forgets upon birth and then has to be *reminded* of.

Since Plato, however, few people have taken the nativist approach. Most rationalists are **intuitionists**, in the following sense (but note that the word "intuitionism" has other uses in philosophy): They think that our synthetic a priori knowledge comes from a non-observational cognitive faculty, that is, one that is distinct from the five senses, introspection, and memory. This faculty is sometimes called "reason" or "the intellect" or "the understanding". The *faculty* is innate (just as the capacities for sense perception, introspection, and memory are innate), but the *particular deliverances* of it are not innate but acquired. You have to exercise your faculties at some time after your birth in order to acquire any particular items of knowledge.

10.5.2. Examples of Synthetic A Priori Knowledge

The irony of the empiricism/rationalism debate is that the empiricists base their view on a priori reasoning, while the rationalists base their view on empirical reasoning. I've explained the first part of that above (§10.2.3). Here's what I mean by the second part: The main reason people are rationalists is not that they thought about it and saw intuitively that synthetic, a priori knowledge was possible. The main reason is that they *looked* for examples of knowledge, and they saw some that appear to be synthetic, a priori.[88]

The axioms of a mathematical system are good examples. In general, these axioms are not analytic, since otherwise one wouldn't bother to state them as axioms; one would just state the definitions and then deduce the "axioms" from them (in which case the so-called axioms would actually be *theorems*, not axioms). Thus, the following look like synthetic a priori truths:

> The shortest path between two points is a straight line.
> For any numbers x and y, $(x+y) = (y+x)$.
> The probability of (A & B) equals the probability of A times the probability of B given A.
> For any things x and y, there is a set containing just those things, $\{x, y\}$.

Those axioms are from geometry, arithmetic, probability theory, and set theory, respectively. Axioms like these are needed to develop mathematical systems.

Another example is the field of ethics. For example:

> One should not cause harm for no reason.
> Other things being equal, it is better to have more enjoyment rather than less.
> One should not cause injustices for no reason.
> It is unjust to punish a person for a crime he did not commit.
> Honesty is a virtue.
> If x is better than y and y is better than z, then x is better than z.

---

[88] Admittedly, you don't literally see this with your eyes, so it's not completely empirical. But the approach of generalizing from examples is broadly empiricist in spirit, as opposed to the approach of laying down general axioms from which to deduce what must be the case.

None of the above statements can be derived from the laws of logic with substitution of synonymous expressions. So those are all synthetic. Furthermore, you can't perceive evaluative properties, such as goodness, virtue, or ought-to-be-done-ness, with the five senses. (Goodness doesn't look like anything, etc.) You also can't infer evaluative conclusions solely from descriptive, non-evaluative premises (see §15.3). So our evaluative knowledge has to be a priori. So the above are examples of synthetic a priori knowledge.

There are also a large number of miscellaneous necessary truths about various different subject matters, e.g.,

> Nothing can be completely red and also completely blue.
> If x is inside y and y is inside z, then x is inside z.
> All green things are extended.
> Time is one-dimensional.
> For any two moments, one is earlier than the other.
> The truths of arithmetic are necessary.
> There could have been ten planets in the solar system.

Again, you can't turn any of those into a logical truth by substituting synonymous expressions.

10.5.3. The Case for A Prioricity

Wait—why should we regard all those things as *a priori*? The basic, intuitive idea is that you don't have to make any observations to check on those things because you can see that they are all necessary; they could not be otherwise. For instance, you know in advance that you're never going to find anything completely red and completely blue. No matter what an object looks like, you won't say that it's both red and blue all over, so there is no need to look.

Here is a more developed and maybe sharper argument. First, note that in general, if p depends on q for its justification, then if q is false, p does not constitute knowledge. This is the lesson of the original Gettier cases (§2.4): In the Gettier cases, a person has a justified, true belief that is based on a false (though justified) premise. Everyone agrees that this isn't knowledge.

Therefore, *if* some belief depends for its justification on observations, then if those observations are false, the belief doesn't count as knowledge. Take, for example, my belief that nothing can be completely blue and completely red. *If* that belief is justified on the basis of some observations, then if those observations are false, I don't really know that nothing can be completely blue and completely red.

You can imagine a situation in which *all* my observations would be false. For instance, maybe I am (and always have been) a brain in a vat. Obviously, I don't think this is plausible, but it is *possible*, and that's all that matters right now. Given what we've said above, we can conclude: If empiricism is true, then if I'm a brain in a vat, I don't know that nothing is completely red and completely blue.

But it's false that if I'm a BIV, I don't know that. Of course, if I'm a BIV, then I don't know whether there actually *are* any red things or blue things in the real world outside my vat. But I still know that *if* there are any red things, they aren't blue. Since I know that's true whether or not I'm a BIV, it must be that my justification for "Nothing is completely red and completely blue" does not depend on observations. So it's a priori.

In case you want to see the formalization of the argument: Let

$E =$ [My knowledge that nothing is completely red and completely blue is empirical].
$F =$ [All my observations are false].
$B =$ [I am a brain in a vat].
$K =$ [I know that nothing is completely red and completely blue].

1.	$E \to (F \to \sim K)$.	Premise.
2.	$B \to F$.	Premise.
3.	$E \to (B \to \sim K)$.	From 1, 2.
4.	$\sim(B \to \sim K)$.	Premise.
5.	$\sim E$.	From 3, 4; modus tollens.

10.5.4. But How Can That Be??

As indicated earlier (§10.2.2), the main reason people resist rationalism isn't that they can't think of any examples of synthetic a priori knowledge. It is that they can't see, theoretically, how it is possible to have synthetic a priori knowledge. For all that I've said so far, I still haven't answered that. ☹

The rationalist's answer to that is the least satisfying part of the rationalist program. Typically, we rationalists just say some vague stuff about "grasping the natures of abstract objects" and such like. I'm no exception—that's just what I'm about to do here.[89]

First, though, let me tell you a bit of rationalistic metaphysics. There is a famous distinction between *universals* and *particulars*. A particular is what it sounds like—just an individual thing or event or state of affairs, the sort of thing that exists or occurs at a particular place and time.[90] A universal, on the other hand, is something that multiple other things can *have in common*. A universal, in other words, can be *predicated of* more than one thing. For instance,

---

[89] I roughly follow Bertrand Russell's account from *The Problems of Philosophy*.
[90] Except mental particulars, which might be non-spatial.

yellow is a universal, because yellow can be predicated of, e.g., the sun and a lemon. That's a fancy way of saying they can both be yellow.

Particulars, on the other hand, can't be predicated of anything; they are only *subjects* of predicates. That is, a particular has properties and relations to other things but is not itself a property or relation that anything else has. For instance, the Empire State Building is a particular; it has properties and stands in relations to things, and it isn't itself a property of something, nor is it a relationship between anything and anything else.

There is a debate in metaphysics about whether universals really exist and whether they are mind-independent. This isn't a metaphysics book, so I won't go into that debate in detail. Here, I'll just say briefly that I believe in universals because of trivial arguments like this:

1. Yellow is a color. (Premise.)
2. [Yellow is a color] entails [yellow exists]. (Premise.)
3. So yellow exists. (From 1, 2.)
4. The sun and lemons are yellow. (Premise.)
5. So yellow can be predicated of more than one thing. (From 4.)
6. So yellow is a universal. (From 5.)
7. So at least one universal exists. (From 3, 6.)

The conclusion is highly controversial; nevertheless, I think it's trivially true.[91]

Once we accept that universals exist, we can wonder how we are aware of them. Briefly, I think that when one understands a concept, one is thereby grasping, or being directly aware of the nature of, a universal. For instance, when you understand the concept YELLOW, you are grasping the nature of yellowness. When you understand the concept FOUR, you grasp the nature of fourness. (And yes, in my view, fourness is a universal: It is the property that any four things have in common with any other four things.[92]) Of course, it is possible to have a better or worse understanding of a concept, and hence of the universal the concept refers to. So merely possessing a concept does not guarantee one perfect knowledge. But one must understand a universal to some degree in order to count as having a concept.

You should accept that we grasp some universals, because otherwise all knowledge would be impossible. Knowledge (in the sense we're talking about throughout this book) is always knowledge *of some proposition*, and every

---

[91] Conclusion (7) is compatible with the view that universals exist only *in* particulars, or dependent on particulars. I, however, hold that universals exist necessarily (this view is sometimes called "**Platonism**"). This is because I think premises (1) and (2) are not only true but *necessary*; hence, yellow exists necessarily. So yellow would exist even if no yellow particulars existed.

[92] See Byeong-Uk Yi's "Is Two a Property?" in the *Journal of Philosophy* (1999).

proposition must contain at least one predicate, which is or contains a universal. If you did not grasp the universal, you couldn't grasp (and so could not know) the proposition. For instance, even to possess the humble knowledge that Donald is fat, you must understand the proposition [Donald is fat], which means that (among other things) you must understand *fatness*, which is a universal.

Some people resist this conclusion. As near as I can guess, the main reason is a quasi-emotional sense that all this talk of "grasping universals" *sounds weird*. This vague feeling distracts people from the fact that the actual, literal content of the talk is obviously, trivially true. If you're being bothered by the feeling of weirdness right now, I'd like to suggest that the "weirdness" is probably not an objective property but just a subjective feeling in you, and further that it probably is not particularly evidentially relevant to the actual facts. (I've had a hard time getting people to explain exactly what "weirdness" is or how it's supposed to be evidentially relevant.)

Now, when one understands the nature of some universal, one is thereby inherently in a position to see some of the properties that it has and some of its relations to other universals that one grasps. For example, if you grasp YELLOW and you grasp RED, then you can directly see that yellow and red are incompatible properties. Therefore, you can know that nothing is completely yellow and completely red. Someone who could not see this would have to not know what yellow is or not know what red is.

All a priori knowledge is like this: It is, or derives from, knowledge of the properties and relations of universals. This is equally true of the analytic as of the synthetic a priori. For instance, if you understand what *being a bachelor* is, then you can see that it contains the property of *being unmarried*; this is a relationship between the universals *bachelorhood* and *unmarriedness*. On this view, *pace* the empiricists, analytic and synthetic a priori knowledge have the same source.

10.6. Kantianism

10.6.1. The Two-Page Summary

The third major view about a priori knowledge, besides empiricism and rationalism, is known as **Kantianism**, after Immanuel Kant. Kant's philosophy is incredibly confusing and complex, but here I'll give you a simplified and only moderately confusing rendition of it. It contains the following major ideas.

i. *There is synthetic a priori knowledge.* He agrees with the rationalists about that. As examples, he cites arithmetic (though most people disagree with Kant about that one, as most think arithmetic is analytic), geometry, and some metaphysical principles, such as that every change must have a cause. He even cites conservation of matter as synthetic a priori (of course, most people today think that's empirical).

> **Interlude: Immanuel Kant**
>
> Immanuel Kant (1724–1804) was a great German philosopher who spent his entire life in one town and was very anal. People set their clocks by him because his daily routine was so predictable. He defended a very staunch, absolutist conception of morality that included such ideas as that it is *always* wrong to tell a lie, no matter what the consequences (even if, for example, the lie could save many lives). He claims that this absolutist morality follows from the nature of rationality. Despite its insanity, his is one of the major theories that is regularly taught (alongside utilitarianism) in ethics classes.
>
> More importantly for us, he produced a fascinating and highly original work called the *Critique of Pure Reason*. The book introduced the analytic-synthetic distinction, argued that we have some synthetic a priori knowledge, and tried to explain how this is possible. More about this in the main text.
>
> If you're thinking of reading Kant's work, however, you should be warned that nearly everything he wrote is incredibly confusing, partly because the ideas are abstract and complex, but also partly because it is absolutely horribly written. He is a master of the long, complicated sentence filled with idiosyncratic, abstract jargon (and the jargon doesn't always have a consistent use[93]). Some people spend their careers arguing about what the hell Kant meant. If you want to know Kant's views, a better bet would be to read some secondary literature, such as C.D. Broad's exposition, *Kant: An Introduction*.

ii. *The existence of synthetic a priori knowledge is a huge mystery*, and the rationalists have not adequately explained it. Kant basically agrees with the empiricists that, in order to have knowledge of mind-independent reality, one would have to rely on experience. In fact, the argument of section 10.2.2 above is inspired by Kant.[94]

---

[93] Here's an example. The following two passages appear one page away from each other: (1) "A priori modes of knowledge are entitled pure when there is no admixture of anything empirical. Thus, for instance, the proposition, 'every alteration has its cause', while an a priori proposition, is not a pure proposition…"; (2) "[I]t is easy to show that there actually are in human knowledge judgments which are … pure a priori judgments. … If we seek an example from the understanding in its quite ordinary employment, the proposition, 'every alteration must have a cause', will serve our purpose" (*Critique of Pure Reason* [1787], Kemp Smith translation, B3, B4). I charitably suppose that he was merely using "pure" inconsistently.

[94] *Critique*, Bxvi-Bxviii.

iii. *Synthetic a priori knowledge reflects a structure the mind imposes on the world.* This is the distinctive Kantian idea. We can't simply perceive objects as they are in themselves; we can only perceive them through the particular cognitive faculties that we possess, and certain features of our experience of the world are explained by the nature of our own cognitive faculties, rather than by the external world itself. The synthetic a priori truths are things that have to be true about everything that we experience *because* our minds are structured so as to always represent things in accordance with those principles. For example, space is not an entity that exists apart from us but rather an artifact of our way of representing the world. Our minds use a Euclidean space to represent external objects, and that is why Euclidean geometry is necessarily true of everything that we can observe. Similarly, time doesn't exist apart from us but is a structure created by our minds to represent mental states themselves.

iv. *We can never know things in themselves.* This is a corollary of the previous point. Because we always represent things using space and time, but things in themselves are non-spatial and non-temporal, we can never truly understand things in themselves. The synthetic a priori truths are only guaranteed to be true within the realm of possible human experience and cannot validly be applied beyond that range.

Here are some quotations apropos of points (*iii*) and (*iv*):

> If intuition must conform to the constitution of the objects, I do not see how we could know anything of the latter a priori; but if the object (as object of the senses) must conform to the constitution of our faculty of intuition, I have no difficulty in conceiving such a possibility.

> [W]e can know *a priori* of things only what we ourselves put into them.

> [W]e can never transcend the limits of possible experience.[95]

Notice that Kant occupies a middle ground between the traditional empiricist and the traditional rationalist: The empiricist said that there is no a priori knowledge of mind-independent reality, so there is no synthetic a priori knowledge. The rationalist said there *is* synthetic a priori knowledge, so there *is* a priori knowledge of mind-independent reality. Kant says there is synthetic a priori knowledge but there *isn't* any a priori knowledge of mind-independent reality.

---

[95] *Critique*, Bxvii, Bxviii, Bxix.

10.6.2. The Glasses Analogy

Point (*iii*) in my summary of Kantianism is the most important and the most difficult to grasp part of Kant's philosophy. One analogy people sometimes use to help explain it is this. Suppose you find that everything in the world is green. You wonder why this is. Then you discover that you're wearing green-tinted glasses. Due to the glasses, everything you can see is automatically going to be "green" (i.e., it will appear to you as green). Suppose further that the glasses are permanently glued to your face. Then you would never be able to know the real colors of things but only the colors they appear to you.

Though that example is somewhat helpful, there are some disanalogies. In the green glasses example, you would be *misperceiving* the colors of things. E.g., you would think that a banana was green when in fact it is yellow. But Kant does not want to say that we are *misperceiving* objects around us; we're not just suffering from sensory illusions, nor is there some other way that we could have perceived things that would have been more "accurate". We are generally (except when you're on drugs, etc.) correctly perceiving things given our cognitive faculties. Also, in the green glasses example, you wouldn't have the sense that everything was *necessarily* green, in the way that synthetic a priori truths are supposed to be necessary. So the analogy is at best imperfect.

10.6.3. Primary and Secondary Qualities

Here is another analogy. What Kant thinks about external reality in general is like what some philosophers (e.g., Locke) thought about *some aspects* of the world, particularly what they called **secondary qualities**.[96] Traditionally, the "secondary qualities" of objects are said to include such properties as color, smell, taste, sound, and temperature. This is contrasted with the **primary qualities**, which include such properties as shape, size, motion, mass, and number.

What's the difference between these two sets of qualities? Well, roughly speaking, a lot of people have thought that the primary qualities are more real, or more objective, or that our perceptions of them are more true to their natures, than is the case for secondary qualities. People put the point in different ways. Sometimes, people say that external objects aren't really colored and color is only in our minds. Or that red is just a disposition to cause a certain kind of sensation in us. Or that secondary qualities are constituted and explained by primary qualities in the atoms and molecules that things are made

---

[96] Kant himself draws this comparison in the *Prolegomena to Any Future Metaphysics* (1783), remark II.

up of, where these primary qualities are the fundamental properties in the world.

Why would we think that primary and secondary qualities differ in some such way? Well, one point is that our fundamental scientific theories explain everything using primary qualities. Atoms have locations, sizes, shapes, masses, and speeds; they do not have colors, tastes, smells, or temperatures. When scientists explain why you see a tomato as red, the most fundamental explanation will be in terms of primary qualities, not secondary qualities—it will have to do with wavelengths of light, and energy levels of photons, and electrical discharges in your neurons, and so on. They don't actually have to use the concept RED.

Now, I don't want to have a debate about whether this view about secondary qualities is *right*. That's not our point here. I just want you to see how someone might think that secondary qualities are somehow less objective than primary qualities. Imagine that that is your view. You don't exactly want to say that secondary qualities are illusory, though; that is, you want to distinguish between a normal perception of a banana in which the banana looks yellow, and a distorted perception in which, say, it looks green because someone has put on green tinted glasses. The latter is the "illusion", the former the "correct perception". But you want to say nevertheless that even the "correct" color perception does not represent the real, underlying, objective nature of the object as it is in itself. You might think that what is in the banana in itself is just some chemicals with dispositions to reflect various different proportions of light at different frequencies (a "spectral reflectance distribution", to those in the know)—but that's not what our experience immediately presents.

Now imagine Kant comes along and says: "Oh yeah, I agree with you about the secondary qualities. But I have news for you: *The primary qualities are like that too!* Our perceptions of shape, size, location, and motion *also* fail to represent the real, underlying, objective nature of the object as it is in itself. Just as *you* think that a collection of primary qualities explains the appearance of secondary qualities, I think that there are some *other* properties (unknowable to us) that explain the appearance of both primary and secondary qualities."

Kant would not want to say that all our perceptions are illusions; that is, he'd make a distinction between a "correct perception" in which your sensations are being caused by the sort of (unknowable, thing-in-itself) properties that normally cause sensations of that type, and a "distorted perception", a.k.a. "illusion", in which your sensations are caused in some abnormal fashion.

10.6.4. Another Analogy

Here is a final analogy. Let's say that I draw a graph showing the correlation between IQ and height (figure 5). I collect data on a bunch of people and plot their locations in the IQ-height space. To make things interesting, let's suppose that I use an unusual scale for the IQ dimension, such that an IQ of 100 gets plotted at position 1 on the y-axis, an IQ of 200 gets plotted at position 1.5, 400 would get plotted at 1.75, and so on. (And I do everything else consistent with that.) I do this to guarantee that all IQ's, however smart someone might be, fit between $y = 0$ and $y = 2$ on my graph. (I have a limited amount of paper, you see.)

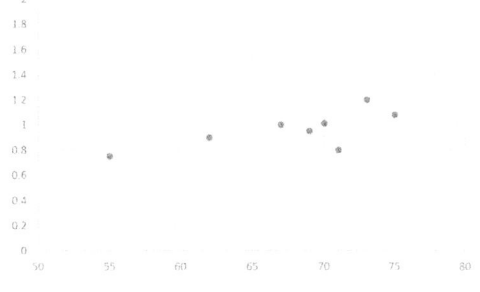

Figure 5: The height-IQ space

Then it will be a *necessary truth* that everyone is between $y = 0$ and $y = 2$ in the IQ-height space, as represented by me. But this necessary truth doesn't reflect any substantive fact about the people whom I am graphing. It is just an artifact of my graphing conventions, i.e., my method of representing the IQ-height combinations of people. So that is like how, in Kant's view, the synthetic a priori truths reflect something about our way of representing objects.

Now suppose there was someone who couldn't ever meet the people my graph was based on and in fact had no independent knowledge of what "IQ" or "height" was. *All* this person knows about the IQ-height space is my graph. This person could know some things about people and how their IQ's and heights are related. He's not suffering from *illusions*—all the information in my graph is correct. I really got everyone's IQ and height, and I plotted everyone's data correctly, given my graphing conventions. At the same time, in an important sense, the person would not be able to understand the true reality underlying the graph. That's like how, on Kant's view, we cannot understand the true reality underlying our experiences of the external world.

10.6.5. Weird Things about Kant

That's enough explanation of Kant's central idea. Now here are some weird things about Kant's views:

i. *His causal subjectivism:* In Kant's view, causation is not an objective phenomenon, any more than space and time are. So "things in themselves" can't really *cause* our experiences. This makes it hard to understand how things in themselves are supposed to be related to our experiences such that our experiences count as appearances *of* those things-in-themselves.

ii. *His psychological subjectivism:* Kant denies that we are directly aware even of our own minds as they are in themselves; he says we can only know how our minds *appear* to us. This is super-weird on its own, and it also makes it hard to understand what an appearance is supposed to be.

iii. *Weird views about time:* Kant claims that *time* is our way of representing the internal (mental) world, as opposed to the external world. He also says that arithmetic is knowledge about time. It's hard to see how these things are supposed to be true. Hypothesis: Kant liked symmetry too much. He had two main branches of mathematics to explain. He knew *geometry* was about *space*, which is where *external* objects appear; so, out of sheer love of symmetry, he decided that *arithmetic* must be about *time*, and that is where *internal* objects appear.

10.6.6. Objections

Kant is the most interesting thinker in history who is completely wrong. Here are a few objections.

i. *What is the problem with synthetic a priori knowledge?* Kant's whole program is motivated by the idea that synthetic a priori knowledge is mysterious and couldn't exist if our minds had to conform to reality. But there is little to no argument for that assumption, which rationalists reject.

ii. *How can Kant talk about things in themselves?* Kant says that we can't know anything about things in themselves, which raises the question of how he can even say that *there are* any such things. It's hard to see how we can even refer to, let alone have compelling evidence for, something that we have no knowledge or understanding of.

iii. *Synthetic a priori knowledge* does *apply to things in themselves*. On Kant's view, synthetic a priori truths, including arithmetic, fail to apply to things in themselves. This seems wrong: One thing-in-itself plus two things-in-themselves must equal three things-in-themselves (whether or not things-in-themselves are perceivable). My reason for believing that is *the same* as my reason for believing that one cat plus two cats equal three cats—those seem equally obvious, in the same way. So there's no reason why we would accept arithmetic as necessary and synthetic a priori to begin with yet not accept that it applies to things in themselves.

iv. *Why are the synthetic a priori truths a priori and necessary?* Kant claims to explain this by appealing to the idea of structures that the mind imposes on experience. Let's say that's true—say the human mind imposes some kind of structure on everything we experience. It doesn't follow from that that we would have any a priori knowledge about that, nor that any of it would be necessary. As cognitive scientists will tell you, most facts about the human mind are contingent and can only be known empirically. Why wouldn't it just be a contingent, empirical truth that our minds impose such-and-such structure? And if that's the case, then the supposedly synthetic a priori truths that result from that structure should themselves be contingent and empirical.[97]

v. *Kant doesn't explain all examples of synthetic a priori knowledge.* He picks certain interesting and important examples and tries to explain them, notably arithmetic, geometry, and metaphysical principles about time, causality, and morality. But there are synthetic a priori truths all over the place, not just in those areas (see §10.3.2). And by the way, although he allegedly explains (what he considers) the fundamental principle(s) of morality, the "categorical imperative", he doesn't explain all the other necessary evaluative truths that ethicists have noticed (see §10.3.2 again).

vi. *What are "appearances" and "things-in-themselves"?* Kant talks all the time about "appearances", which are supposedly all we can know, and "things in themselves", which we supposedly can never know. But he is never very clear about what these things are. Sometimes, it sounds like they are two separate classes of objects; other times, it sounds like they are two ways of viewing the same set of objects. Sometimes, it sounds like appearances are mental representations that things-in-themselves cause in us; other times, it sounds like appearances are the things we are aware *of*, the *objects* of those representations. Probably Kant was not clear on this in his own mind.

10.7. Conclusion

Is there a priori knowledge? Yes, plenty. First, almost everyone agrees that there is *analytic* a priori knowledge, knowledge of things that are true by definition, such as that all grandmothers are mothers.

Some philosophers, following Quine, reject the notion of analyticity because analyticity is allegedly hard to define. However, this argument depends upon implausibly claiming that the ordinary notions of SYNONYMY and MEANING are obscure. Some also cite allegedly difficult-to-classify sentences, such as "all green things are extended". But these cases are not that difficult to classify, and anyway many perfectly good concepts have borderline cases.

The main issue is whether there is *synthetic* a priori knowledge. Empiricists think there is none because it is hard to understand how we could have it. However, this argument appears self-defeating, as it is an a priori argument for

---

[97] Objections (*iii*) and (*iv*) appear in Russell's *The Problems of Philosophy*, ch. 8.

a synthetic claim. More generally, normative epistemological claims, including empiricism itself, are synthetic and non-empirical.

Logical positivists combine empiricism with the verification criterion of meaning, which claims that sentences are meaningless if they cannot be empirically tested. This principle may rest on a confusion between truth and verification. It also conflicts with the compositionality of meaning, and there seem to be many counter-examples to it.

Immanuel Kant argued that there is synthetic a priori knowledge and that it could only be explained by the hypothesis that the human mind inherently imposes some structure on everything that we are aware of. The synthetic a priori truths are artifacts of this structure. A corollary is that we can only know things as they appear, not things in themselves.

However, this view makes it mysterious how we can even refer to "things in themselves" or know that they exist. Kant only directly tries to explain *some* examples of synthetic a priori knowledge, and it's not clear how one would explain the rest. It's not even clear that the theory explains the cases it is directly designed for, as the existence of a structure that our minds impose on the world would seem to be a contingent, empirical fact. Lastly, Kant's theory can't explain the fact that arithmetic applies to everything, including "things in themselves", if such there be.

The rationalists, in my view, have the best position. They give various examples of synthetic a priori knowledge, such as the knowledge that the shortest path between two points is a straight line, that nothing can be entirely red and entirely blue, and that "better than" is transitive. These things are synthetic since you cannot derive them from laws of logic by substituting synonymous expressions. You can see that they are also a priori since, even if all your observations are false (e.g., because you're a brain in a vat), you still know these things to be true.

The most popular rationalist explanation of the a priori is that a priori knowledge (whether analytic or synthetic) is or derives from knowledge of the properties and relations of abstract objects known as "universals". Universals are things that can be predicated of multiple particulars. All knowledge requires grasping universals, since a universal always features in the predicate of a proposition. When one intellectually grasps a universal, one is thereby able to see some of its properties and relations to other universals.

The underlying issue we've been dealing with is: What is the role of *reason* in human knowledge? Does reason produce some substantive knowledge of its own, or does it only make inferences starting from information provided by observation? Empiricists embrace the latter answer. From what we've said in this chapter, however, the former answer seems correct.

11. Memory

In this chapter, we discuss how you're justified in believing what you remember.

11.1. The Puzzle of Forgotten Evidence

I know a lot of things about the world for which I am not currently entertaining the evidence. I know, for instance, that Sudan is located in Africa. I don't know when or how I learned that. I assume it was because someone told me, or I saw it on a map, or I read it in a book, but I don't remember who or what the source was or why I thought it was reliable. I just remember that Sudan is in Africa. Since I first learned that, I probably had many experiences corroborating it, but I don't specifically remember any of them either. This raises the question: How do I really know that Sudan is in Africa?

Let's assume that taking the word of other (trustworthy) people is a legitimate way of acquiring knowledge and justified belief. Still, even if my belief was justified at the time I acquired it, it is not exactly clear why I am *right now* justified in believing that Sudan is in Africa, given that I don't even know how I learned it to begin with and certainly don't have my initial evidence (whatever it was) before my mind at the moment. If a skeptic challenged me, I would have essentially nothing to say to her. Fortunately, skeptics rarely challenge specific memory beliefs like this, preferring instead to attack sensory perception in general. They seem oddly content to assume that *if* we have knowledge of the external world in general, then there's no problem about knowing where Sudan is located. In fact, this isn't obvious at all.

Notice how far-reaching this problem is. *Most* of the things that I know are things that I learned in the past and no longer have the original evidence for before my mind. Most of the time, I don't recall what the evidence was. So this is a puzzle for most human knowledge.

11.2. Four Theories of Memory Justification

I can think of four accounts of how memory beliefs are justified.[98] Let's consider how each might address the above puzzle.

11.2.1. The Inferential Theory

First, perhaps memory beliefs require inferential justification. That is, memory beliefs, if and when they are justified, are justified because you can construct some kind of argument for the reliability of your memory.

Well, this really is an ill-fated theory. It is extremely difficult to think of how such an argument could go without begging the question. You might try testing your memory and then, if things go well, making an inductive inference. For instance, I seem to remember where I live. I go to that location and find a place that looks the way I was expecting. Later, I seem to remember a certain person's name. I call the person by that name, and they respond appropriately. And so on. After numerous experiences like this, I conclude that my memory is reliable.

The problem: All of this *relies on memory*. I can't do all these tests simultaneously, so when I come to make the inductive inference, I have to *remember* that I have successfully tested my memory on many occasions. This looks circular. If I don't, at time t, already know that my memory is reliable, then I can't rely on my memory of having tested my memory.

Furthermore, I can't be going through this argument *constantly*, every time I want to rely on memory for something (if I had to do that, I would be unable to go through any other reasoning to learn anything else). So, after establishing the reliability of memory, I would subsequently have to *remember* that I had done so. At time t_2, when I am no longer thinking of the argument for the reliability of memory, I would need to rely on my memory that my memory is reliable. That again looks circular.

Even if I came up with some other argument for the reliability of memory, there is a threat that it, too, would be epistemically circular (in the sense defined in §6.3.2). If the argument was even slightly complex, so that I could not hold the entire argument in my mind at once, I would have to rely on memory in order to carry out the reasoning. E.g., when I got to step 3, I would have to rely on my memory that I successfully justified step 2.

---

[98] The Foundational and Preservation theories discussed below appear in the epistemology literature. I know of no one who holds the Inferential theory. The Dualistic theory is my own, from "The Problem of Memory Knowledge" (*Pacific Philosophical Quarterly*, 1999).

So all this really doesn't seem like it is going to work out. That is, *if* I need an argument for the reliability of memory in order to be justified in any beliefs that rely on memory, then there is no way that I am going to get that argument.

In case you're thinking that you'll just become a memory skeptic now, I'd like to point out that *that* conclusion would also be undermined. Since it took a nontrivial amount of time to go through the preceding reasoning, you'd have to rely on your memory to know that you completed an argument for memory skepticism. So the memory skeptic's position is worse than epistemically circular; it is self-undermining.

Now you might wonder why I'm complaining about epistemic circularity in this section, since I seemingly accepted some epistemic circularity as benign earlier (§6.3). Well, no one accepts *all* epistemic circularity. In particular, epistemic circularity could only be acceptable, at most, in the cases in which the belief-forming method you are using is foundational (it produces justification without the need of independent arguments for its reliability). And the Inferential Theory we're talking about in this subsection explicitly denies that memory is foundational. So on this theory, you should not be allowed to rely on memory in constructing an argument for the reliability of memory.

By the way, note also that it is possible to legitimately get evidence for thinking that your memory is *more* or *less* reliable than you initially thought it was, by doing the sort of tests described above. If the things you seem to remember frequently clash with other evidence, you should downgrade your opinion of your memory's reliability. If the things you seem to remember are often corroborated by other evidence, you should upgrade your opinion of your memory's reliability (if it wasn't very high to begin with). None of what I have said is meant to deny that. What I am denying is that you could start out with *no trust whatsoever* in your memory, and from there construct a cogent argument that memory is reliable.

11.2.2. The Foundational Theory

If the Inferential Theory fails, perhaps we should say that memory provides *foundational* justification for beliefs. This would address the problem of forgotten evidence: If I don't remember how I learned that Sudan is in Africa, that's okay, since I have the memory that Sudan is in Africa, and that memory itself gives me non-inferential justification to believe that Sudan is in Africa. Of course, this might be fallible and defeasible justification, so if I acquire specific reasons to doubt that Sudan is in Africa, that can override my memory. But in the absence of such reasons, the memory justifies the belief. (Compare §5.2.1.)

This view seemingly gives the right result in the Sudan example. But it seems to give the wrong result in two other kinds of cases. First:

> *Unforgotten Evidence:* I read an argument for mind/body dualism, which justifies me in believing dualism. A minute later, while still holding that argument in my mind, I also *remember that* dualism is true. On the Foundational Theory of memory, I now have *two* justifications for believing dualism: the inferential one (from the argument) and a new, foundational one. So now I am justifiably *more certain* (I have a higher degree of justification) that dualism is true.

This result seems wrong. In the (perhaps unusual) case where you still have your original justification for believing something in mind, your memory of that same proposition does not increase its justification.

Second:

> *Forgotten Irrationality:* I initially adopt the belief that I am immortal in a completely unjustified way—say, by wishful thinking. Later, I forget how I acquired the belief, but I continue to hold the belief in memory. (Stipulate that I also have no specific reasons to doubt my immortality.) On the Foundational Theory of memory, this *initially* unjustified belief is now *justified* because it now has a foundational source of justification, my memory, and I have no grounds for doubting the belief since I've forgotten that I adopted it irrationally.

This result, again, seems wrong. An irrational belief does not become rational when you forget how you adopted it.

11.2.3. The Preservation Theory

The preceding cases seem to support a third theory: Memory is not a source of justification at all; rather, memory merely *preserves* whatever justification one had for a belief at the time one adopted it. Thus, if a belief started out justified, then as long as you continue to remember it, it remains justified. The degree of justification cannot increase, nor can an unjustified belief become justified, since memory isn't a source of justification in itself. It just passes forward the initial degree of justification, so to speak. The degree of justification might even diminish over time, as memory is an imperfect preserver (as time passes, you should often become less certain of the things you remember, because you can't be sure you aren't misremembering).

The Preservation Theory clearly explains the Unforgotten Evidence case and the Forgotten Irrationality case. But now here is another case that it does less well with:

> *The Five Minute Hypothesis:* Imagine that "the world sprang into being five minutes ago, exactly as it then was, with a population that 'remembered' a wholly unreal past."[99] What would we now be justified in believing about our past?

I hope you agree that, if rational, we would still believe exactly what we now actually believe about the past—that Russia invaded Ukraine in 2022, that Barack Obama was elected President of the U.S. in 2008, and so on. In the five-minute hypothesis, everything would appear exactly as it does now, with no evidence whatever suggesting the world's recent origin, since the world would be in exactly the state that it is currently actually in. So if someone *didn't* accept these sorts of beliefs about the past, that person would have to be suffering from a psychotic break, just as someone in the actual world would be psychotic if they thought the world appeared five minutes ago.

This poses a problem for the Preservation Theory. On the Preservation Theory, memory can only preserve the justification we originally had for acquiring a belief. But in the Five Minute Hypothesis, we *had no* original justification for acquiring any of the beliefs that we "remember" from before 5 minutes ago. We did not ever learn of the Russian invasion of Ukraine on a newscast; that's just a false memory. If memory cannot produce justification, it must be that we would be unjustified in believing that Russia invaded Ukraine.

11.2.4. *The Dualistic Theory*

On the dualistic theory, there are two components to the justification of a belief: the subject's justification for *acquiring* the belief, and the subject's justification for *retaining* the belief. To say that a belief is justified *full stop* is to say that (*i*) the person was justified in acquiring the belief at some time, and (*ii*) the person was justified in keeping the belief since then.

How do we get justification for acquiring beliefs? Well, you can use your favorite theory of justification for that, whatever it is (see chs. 4–5). That isn't (normally) anything to do with memory. As to justification for *retaining* beliefs, that is easy to come by: You're justified in holding onto your beliefs as long as you continue to remember them and you have no specific reasons to change them.

This theory explains the above cases. I'm justified in thinking that Sudan is in Africa as long as I acquired that belief in a rational way, I've kept it in memory since then, and I haven't gotten any particular reasons to change it. All of these conditions are perfectly realistic.

---

[99] This is from Bertrand Russell, *The Analysis of Mind* (1921), lecture 9.

In the Unforgotten Evidence case, when the belief passes into memory I don't acquire a new, independent justification for it. Rather, I retain my original justification for *acquiring* the belief (but since I already have the belief at that point, there's nothing for me to do on that front), and I acquire a new justification for *retaining* it. Thus, the theory simply recommends that I *keep* the belief, not that I increase my confidence.

In the Forgotten Irrationality case, I have justification to retain the belief but I lacked justification to acquire it in the first place, so the Dualistic Theory says that the belief is unjustified overall.

In the Five Minute Hypothesis case, our beliefs about the past (from before 5 minutes ago) were all acquired five minutes ago when the world popped into existence. (Or perhaps each one is acquired when we first activate our dispositional memories about the things the belief is about?) In this case, the beliefs are *acquired by memory*. This is highly unusual, as memory normally only operates to retain a belief after one has acquired it by some other cognitive faculty. But in the case where you have false memories implanted into you, those memories are the actual source of your beliefs.

So to get the right verdict about the case, we just need to add the postulate that seemingly remembering something counts as a justified way of acquiring a belief, if indeed that is how one acquired it. Why might this be true? Perhaps because a memory is a kind of appearance, and we are justified in general in assuming that things are the way they appear (see §5.2).

This postulate does not reintroduce the problem with Forgotten Irrationality, because in the Forgotten Irrationality case, I didn't *acquire* the belief via memory. I acquired it via wishful thinking, then merely *retained* it via memory. So it remains the case that the belief had an unjustified acquisition method, despite its justified retention method.

Now here is a possible problem case for the Dualistic Theory:

> *Election:* It's 2020, and I'm looking forward to the U.S. Presidential Election. I'm completely convinced that Joe Biden is going to win. This belief is purely based on wishful thinking and my overwhelming hatred for the other major candidate. So my belief is clearly acquired in an irrational manner. I then hold on to this belief through election night (when it becomes the still-wishful belief that Joe Biden *has* won) and beyond. Over the succeeding months, I see many newscasts reporting Joe Biden as the winner. In January, I watch Joe Biden's inauguration. Over the next few years, I see many news items referring to Joe Biden as the President. Etc.

In this case, my belief starts out unjustified. It is perhaps still unjustified on election night (when the vote totals are very close and the other candidate claims to have won). But surely at some point, with the overwhelming evidence I receive, my belief becomes justified. A year into Biden's term, it would be ridiculous to say I still don't know who won the election.

But the Dualistic Theory seems to give the wrong result, since it says that, to be justified in thinking Joe Biden won, I must have had justification for acquiring the belief, and in this case my initial acquisition was unjustified.

This case calls for some reinterpretation/modification of the dualistic theory. The theory says that, to have a justified belief that p, one must have had *justification to acquire* the belief at some point. Interpret this as meaning that there must have been a time when one had some source of justification that, if one didn't already believe p at that time, *would* have justified one in adopting the belief. In the Election case, though my initial acquisition was unjustified, there is a later time (say, when I'm watching Biden being inaugurated on television) when, if I didn't already believe Biden was the election winner, I would be justified in adopting that belief based on the evidence I acquired at that time. Since that time, I was justified in retaining the belief. So the belief is justified overall.

That accounts for my *propositional* justification for [Joe Biden won the election]. My *doxastic* justification could be accounted for by saying that, although the compelling evidence that Joe Biden won didn't cause me to initially adopt the belief, it *reinforced* the belief and became a further source of my confidence that Biden won; in that sense, it was part of the basis for my belief. (See §2.3.3 on propositional vs. doxastic justification.) Alternately, if this isn't true—if the compelling evidence *doesn't* become part of my basis for thinking Biden won, then my belief remains doxastically unjustified.

11.3 Conclusion

Most of our knowledge at any given time consists of memories of things we learned previously. Usually, we no longer have the original justification for the belief available. Why are these memory beliefs justified?

One theory is that we need to construct an argument that memory is reliable. But there's no apparent way of doing that without relying on memory.

A second theory is that memory is a source of foundational justification. But that seems to imply that if you adopt a belief irrationally, then as soon as you forget how you adopted it, it becomes rational.

A third theory is that memory merely preserves the original justification for a belief, rather than producing any justification of its own. But this theory implies that in the Five Minute Hypothesis, all of our beliefs would be irrational.

The best theory holds that a belief is justified if and only if it was initially acquired in a rational way (where having false memories implanted into you counts as a rational way), *and* it was rationally retained since then (where the normal operation of memory counts as a rational retention method). This theory gives the right answers in the above cases.

12. Induction

In this chapter, we talk about whether and how inductive reasoning justifies beliefs.

12.1. The Problem of Induction

12.1.1. Background Concepts

In any piece of reasoning, you start from some information (your *premises*) and you draw some *conclusion* that you take to be supported by those premises.[100] There are two kinds of reasoning: deductive and non-deductive. In deductive reasoning, or **deduction**, you have some premises which allegedly *guarantee* the truth of your conclusion. (I said "allegedly" because there is such a thing as a *fallacious* deduction, in which the premises don't really support the conclusion in the way they're supposed to.) That is, it is (allegedly) logically impossible for the premises to be true and the conclusion to be false.

In **non-deductive** (or "non-demonstrative") **reasoning**, your premises are supposed to support the conclusion without absolutely guaranteeing it. That is, if the premises are true, then the conclusion is (allegedly) *more likely* to be true, but it wouldn't be absolutely impossible for the conclusion not to be true.

Maybe the most common kind of non-deductive inference is **induction**. Induction is a kind of reasoning in which you generalize from particular cases. You have premises that say that certain things have a certain property, and you conclude that some wider group of objects than just the ones mentioned in the premises possess that property.[101]

---

[100] Technically, some reasoning lacks premises. This can happen if you only use *assumptions* (as opposed to *premises*) for *reductio ad absurdum* or conditional proof. But this is a needlessly technical point for the main text. Anyway, this kind of reasoning only generates tautologies.

[101] By the way, note that the definition of "induction" is different from the definition of "non-deductive inference". Some books confusingly define induction to be the same as non-deductive inference. Some even give two different definitions of

Standard examples: You see the sun set every day of your life (that you've looked), so you conclude that the sun will set tomorrow as well. You observe 100 honey badgers, you find them all to be mean, so you infer that all honey badgers are mean. You read some student essays that begin with "Since the dawn of time, man has pondered …" and you conclude that a lot of students like talking about what has been pondered since the dawn of time.

This is an extremely common way of reasoning and is probably involved in almost all our knowledge. (But it actually *hasn't* been pondered since the dawn of time, in case you were wondering. Sorry if that makes you no longer interested.)

12.1.2. Hume's Skepticism

The Great Skeptic, David Hume (whom you remember for his defense of indirect realism in §9.3.1 above) came up with a famous argument for **inductive skepticism**, the thesis that the premises of an inductive argument never provide any support at all to the conclusion.[102]

> **Interlude: Hume's Psychology**
>
> Hume is standardly read as defending inductive skepticism, as discussed in the rest of this section. However, Hume never explicitly mentions "justification", nor does he say that we should give up our inductive beliefs or anything like that. His explicit thesis is a purely *psychological* one: It is that inductive beliefs are not *produced by the faculty of reason*; instead, we simply have an instinctive disposition to expect future events to develop in roughly the way things have gone in our experience.
>
> However, other philosophers (myself included) have found this psychological claim a lot less interesting than the skeptical thesis that Hume's discussion seemingly suggests. Hence, we like to read Hume as saying the more interesting thing, and that's what we talk about.

The original argument is a bit complex, but I'm going to skip some parts and boil it down to its essence. (Hume's discussion goes on for a while about the relation of cause and effect, but as you'll see, we don't need to go into that

---

induction—first saying basically that induction is non-deductive reasoning and then saying that induction is generalizing from cases. This is because even some professional philosophers are confused. They probably got confused by reading David Hume.

Another, smaller error is to define induction as generalizing from *observations*. The premises of an induction need not be observational, e.g., you can have an inductive argument for thinking that every even number is the sum of two prime numbers. You check instances of the generalization by purely intellectual reflection, not observation.
[102] See his *Enquiry Concerning Human Understanding* (1748), §§IV-V.

to see the main problem.) Hume first distinguishes between "relations of ideas" and "matters of fact". **Relations of ideas** are basically (as we would say today) statements that are *analytic* and *a priori*. **Matters of fact** are statements that are *synthetic* and *empirical*. (Hume doesn't recognize the possibility of synthetic a priori knowledge.)

Among matters of fact, some are directly observed to be true, and some are not. The latter we can call "unobserved matters of fact".

Hume says that beliefs about unobserved matters of fact are always based on induction. E.g., suppose you believe that the next U.S. President is going to be a tall liar. This is a synthetic and empirical claim (so a "matter of fact" in Hume's terminology), but you have not *observed* this to be true since it concerns the future. Your belief would instead be based on induction: All U.S. Presidents for the past 40 years have been tall liars, so probably the next one will be too.

Or suppose you think that Nepal is in Asia. Again, that's a matter of fact, but you haven't observed that to be true with your own eyes. Rather, you believe it because someone told you that. This, Hume would say, is also based on induction: You've had many past experiences with other people saying true things, so you have formed the inductive belief, roughly speaking, that people usually tell the truth. Thus, when someone told you that Nepal is in Asia, you took that to be true.

So now we have to ask about the basis for induction. It seems that all inductive inferences presuppose what we might call "the **Uniformity Principle**" (UP), namely, that the future will resemble the past, or that the course of nature is uniform, or that the things you haven't so far observed are similar to the things you *have* observed. If you *don't* assume that, then there's no reason to make an inductive inference. For instance, when you infer that the next President will be a tall liar, you're assuming that the future President will be similar to past Presidents. But why should we assume that?

Well, let's look at the claim:

UP Unobserved things resemble observed things.

What kind of statement is that? That's clearly not a relation-of-ideas claim—it's not true by definition, nor could you know that a priori. Unobserved things *could* turn out to be very different from observed things. So UP is a matter-of-fact claim.

It's also not an observation. You can tell this because the statement is explicitly about *unobserved* things. By definition, you haven't observed the unobserved things at all, so you certainly haven't observed them to be similar to the observed things.

So UP is an unobserved matter of fact. This means that UP must itself be based on induction, as we said above that all unobserved matter-of-fact beliefs rest on induction.

But UP can't be justified by induction! Suppose, for instance, that you reason, "The UP has generally turned out to give us correct predictions in the past, so it'll probably continue to work in the future." That would be circular, since that argument, like all inductive arguments, presupposes UP.

Therefore, UP can't be justified, and so *induction* can't be justified. To summarize:

1. All unobserved matter-of-fact claims depend on induction for their justification.
2. Induction presupposes the Uniformity Principle (UP).
3. Therefore, induction is justified only if UP is justified. (From 2.)
4. UP is an unobserved matter-of-fact claim, for:
   a. It's not a relation-of-ideas claim.
   b. It's not an observation.
   c. All claims are either relations of ideas, observations, or unobserved matters of fact.
5. UP can't be justified by induction. (From 2, due to circularity.)
6. UP can't be justified. (From 1, 4, 5.)
7. Therefore, induction can't be justified. (From 3, 6.)

12.1.3. Comment

Notice how radical this conclusion is. This isn't something you could happily embrace and then coherently just go about your life like normal. This is a belief-system-destroying conclusion. *Almost everything* that you believe about the world is under attack by this argument, for the argument claims that the only things you can possibly be justified in believing are the things you are right now directly observing. You don't know whether fire is generally hot, whether you live on the Earth, whether you have parents, or whether anything at all exists outside the room you're now in. If you believed all this *and you acted as if you believed it*, you would be psychotic.

Fortunately, few if any people have ever behaved as if they believed inductive skepticism (for example, by refusing to accept any beliefs about the world outside the room they are presently in). You'd be surprised, though, at how many philosophers verbally embrace inductive skepticism.

In the rest of this chapter, we'll try to figure out how induction might be justified despite Hume's argument.

12.2. Weak Responses

Let's start with some failed responses to Hume. I'm grouping together in this section the five responses that I don't want to spend a lot of time on.

12.2.1. *"Hume Misuses 'Reason'"*

Some people object that the inductive skeptic is misusing the word "reason" when he says we have *no reason* to believe inductive conclusions.[103] Of course, we have no *deductively conclusive* reason to believe inductive conclusions. We do, however, (trivially) have *inductive* reasons to believe inductive conclusions. These are reasons that make our conclusions more likely without guaranteeing their truth. The skeptic is just redefining the word "reason" to give it a much more restrictive sense. It's as if someone defined "physician" to mean "person who has a medical degree and can cure any conceivable illness in less than two minutes" and then concluded that there are no physicians in New York. The conclusion sounds amazing, but that is only because the person is using words in a bizarre way.

This is not a good take on Hume's argument. I mention it only to ensure that you don't fall prey to this confusion. Hume *is not* using "reason" to mean "deductively conclusive reason", nor are any of the other inductive skeptics. Their point is not just the trivial point that we do not have *absolutely conclusive, infallible* justification for inductive conclusions. They really are saying that there is *no reason whatsoever*, of any kind, of any strength, for believing an inductive conclusion. The belief that the sun will rise tomorrow is exactly as well justified, on the skeptics' view, as the belief that the sun will turn into a giant pear tomorrow.

Why interpret the skeptic in that way? Two reasons. First, because if you look over the argument of section 12.1.2, it simply does not contain the assumption that all reasons are deductively conclusive. The argument works fine when you take "reason" and "justification" to include fallible reasons and justification. For example, if you're going to have some fallible justification for accepting inductive conclusions, then it seems that you should at least have some fallible justification for believing the Uniformity Principle. And presumably fallible justifications can't be circular, any more than infallible ones can.

Second, in the passage introducing inductive skepticism, David Hume *explicitly discusses* the possibility of probabilistic reasons for the Uniformity Principle. He argues that we don't have any such reasons because probabilistic

---

[103] This is based on Paul Edwards' article, "Russell's Doubts About Induction" (*Mind*, 1949). Edwards is responding to Russell rather than Hume, but the issues are the same.

reasons depend on UP itself. This shows that he wasn't simply *defining* "reasons" to be deductively conclusive.

12.2.2. "The Skeptic Begs the Question"

Here is a better thought in the neighborhood of the previous objection: Even if Hume isn't just defining reasons to be deductively conclusive, his argument covertly assumes that only deductive reasons count. Consider an inference such as this:

> All observed squirrels have been furry.
> ∴ All squirrels are furry.

The skeptic says that this inference requires a hidden assumption, something like "unobserved squirrels are similar to observed squirrels". But notice that that premise is just what you would have to add to the inference to turn it into a *deductive* inference. If all observed squirrels are furry, and unobserved squirrels resemble observed squirrels (in particular, with regard to furriness), then it deductively follows that unobserved squirrels are furry, and thus that all squirrels are furry. So the skeptic, by claiming that induction "presupposes the Uniformity Principle", is really presupposing that induction has to be deductive.

The skeptic's best response would be to swap the previous formulation of UP for something more like this:

UP*   Unobserved objects *tend to be* similar to observed objects.

In other words, the new version of the Uniformity Principle, instead of saying that the unobserved objects are definitely like the observed ones, only says that if observed objects of a given kind are a certain way, that makes it *more likely* that unobserved objects of that kind will be that way. Notice that when we include this weaker assumption, we are not turning the inductive argument into a deductive one—now it is explicit that the conclusion would only be probabilistically supported. It's also plausible that UP* is presupposed by inductive inferences—if you don't think there is at least a *tendency* for unobserved things to resemble observed things, then why would you generalize from observations to conclusions about unobserved things?

Notice also that UP* still looks like an unobserved matter-of-fact claim. So again, on pain of circularity, UP* can't be justified by induction, and so we still have a skeptical problem on our hands.

12.2.3. "Induction Is Basic"

Maybe induction is a basic form of inference. What I mean by that is that it's a form of inference that is inherently compelling, without the need for any further reasoning to explain why it is good. There must be some basic forms of inference, since otherwise, every time we made an inference we would have to complete an infinite series of inferences to show why the first inference was cogent. A plausible example of a basic form of inference would be *modus ponens* ("*A*. If *A* then *B*. Therefore, *B*."). You don't need any further reasoning to explain why you're entitled to infer "*B*" from "*A*" and "*A* → *B*"; it's just obvious.[104]

So maybe induction is like that. If so, it's a mistake for the skeptic to say that induction presupposes the Uniformity Principle and that we need a justification for UP. Rather, the premise of an inductive conclusion, by itself, just inherently supports the conclusion, without the need to add any more premises.

This is a coherent and not-unreasonable point of view. However, in general you want to be careful about claiming that things are "basic" and in no need of explanation. You need to be careful because it is so easy to make the claim about whatever you want to believe that you can't think of any other way of defending, and it is so hard to refute the claim regardless of whether it is true.

In this case, we have to ask ourselves: Is it really self-evident, with no need of explanation, that observing some pattern justifies you in extending the pattern to other cases? This just doesn't strike me as fundamental and obvious in the way that, e.g., modus ponens is fundamental and obvious. It strikes me as the sort of thing that could be explained and should be explained. Anyway, some people have in fact tried to explain it, so let's see some of those explanations before we throw up our hands and declare that there's no explanation.

12.2.4. *The Pragmatic Defense*

The pragmatic defense of induction claims that it makes sense to use induction because we have certain cognitive goals, and we can know a priori that *if* there is any method that will attain those goals, inductive reasoning will do so. Importantly, this defense does not claim that we have any good reason to believe that induction (or anything else) will actually get us what we want. It just claims that induction will work *if* anything will, so we might as well give induction a try.[105]

---

[104] This is one of the lessons of Lewis Carroll's famous article, "What the Tortoise Said to Achilles" (*Mind*, 1895).
[105] See Hans Reichenbach's *The Theory of Probability* (1949), 469–82.

What is the goal that induction might help us achieve? According to Hans Reichenbach's classic account, our goal in scientific investigation is to identify the long-run frequencies of certain characteristics. For instance, if you're a medical researcher, you might want to know what is the risk for smokers of developing cancer. This is a question about a long-run frequency: If you have an indefinite series of people smoking cigarettes, about what percent of the time will those people get cancer? Reichenbach argues that *if* there is a long-run frequency (that is, a value that the frequency approaches as a limit as the series continues), then inductive reasoning will identify that limit. If there *isn't* any determinate long-run frequency (e.g., the frequency fluctuates randomly), then induction won't get you what you want, but neither will anything else. So you might as well try induction.

This defense of induction has problems. First, it turns on a narrow and quite weird account of what our goals are. I suppose sometimes we're aiming to identify long-run frequencies. But there is a lot more that we care about. Much more saliently, I should think, we often want to know what will happen in specific cases. E.g., when you build a bridge, you want to know whether *that bridge* is going to collapse. If you care at all about the long-run frequency with which bridges would collapse in an indefinitely extended series of bridges, that concern would only be derivative, insofar as you think the long-run frequency bears on what *this* bridge is likely to do. Reichenbach actually denies that you have any reason at all for believing any prediction about any particular bridge (he agrees with Hume's skeptical argument). So the pragmatic defense of induction is cold comfort for bridge-builders.

We should really take a second to appreciate what an extraordinarily implausible position that is. On the skeptic's account (including Reichenbach's view), when someone builds a bridge, they never have any reason whatsoever for thinking that the bridge will support anyone's weight. Any such reason would have to rely on induction. So, on the skeptic's view, there's no more or less reason to think the bridge will stand up than there is to think, say, that a bridge made entirely of toilet paper would stand up. If one really thought that, I don't think one would be rational to try walking across the bridge.

This points up the important lesson that most inductive conclusions are only *pragmatically* justified if they are *epistemically* justified. That is, it is only *useful* to rely on these conclusions if the conclusions are *likely to be true*. If your inductively-based predictions about bridges, and food, and airplanes, and so on don't actually come true, then a lot of your practical goals are going to be frustrated in a really bad way. Reichenbach was able to miss this point only because of his weirdly restricted choice of goals to consider.

So we really need an account of why induction is epistemically justified; we can't substitute a pragmatic account.

12.2.5. Appeal to the Synthetic A Priori

Immanuel Kant famously said that it was David Hume who woke him (Kant) from his "dogmatic slumbers". He was talking about Hume's skepticism concerning causation and induction. Part of what Kant wanted to do in developing his whole complicated philosophical system was to answer Hume's skepticism.

Kant noticed that Hume had collapsed two distinctions (analytic/synthetic and a priori/empirical) into one (relations of ideas/matters of fact). In so doing, Hume overlooked the possibility of synthetic a priori knowledge, which of course Kant made a huge deal about (§10.6). Kant took himself to have explained, in particular, how we know the Law of Causality (that every change must have a cause) a priori, even though it is a synthetic claim. He also thought that conservation of matter and Newton's Third Law were synthetic a priori.

There are two main problems with Kant's approach. First, as everyone knows, Kant kinda went overboard with what he considered synthetic a priori. (It's sort of like how, when you get a hammer, everything starts to look like a nail.) Almost everyone today recognizes that conservation of matter and Newton's Third Law are contingent and empirical. It's not the case that our mind imposes those laws on experience in such a way that it would be impossible for us to experience violations of those laws. Some of the things Kant considered a priori have even been rejected by later science. Euclidean geometry has been replaced in General Relativity with non-Euclidean geometry, and the conservation of matter has been replaced with a more general conservation of energy principle, recognizing that matter can be converted into (other forms of) energy.

Second and more importantly, Kant's synthetic a priori principles would not help with the vast majority of inductive inferences. Let's say I observe a series of geckos, all of whom are green. I want to draw the inductive conclusion that all geckos are green, but then I remember Hume's argument, I start to wonder if the Uniformity Principle is justified, and so on. Now Kant comes along and tells me: "Oh, don't worry, Mike. You see, it's a priori that all events have causes. Also, Newtonian physics and Euclidean geometry are a priori." Let's say I even believe him. So what? I mean, that's all very interesting and all, but how does that tell me whether the unobserved geckos are the same color as the observed ones?

Kant's general approach could perhaps work if he was willing to say that *the Uniformity Principle* is synthetic a priori. However, he would not want to say that because it really doesn't fit with the rest of what he says about synthetic a priori truths. He says that synthetic a priori truths are *necessary*, that they're strictly *universal*, and that we know them with *certainty*. None of that is true of the Uniformity Principle. It's not necessary since there could be a world in which the unobserved things are very different from the observed things. It's not universal, since there are actual cases in which hitherto-unobserved things have turned out to be different from hitherto observed things. (Think about the time when people had inductively inferred that all swans were white, based on long experience with lots of swans. Later, it turned out that there were black swans in Australia.) And it's not certain, since it *may* turn out in any given case that the unobserved things will be quite different from the observed things. That's why it's universally recognized that inductive conclusions are only probable, not absolutely certain. So UP does not look like a synthetic a priori truth.

12.3. Basics of Probability

12.3.1. A Smart Idea

Non-deductive reasoning is widely described as reasoning that shows its conclusion to be *probable* (or at least *more* probable than it would be if the premises were not true). And, come to think of it, there is an actual, well-developed branch of mathematics that's about probability. So a smart idea would be to consult probability theory and see if it can help explain why inductive conclusions are likely to be true.

We're not the first to think of this! Some philosophers have done that. In the next three sections (12.4–12.6), we discuss three variants of the appeal to probability theory. In terms of Hume's argument from §12.1.2, this approach would involve rejecting Hume's second premise ("Induction presupposes the Uniformity Principle"), since induction rests on the principles of probability, where UP isn't one of those principles. Hume's first premise ("All unobserved matter-of-fact claims depend on induction for their justification") is also false, since there are other kinds of non-deductive reasoning besides induction.

12.3.2. The Laws of Probability

There are four main axioms of probability theory (known as the "**Kolmogorov axioms**"):

Axiom I: $P(a) \geq 0$, where a is any proposition.
Axiom II: $P(t) = 1$, if t is a tautology (an analytic truth).
Axiom III: $P(a \vee b) = P(a) + P(b)$, if a and b are mutually exclusive alternatives.
Axiom IV: $P(a \& b) = P(a) \times P(b \mid a)$, where a and b are any propositions.

The last one requires some explanation: "P($b|a$)" is read "the probability of b given a", and it refers to the probability that b is true *if a is true*.[106] So the probability of two propositions both being true equals the probability of the first one being true times the probability of the second one being true if the first one is. (And please note that "|" is *not a division symbol*. That does not say "b over a", which would make no sense!) With that stated, I hope you find all four axioms self-evident. If not, that's too bad, because they're axioms!

On these axioms rests the branch of mathematics known as probability theory. I will just mention two theorems that are going to be particularly interesting for us. First, there is **the law of large numbers**, which states that if outcome O has probability p of occurring in circumstances C, then if you repeat C over and over, the frequency with which O occurs will approach p, with increasing probability. I.e., the more times you repeat C, the more likely it is that the frequency will be close to p, and the closer you should expect it to be.

So, say you have a coin with a 52% probability of coming up heads when flipped. If you flip it a thousand times, you'll probably get heads about 52% of the time. (This isn't guaranteed, of course; it *could* come up heads every time, but that's very unlikely.) If you flip the coin a *million* times, it is even *more certain* that you'll get heads about 52% of the time, and furthermore, the frequency will probably be even *closer* to 52%. If you keep flipping the coin forever, then, with probability 1, the frequency of heads will approach 52% as a limit. Most people find this theorem very intuitive on its face.

The second really important theorem is this:

Bayes' Theorem: $P(h|e) = \frac{P(h) \times P(e|h)}{P(e)}$

Bayes' Theorem is named after the Reverend Thomas Bayes (and please don't call him "Bay" or "Baye"). Here is a simple proof[107]:

1. $P(e\&h) = P(h\&e)$ Obvious.
2. $P(e) \times P(h|e) = P(h) \times P(e|h)$ From 1, Axiom IV.
3. $P(h|e) = \frac{P(h) \times P(e|h)}{P(e)}$ From 2, dividing by P(e).

We'll talk later about why this theorem is important for the problem of induction. For now, I'm just telling you some principles of probability. Here is another form of Bayes' Theorem that is sometimes useful:

---

[106] Some people (not me) regard Axiom IV as a *definition* of conditional probability.
[107] This isn't the full proof, because I didn't prove step 1. But I'm pretty sure you'll grant me that step. Also, obviously, step 3 only holds assuming P(e) is nonzero.

Bayes' Theorem 2.0: $P(h|e) = \frac{P(h) \times P(e|h)}{P(h) \times P(e|h) + P(\sim h) \times P(e|\sim h)}$

In that formulation, the thing in the denominator is equal to P(*e*).[108]

12.3.3. *What Is Probability?*

What the heck is a "probability" anyway? So far, all we know is that probabilities are numbers that satisfy the Kolmogorov axioms. But what do these numbers measure? There are several theories:

i. *Frequencies:* Perhaps the probability of an event occurring in circumstance *C* just means the frequency with which the event would happen if *C* were repeated many times.

   Problem: It's not guaranteed that the frequency would match the probability. Example: Assume that the probability of a coin coming up heads is 50%. From that assumption, you can calculate the probability that in 100 flips, exactly 50 would be heads. It's only about 8%. So standard probability theory tells us that the *actual frequency* of heads probably will not equal the *probability* of heads in each case. So those two things certainly aren't definitionally equivalent.

   Possible fix: Say that the probability is the frequency in an *infinite* series of trials.

   Problems: (*i*) Even in an infinite series, it's still *logically possible* that you'd get all heads. (*ii*) It's impossible to flip a coin infinitely many times (at some point, the coin would be worn down by excessive handling, etc.). It's odd to think that when I talk about a coin's probability of coming up heads, I'm saying something about the impossible scenario in which the coin was flipped infinitely many times. Why would we care about that?

ii. *Propensities:* **Propensities** are, roughly, degrees of causal influence. Sometimes, a set of causal factors *guarantees* some outcome; in that case, the propensity of that outcome is 1. Other times, a set of causal factors *precludes* some outcome; then the outcome has a propensity of 0. But also, sometimes a set of causal factors has some stronger or weaker *tendency* to produce a certain outcome. In that case, the propensity is something in between 0 and 1. In this interpretation, chance is objectively present in nature. This, by the way, is the kind of probability used in (indeterministic

---

[108] If you want to see why that's true: *e* is logically equivalent to [(*h* & *e*) ∨ (~*h* & *e*)]. The two disjuncts there are mutually exclusive, so by Axiom III, P[(*h* & *e*) ∨ (~*h* & *e*)] = P(*h* & *e*) + P(~*h* & *e*). Applying Axiom IV to that (twice) gives you P(*h*)×P(*e*|*h*) + P(~*h*)×P(*e*|~*h*).

interpretations of) quantum mechanics, e.g., when a radioactive atom is said to have a 50% probability of decaying in a given time period.

Comment: I don't have anything against this interpretation of probability *for certain cases*. But it doesn't work well for the uses of probability in epistemology. For instance, when I say that an inductive conclusion is likely to be true given the evidence, this is not referring to a degree of causal influence.

iii. *Degrees of Belief:* Maybe when you say something is "90% probable", what you're doing is reporting your *degree of belief* in that thing—you're saying you're 90% confident that the thing is true. Degrees of belief are often referred to as **subjective probabilities,** or **credences**.

Problem: Subjective "probability" doesn't satisfy the axioms of probability theory. E.g., Axiom II says the probability of a tautology is 1, but no actual person is maximally confident of every tautology (some tautologies are very hard to recognize). There are also psychology studies in which they get people to assign a higher probability to a conjunction than to one of the conjuncts, thus violating standard probability theory. Since people's actual credences don't satisfy the laws of probability, they are not probabilities.

Possible fix: Say that the probability of a proposition is the credence that a *fully rational* person would have. Or say that the probability of a proposition is relative to a person, and the probability *for you* is the credence *you* would have if you were fully rational.

Problem: Different fully rational people might have different credences. There is not even a fact about what credence *you* would have in a given proposition if you were fully rational, because there are many different ways that you could become fully rational, and these different ways would involve your having different credences. (Don't feel bad about being called irrational; everyone is "irrational" to some degree by the standards of epistemologists.)

iv. *Degrees of Justification ("epistemic probabilities"):* The **epistemic probability** of a proposition is a measure of how much justification there is for the proposition, or how strongly your current evidence supports it. On this view, a proposition can have different probabilities for different people, since different people have different evidence available to them. If you have conclusive justification to believe A, then $P(A) = 1$ (for you). If you have conclusive justification to *deny* A, then $P(A) = 0$. Most of the time, you have some weaker degree of justification, in which case the probability is something in between 1 and 0.

Comment: This interpretation does a good job of explaining what we're talking about in epistemology when, e.g., we say that inductive conclusions are likely to be true.

v. *Degrees of Entailment ("logical probabilities"):* **Logical probabilities** are something like degrees of entailment. More precisely, there is a logical relation that comes in degrees, such that the maximum degree of this relation is entailment, and the minimum degree is contradiction. I.e., if A entails B, then $P(B|A) = 1$; if A contradicts B, then $P(B|A) = 0$. If A has some weaker degree of support for B, then $P(B|A)$ will be something in between 0 and 1.

Another way to think of it, if you like "possible worlds" talk: If B is true in all the possible worlds in which A is true, then we say that A entails B and $P(B|A) = 1$. If B is true in, say, 90% of the possible worlds in which A is true, then we can say that A non-deductively supports B and $P(B|A) = 0.9$.[109]

This account is very similar to the previous one. The difference is that the epistemic interpretation (*iv*) makes probabilistic facts normative *epistemological* facts, about justification for belief. The logical interpretation (*v*), on the other hand, makes probabilistic facts *metaphysical* facts. E.g., maybe they're facts about proportions of possible worlds (which could obtain whether or not there were any believers).

Comment: This interpretation also works for epistemology.[110]

---

[109] By the way, this is closely related to the so-called **classical interpretation of probability**, which says that the probability of an event = (the number of favorable cases)/(the number of possible cases), that is, the ratio of the number of possible outcomes in which the event occurs to the total number of possible outcomes. This account fails when you have an infinite number of possibilities or when some possible outcomes are more likely than others.

[110] Technical aside: The possible worlds interpretation *sounds* illuminating, but in fact it may be empty. There are typically going to be *infinitely many* possible worlds in which A holds (the "A-worlds") and infinitely many in which B also holds (the "B-worlds"), usually the same order of infinity. In such a case, "the ratio" of one set to the other is not well-defined. You can of course have *a measure* on the set of A-worlds, and that measure could tell you "what proportion" of that set are also B-worlds. Indeed, that is just what a probability distribution is (sc., a measure wherein the measure of the set of all possible worlds is 1). But there will in general exist *many different* measures, which will assign different numbers to the set of A-worlds that are also B-worlds. So, to genuinely explain logical probability, you would have to explain what makes one of the many possible measures *special*. However you do that is probably going to amount to an independent account of probability. In spite of all this, I still like logical probabilities.

12.4. Proportional Syllogism and the Law of Large Numbers[111]

12.4.1. Background: Proportional Syllogism

Induction is a *species* of non-deductive inference, but it isn't the only species. Importantly, the argument for inductive skepticism is an argument for skepticism specifically about *induction*, not about other kinds of non-deductive inference. So one perfectly good way of responding to the skeptic would be (if we can manage this) to show that induction is dispensable; that is, that we can get inductive conclusions using other forms of inference that are not in dispute.

One such form of non-deductive inference is known as **proportional syllogism**. This is a kind of inference in which you reason from a premise about the proportion of some trait in a population, to a conclusion about some particular member of the population. E.g., you know that 90% of A's are B, and x is an A, so you conclude (with 90% confidence) that x is B. Notice how this differs from induction: In induction, you reason from premises about particulars to a conclusion about the general population; in proportional syllogism, you reason from a premise about the general population to a conclusion about a particular. Some examples:

Normal syllogism (deductive)	Proportional syllogism	Induction
All A's are B.	90% of A's are B.	x is an A and x is B.
x is an A.	x is an A.	y is an A and y is B.
$\therefore x$ is B.	$\therefore x$ is B.	...
		$\therefore$ All A's are B.

The proportional syllogism is non-deductive because the conclusion is not guaranteed by the premises; in the above case, the premises only support the conclusion with 90% confidence. (By the way, that's only true if you have no other information about x. If you have other information, it could indicate that x is either more or less likely to be B than the average A. So to avoid complications, let's just stipulate that all we know about x is that it is an A.)

12.4.2. Background: Populations, Samples, and Representativeness

Some more terminology: Suppose there's a large group of objects of some kind. The whole group, including both observed and unobserved objects, is known as "the population".

Say you observe some but not all of the members of the population. The set of objects you observed is known as a "sample" from the population.

---

[111] The argument of this section derives from David Stove, *The Rationality of Induction* (1986), ch. 6.

Lastly, let's say that you are interested in the frequency of some trait in the population. We can say the sample is "representative" (with respect to that trait) provided that the frequency of the trait in the sample is approximately equal to the frequency of the trait in the population. (This is something that you'd want to be true, though you generally can't know for certain whether it is.) E.g., depending on how strict you want to be, you might want to say the sample is representative with respect to trait T iff the frequency of T in the sample is within 5 percentage points of the frequency in the population; or maybe 3 percentage points, or 1, etc.

12.4.3. The Argument for Induction

Now we can state the basic argument in defense of induction. To make it easier to follow, let's take an example. You're considering moving to California, and before moving, you want to know what proportion of the restaurants in California serve vegan food. (Interpret that to mean that they have at least one vegan entrée.) You take a random sample of 1,000 California restaurants, examine their menus, and see how many have at least one vegan entrée. (You're really diligent when it comes to moving decisions!) Let's say the proportion comes out to 50%. You infer that, among California restaurants *in general* (not just in your sample), about 50% have vegan food. This is a clear example of an inductive inference.

Stipulate that you didn't make any mistakes prior to the last step—you really did sample the restaurants randomly, you have no reason to think your sample is biased, you can trust the menus to correctly report what the restaurants have, etc. The only issue is whether you can make the jump from what's true of *a sample* to a conclusion about *the population*. The inductive skeptic's claim is that, even in the best of cases, with everything going as well as possible, you still have no reason to infer anything about the population outside your sample.

So here is how we can argue against the skeptic:

1. We took a random sample of 1,000 restaurants. (Empirical premise.)
2. Nearly all samples of 1,000 or more items are representative. (Premise.)
3. So (probably) our sample was representative. (From 1, 2.)
4. In our sample, 50% of restaurants had vegan food. (Empirical premise.)
5. So about 50% of restaurants in the population have vegan food. (From 3, 4.)

Premises 1 and 4 are stipulated to be true. The inference from 1+2 to 3 is proportional syllogism, which, as we've said, is not in dispute. The inference from 3+4 to 5 is just deductive (given the meaning of "representative"), so that's not in dispute either.

So the only thing that remains to be justified is step 2. Step 2 is a perfectly general thesis about any population that contains more than 1,000 items, and any sample size greater than or equal to 1,000. How can we know premise 2 without relying on induction? That's the key question.

12.4.4. The Key Premise

The answer, it turns out, is that premise 2 is an a priori *mathematical theorem*. It's actually a version of the law of large numbers. I'm not going to give a complete proof of the theorem (which would be very tedious), but I'm going to explain enough so that you'll be able to see how this would be an a priori mathematical truth.

The first thing to understand is that in general, if you have a population of a given size, with a given proportion of some trait, then for any given sample size, you can calculate, just by arithmetic, how many samples of that size would be representative and how many would not. This doesn't require any induction, and it doesn't require any disputable philosophical premises.

Example: Let's say there is a "population" of four marbles in a bag, call them A, B, C, and D. Stipulate that A and B are black, while C and D are white. You're going to take a random sample of two marbles from the bag. What proportion of the possible samples are representative? Well, since the proportion of black marbles in the population is 50%, the sample will be representative if and only if it contains about 50% black marbles, i.e., "about" 1 black marble and 1 white one. There are 6 possible samples:

$\{A, B\}$
$\{A, C\}$
$\{A, D\}$
$\{B, C\}$
$\{B, D\}$
$\{C, D\}$

The *representative* ones are $\{A,C\}$, $\{A,D\}$, $\{B,C\}$, and $\{B,D\}$ (those each contain one black marble and one white one). The unrepresentative samples are $\{A,B\}$ and $\{C,D\}$ (all black or all white). So *most* (sc., two thirds) of the possible samples are representative. Notice how that's just a mathematical fact about this scenario. It's not an induction, and it's not a philosophical opinion.

You can generalize to cases with larger populations. For instance, if we take a population of 6 marbles, again with half of them being black, and we take a sample of two, then 9 of 15 possible samples are representative. As you go to larger populations and sample sizes, the calculations get much hairier (the number of possible samples explodes). Also, at some point you have to decide exactly how strict to be about what counts as "representative" (must the sample frequency match the population within 5%, or 1%, etc.). But, given a threshold for "representativeness", the number of samples that are representative is always just a matter of arithmetical fact, however complicated the calculations may be.

Now, it turns out that, as you get to larger and larger sample sizes, the *proportion* of samples that are representative increases, approaching 1 as a limit. With sample sizes over 1,000, the proportion is *always* very high. This continues to be true, by the way, no matter what the frequency of the trait is in the general population; i.e., for *any* possible frequency that the trait could have in the general population, the overwhelming majority of large samples are going to be representative. (The case where half of the population has the trait is actually the worst case. If the proportion of the population with the trait is closer to 1 or 0, then the proportion of representative samples goes up.)

This is also true no matter how big the population is. A sample size of 1,000 is enough to guarantee that the overwhelming majority of possible samples are representative, regardless of how big the total population is. Some people find this counter-intuitive, so let me give you an explanation that will make it more intuitive. This explanation also shows what all this has to do with the Law of Large Numbers.

Say you randomly pick an individual from some large population. It doesn't matter how large; could be infinite. The *probability* of getting an individual with feature F is equal to the *frequency* with which F occurs in the general population. Now, by the Law of Large Numbers, if you do this many times (i.e., pick many individuals randomly), you should expect the frequency with which F occurs in your sample to roughly match the probability of getting F on each occasion. Therefore, the frequency of F in the sample should roughly match the frequency of F in the population.

So that explains why, if you take a large random sample, it is probably going to be representative. Which explains why you can then make an inference from the sample to the population. So induction is justified after all.

12.5. Subjective Bayesianism

12.5.1. *The Subjective Bayesian Creed*

Bayesians are basically people who think all cogent non-deductive reasoning is explained by the principles of probability, especially Bayes' Theorem. They think we have degrees of belief (credences), that the laws of probability provide rational constraints on our credences, and that when we acquire new evidence *e* that bears on hypothesis *h*, we should update our credence in *h* from P(*h*) to P(*h*|*e*).

Subjective Bayesians think that the Kolmogorov axioms plus the principle about updating when you get new evidence are the *only* constraints (or *almost* the only constraints[112]) on rational credences. This contrasts with the **objective Bayesians**, who think there are substantial additional constraints (to be discussed later).

On the subjective Bayesian view, then, perfectly rational people could have radically different credences, even when they have the same evidence. As long as you're respecting the axioms and reasoning consistently with your starting credences, you're rational. The only propositions whose probability everyone must agree on are tautologies and contradictions.

12.5.2. Why Obey Probability?

Why think that rational credences must satisfy the axioms of probability? If you don't find that self-evident off hand, there's a famous set of arguments called "Dutch Book Arguments" (the name seems to be based on some kind of racist stereotype about Dutch people being good bookies—quite shocking, really). These are arguments that show that if you have credences that violate the laws of probability, and you're willing to place bets based on those credences, then it's possible for someone to offer you a series of bets that you would accept in which you would be *guaranteed* to lose money overall. Here, I'll just give one example to illustrate the idea.

Axiom III says P($a \vee b$) = P(a) + P(b), if a and b are mutually exclusive alternatives. Suppose you violate that. Say you assign credence 0.3 to A, 0.3 to B, and 0.8 to ($A \vee B$), where A and B are two mutually exclusive alternatives. A Dutch bookie comes along and offers you three bets. For each bet, the bookie specifies three things:

i. A proposition that you may bet for or against;
ii. How much money you win if you bet in favor of the proposition and it turns out to be true (this is also the amount that you *lose* if you bet *against* the proposition and it turns out true); and
iii. How much money you win if you bet *against* the proposition and it turns out to be *false* (this is also the amount that you lose if you bet in favor of the proposition and it turns out to be false).

---

[112] I think you can still call yourself a "subjectivist" if you incorporate some minor additional constraints, e.g., that one isn't allowed to assign prior probability 0 to a contingent theory that some experts seriously advance.

You get to decide which propositions to bet on, and whether to bet for or against each.

So here are the three bets the bookie offers you:

Proposition	Winner's payout if true	Winner's payout if false
1. A	$65	$35
2. B	$65	$35
3. $(A \vee B)$	$25	$75

So, e.g., if you bet *in favor of* A, then you win $65 if A is true and lose $35 if A is false. If you bet *against* A, then you lose $65 if A is true and win $35 if A is false. Etc.

If you make bets based on your credences, then you would bet *against* A, *against* B, and *for* $(A \vee B)$. These would be the bets that, according to your credences, have positive expected value. Based on your 0.3 credence in A, the bet against A has an expected value of $(.3)(-\$65) + (.7)(\$35) = \$5$. The bet against B likewise has an expected value of $(.3)(-\$65) + (.7)(\$35) = \$5$. The bet *for* $(A \vee B)$ has an expected value of $(.8)(\$25) + (.2)(-\$75) = \$5$. Since $5 is greater than 0, you regard all these as favorable bets.

Now what happens? One of three things happens: A turns out to be true and B false, or B turns out to be true and A false, or both turn out to be false. (They can't both be true, since we said A and B are mutually exclusive.) Here are your payouts in each of these possibilities:

Outcome	Payout from bet against A	Payout from bet against B	Payout from bet for $(A \vee B)$	Total payout
A & $\sim B$	–$65	$35	$25	–$5
$\sim A$ & B	$35	–$65	$25	–$5
$\sim A$ & $\sim B$	$35	$35	–$75	–$5

So no matter what, you lose $5! This is taken to show that your set of credences was irrational.

This result generalizes: If your credences violate *any* of the Kolmogorov axioms, in any way, and you place bets based on those credences, then there will always be a possible set of bets that you would make even though they imply a guaranteed loss.

The moral of the story: Respect the axioms!

12.5.3. Conditionalization

When you acquire new evidence, according to Bayesians, you should update all your beliefs that the evidence bears on by **conditionalization**. To explain that: Say you start out with an initial credence function C_i. For any proposition x,

$C_i(x)$ is your level of confidence in the truth of x. You also have conditional credences; $C_i(x|y)$ is how confident you are that x is true *if* y is true.

You're going to learn some new evidence, e, whereupon you will change your credence function from C_i to C_f. For any proposition x, $C_f(x)$ represents your final level of confidence in x, after taking account of e.

So here is the principle of conditionalization: $C_f(x)$ should equal $C_i(x|e)$ for each x. Hopefully, you find that intuitive. Example: You don't know whether it's raining or not right now. I ask you, "Hey, *if* it's raining now, how likely do you think it is that it will still be raining in two hours?" Suppose you answer "40%". Then you look outside and see that it is in fact raining. (And that's all you learn.) I ask you, "Now how likely do you think it is that it will be raining in two hours?" If you're rational, you answer "40%".

If that's not obvious enough for you, there's also a Dutch Book argument for conditionalization.[113]

12.5.4. Bayes' Theorem

Here, again, is Bayes' Theorem:

$$P(h|e) = \frac{P(h) \times P(e|h)}{P(e)}$$

Here is how people often apply the theorem, especially in philosophy of science. Say you have a hypothesis h and a piece of evidence e. You want to know how likely your hypothesis is in the light of that evidence. That's given by $P(h|e)$. So if you find out for certain that e is true, you should revise your credence in h by changing it from $P(h)$ to $P(h|e)$.

Looking at the right-hand side of Bayes' Theorem, you can see that three things determine $P(h|e)$. First, it's proportional to the **prior probability** of h, $P(h)$ (in other words, how likely h was to be true before you learned e, or how likely you would say it was if you didn't know e). The more probable the theory starts out, the more probable it ends up. (Sort of like how the easiest way to become a millionaire is to start out with $999,999.) This also supports the slogan "extraordinary claims require extraordinary evidence", which basically means that if you have a hypothesis that is super-implausible to begin with, then you're going to need a lot of evidence before it becomes believable. Whereas if you started out with a plausible hypothesis, then you don't need as much evidence.

Second, it's good if $P(e|h)$ is high. $P(e|h)$ is sometimes called (a bit weirdly) the **likelihood** of h. Higher likelihoods engender better support for h.

---

[113] See David Lewis, "Why Conditionalize?" in *Papers in Metaphysics and Epistemology* (1999).

Intuitively, if you want to support a theory, you want the theory to *strongly predict* some possible evidence, where that evidence then occurs. To strongly predict something is to imply that that thing is very likely. Thus, you want the probability of some evidence on your theory to be high, and then that evidence to occur.

Third, it's good if P(*e*) is *low*. You can see from the theorem that as P(*e*) goes down, P(*h*|*e*) goes up. Combining this with the previous point, we can say: You want a theory that strongly predicts evidence that is *otherwise* highly unlikely. In other words, you want *e* to be much more likely if *h* is true than otherwise.

Here's an illustration. People used to debate whether light was a wave or a stream of particles. The French physicist Fresnel thought light was a kind of transverse wave (oscillating in a direction perpendicular to its motion). Looking at Fresnel's theory in detail, people figured out that one prediction of this theory was that you could have a beam of light shining on a small, round object, casting a shadow on a screen, and a spot of light would appear *in the center of the shadow*. (Never mind why; it's some weird stuff about diffraction and wave interference.) At first, people thought this was an absurd result; everybody knows that that doesn't happen.[114] You can interpret this as meaning that P(*e*) was very low. Then someone decided to actually do the experiment … and the prediction turned out to be *correct*—you *can* make a dot of light appear in the middle of the shadow. When this happened, everyone had to admit that Fresnel was the boss and the wave theory of light was triumphant.

In the above formulation of Bayes' Theorem, there are three quantities on the right hand side. But you can also represent P(*h*|*e*) as a function of two quantities: the prior probability of *h* (that's P(*h*)), and the **likelihood ratio**, which is P(*e*|*h*)/P(*e*|~*h*). In Bayesian reasoning, the likelihood ratio is key to evidential support: If your likelihood ratio is greater than 1 (meaning that *e* is more likely if *h* is true than if it's false), then *e supports* (raises the probability of) *h*. If the likelihood ratio is less than 1 (meaning *e* is less likely if *h* is true than if *h* is false), then *e undermines* (lowers the probability of) *h*. If the likelihood ratio equals 1, then *e is irrelevant to* (neither raises nor lowers the probability of) *h*. Here's another equation that's a variant on Bayes' Theorem:

$$P(h|e) = \frac{Lp}{Lp + 1 - p}$$

---

[114] By "people" here, I mean the French physicist Poisson, who supported the particle theory of light.

Where *p* is the prior probability and *L* is the likelihood ratio. (If you plug the definitions of those things into the above equation and simplify, taking note that 1 − P(*h*) = P(~*h*), you're going to get back Bayes' Theorem, Version 2.0.)

12.5.5. Subjectivist Induction

I know what you're thinking: "Great, now I know a bunch of equations and junk! But how does all this help me refute David Hume?"

The first thing to get is that, on the subjective Bayesian view, there is no *one* rational response to a set of evidence. It all depends on your initial credences, your **priors** as we call them (short for "prior probabilities"). As long as your priors satisfy the axioms of probability, and you update by conditionalization, you're rational. So the subjective Bayesian isn't going to say that inductive skepticism is irrational per se; it could be rational for some people, depending on their priors. But the subjective Bayesian is going to say that induction is also rational for some other people, probably including all or nearly all actual people.

How would induction be rational? Suppose you start out assigning a prior probability of 0.01 to the hypothesis "All ravens are black" and a prior probability of 0.1 to the proposition "The next raven I observe will be black." Letting *h* = [All ravens are black], *e* = [The next raven I observe will be black], you have P(*h*) = 0.01, P(*e*|*h*) = 1, and P(*e*) = 0.1. By Bayes' Theorem:

$$P(h|e) = \frac{P(h) \times P(e|h)}{P(e)} = \frac{(.01)(1)}{(.1)} = 0.1$$

So if the next raven you observe turns out to be black, then, by conditionalization, you update your credence in *h* from 0.01 to 0.1. So the hypothesis is supported by that evidence (its probability increases by a factor of ten). As you keep doing this, the probability is going to keep going up (though there are diminishing returns).

As a perfectly general matter, as long as P(*e*|*h*) > P(*e*), your hypothesis will be supported if *e* turns out to be true. This is almost always the case for inductive conclusions, because P(*e*|*h*) = 1 (since the evidence is just an instance of the inductive generalization), and P(*e*) is usually less than 1 (because you're not absolutely certain of what the evidence will be before you observe it). So inductive generalizations are almost always supported by inductive evidence.

There are possible exceptions. A skeptic might start out assigning probability zero to every inductive generalization. This can't be ruled out, since nothing in the axioms says that these generalizations must have nonzero probability. If you have a probability distribution like that, then skepticism is true of you: *You* have no reason to believe inductive conclusions. But other people, with less extreme prior probabilities, *can* get probabilistic reasons to believe inductive generalizations.

12.5.6. Objection

I have one major objection to subjective Bayesianism: It is too subjective. The subjective Bayesian can't recognize any objective facts about what conclusions are supported by what evidence; all facts about (non-deductive) evidential support are, on their view, relative.

Note that I am not assuming that there is always a perfectly determinate fact about how you should respond to some evidence. Maybe in some cases, there is a *range* of credences that are rational, and maybe sometimes rational people can form conflicting interpretations of the same evidence. All I am saying is that there are *at least some cases* in which *some* credences would count as irrational responses to the (non-deductive) evidence.

For example, I think that, in light of all the evidence we currently have, you could not rationally think that the Earth rests on the back of a giant turtle. That isn't a possible justified response to the evidence. But on the subjective Bayesian view, it is. All you have to do is assign a super high prior probability to chelonian cosmology.[115] (Yep, there's a word "chelonian", meaning "turtle-related". I brought up this example just so I could use that word.)

Here is a graph I made to illustrate how confirmation works (fig. 6).[116] L is likelihood ratio, and Posterior Probability is $P(h|e)$. The graph shows how $P(h|e)$ varies as a function of both the prior ($P(h)$) and the likelihood ratio.[117] As you get

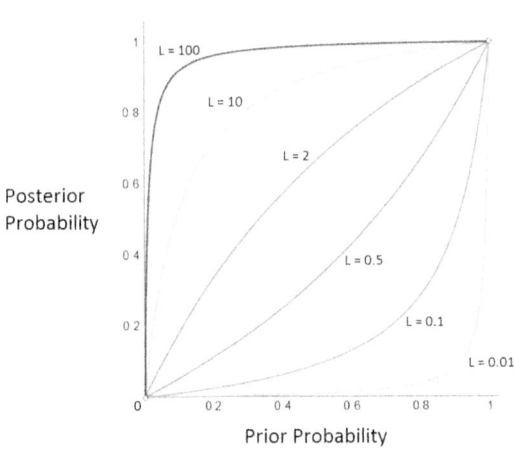

Figure 6: Posterior probability as a function of prior probability and likelihood

---

[115] I'm assuming that our evidence does not literally, deductively entail that the Earth isn't on a giant turtle. If you disagree with this, just take another example of a ridiculous theory that doesn't literally contradict our evidence.
[116] Taken from my paper, "There Is No Pure Empirical Reasoning" (*Philosophy and Phenomenological Research*, 2017).
[117] This is based on the equation from §12.5.4, $P(h|e) = Lp/(Lp + 1 - p)$.

more evidence, you tend to get a more extreme likelihood ratio for the total set of evidence, and thus the curves bend away from the center of the graph. But here's the key point: All of the curves, regardless of the value of L, pass through *every value on the* y *axis* between 0 and 1 inclusive. That means that, for any value of L, there are always prior probabilities that give you *any* chosen posterior probability. Since, on the subjective Bayesian view, any prior probability is permissible, that means that *any posterior probability is permissible* (i.e., cannot be ruled out by norms of rationality).

Why are subjective Bayesians so permissive? Basically, they think that a "rational" belief is just a belief that does not violate any norms of rationality. They think that there are compelling reasons to accept the Kolmogorov Axioms and the rule of Conditionalization as rational constraints. But they just don't think there's a compelling case for any much stricter constraints than that. Hence, you're being rational as long as you satisfy the Axioms and Conditionalization.

I disagree, essentially because I think rationality is more demanding. I don't think a belief state is presumed rational as long as there's nothing in particular wrong with it; rather, I think a belief state is *irrational* by default unless there is something that justifies it.

12.6. Objective Bayesianism

12.6.1. The Objective Bayesian Creed

Objective Bayesians also think probability theory explains non-deductive reasoning, but they think there are substantial additional constraints on rational credences, beyond the Kolmogorov axioms and the rule of conditionalization. The main motivation for saying this is to avoid the excessive subjectivism I just complained about.

What might these constraints be?

Here, I'll just mention one of the most popular candidates. Many people have endorsed the **Principle of Indifference**, which states that we should by default assign equal probabilities to all the possibilities, unless there is some reason not to do so, i.e.:

PI   If there are no reasons favoring A over B or B over A, then $P(A) = P(B)$.

Here is an illustration.

> *The Two Envelopes:* I show you two envelopes and tell you that one of them contains $100 and the other contains nothing. The two envelopes are indistinguishable to you. One of them isn't fatter than the other, I'm not holding one of them closer than the other, etc.; they're just completely

> indistinguishable in all relevant respects. What probability should you assign to each envelope containing $100?

Everyone can work this one out: Each envelope has a 50% chance of containing the money. That's an application of the Principle of Indifference.

Subjective Bayesians would demur. They would say that you could assign *any* pair of credences to the two envelopes, as long as they add up to 1. So 50/50 is permissible, but 90/10 is equally permissible (it doesn't violate the Kolmogorov axioms!). I think that's crazy.

12.6.2. Wherefore Indifference?

The above example provides one of the central motivations for the Principle of Indifference: It is extremely intuitive in certain cases.

Another motivation is that the PI looks close to analytic, if you take an epistemic interpretation of probability. (Obviously, the PI does not hold under a frequency or propensity interpretation!) On the epistemic interpretation, the PI just says that if there is no reason for favoring A over B or vice versa, then A and B are justified to the same degree. Think about the converse: If one of them was justified to a greater degree than the other, wouldn't that have to mean that there was a reason to favor the one that was more justified?

In fairness, the preceding reasoning assumes that there is such a thing as the degree of justification that A has, and similarly for B, i.e., it assumes that both have determinate epistemic probabilities. Someone who rejected the PI (such as a subjective Bayesian) would deny that there is any unique epistemic probability for A or B.

Some people think that there is no way of assigning probabilities a priori, and that you can only assign probabilities based on empirical evidence. Call this the *empiricist* view of probability. Empiricists think that you are justified in assigning equal probabilities to a set of alternatives only if you have empirical evidence that the alternatives are equally probable—for instance, if you thoroughly shuffle a deck of cards, *then* you have reason to think that every possible card is equally likely to be drawn. In the absence of such evidence, either there are no probabilities, or we can't know them, or all probability assignments are equally good. Importantly, though, most of these empiricists would *not* want to say that *nothing ever* has any probability; e.g., they would accept that the probability of getting double sixes when throwing a normal pair of dice is 1/36.

In fact, however, the "empirical" probability judgments that empiricists accept *depend upon* a priori probability judgments that empiricists reject. Say you shuffle a deck of cards. There are many particular, exact ways of moving your hands and a deck of cards that count as "shuffling the deck". Some of those possible shuffling motions would put the ace of hearts on top, some would put the three of diamonds on top, and so on, for every possible card. (If there is randomness in quantum mechanics, it doesn't apply to macroscopic things like hands and cards.) Now, these different classes of deck-shufflings are indistinguishable to normal human observers, so you have *no more reason* for thinking that you did a shuffling-that-puts-the-ace-of-hearts-on-top, than to think you did a shuffling-that-puts-the-3-of-diamonds-on-top, etc. Thus, you assign equal probabilities to each possible type of shuffling that you might have done. That's why each card is equally likely to be on top after shuffling. And that's an application of the Principle of Indifference.

You might think that we can avoid this by collecting inductive evidence about the frequencies of different kinds of shufflings. But inductive reasoning in general relies on the Principle of Indifference. In inductive reasoning, you take a (hopefully large) sample from a population. You know that the great majority of large samples that could be taken from that population are representative (per §12.4). So *if* you assume that each possible sample is equally likely to be drawn, then you can infer that your sample is highly likely to be representative. If you *don't* assume that, then you *can't* infer that—maybe the unrepresentative samples are somehow much more likely to be drawn, in which case your induction fails. So what's the justification for treating each sample as being equally likely? It's the Principle of Indifference—we take them as equiprobable when we have no evidence of some types of samples being more likely to have been chosen than others.

12.6.3. Inconsistencies in the PI

Now I'll tell you the main objection to the PI: It is that the PI supports contradictory probability assessments. Here is an example.

Traveling Sue: You are informed that Sue took a journey of 100 miles. Assume you have no other relevant information about the case. You are then asked to answer two possible problems:

Problem 1: Assuming that Sue's trip took between 1 hour and 2 hours, what is the probability that it took between 1 and 1.5 hours?

Problem 2: Assuming that Sue's average velocity was between 50 and 100 mph, what is the probability that it was between 66.7 and 100 mph?

These are seemingly easy questions to answer using the Principle of Indifference.[118] Problem 1: The interval from 1 to 1.5 is half of the range of

---

[118] Just stipulate that it's part of the PI that, when you have a continuous range of

possible times, so the probability of the time falling between 1 and 1.5 is ½. (1 − 1.5)/(2 − 1) = 0.5.

Problem 2: The interval from 66.7 to 100 is two thirds of the range of possible velocities, so the probability of the velocity falling between 66.7 and 100 is ⅔. (100 − 66.7)/(100 − 50) = 0.667.

Great. Now, the only problem is that these two answers are inconsistent. Given a distance of 100 miles, $t = 1$ hour if and only if $v = 100$ mph, $t = 2$ hours if and only if $v = 50$ mph; and $t = 1.5$ hours if and only if $v = 66.7$ mph ($v = d/t = 100/1.5 = 66.7$). So to say that t was between 1 and 2 is equivalent to saying that v was between 50 and 100, and to say that t was between 1 and 1.5 is equivalent to saying that v was between 66.7 and 100. Hence, Problem 1 and Problem 2 are the same problem.

The same problem can't have two different answers. The probability can't be both ½ and ⅔. Since we worked out these answers by applying the Principle of Indifference, the PI must be false.

There are many examples like this. Another example involves a cube about which you know only that its side is between 0 and 2 inches, and you have to calculate the probability that the side is between 0 and 1 (you get different answers depending on whether you frame the problem in terms of the length of the side or the volume of the cube). Another involves choosing a random chord in a circle and trying to calculate the probability of the chord being shorter than the radius (you get different answers for different ways of choosing "a random chord").[119]

12.6.4. Defenses of the PI

Is there any way of rescuing the PI?

The general problem is that there are different ways of describing the same set of possibilities—different ways of dividing up the possibility space, or different sets of variables that can capture the same possibilities—and what counts as a uniform probability distribution under *one* description may be nonuniform under another description. Some of these different descriptions, of course, are unnatural—e.g., if I proposed describing the Traveling Sue problem in terms of the *cube root* of the velocity, that would also generate a different answer to the problem, but you would probably have just found that silly, because cube root of velocity is an unnatural, arbitrary choice of variable.

---

possibilities, with no evidence favoring any subset of the range over any other, equal-sized subset, then the probability of the truth falling within a given range is proportional to the size of that range.

[119] For discussion of these examples, see Bas van Fraassen, *Laws and Symmetry*, ch. 12.

That's why I chose velocity and time—because those strike most people as equally natural variables in terms of which to state the problem.

So one way of trying to (partially) save the PI would be to restrict it—maybe the PI applies only when there is a uniquely natural description of the possibilities, as in the Two Envelopes example (§12.6.1). Another approach is that, when there are multiple natural descriptions, we could apply a meta-PI, so to speak: We could treat each of the natural descriptions as being equally good, and thus average the answers that we would get from each of them. So in the Traveling Sue example, we might average the ½ and ⅔ answers.

A third approach would be to find a reason for privileging some description of a set of possibilities, to say, "this is the right description". This is my preferred approach. I say that the right description is the one that uses the most explanatorily fundamental variables. Example: In the Traveling Sue case, I claim, the velocity at which one travels *explains* the duration of the trip (given a fixed distance), but not vice versa. (The trip took a certain amount of time *because* the person was traveling at a certain speed, not vice versa.) So the velocity formulation is privileged.[120]

12.6.5. The Problem of the PI Is the Problem of Induction

Here's something you probably didn't notice: The problem with the Principle of Indifference is kind of the same problem as the Problem of Induction.

Say you're flipping a coin, and you have no previous knowledge about coins. (So you have no evidence or opinions about whether the coin is fair.) All you know is that it must come up "heads" or "tails" each time. Now say you flip it ten times and it comes up heads all ten times. What credence should you have that it will come up heads the next time you flip it?

The skeptic (at least one kind of skeptic) is going to say: 50%, the same as the probability before you flipped the coin at all. No matter how many times you get heads in a row, the next flip always has a 50% chance of yielding heads and a 50% chance of yielding tails. This can be justified by the Principle of Indifference: There are 2,048 (that's 2^{11}) possible outcomes for a sequence of 11 coin flips. By the PI, we assign an equal probability to each of those outcomes. Of the 2,048 possibilities, there is exactly one in which the coin comes up heads the first ten times and then heads the eleventh time, and one in which the coin comes up heads the first ten times and then tails the eleventh time. Since we assign each possible sequence an equal probability, that means that, given that you get heads on the first ten flips, there is a 50% chance of heads on the eleventh flip and a 50% chance of tails.

---

[120] See my paper, "Explanationist Aid for the Theory of Inductive Logic" from the *British Journal for the Philosophy of Science* (2009).

Now, here is a different answer. The coin has some objective chance of coming up heads when flipped, based on its physical properties. This objective chance is not to be confused with the *epistemic probability* of its coming up heads; the objective chance is supposed to be a physical property of the coin, which you start out completely ignorant of but you can gather information about. Since you start with no knowledge about the coin, you apply the Principle of Indifference to the possible values of the objective chance of heads. Each time you flip the coin, that gives you probabilistic information about the value of that objective chance. Getting ten heads in a row causes you, by Bayesian reasoning, to revise upward your estimate of the objective chance, which in turn causes you to expect the coin to come up heads in the future. I don't want to put too much math here, so I'll just tell you that if you do the calculations, you get a probability of 11/12 for the next flip being heads, given that the first ten were all heads.[121]

So you see that you can derive either a skeptical conclusion or an inductivist conclusion by applying the Principle of Indifference to different descriptions of the possibilities. So the problem of induction becomes one of explaining why the latter application of the PI (or something like it) is better than the skeptic's application. So the problem of induction turns into a problem of interpreting the PI.

Last comment on this: My answer is that the objective chance is more explanatorily fundamental than the particular sequence of outcomes; hence, the correct application of the PI is the one that applies the PI to the objective chance.

12.7. Inference to the Best Explanation[122]

12.7.1. The IBE Theory of Induction

Here is something that a lot of people have noticed: When you have a heavy object that is unsupported near the surface of the Earth, it moves downward.

---

[121] For mathophiles, here is how I got that. Let H_n be the proposition that all of the first n flips come up heads, let c be the objective chance of heads on each occasion, let ρ be the (epistemic) probability density function over c, and let $C=c$ be the proposition that the correct objective chance is c. In general, $P(H_n) = \int_{c=0}^{1} \rho(c) \times P(H_n | C = c) dc = \int_0^1 \rho(c) \times c^n \, dc$. ρ is everywhere 1 from the Principle of Indifference, so $P(H_n) = \int_0^1 c^n \, dc = \frac{1}{n+1}$. Now, what we want is $P(H_{11} | H_{10})$, which, by Axiom 4, equals $P(H_{11} \& H_{10})/P(H_{10})$, which $= P(H_{11})/P(H_{10})$, which (from the above-derived formula) equals $\frac{1}{11+1} / \frac{1}{10+1} = \frac{11}{12}$.

[122] This section is based on John Foster's "Induction, Explanation, and Natural

We could call this phenomenon "gravitational behavior". Because gravitational behavior has been observed very many times, by very many people, all over the world, in a wide variety of circumstances, it is not plausible that it is a mere coincidence. There must be some explanation.

Here is an explanation: There is a law of nature according to which bodies must behave gravitationally. In that case, we would not have to posit a giant coincidence. If this is the best explanation we can find (which seems plausible), then it would be reasonable to think that something like this is probably correct. If this explanation is true, bodies will also have to behave gravitationally in the future. So bodies will probably behave gravitationally in the future.

The preceding line of thinking illustrates the *inference to the best explanation* (IBE) approach to justifying induction. We started from some inductive evidence (bodies have been observed to behave gravitationally in the past, in a wide variety of circumstances), and we got to an inductive conclusion (bodies will behave gravitationally in the future). We don't draw the inductive conclusion *directly*; rather, we first make an intermediate step, which is an **inference to the best explanation**. This is an inference in which you start from some evidence that would be improbable if there were no explanation, identify the best available explanation, and infer that that explanation is likely correct. After making this inference, you then deduce the consequences of that explanation for other cases. Here's a diagrammatic representation:

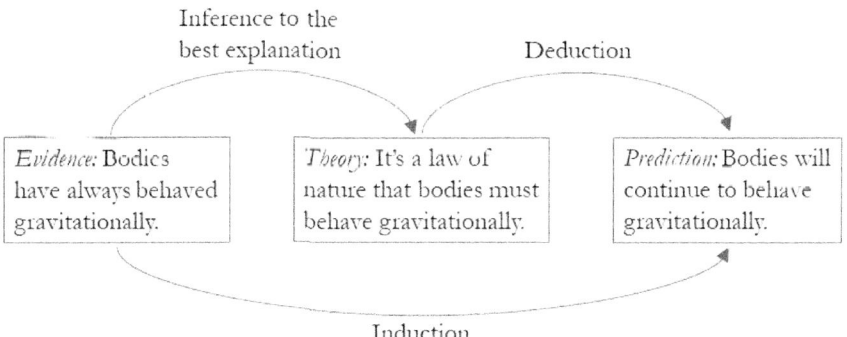

Some comments about the proposed explanation. It's important that the hypothesis is of a general *law* that *requires* gravitational behavior (it says bodies *must* behave gravitationally), not of a mere coincidental generalization. This matters because only the former actually *explains* the observations. However, the explanation is intentionally phrased in a vague way; I did not specify the

---

Necessity" (*Proceedings of the Aristotelian Society*, 1982-1983), though I have departed somewhat from Foster in responding to skeptical alternatives.

exact law of nature, only that there is *some* law according to which bodies must behave gravitationally. This would include Newton's Law of Gravity, Einstein's Field Equations, or numerous other possible laws of gravity. Any law that would require heavy objects to fall when dropped counts. I define our theory in this expansive way because we can't be sure just from watching gravitational behavior exactly what the law is, but we also don't *need* to know that in order to draw the desired inductive conclusion.

12.7.2. Alternative Explanations

A skeptic's main response would probably be to deny that the proposed theory is really the best explanation; the skeptic would likely propose some alternative explanation that wouldn't support inductive predictions. Let's look at some of those.

Alternative #1: Maybe the observed gravitational behavior is just a matter of chance. (Note: Perhaps this isn't an alternative *explanation* but rather a *rejection* of any explanation. But let's not worry about that.)

Reply: This is *logically possible*, but, obviously, ridiculously unlikely. No defender of induction claims to have *100% certainty* in inductive conclusions; we at most claim to have highly probable conclusions, and that's what the inductive skeptic is doubting. So it's not enough for the skeptic to point to an extremely unlikely logical possibility.

Alternative #2: Maybe there is a law of nature, but it only says that bodies behave gravitationally *up until the year 2100*. This law would explain all of our observations thus far but would not enable us to predict anything about what will happen after 2100 A.D.

Reply: I think this alternative law is metaphysically impossible. The *current time* cannot itself be a causally relevant factor. One reason for this is that all times are intrinsically, qualitatively identical to each other. Also, what produces effects are events and states of affairs. Events and states are things that *happen at* particular times; times are not themselves events or states of affairs.

Alternative #3: Maybe there is a law of nature that says "All bodies must behave gravitationally", but the law itself ceases to exist in the year 2100 A.D.

Reply: I think this is also metaphysically impossible. Laws are not ordinary objects, like a table, that could be destroyed. There is not some ethereal object floating around the universe *making* things behave in a certain way, such that if that object goes away things will be free to behave differently; there are only the ordinary physical things themselves, and it is only *their own* properties that make them behave in the way they do. Laws are just propositions that correctly describe the fundamental causal powers of certain features of events and states of affairs. Thus, if gravitational behavior is to stop in 2100 A.D., there must be some actual event that happens or state of affairs that changes at that time.

Alternative #4: Maybe there is some unknown-to-us condition C, which has obtained throughout human history, and the true law of nature says that *in condition C*, bodies must behave gravitationally. But also, maybe condition C is shortly going to stop obtaining. (Perhaps this is what Alternatives #2 and #3 were really getting at.) This theory would explain all past observations of gravitational behavior without letting us make inferences about the future.

Reply: Is condition C a common condition or a rare condition, in the universe as a whole? (Or: Does C have a high objective (physical) probability, or a low one?) If C is a rare condition, then it's highly unlikely that C would happen to have obtained every time that humans have checked for gravitational behavior in the past. If C is a common condition, then it's unlikely that it is about to stop obtaining. Thus, the alternative hypothesis either fails to explain our evidence, or it supports the inductive conclusion that bodies will probably behave gravitationally in the future. This point remains true as long as the skeptic has no specific reasons for thinking that the current time is special (and thus for thinking that C would stop obtaining now of all times).

Alternative #5: Maybe there is a law of nature that in Φ-circumstances, bodies must behave gravitationally.

This one requires explanation. Take the exact, complete state that the world was in the first time someone observed gravitational behavior. Call that condition "Φ_1". Similarly, the state the world was in the second time someone observed gravitational behavior is condition Φ_2, and so on, all the way up to condition Φ_n, the state the world was in the most recent time that someone observed gravitational behavior. Let "Φ-circumstances" be defined as circumstances in which Φ_1 or Φ_2 or ... or Φ_n obtains. Now you can see that we can explain all previous observations of gravitational behavior by the hypothesis of a law that *in Φ-circumstances*, bodies must behave gravitationally. However, we can't extend this to any inductive conclusions, because Φ-circumstances will probably never obtain again (or at least not for an extremely long time!), since the universe is not going to repeat the exact state that it was in at one of those previous times.

Reply: This hypothesis succeeds in explaining our past observations, but only by a ridiculously complex theory that posits distinct causally relevant factors for each past observation of gravitational behavior. Other things being equal, the simplest explanation of a set of evidence is best. Since there is no reason for introducing the additional complexity in this case, and since the normal law of gravity is vastly simpler, it is vastly superior to the "Φ-circumstances" theory.

A related point (which may also explain why the simplest explanation tends to be the best) is this. If the true law of gravity were an incredibly complex law, such as the skeptic proposes, with n different, highly specific and complicated conditions in it, then it would be an amazing coincidence that all the previous times when we humans have been observing, the actual state of the world just happened to be one of those incredibly complicated and super-specific conditions that appears in the law. What's the probability of such a coincidence? Pretty much zero. Why? Because the Φ-circumstances were deliberately constructed by the skeptic to constitute 0% of the space of possible states of the world—that's how we know that Φ-circumstances are not going to obtain again.[123]

12.8. The Grue Puzzle

12.8.1. Goodman's New Color

Many years ago, Nelson Goodman discovered a new color, so to speak.[124] It is the color **grue**, and it is defined as follows:

x is grue $=_{df}$ [(x is first observed before the year 2100 A.D. and x is green) or (x is not first observed before 2100 A.D. and x is blue)].

("$=_{df}$" is the symbol for "is defined as".) *Note:* I do not care whether you think this actually counts as "a color" or not, so don't try to argue with me about that. I also don't care that you hate this concept because it contains a disjunction in its definition. That is just a stipulative definition, so there is no sense in complaining about it. Nelson Goodman made-up the word "grue", so it means whatever he says it means.

Notice that many objects in the world are verifiably grue. For instance, as of this writing, every emerald that anyone has ever seen has (I assume) been grue. You can tell that because they have all been observed before 2100 A.D., and they have also all been green; hence, they satisfied the first disjunct in the

---

[123] Another way to put the point: If the true law of gravity were of the general form that the skeptic proposes, with this very long disjunction of extremely specific conditions, it could have just as well been *any* similarly specific conditions. But there are very many (infinitely many, in fact) such sets of conditions. So the probability of its being exactly the set of conditions needed to explain our actual observations is zero. So the skeptic's hypothesis has a prior probability of zero. Alternately, if you believe in "infinitesimal" numbers, the skeptic's hypothesis has an infinitesimal probability.
[124] See his "The New Riddle of Induction" in *Fact, Fiction, and Forecast* (1955).

definition, so they were grue. And please don't sit there and insist, "They weren't grue, they were green!" This is a dumb thing to say, since of course the fact that they were green is part of what *made* them grue, not something that *prevents* them from being grue. If you're denying that some emeralds are grue, you have to be either (*i*) denying that they are green, or (*ii*) denying that they've been observed. Because, again, that's what the definition says, and Nelson Goodman gets to define his made-up word however he wants.

Notice also that many objects in the world are verifiably non-grue. For instance, every sapphire that has ever been observed has (I assume) been non-grue. For (I assume) none of them have been green, so they violated the first disjunct in the definition; and all of them were observed before 2100 A.D., so they also violated the second disjunct in the definition.

When it comes to the objects that are going to be first observed in 2100 and after (say, the emeralds that are going to be excavated then), we don't know for sure whether they will turn out to be grue or not. If the emeralds we dig up in 2100 A.D. are green, then they will *not* be grue. If they are blue, then they *will* be grue. (Again, look at the definition.)

12.8.2. The Puzzle

As noted, every emerald that has ever been observed thus far has been verifiably grue. (Unless maybe you're reading this after the year 2099, which I doubt.) I learned from other philosophers that there is this thing called induction, whereby, if all observed *A*'s have been *B*, you get to infer that all *A*'s are *B* (including the unobserved ones). So I guess we can now infer that all emeralds are grue, right?

No, wrong. The observation of grue emeralds in the past is *not* evidence for new emeralds found in 2100 A.D. and after being grue. In fact, it is evidence *against* that. In fact, it is *inductive* evidence against that. So induction *isn't* really just generalizing from observations. Sometimes, proper inductive reasoning leads you to *deny* that future things will have the same properties as the things you've observed (if, e.g., one of those properties was grueness). Comparing these two inferences:

All observed emeralds have been green.
∴ All emeralds are green.

All observed emeralds have been grue.
∴ All emeralds are grue.

The first one is induction; the second is not induction and not any legitimate kind of inference at all.

So here's the puzzle: Try to give a complete characterization of "the rules of induction"—what you get to infer from what—that allows the first inference but excludes the second.

12.8.3. What's Wrong with Grue?

Your first reaction is probably that there is something wrong with the predicate "grue", and that sort of predicate needs to be excluded. But what might be wrong with it?

You might want to say that what's wrong with it is that the definition of "grue" contains a reference to a particular time, the year 2100 A.D. Goodman's response to this is to say that the word "green" can also be defined in a way that refers to a particular time. To see this, I first have to explain another color term that Goodman invented:

x is **bleen** $=_{df}$ [(x is first observed before the year 2100 A.D. and x is blue) or (x is not first observed before 2100 A.D. and x is green)].

It's just like grue, but with blue and green switched. Now let me tell you Goodman's definition of "green":

x is green $=_{df}$ [(x is first observed before the year 2100 A.D. and x is grue) or (x is not first observed before 2100 A.D. and x is bleen)].

(Notice that that works out logically.) So now you can see that "green" also contains a particular time in its definition. So you haven't identified anything that really differentiates "green" from "grue". (One imagines Goodman having a good laugh at our expense as he declares this.)

Goodman's own "solution" was to say that the relevant difference is that "green" is a more **entrenched** predicate than "grue". And what that means is basically that "green" has been used a lot more than "grue" has in actual people's reasoning in our society. I think this is such a lame thing to say that I'm not going to talk about that any more.

Here is another thing you might say. Green is an observable property, while grue is not. If you look at a thing, you can tell, just by how it looks, whether it's green (in normal circumstances). But you cannot tell just by looking at a thing whether it is grue. You have to also find out what time it is, and if it is now 2100 A.D. or later, you have to do historical research to find out whether anyone else observed this object previously. Maybe that has something to do with why grue is not a suitable property to use in inductive reasoning.

Lastly, perhaps the right thing to say is the obvious thing: The concept GREEN groups things together based on actual, objective similarities. The concept GRUE does not do this. The GRUE concept includes some objectively dissimilar things, while refusing to include some things that are more similar. To state that more precisely: In the GRUE/BLEEN conceptual scheme, you can have objects x, y, and z, where x and y objectively resemble each other more than x and z do in any qualitative respect, yet x and z both get grouped together as part of the same category, while x and y do not. It's plausible that, if you're going to be making inductive inferences, you need to classify things according to their objective, qualitative resemblances.

By the way, it's not like Goodman didn't think of this. He disagrees with it because of a broader sort of metaphysical subjectivism. That is, he doesn't believe in objective degrees of similarity; he thinks there is only similarity relative to a conceptual scheme.

12.9. Conclusion

Of course David Hume is wrong. Come on, you didn't think that a philosopher 300 years ago refuted the entire scientific method, as well as most of the reasoning of every human being who ever lived, did you? You didn't think that the success of science has been a complete coincidence … and, even more ridiculously, that every regularity we've ever observed is a total coincidence that can't be expected to continue?

No, you didn't. But it's still philosophically interesting and important to understand how inductive reasoning works to render its conclusions probable. There are three plausible accounts of this: Proportional Syllogism, (objective) Bayesianism, and Inference to the Best Explanation. Let's conclude by thinking about how these relate to each other.

You could think of the "proportional syllogism" approach as an instance of Inference to the Best Explanation, rather than as a competing approach. The evidence you start with is the distribution of a certain trait in some large sample—trait T has a frequency of x% in the sample. This evidence would be improbable if the *population* did not have a frequency of about x%. The best explanation of the evidence, you might say, is that the population frequency is about x%. The probabilistic argument we gave in §12.4 can be construed as striving to show that this is indeed the best explanation.

(By the way, this isn't *always* the best explanation. In some cases, a better explanation might be that there was a defect in your sampling method, such that your method either preferentially selects items with T, or preferentially selects items without T. People in statistics have techniques for avoiding this, and these are designed to make it so that the best explanation of the sample data really is that the population has approximately the distribution of traits found in the sample.)

Turning to the Bayesian approach, you can think of Inference to the Best Explanation as a kind of Bayesian reasoning. You start from some evidence that would be improbable if there were no explanation. Plausibly, an explanation is going to be something that, if true, would render that evidence more probable. So P(*e*|there is an explanation) > P(*e*|there is no explanation). So by Bayesian reasoning, you infer that there is an explanation. Trivially, if there is an explanation, then the *best* explanation is the one that is most likely to be correct. Hence, you have probabilistic reason to accept the best explanation. So the Bayesian approach helps motivate inference to the best explanation. At the same time, the explanationist approach helps fill out the Bayesian approach, because explanatory considerations help the objective Bayesian figure out how to apply the Principle of Indifference (§12.6.5).

Since the proportional syllogism approach is explicitly formulated in probabilistic terms, it is obvious how it coheres with Bayesianism. As noted earlier (§12.6.2), the proportional syllogism argument implicitly applies the Principle of Indifference by assigning equal probabilities to each possible sample of a given size that could be drawn from the population.

So this is all to say that the right answer to the problem of induction might be proportional syllogism, *and* Bayesianism, *and* inference to the best explanation.

13. Testimony

In this chapter, we talk about how you get justified beliefs from **testimony**, which is what philosophers call it when other people tell you things.

13.1. The Centrality of Testimony

Almost all of my interesting knowledge about the world is based on testimony. I know, for example, that the Earth is about 4.5 billion years old, that Japan is a country, that the United States originated from British colonies, that tables are made of atoms, and that the stars in the night sky are distant suns. I didn't figure out any of that myself; I learned all of it from other people. Without testimony, practically none of my current beliefs would be justified.

Fortunately, we have very smart, diligent, rational people to figure out stuff like that for us—we have scientists, historians, and other experts. These experts figured out those things for themselves; *they* presumably didn't just rely on other experts. Or so people say. I know something about how they figure stuff out—using the scientific method, for example (see ch. 14). When the experts' methods are described, you can see why they're good methods. And how do I know that they really use those methods? Well, I learned that from other people too.

The world's oldest scientific academy, the Royal Society of London, was founded in 1660. Shortly after its founding, they adopted the motto, "*Nullius in verba*" (Latin for "On no man's word"), which is still their motto. This motto expressed the Enlightenment spirit of independent thinking. These were serious researchers who wanted to genuinely understand reality, not just confirm their biases. They wanted to get away from the appeals to authority that, in their view, were all too common in medieval philosophy (if you ever look at some medieval philosophy, there are a lot of appeals to Aristotle and the Bible). Instead of taking someone's word, they were going to verify everything for themselves.

Those are admirable sentiments. But to modern ears (at least to mine), the motto comes across as foolishly naïve. Were these scientists really claiming that they don't trust anyone's word on anything? That's clearly false; they at least trusted other scientists. If we were to take up the Royal Society's motto, we'd have to throw out almost everything we currently know. Every scientist would have to verify every piece of accepted scientific knowledge for himself. Anyone who wanted to be a physicist would have to redo every important experiment in the history of the subject. It would take the rest of his life to do the first ten thousandth of this work, so he'd never get around to doing anything new. Scientific knowledge, in reality, is almost 100% based on authority, even for the scientists themselves—any scientist takes almost all of his understanding of his subject from textbooks, articles, and lectures by other people.

All of which is to say that testimony is a crucial source of knowledge and justified belief, which we can't do without.

13.2. The Inductive Account

So here's a simple, natural account of how testimony justifies beliefs: You hear someone say that p. You believe that person is probably reliable about p. Therefore, you infer that p is probably true.[125]

The key question would then be why you think that person is reliable about p. Perhaps you have heard this person speak about p-related matters before, you have frequently checked on her p-related assertions, and you have generally found them to be correct. Thus, you inductively inferred that this person is reliable about things related to p.

This scenario, however, hardly ever happens. I rarely check up on anyone's assertions, and I certainly don't check up on a *large number* of assertions by the same person on the same topic, as would seem to be necessary for an inductive inference. And by the way, on those rare occasions when I do try to check on someone's assertions, the way I do it is almost always by checking them against *someone else's assertions*—e.g., I check my neighbor's claims against claims from some news source. So I must already accept testimony in some more general sense. Furthermore, the range of topics on which I can readily test people's assertions is very limited. There are entire, broad fields of knowledge in which I have *never* acquired any non-testimonial knowledge. For instance, I have never verified a single historical claim by non-testimonial means.

Maybe I don't need to check on the reliability of each testifier for each topic. Maybe I have checked on many other people's assertions about various things in the past, I generally found them to be correct, and thus I have inductively inferred that *people in general* tend to tell the truth about most things. Thus, when a new person tells me something, I may assume that that person's

---

[125] This is David Hume's view of testimony. See his section on miracles in the *Enquiry Concerning Human Understanding* (1748).

assertion is probably trustworthy, as long as I have no special reasons for doubting that person's statement or for thinking that person less reliable than the average person.

Even this story, however, is overly optimistic. Sad to say, I really haven't checked on very many people at all. I haven't taken a large, random sample of assertions by various humans and verified their truth, as would seem to be required for an inductive inference to the general veracity of people's statements.

Children are in an even worse state: They haven't had a chance to check on almost any assertions that they receive from adults. They just start out credulous, instinctively believing most of what adults (and even other children!) tell them. This natural credulity may be necessary to develop a complex enough belief system to be able to assess whether a new claim that one hears is plausible or not. So if you don't start out trusting testimony by default, you might never be able to develop a sophisticated belief system at all.

The only kind of claims that I have frequently checked on are claims about directly observable features of my immediate environment. E.g., you tell me it's raining, then when I go outside I see that it is. You say there's some beer in the fridge, and when I open it, I find it there. So, on the inductive theory of testimonial knowledge, we might have adequate grounds for trusting assertions that other people make about directly observable matters of fact.

But that's only enough to support a tiny portion of our understanding of the world. And it's really not obvious why you could infer, from people's being reliable about immediately observable facts, that they're reliable about all the much more difficult-to-discover, non-observable facts that we commonly learn from others. It would be hard to see, for instance, why I would be justified in believing that the Earth is 4.5 billion years old, that tables are made of atoms, or that the U.S. was founded by former British colonies.

13.3. The Default of Credulity

Motivated by the sort of problems just discussed, some philosophers propose that testimony is a basic source of justification—meaning that you're justified in trusting testimony by default, without the need of any argument for its reliability, as long as you have no specific grounds for doubt about a given piece of testimony. There must be *some* knowledge sources that one may trust by default in this way; otherwise, all knowledge would be impossible (see §6.2). Introspection, memory, intuition, and perhaps sensory perception are good examples of such basic sources. Maybe testimony is another one.

13.3.1. Natural Inclination to Believe

Why would we be entitled to trust testimony by default? The first account of this is Thomas Reid's. Reid basically thought that if you have a natural inclination to form beliefs in a certain way, then you're justified in holding those beliefs by default. You get to just start out trusting your natural faculties until you have a reason not to. He also thought that accepting testimony was one of these natural belief-forming mechanisms. Human beings are born with a pair of instincts that go well together: We have an instinct to tell the truth as we see it, and we also have an instinct to accept the statements of other people. So we're justified in accepting testimony by default.

> **Interlude: Thomas Reid**
> Thomas Reid was a Scottish philosopher of the 1700s. He spent a lot of time defending common sense and criticizing "the theory of ideas", by which he meant the view that the immediate objects of our awareness are always ideas in our own minds, as argued by Locke, Berkeley, and Hume. He thought instead that we could be directly aware of external objects. He was kind of the anti-Hume, and he has some choice passages making fun of Hume (and other philosophers). E.g., after mentioning Hume's theory that the self is an illusion, he writes:
>
>> [I]t is certainly a most amazing discovery, that thought and ideas may be without any thinking being. A discovery big with consequences which cannot easily be traced by those deluded mortals who think and reason in the common track.... It seemed very natural to think, that the *Treatise of Human Nature* required an author, and a very ingenious one too; but now we learn, that it is only a set of ideas which came together, and arranged themselves by certain associations and attractions.[126]
>
> About common sense, he writes:
>
>> [P]hilosophy ... has no other root but the principles of common sense; it grows out of them, and draws its nourishment from them: severed from this root, its honours wither, its sap is dried up, it dies and rots.[127]

Skeptics are basically people who accept some argument for distrusting one or more of our natural belief-forming mechanisms, such as testimony or sensory observation. But then the skeptic is placing trust in his own *reasoning*, which is just another natural belief-forming mechanism. Reid thought there

---

[126] From the *Inquiry into the Human Mind* (1769), II.6.
[127] *Inquiry*, I.4.

was no principled rationale for accepting *some* of our natural faculties but not others. So it doesn't make sense to trust reasoning but not trust, e.g., testimony.

This is an interesting line of thinking, but it is not entirely persuasive. It's not obvious that the only relevant epistemological distinction one can draw among beliefs is between those that are and those that are not produced by a natural faculty. Maybe some but not all natural mechanisms produce justified beliefs. Here's an example: Recent research in psychology shows that people tend to have very strong self-serving biases. E.g., large majorities of people think themselves to be smarter, more moral, better drivers, better at getting along with people, and of course *less biased* than the average person. This may be a natural belief-forming mechanism; let's suppose it is. We wouldn't want to say this makes all these self-serving beliefs epistemically *justified*, would we?

In an earlier chapter, we mentioned some theories about which beliefs have foundational justification (ch. 5). "Beliefs formed by natural faculties are foundational" is not the only possible theory! For instance, you might think that a belief has foundational justification when we are directly *acquainted with* the fact that makes it true. Perhaps we enjoy such acquaintance with our own mental states and some universals. However, upon hearing a piece of testimony, we do *not* thereby enjoy direct acquaintance with the fact to which the speaker is attesting, nor are we directly acquainted with the speaker's reliability. Thus could we justify trusting introspection and reason by default but not testimony.

13.3.2. Intelligible Presentation as True

Some philosophers think that we are entitled by default to believe any proposition that is presented to us as true, simply because it is intelligible and presented as true.[128] The thought is that, first, if a statement is intelligible (you are able to understand what it says), that is enough for you to presume that it came from a rational being. (Notice that sounds produced by inanimate nature or non-intelligent animals are generally not intelligible.) Second, you're also entitled to assume that rational beings are probably right about things unless there's some reason to think otherwise, because rationality itself is inherently truth-oriented. This principle applies to yourself (when you use your own faculty of reason) as well as others (when you listen to other people's ideas). Notice, by the way, that if you don't assume this, then you're going to be epistemically screwed, i.e., you'll be permanently trapped in skepticism. You won't be able to reason your way out of skepticism, because you won't trust

---

[128] By "some philosophers", I mean Tyler Burge ("Content Preservation", *Philosophical Review*, 1993).

your own faculty of reason to start with. Assuming (as we do) that skepticism is wrong, we're entitled to treat reason as a source of truth.

Problem: Sure, reason is a source of truth. But it's also often rational to lie to others. So maybe this "rational source" that you're listening to is rationally misrepresenting the facts to you.

I can't think of a good response to this problem, so I'll just mention Tyler Burge's bad response. He says that "[o]ne of reason's primary functions is that of presenting truth, independently of special personal interests. Lying is sometimes rational in the sense that it is in the liar's best interests. But lying occasions a disunity among functions of reason."[129] He reasons that since presenting truth is at least *one* of reason's functions, there is *at least some* prima facie reason to think that a proposition presented as true by a rational being would be true, unless there's some reason to think it would be in the being's interests to lie. (This is a weak conclusion, but that's all Burge is going for.) Why I don't find this persuasive: I agree that uncovering truth *for oneself* is a primary function of reason, but I don't see how presenting truth *to other people* is a primary function of reason.

13.3.3. *The Principle of Charity in Interpretation*

Some philosophers think that you can derive a default entitlement to accept testimony by thinking about how we interpret language.[130] People who think about this sort of thing generally endorse the **Principle of Charity** in interpretation, which holds that one must try to interpret other people's words in a way that makes their statements by and large correct, or at least reasonable.

Suppose you see me point to a table and say, "Look, there's a flurge." You've never heard the word "flurge" before and have no clues to its meaning other than my usage. Several more times, you notice me apparently calling tables "flurges". How are you going to interpret the word "flurge"?

It seems obvious that you should interpret it to mean "table", or something like that (maybe "tabletop", or "undetached table part", or "table time slice"[131]). You wouldn't interpret it to mean "giraffe" or "planetoid". Why not? Because there *was no* giraffe or planetoid in the places where I said there was a "flurge". Notice, then, that your method of interpretation presupposes that I should be interpreted, if possible, as saying something *true*. If you don't assume

---

[129] "Content Preservation," 475.
[130] See C.A.J. Coady's "Testimony and Observation" (*American Philosophical Quarterly*, 1973).
[131] The last two suggestions are inspired by Quine's discussion of indeterminacy of translation in *Word and Object* (1960).

that, then the "giraffe" interpretation is just as good as the "table" interpretation.

Interpretation would be impossible without this assumption. If you don't by default assume that I'm probably saying apparently true things, then there are no constraints on what "flurge" might mean. The point generalizes to language in general, so that you could not even learn any language in the first place without using the Principle of Charity. In the "flurge" case, you might be tempted to think that you could avoid reliance on the Principle of Charity by simply *asking* me what "flurge" means. But then you'd have to assume that I was telling the truth about what "flurge" means. Moreover, asking me what I mean only works if you have already learned language in general, which could not have taken place by your asking people what every word means.

So the idea that *people usually say true things* is built into one's ability to interpret language, which is to say, it is built into one's understanding of people as *saying things* at all. So there would be something deeply strange and self-undermining about holding that one should start out by default mistrusting people's statements and that one needs special evidence for thinking their statements are true.

The above doesn't really explain *why* it makes sense to assume that people's statements are by and large true, though. The fact that we couldn't learn language without this assumption doesn't entail that the assumption is justified. One thought is that the Principle of Charity in interpretation is just a special case of the broader principle that one should interpret other beings as doing things that at least somewhat *make sense*. (But a problem for this thought is that, as noted earlier, it often makes sense to lie.)

Another thought is that the way word meanings are constituted requires general truth-telling. Suppose that people start calling giraffes "tables", and we stop calling tables "tables". At first, we're making a lot of false statements. But if this new way of talking becomes well-established, our statements are going to stop being false—the word "table" will just come to *mean* "giraffe", at which point our statements using the word "table" will be true again. This is how word meanings work in general, so that guarantees that our statements are by and large true.

Some caveats: Obviously, not all statements are true. Sometimes we lie or make mistakes. The claim is only that *most* statements, under normal circumstances, are correct. Or perhaps better, most statements are rational, or apparently correct given the speaker's evidence at the time. This is just to establish a prima facie presumption in favor of testimony, which of course can be defeated if you have reasons for thinking a particular statement is unreliable.

Also, there can be particular words that are regularly used to make false statements. Back when people believed in witches, they regularly applied "witch" to people who were not witches. As a matter of fact, every single time the word was applied to someone, it was misapplied! This did not make the word lose its meaning or come to mean something like "woman whom we don't like and want to burn". The reason is that people accepted an explicit definition of the word, along the lines of "woman who has acquired supernatural powers by intercourse with the Devil", and they accepted lots of statements about "witches" that cohered with that definition. These other statements helped to fix the meaning of "witch". But this only works because we have a large number of *other* words that have already acquired meanings, and those other words *by and large* acquired their meanings from their contexts of usage, such that our sentences mean things that make sense to say in the contexts in which they are used.

I think the above line of thinking is basically right, as regards statements about our immediate environment. However, it leaves open the possibility that people are only reliable about immediately observable facts—that would be enough for us to have a meaningful, understandable language. We might at the same time be radically unreliable about not-directly-observable matters. This is important, because most of our worldview concerns matters that we can't directly observe (see the examples in §13.1).

13.4. Coherence

The above ideas resolve *some* of the problem of testimony. Plausibly (well, it's plausible to me, anyway), the point about the Principle of Charity shows that it's reasonable to assume that people by and large tell the truth about mundane, observable matters. This conclusion is also supported by induction from ordinary experiences: We often have occasion to check on things that other people say about the observable world. When someone remarks on the weather, when they talk about the buildings around us, when they mention a sound or a smell in the environment, etc., my experience is that what they say usually makes sense in light of what I myself can observe. I bet you have the same experience. It basically never happens that other people talk about observable things that I can't observe (if I'm in the appropriate place to observe them).[132]

That's enough to establish at least some small presumption in favor of believing things that other people tell you in general, unless you have a reason for thinking that a particular statement is likely to be false. I think there are two remaining problems. First: How do we get a *very high* degree of justification for some claims about *unobservable* facts? For instance, I know that America had its

---

[132] Exception: If your friends are into hallucinogens.

origin in colonies that rebelled against Britain. That is not just a plausible conjecture for me, slightly more likely than not; that is something about which I have no serious doubts at all, even though my knowledge is purely testimonial. If I meet someone who expresses doubts about it, I will dismiss the person as not serious. So, how is this so certain for me?

Second: How is it that children have strong justification for testimony-based beliefs, given the very limited experience from which they can draw for inductive reasoning?

I think the best answer to the first question is essentially to appeal to coherence. I don't just have a simple inductive inference from the testimonial claims that I have checked via non-testimonial evidence. I can also compare testimonial claims to each other. The standard views about history (and various other matters) that I have acquired from others *fit together* in a way that would make it hard for just one to be false, particularly one as central as the belief about the origin of the U.S. (Some less central beliefs could of course be mistaken without causing too much trouble for the rest of the system.) The coherence of the system means that it is highly likely to be by and large correct, and that the particularly central beliefs are particularly probable (see the discussion of coherence in §4.3).

And it's not just my beliefs *about history* that figure in this coherent system. It's also my beliefs about the present, especially my beliefs about other people. My understanding of where the standard historical doctrines came from—i.e., from professional historians who do research, from documents and artifacts that have been passed down, etc.—fits with their being by and large reliable, especially about things like where the U.S. came from (which is not a particularly difficult thing to know).

By contrast, if I hypothesize that we're radically mistaken, or that the historians are lying, about this kind of thing, I have no way of explaining how that works. I have no plausible account of how people would make such a colossal error without anyone finding out, or how and why historians would conspire to deliberately hide the truth from the rest of us. Any account I try to invent of how it might be that I'm radically wrong about how the U.S. was founded involves super-implausible, paranoid-delusion-style stories. It requires supposing that historians (or some other nefarious actors) are unlike the normal people I've met in my actual life. All this is summed up by saying that my belief system is a lot more coherent with the belief that the U.S. was founded by rebellious British colonists than with its denial.

Now you might want to ask: "But Mike, didn't you reject the coherence theory of justification in chapter 4?" Why yes, I did. But not on the grounds that coherence doesn't justify. My objection was that coherence justification *depends upon foundational justification*. So *if you reject foundational justification* (as coherentists do), then you've got no account of how coherence justifies anything. But if you *accept* foundational justification, as I do, then coherence can very well provide additional justification, and we're all good. By the way, I think that pretty much all foundationalists accept this. The dispute between foundationalists and coherentists never was about whether *coherence* can justify; it was always only over whether *foundations* exist.

One last issue: Children start out very credulous from a very young age, before they've had enough experiences to construct compelling inductive arguments, and before they have sufficiently complex belief systems to construct compelling coherence-based arguments. Indeed, children can be convinced of some extremely improbable things that *don't* fit with the rest of the things that adults say—e.g., beliefs about Santa Claus and perhaps some religious beliefs—because children are so uncritical in their reliance on testimony. In pre-scientific societies, people often hold onto systems of mythology, passed down through generations, that lack grounding in observable reality. This doesn't sound so great, but the upside is that children are able to quickly learn information that is of crucial practical import. That may be why humans evolved this natural credulity—you don't want young humans practicing scientific skepticism when parents tell them that snakes are dangerous, for example. So why are the testimonial beliefs of young children justified?

Perhaps the best answer is that they are not. Our testimonial beliefs start out unjustified (or rather, not *very* justified—the degree of confidence we repose in them is higher than warranted). Over time, as we acquire more sophisticated belief systems and a better understanding of other human beings, some of those beliefs become much more justified, as they come to be supported by increasingly complex networks of belief. Not all of our testimonial beliefs become equally justified, by the way. Some of them turn out *not* to fit very well with the rest of our beliefs (e.g., the belief in Santa Claus—that's why people usually give it up before too long).

13.5. Conclusion

Testimony is a super-important source of knowledge. But it's puzzling because we believe a lot of things on testimony in fields where we have never or almost never tried to verify anything by non-testimonial means. So why is it reasonable for us to think testimony in those areas is reliable?

One answer is that this is reasonable simply because it is our natural inclination. But this is doubtful since it suggests that any bias that is natural thereby becomes rational—e.g., it would be rational for average people to think they're smarter than average, merely because they have a natural egotistical bias.

Another answer is that, as long as a statement is intelligible, it is reasonable to assume that it was produced by a rational being. Since we're entitled to assume that reason is reliable in general, it's okay to assume that another rational being is a reliable source of information, unless we have reasons to doubt that. This account, however, doesn't give us a good answer to why we should assume that other people aren't simply lying.

A third answer is that the rational way of interpreting language, using the Principle of Charity, inherently presupposes that most statements are true, or at least apparently true given the speaker's evidence. This seems to be built into the nature of language, since the meanings of words (with occasional exceptions) are typically determined by their normal usage.

To account for our very high degree of justification for testimonial beliefs about unobserved matters in science, history, and so on, the above answer needs to be supplemented by appealing to coherence. As children, we start out forming a lot of beliefs that are a lot more confident than is justified. But over time, we develop complex systems of beliefs that fit together well. The beliefs that are central and well-connected get to be highly justified due to the coherence of the system and the lack of coherent alternative theories that could explain our being systematically mistaken.

Part III: Areas of Knowledge

14. Scientific Knowledge

In this part of the book, we discuss some areas of knowledge that have attracted particular philosophical attention. We start with scientific knowledge: How does it work, what makes a scientific theory a good one, and do we really know our scientific theories to be true?

The main issue about scientific knowledge is really the problem of induction, which we have already discussed (ch. 12). Here we will address some further issues about scientific reasoning that are also interesting.

14.1. Confirmation Puzzles

14.1.1. *The Idea of Confirmation Theory*

In the philosophy of science, people try to figure out how scientific reasoning works to produce knowledge, or at least justified beliefs. It is common to use the word "**confirms**" to mean "provides at least some amount of support for". E.g., the observation of a white raven *confirms* [All ravens are white] (albeit only slightly!). Please note that this is a technical use of "confirm" and that "confirm" does *not* mean "to provide conclusive evidence for"!

So one thing we'd like is a theory of when some evidence, e, confirms some hypothesis, h. In the twentieth century, some people tried to articulate qualitative conditions for this, and it led to paradoxes.[133]

14.1.2. *Does Everything Confirm Everything?*

Here are two plausible qualitative conditions for confirmation:

1. If h entails e, then e confirms h.
   Comment: Scientific method tests theories by testing their observational *predictions*, i.e., the things that the theory entails about what we should observe in particular circumstances. When a prediction is found to be true, that counts as support for the theory.
2. If e confirms h, and h entails x, then e confirms x.

---

[133] See Carl Hempel's "Studies in the Logic of Confirmation" in *Aspects of Scientific Explanation and Other Essays in the Philosophy of Science* (1965).

Comment: If you have evidence for a theory, then you thereby also have at least some evidence for the other things that that theory predicts.

You might want to add some qualifications to condition (1), e.g., that *e* can't be a tautology. This eliminates the problem where a hypothesis would be confirmed by any tautology (since everything entails a tautology). We could also stipulate that *h* cannot be contradictory; this eliminates the case where a contradictory hypothesis would be confirmed by any evidence (since a contradiction entails anything). We could add similar qualifications to condition (2); these qualifications are not important to the problem we're about to discuss.

Here is the problem: Conditions (1) and (2) entail that every proposition confirms every other proposition (with minor qualifications, if you want). Let *A* and *B* be any two randomly chosen (non-tautological, non-contradictory) propositions. Note that (*A* & *B*) entails *A*. Therefore, by condition (1), *A* confirms (*A* & *B*). Now, since (*A* & *B*) entails *B*, by condition (2), *A* also confirms *B*. That seems wrong, to put it mildly.

14.1.3. The Ravens Paradox

Here are two more plausible conditions on confirmation:

I. **Nicod's Criterion**:[134]
   a. Observation of an *A* that is *B* confirms [All *A*'s are *B*].
   b. Observation of an *A* that is non-*B* disconfirms [All *A*'s are *B*].
   c. Observation of a non-*A* is irrelevant to (neither confirms nor disconfirms) [All *A*'s are *B*].
II. **The Equivalence Condition**: If *p* and *q* are logically equivalent, then whatever confirms *p* confirms *q*.

I take condition II to be self-evident. To illustrate condition I, if you see a black raven, that supports "All ravens are black." If you see a white raven, that refutes "All ravens are black." And if you see a white shoe, that is irrelevant to "All ravens are black."

Problem: Let's think about that white shoe again. It isn't black, and it also isn't a raven. That is, it is a nonblack nonraven. So by condition Ia, it *confirms* "All nonblack things are nonravens." But "All nonblack things are nonravens" is *logically equivalent* to "All ravens are black." So by condition II, it actually *is* evidence for "All ravens are black." But this contradicts condition Ic.

---

[134] Named after the French philosopher and logician Jean Nicod (pronounced "nee-so") (1893–1924), who proposed this in his *Foundations of Geometry and Induction*.

14.1.4. Bayesian Analysis

The leading responses (which are also the correct responses) to the above problems are probabilistic. First, Bayesians define confirmation in terms of raising the probability of a theory:

Bayesian Account of Confirmation:
  e confirms $h =_{df} P(h|e) > P(h)$.

Now we can analyze the proposed qualitative conditions of confirmation in terms of probability theory.

"*If h entails e, then e confirms h*": This is true as long as P(e) and P(h) have non-extreme (neither 0 nor 1) probabilities. You can see this from Bayes' Theorem: $P(h|e) = \frac{P(h) \times P(e|h)}{P(e)}$. Since h entails e, P($e|h$) is 1. Assuming P(e) is less than 1, P($e|h$)/P(e) is going to be greater than 1, so the whole right hand side is greater than P(h), so P($h|e$) > P(h).

"*If e confirms h, and h entails x, then e confirms x*": This is definitely false. Evidence may raise the probability of a theory but fail to raise, or may even lower, the probability of *some* of the theory's consequences. To take an intuitive example, let's say you know that either Jon, Sue, or Mike stole some money from the cash register during the lunch hour. Then you view a security video which shows Mike peacefully eating a salad during the time that the money was stolen, so it could not have been Mike. This evidence confirms that it was Jon, and also confirms that it was Sue (i.e., it raises the probability of both of those hypotheses). But note that [It was Jon] entails that it *wasn't* Sue. So the evidence confirms a hypothesis ([It was Jon]) while also *lowering* the probability of a logical consequence of that hypothesis ([It wasn't Sue]).

"*If p and q are logically equivalent, then whatever confirms p confirms q*": This is correct. It's a theorem of probability that logically equivalent propositions always have the same probability (including the same probability conditional on any chosen evidence).

"*Observation of an A that is B confirms [All A's are B]*": This is typically true, but it depends upon how the observation was made. Say there's a giant bag labelled "Ravens", and another giant bag labelled "Black Things". You can reach in and randomly pick an object from either bag. If you pick a random raven from the raven bag and it turns out to be black, that confirms [All ravens are black]. But if you pick a random black thing from the Black Things bag, and it turns out to be a raven, that's irrelevant to [All ravens are black],[135] since

---

[135] Of course, you could *imagine* probability distributions on which this wouldn't be true, but I'm assuming an intuitively natural probability distribution.

you knew in advance that you had no chance of getting a nonblack raven from *that* bag, even if nonblack ravens existed.

"*Observation of an A that is non-B disconfirms [All A's are B]*": Obviously true.

"*Observation of a non-A is irrelevant to [All A's are B]*": Again, this depends on how the observation was made. Say there's a giant bag of Nonblack Things and a giant bag of Nonravens. If you randomly sample from the Nonblack Things and get a white shoe, then yes, that *does* support [All ravens are black] because, if there were nonblack ravens, there was a *chance* that this observation would have turned one up. Since it didn't, you have a tiny bit of evidence that there aren't any nonblack ravens (it's tiny since nonblack ravens would be such a small portion of the set of all nonblack things that you'd have been very unlikely to find one). On the other hand, if you randomly sample from the Nonravens and you turn up a white shoe, that's irrelevant to [All ravens are black] since this method had no chance of turning up a nonblack raven.

14.2. Falsifiability

14.2.1. The Idea of Falsificationism

Many people today believe that scientific method has a lot to do with **falsifiability**. It is said that any scientific theory must be capable of being tested so that, if it were false, we could prove that it was false. People are often criticized for advancing "unfalsifiable" theories, which is generally treated as in some way fallacious or otherwise bad. This view is popular not only among lay people but also among scientists. To illustrate the idea:

> *The Elusive Psychic:* Uri claims to have psychic powers. You propose to do some scientific tests to determine whether this is true. Uri then explains that the psychic powers don't work in the presence of skeptics. Hence, if you do your tests, the psychic powers won't show up; nevertheless, he insists, they are perfectly real.

You would probably see Uri for the scammer that he is. Methodologically, the problem is that Uri has designed his theory so as to make it untestable, or at least very hard to test, which makes it unscientific.

14.2.2. The Origin of Falsificationism

The source of this view of science is the 20th-century philosopher of science, Sir Karl Popper. Few people who use his idea, however, know what motivated it. Popper's fundamental motivation was *inductive skepticism*. He thought David Hume was right and thus that there is *never any reason whatsoever* to believe *any* scientific theory.

By the way, even though he is completely explicit about it, many people who have been exposed to Popper fail to realize that that is his core view. There are two main reasons for this. First, Popper's *emotional attitude* toward science is highly positive, which comes out in his writing; second, inductive skepticism is so ridiculous that people have a hard time believing that Popper means it when he says it. So in case you don't believe me, I have collected a few quotations from Sir Karl:

"We must regard all laws and theories as guesses." "There *are* no such things as good positive reasons." "Belief, of course, is never rational: it is rational to *suspend* belief." "I never assume that by force of 'verified' conclusions, theories can be established as 'true', or even as merely 'probable'." "[O]f two hypotheses, the one that is logically stronger, or more informative, or better testable, and thus the one which can be *better corroborated*, is always *less probable*—on any given evidence—than the other." "*[I]n an infinite universe [...] the probability of any (non-tautological) universal law will be zero.*"[136]

Now, after deciding that non-deductive reasoning is completely impotent, Popper didn't want to just throw out science. So he had to come up with a way that scientific method is somehow based on *deduction*. And what he came up with was this: Even though it's impossible to establish any scientific theory by deduction, it *is* possible to *refute* a scientific theory by deduction. No amount of evidence ever proves that all swans are white; yet a single observation of a black swan deductively proves that *not* all swans are white. Popper concluded, therefore, that science must all be about *refuting* theories, rather than about confirming them. That led him to posit that a theory is unscientific if it could not in principle be refuted.

Now, you might be thinking that once a scientific theory survives many attempts to refute it, we will then have a reason to believe it, or that the theory will be rendered more probable, or something like that. But that is not Popper's view. He explicitly rejects that; no matter what, you never have any reason to believe a scientific theory.

All of which raises the question: Why on Earth would we care about science? And what, exactly, is good about falsifiable theories?

14.2.3. A Bayesian Account of the Virtue of Falsifiability

Popper was onto something with his emphasis on falsifiability: Unfalsifiable theories really are bad in some way, and that principle really is important to scientific reasoning. (This observation applies to empirical theories in general but not to a priori "theories", such as most philosophical theories.)

---

[136] Sources: *Objective Knowledge* (1972), 9; *The Philosophy of Karl Popper* (1974), 1043; 69; *Logic of Scientific Discovery* (2002), 10; 374; 375; emphasis Popper's.

Unfortunately, Popper was in no position to explain *why* this is the case, because he explicitly rejects all non-deductive reasoning.

The correct account of the virtue of falsifiability is probabilistic. A falsifiable theory is, in essence, a theory that makes definite, non-trivial predictions about the evidence that we should expect to see. If the predictions turn out false, the theory is refuted. On the other hand, if the predictions turn out true, then the theory is supported in accordance with Bayes' Theorem: $P(h|e) = \frac{P(h) \times P(e|h)}{P(e)}$. Since h predicts e, $P(e|h) = 1$. As long as e is something non-trivial, $P(e)$ should be less than 1. So on the right-hand side of the equation, you have $P(h)$ multiplied by something greater than 1, which gives you something greater than $P(h)$. Thus, a falsifiable theory is confirmed (has its probability raised) when it survives a test that could have refuted it.

On the other hand, suppose h makes no predictions at all and is therefore untestable. In that case, the theory is also *unsupportable*. It's a general theorem of probability that $P(h|e) > P(h)$ if and only if $P(h|\sim e) < P(h)$.[137] On the Bayesian account of confirmation, this amounts to saying: e confirms h if and only if $\sim e$ would disconfirm h. So a theory that can't be disconfirmed can't be confirmed.

Note, however, that the Bayesian would broaden the concept of falsifiability. Popper, being an inductive skeptic, defines falsifiability in terms of being able to *deductively prove* that a theory is false. The Bayesian would (rightly) employ the broader notion of being able to *disconfirm* (lower the probability of) the theory. Thus, a good scientific theory must make at least probabilistic predictions, such that the probability of the theory could be raised or lowered by evidence gathered. The sharper the predictions are (that is, the higher $P(e|h)$ for specific values of e), the more confirmable or disconfirmable the theory is.

14.3. Simplicity

14.3.1. Occam's Razor and the Burden of Proof

It is widely agreed in scientific reasoning and much of ordinary life that, other things being equal, the *simplest* explanation of some evidence is most likely to be correct. This, or something close to it, is often dubbed **Occam's Razor**. The other common statement of the Razor is "entities must not be multiplied

---

[137] To see why, note that, from Bayes' Theorem, e supports h iff $P(e|h) > P(e)$. Multiplying by -1 and then adding 1 to both sides gives $1 - P(e|h) < 1 - P(e)$, which is equivalent to $P(\sim e|h) < P(\sim e)$, which in turn is the condition for $\sim e$ to disconfirm h.

beyond necessity."[138] A closely related idea is the **burden of proof principle**, which states that the burden of proof is on those who make positive claims; the presumption rests with negative claims. Here, a **positive claim** is understood as one asserting that something exists or that something has some property, whereas a **negative claim** denies that something exists or that something has some property.

As conventionally understood, these principles postulate an epistemological *asymmetry* between positive and negative claims. In the absence of specific evidence either for or against the existence of some particular thing, the negative thesis (that it doesn't exist) is held to be somehow privileged—more reasonable to believe, more reasonable to have a higher credence in, more reasonable to assume for practical purposes, or something like that. For a randomly chosen possible thing, the default assumption, so to speak, is that it doesn't exist.

14.3.2. Why Accept Occam's Razor?

Before we talk about why Occam's Razor might be true, or even what exactly it means, let's get the motivation for it. That way, we can interpret and explain the principle in a way consistent with that motivation.

The main reason for believing something like Occam's Razor is that there are various examples in which the appeal to simplicity is very intuitively compelling. Perhaps the most famous case is that of Copernican (geocentric) vs. Ptolemaic (heliocentric) astronomy. Back in the 16th century, people were debating the structure of the cosmos. The old, Ptolemaic theory had the Sun and the planets all moving around the Earth. Copernicus proposed instead that the Sun is stationary and the Earth and planets orbit the sun.

It turns out that, in the Ptolemaic system, in order to explain the observed positions of planets in the night sky, you have to complicate your model a bit. You can't just have each planet moving in a circle with the Earth at the center. Rather, the Earth is located *off center* within those orbits. There was no theoretical explanation for this; the distance of the Earth from the center was

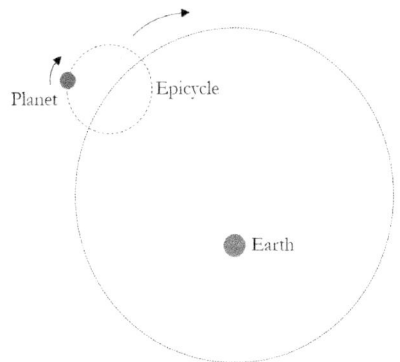

Figure 7: Ptolemaic model of a planetary orbit

---

[138] The principle is named after the medieval philosopher William of Ockham, who used the idea to defend nominalism in metaphysics.

just posited to get the right observational predictions. The other, more famous complication was the **epicycle**: Rather than moving in a simple circle around the Earth, the planets were held to be moving in smaller circles called "epicycles", where the epicycle itself would move around the Earth (fig. 7).

The Copernican model did not require any such epicycles, nor did it place anything off center (the sun was at the center of the cosmos). It thus gave a simpler explanation of the same set of observations. This greater simplicity has long been considered an important advantage of the Copernican theory. Indeed, the term "epicycle" has become a pejorative term for ad hoc complications that someone adds into a theory to try to save the appearances.

It's useful to have a few examples of different types, so here's another case, also from astronomy. The way that Neptune was discovered was that astronomers first noticed some anomalies in the orbit of Uranus—it wasn't moving in exactly the way expected based on Newton's laws and the theory of gravity. The astronomer Urbain Le Verrier figured out that these anomalies could be explained if one posited a hitherto-unobserved planet whose mass was influencing Uranus. This turned out to be correct, and the new planet is now known as Neptune. Now, when Le Verrier wanted to explain the anomalies, he *could* have posited six unknown planets, or seventy-three, or any other number. But he didn't do any of these things, nor would any normal person have done so, given that a *single* planet of the right mass and orbit was sufficient to explain the data.

A similar case is the discovery of the neutrino. The neutrino was originally postulated in order to explain an apparent loss of energy that occurs in beta decay (never mind exactly what that is)—basically, the physicist Wolfgang Pauli proposed that the energy that appeared to be lost was carried away by a new, previously-unobserved particle produced during beta decay.[139] That particle was subsequently detected and named the "neutrino". Notice that Pauli *could* have postulated that during beta decay, seventy-three different kinds of particle are produced, each of which carries away some of the lost energy. That would also have explained the data. But no one would have seriously entertained such a theory, given that a single theoretical particle would suffice to explain the same evidence.

I have one more example, this one from ordinary life. Let's say you're sitting in your apartment, in which you have exactly two electrical devices turned on: a lamp and a computer. Suddenly, both the lamp and the computer shut off. You consider two hypotheses: (*i*) Maybe there was a power failure, or

---

[139] Beta decay is a kind of radioactive decay in which an electron or positron is emitted from the nucleus of an atom. The neutrino also explained an apparent violation of conservation of spin during these events.

(*ii*) maybe the light bulb burned out and the computer crashed at the same time. It seems that the simpler explanation, (*i*), is the more likely.

14.3.3. What Shouldn't We Multiply?

Some say that we should strive to minimize the number of *individual entities* whose existence we postulate. Others say that we should strive to minimize the number of *kinds* of entity that we postulate. And still others say that we should strive to minimize the number of **adjustable parameters** in our theories. Adjustable parameters are essentially numbers whose values could be adjusted (consistent with intuitively still having "the same theory") to try to accommodate the available data. For instance, the gravitational constant in Newton's theory of gravity is an adjustable parameter.

All three of these are natural interpretations of the value of simplicity, and all three are illustrated in the preceding examples. The Neptune example illustrates the virtue of minimizing the number of individual entities (sometimes called "quantitative parsimony"). The neutrino example illustrates the virtue of minimizing the number of *types* of entities (a.k.a. "qualitative parsimony"). And the Copernican Astronomy example illustrates the virtue of minimizing the number of adjustable parameters in a theory. In the Copernican model, you have the radius and speed of each orbit as adjustable parameters. In the Ptolemaic model, you have the radius and speed of the main orbit, plus the radius and speed of each epicycle, plus the distance of the Earth from the center. The computer/lamp example also illustrates this kind of simplicity. The power failure theory has one adjustable parameter, the time of the power failure. The burnout/crash theory has two parameters, the time of the light bulb burnout and the time of the computer crash.

This suggests that all three kinds of simplicity matter for assessing theories. We should avoid multiplying individuals, kinds, or parameters beyond necessity.

14.3.4. Seven Weak Defenses of Simplicity

Although almost everyone accepts the theoretical virtue of simplicity at least in some contexts, most people (even philosophers!) have no clue *why* simplicity is a theoretical virtue, which of course puts one in a poor position to judge *when* it is a theoretical virtue. Let's start by considering some accounts of this that are wrong.

Account #1: The world is simple.

On the face of it, when you hear the statement "other things being equal, simpler explanations are better", it sounds as if the principle is that we get to assume, a priori, that the world is probably simple. But why on Earth would that be? I certainly *don't* think that the world is probably simple; I think it is probably extremely complex. Over the history of science, our accounts of the world have steadily grown more complex as they have become more accurate. Modern physics is way more complicated than Aristotelian physics.

Nobody seems to be able to explain why it makes sense to assume the world is probably simple, so let's consider some other explanations.

Account #2: It is impossible to prove a negative.

If a thing doesn't exist, then there won't be any (positive) evidence left behind by its non-existence. This is supposed to show that the burden of proof must lie on those who assert the positive, since a negative claim in principle couldn't be proved.

There are just two problems with this account. First, it's false. You *can* sometimes prove a negative. If there is no beer in my refrigerator, I can prove this by doing an exhaustive search of the refrigerator. Some people claim to have proved that God doesn't exist by pointing to contradictions in the concept of God.

Second, it's irrelevant even if true. Just because a claim could not be proved false does not mean that it is true. So why would we get to start by assuming negative claims?

Account #3: (A & B) is less likely than A.

This is a theorem of probability: As long as $P(B|A) \neq 1$, $P(A \& B)$ must be strictly less than $P(A)$. Therefore, if you can explain all your evidence by citing A, you should not go on to assert B in addition, because that lowers the probability of your theory.

Problem: This fails to identify any asymmetry between positive and negative claims. The following is also a theorem of probability: As long as $P(B|A) \neq 0$, $P(A \& \sim B)$ is strictly less than $P(A)$. Therefore, if you can explain all your evidence by citing A, you should not go on to *deny* B in addition, since that lowers the probability of your theory. The argument against affirming B is also an argument against denying B. So it does not support any kind of burden of proof or presumption for one side.

Note also that the account, even if it worked, would only apply to a small minority of cases. Though people often appeal to simplicity to justify preferring one theory over another, *virtually never* is one theory equivalent to the conjunction of another theory with some other proposition.

Account #4: We're just saying don't believe unjustified propositions.

Sometimes, people explain Occam's Razor as the trivial principle that if there is no justification for believing a positive claim, then one should not believe that claim. This is entirely consistent with the (presumably equally correct) principle that if there is no justification for *denying* a positive claim, then one also should not deny it.

The only thing to be said about this is that this isn't a defense of Occam's Razor or a burden of proof principle, since this view posits no asymmetry between positive and negative claims or between simple and complex theories. The view would be that entities should not be posited *or denied* unnecessarily; negative claims would have just as much burden of proof as positive claims.

Account #5: Simple theories are convenient and pretty.

Sometimes people propose simplicity as a pragmatic virtue: Simpler theories are easier for us to understand and work with. They might also be more aesthetically pleasing.

The problem is that the pragmatic/aesthetic benefits of simplicity would typically be swamped by the value of truth. We use non-deductive inferences to plan our actions all the time, where what matters is whether our conclusions are true. When you're building a bridge, you want your predictions about how much weight it supports to be *correct*. How aesthetically pleasing or convenient the calculations are is an utterly trivial consideration by comparison.

And indeed, we do not merely think that our theories are aesthetically pleasing or convenient. We clearly think of them as true (at least we think their predictions about future observations are true), given how much we use them to plan our actions. In the examples from §14.3.2, the simpler theories clearly seem more likely to be true. For instance, when your lamp and your computer both shut off, it is *more likely* that there was a power failure rather than that the bulb burned out at the same time that the computer crashed. That is what needs to be explained.

Account #6: There are fewer simple theories.

Maybe the world isn't more likely to be simple than complex. Maybe it's equally likely to have each possible degree of complexity, but there are generally *more* complex theories than there are simple theories. (Example: You're trying to solve a burglary case, and you could hypothesize either one burglar or three. With three burglars, there would be many more ways to fill in how the whole crime might have happened.) Thus, each *particular* simple theory gets a higher prior probability than each complex theory.

The main problem with this account is that we don't have a clear rationale for applying the Principle of Indifference to the possible *degrees of simplicity* of theories, i.e., there is no obvious reason to assume that each degree of simplicity is equally likely.

Account #7: Complexity is unbounded.

The "complexity" dimension is unbounded in one direction. That is, there is a *minimum* possible degree of complexity, but there is no *maximum*. However complex a theory is, it could always get more complex. Now, in the case of any variable that is unbounded in one direction, probability theory *requires* you to assign decreasing probabilities (approaching zero as a limit) as the variable increases. That's the only way to have probabilities add up to something less than or equal to 1. Example: Suppose theories have possible levels of complexity 1, 2, 3, and so on (these might represent, e.g., the number of entities postulated). You can't give an equal probability to each degree of complexity, because then you're going to get the sum of all the probabilities being infinity (or zero). What you could do is give probability ½ to complexity level 1, then probability ¼ to complexity level 2, then ⅛ to level 3, and so on. Then all the probabilities add up to 1. (Of course, there are other ways to do it so that the sum comes out to 1, but they all require the probability to approach zero as complexity increases without bound.)

The above reasoning is correct—the probability of a theory has to approach zero as the degree of complexity approaches infinity. However, this doesn't support Occam's Razor across the board; it is consistent with there being, say, an optimal (most likely) degree of complexity such that theories become less probable as the complexity increases *or decreases* relative to that optimum (see fig. 8). This isn't a totally random thing to suggest, either, as most probability distributions in the real world are like that.[140]

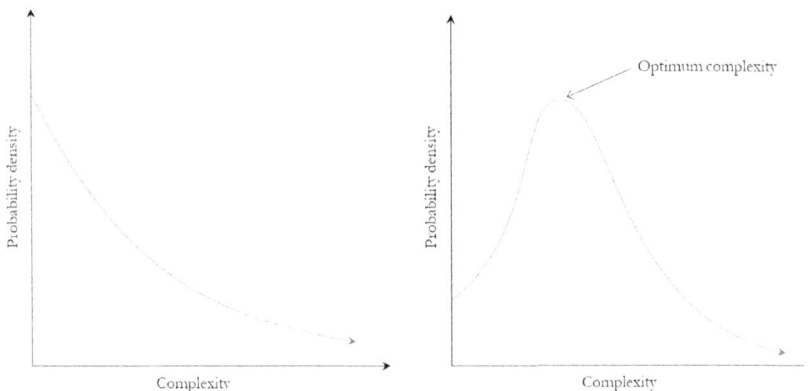

Figure 8: Probability distributions that add up to 1

---

[140] See the Maxwell-Boltzmann distribution in statistical mechanics.

14.3.5. The Likelihood Account

You might be able to guess at this point that a Bayesian account of the virtue of simplicity is coming. Here it is. Simpler theories tend to be *better supported* by evidence that they accommodate, because they tend to have higher *likelihoods*.

In this account, we understand degree of complexity in terms of number of adjustable parameters (see §14.3.3). As a general rule, the more adjustable parameters a theory has, the wider the range of possible data that the theory could accommodate by adjusting those parameters. Thus, in the Ptolemaic system of astronomy (as discussed in §14.3.2), a wide range of possible planetary motions in the night sky could be explained by adjusting the distance of the Earth from the center of the cosmos, the speed and radius of each main orbit, and the speed and radius of each epicycle. The Copernican model has fewer parameters to work with, so it could accommodate fewer possible sets of observations.

This matters because when there is a wide range of possible evidence that a theory accommodates, $P(e|h)$ is correspondingly low for any given e; when there is a narrow range of allowable evidence, then the value of $P(e|h)$ is higher within that range. The reason is that $P(e|h)$ has to add up to 1 for all possible values of e that the theory accommodates (see fig.

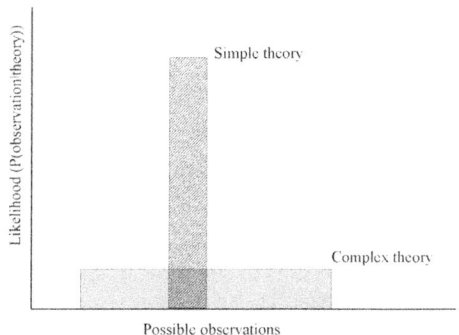

Figure 9: *The likelihood account of simplicity*

9). Another way to describe the situation is to say that simple theories tend to be *more falsifiable* than more complex theories, in that the simpler theories make more specific predictions (see §14.2).

How does this account explain the virtue of minimizing the number of entities (or kinds of entity) that we postulate in a theory? Well, postulating new entities typically introduces new adjustable parameters having to do with the properties of these entities. A wider range of possible evidence can be explained by the postulated causal powers of a larger collection of entities.

This account of simplicity, it should be noted, does not imply that simpler theories are *always* better (even in one respect) than more complex theories. The claim is merely that simpler theories *tend* to have higher likelihoods than more complex theories, though there may be exceptions to this. Note also that simple theories are not held to be *a priori* more probable than complex theories; they are only held to be more easily supported by evidence (but also more easily refuted by evidence—these two traits go together). In the absence of evidence, simple and complex theories are (for all this account says) on a par.

14.3.6. Philosophical Applications

A final issue about simplicity. Some people apply the virtue of simplicity not only to scientific but also to philosophical contexts, suggesting that simpler *philosophical* theories are more likely to be correct, other things being equal—e.g., that physicalism is more likely than dualism, and nominalism is more likely than Platonism. Are these applications legitimate?

Typically no. Mostly they result from philosophers not having thought about why simplicity is supposed to be a theoretical virtue. In most cases, philosophical theories are not at all like scientific theories. When you have a scientific theory, normally there is a specific range of possible evidence that it accommodates, and there is little to no dispute over the fact that it accommodates that evidence. Competing theories accommodate different ranges of possible evidence, so we can perform experiments to discriminate among them.

When you have a philosophical theory, by contrast, typically the theory *either* contradicts pretty much all the evidence, *or* it accommodates all possible evidence; and the core dispute concerning the theory is about whether it does or doesn't accommodate the evidence. This makes the likelihood account of simplicity inapplicable to philosophical theories.

E.g., take the case of nominalism, the theory that universals (as defined in §10.5.4) don't exist. What evidence does this theory predict? There are two views about this:

(1) *Realists* think that nominalism entails that nothing has any characteristics. So one "prediction" of the theory would be that nothing is red. Since some things are red, nominalism fails to accommodate the evidence. Since the virtue of simplicity only applies to theories that accommodate the actual evidence, simplicity is not a reason in favor of nominalism.

(2) Nominalists claim that their theory is compatible with the fact that some things are red. If they're right about this, then their theory is compatible with *any* things being *any* way. So the theory has no predictions whatever. Since simplicity is only a virtue to the extent that simpler theories tend to make sharper predictions, simplicity considerations again fail to support nominalism.

14.4. Realism & Skepticism

Scientific realists are basically people who think that science reveals to us important truths about mind-independent reality. Scientific anti-realists are people who deny this. "Why isn't everyone a scientific realist?" you might wonder. Well, let's see ...

14.4.1. *The Underdetermination Problem*

The **underdetermination** of theory by empirical data is the phenomenon that the available evidence never uniquely determines the correct scientific theory. There is always more than one possible interpretation of the data. This is true because scientific reasoning isn't deductive. If your theory isn't entailed by the evidence, then by definition there are alternative ways the world could be in which the evidence is the same but your theory is false.

Philosophical skeptics like to come up with all-purpose alternative explanations of our evidence, such as that you're a brain in a vat, God is deceiving you, or you're dreaming everything. These suffice to make the point that there are always alternative explanations of the evidence. However, many people find these silly and would prefer more plausible examples. So here you go:

Say you learn that, within the U.S., jurisdictions that have stricter gun laws tend to have higher violent crime rates. (This is true.) A conservative might say: "That's because gun restrictions exacerbate crime, because victims are prevented from defending themselves." A progressive might say: "No, it's because, when leaders see high crime rates, they wisely respond by regulating private gun ownership more." Someone else (a moderate?) might say: "Maybe population density contributes to both variables. Heavily populated places tend to have more crime. They also tend to have more left-leaning voters, which independently causes stricter gun laws."

It's not as if one side is being stupid and ignoring the evidence. Each side has its own scheme for making sense of the same evidence. You could look at other pieces of evidence, but much the same thing is going to happen: People with different theories will come up with their own ways of interpreting the evidence within their system.

A similar situation transpired in the debate between Ptolemaic and Copernican astronomy (§14.3.2). Both systems could explain approximately the same set of data consisting of observations of planetary positions in the night sky, even though they told very different stories about the structure of the cosmos.[141]

---

[141] It is sometimes said that Ptolemaic predictions were actually *more* accurate, but this is not true. Each system had errors, and each did better in certain cases. Copernicus did better in more cases, though not by a huge margin. See Frank Tipler and Wesley Bollinger's "Ptolemy and Copernicus" (*Inference*, July 2015), https://inference-review.com/article/ptolemy-versus-copernicus.

Usually, when you have two interpretations of the same evidence (unless one of them is a skeptical scenario designed to be irrefutable, like the brain-in-a-vat scenario), it's possible to gather further evidence that differentiates between them. In the geocentric/heliocentric cosmology case, we have, e.g., Foucault's Pendulum.[142] This is basically a big pendulum that swings back and forth for a long time. Over the course of many hours, the plane of oscillation of the pendulum can be seen to rotate, with the rate of rotation calculable based on your latitude (it rotates faster near the North or South pole). This is explained by the fact that the Earth itself is rotating. This was unknown to Copernicus (let alone Ptolemy), but it's a pretty powerful demonstration that the Earth rotates.

Does this eliminate underdetermination? Not really. It would be *possible* to maintain Ptolemaic astronomy despite demonstrations like that, provided that you're willing to complicate your physics, e.g., by giving up the principle of conservation of momentum and introducing some more complicated laws of motion that are relative to the Earth's location. No one wants to do that, but it's still philosophically interesting to consider exactly *why* we don't do that.

A more modern example is the different interpretations of quantum mechanics. Here's a very vague, basic outline of the situation. Quantum mechanics provides a certain algorithm for predicting the results of experiments. This algorithm makes use of vectors that are used to represent the physical state of a system. When you do certain mathematical operations on the vectors, you can calculate probabilities for different measurement outcomes, and those probabilities match the statistics you get if you do the measurements.

People have come up with multiple interpretations of what's going on— different theories about why the algorithm works and what the mathematical objects that it uses correspond to in reality. There is the Copenhagen Interpretation, in which objects are regularly in indeterminate states and observers cause them to jump to a randomly chosen determinate state when we make an observation. There is the Many-Worlds Interpretation, in which the universe is constantly splitting into many universes, where each possible thing that might happen happens in some universe. There is Bohm's Interpretation, in which a physical system is a particle located in a definite but unknowable-to-us position in a many-dimensional space, and the particle is deterministically pushed around by the wave function. And there are multiple others.

---

[142] Named after the 19th-century French physicist Léon Foucault. Not to be confused with Umberto Eco's novel of the same name!

I'm not going to explain those theories. Here's what matters for our purposes: Those are all theories that use *the same algorithm* for predicting experimental results, so they explain the same evidence.[143] But they're incompatible with each other. So how, if at all, could we distinguish among them?

This last example (quantum mechanics), despite being esoteric, is a good example of the underdetermination problem because the alternative interpretations are seriously advanced by actual scientists (unlike skeptical scenarios, which no one believes), and we don't have any evidence that can differentiate among them (unlike the Ptolemy/Copernicus example).

14.4.2. Scientific Anti-Realism

Scientific anti-realists take a skeptical lesson from the underdetermination problem: They think there is no objective, purely rational way of choosing among different interpretations of the same evidence. Of course, we make choices anyway—scientists adopt particular theories, often forming a consensus in a given field as to the "right" theory. Since the evidence underdetermines theory, *by definition* these choices aren't dictated by the evidence. So instead they must be based on subjective, non-rational factors— our preferences, intuitions (where these are not viewed as genuine evidence), aesthetic tastes, and intellectual fashions. Because of this, anti-realists think, we can't view accepted scientific theories as rationally justified portrayals of the objective truth. Thomas Kuhn got famous for advancing this sort of view in *The Structure of Scientific Revolutions*, which became literally the most cited book in the world.[144]

14.4.3. A Realist Interpretation

How should scientific realists respond to the underdetermination problem? They should say different things about different kinds of cases.

(*i*) One kind of case is the general skeptical scenario. Here, I have in mind things like the brain in a vat scenario, or the hypothesis that all emeralds are grue. (Once you've understood "grue", you can see how to generate skeptical theories rivalling any inductive generalization.)

---

[143] At least, they explain the same currently existing evidence. In principle, theories that include a collapse of the wave function could be experimentally distinguished from no-collapse theories, but it would be extremely difficult to do the experiments. See David Albert, *Quantum Mechanics and Experience* (1994), 84–92.

[144] As of this writing, Google Scholar records 139,699 citations for it. Which is a lot. Probably because humanists and social scientists loved the opportunity to attack the hard sciences, which had been getting all too much respect lately.

These general skeptical arguments really do show that theory is underdetermined by data. But that only means that our evidence does not *entail* our conclusions, which should only worry you if you're a **deductivist**, i.e., you think only deductive reasoning is legitimate. It doesn't show that we can't *inductively* or otherwise *non-deductively* infer our conclusions from our evidence. Realists may cite partly a priori reasons why our actual beliefs are superior to the skeptical theories, e.g., that the skeptical theories are needlessly complicated, that they're less falsifiable, and generally that they're improbable. (See ch. 12 and §§8.3, 14.2, 14.3.)

(*ii*) There are also some alternative theories that are not general skeptical scenarios but also would not be seriously advanced by any scientist—e.g., a Ptolemaic theory of astronomy conjoined with an alternative physics designed to explain away Foucault's Pendulum (and all other evidences of the Earth's motion). It would be possible to construct such a theory, but it would be full of silly ad hoc complications. About cases like this, the scientific realist should and would say that the alternative theories are just extremely improbable due to all the needless complexities.

(*iii*) Another kind of case (and the kind most often discussed) concerns serious scientific theories for which we do not have enough evidence to decide between them, as in the case of Ptolemaic and Copernican astronomy in the 1500s. In these cases, it is still plausible that a priori considerations might strongly favor one theory over another, as the simplicity of Copernican astronomy favored it over Ptolemaic astronomy.

If no such a priori reasons can be found, it is open to the realist to say that we should suspend judgment until further evidence is gathered. In some cases, as in that of the interpretations of quantum mechanics, we may never gather enough evidence to know which theory is correct.

This last situation is the only one that should seriously bother us. However, it does not pose a threat to scientific realism in general, because it only occasionally occurs. (Obviously, scientific realists don't hold that science is omniscient.) In advanced, theoretical physics, there may indeed be serious alternatives that we cannot now decide among and even will never be able to decide among.

But this really does not generalize across science. In biology, there is no serious alternative to the theory of evolution. No one has some other, completely different account that explains the same evidence (without being a skeptical scenario). In astronomy, there is no serious alternative to heliocentric cosmology—no one seriously thinks anymore that the planets might be orbiting the Earth, or that they're all orbiting Jupiter, etc. In chemistry, there is no serious alternative to the theory that water is H_2O. In geology, there is no serious alternative to plate tectonics. In all these cases, no one has any examples of underdetermination, unless one wants to resort to *general* skeptical theories or silly theories that no scientist would seriously advance. So it remains open to us to maintain that science has told us *a lot*, though not *everything*, about the objective nature of the world we live in.

14.4.4. The Skeptical Induction

The best reason for being skeptical about science is history: Ever since human beings started theorizing about nature, we have been wrong. More precisely, almost every theory that people have ever held about natural phenomena has later been rejected. A good example is how Aristotelian physics, after holding sway in Western science/philosophy for many centuries, was superseded by Cartesian physics, which was then superseded by Newtonian physics, which was superseded by relativity and quantum mechanics, which may themselves be superseded by string theory. It would be foolish to think that you just happen to be born in the first time ever that human beings correctly understood how the world works. So probably our current theories are going to be rejected by future generations too. And thus, we shouldn't take our current theories as telling us the true nature of reality.

Some people concede that we don't currently know the actual truth about the world, but they maintain that we are getting *closer* to the truth. You could consider this a weaker form of scientific realism: Science tells us the *approximate* truth about objective reality, and it is becoming more accurate (a closer approximation) over time. People with this view like to point to how, as our basic physical theories advanced, we got more precise predictions. Newtonian physics gives you very accurate predictions for most cases and gives significant errors only in unusual cases, such as for very fast moving or very tiny objects. Relativity and quantum mechanics then make good predictions for all the cases that Newtonian physics works for, *plus* also the cases of very small and very fast-moving objects. But maybe they don't work so well for some even weirder cases, like explaining what goes on in a black hole or at the beginning of the universe. Then maybe string theory gets those cases right. Etc.

This, however, isn't such a great response. It confuses accuracy of observational predictions with accuracy of the underlying *explanation*. Two theories may give only slightly different quantitative, empirical predictions from one another, yet give radically different *explanations* for those predictions. Take the case of Copernican and Ptolemaic astronomy. These theories give extremely similar predictions; there are only slight differences in where you would expect to see a planet in the sky if you used these two theories (and both gave you small errors). Yet the underlying stories they tell about how the cosmos is structured are *completely different*. So, from the standpoint of

Copernican astronomy (which really is approximately correct), Ptolemaic astronomy is *not* approximately correct. It's totally wrong, because none of the planets is in fact circling the Earth, nor is any of them doing anything *close* to circling the Earth.

The same is true about classical physics and quantum mechanics. True, QM only makes significantly different *observational predictions* from classical physics in certain special circumstances, with very small systems. But it (in most interpretations) gives a totally different picture of the underlying reality. For example, if observers create reality, or if there are infinitely many parallel worlds appearing at every instant, that really is not at all close to anything that classical physicists thought. Thus, from the quantum mechanical standpoint, the classical picture is *not* approximately correct.

The implication seems to be that, if and when our current theories are overthrown by some revolutionary future theory, that future theory will probably also judge our current theories as not even close to correct.

A better response to the Skeptical Induction from the history of science is to point out that—like the underdetermination problem—it only has plausibility in certain areas, particularly advanced, theoretical physics. It is completely implausible, for example, that the Theory of Evolution is going to be overthrown by some alternative biological theory that explains the same evidence without relying on anything like genes or natural selection. It is similarly implausible that a future scientific revolution will overthrow plate tectonics, heliocentric cosmology, the theory that water is H_2O, the germ theory of infectious disease, the theory that lightning is an electrical discharge, the DNA theory of genes, etc.

Apropos of which, there really haven't been that many scientific revolutions in very many areas. Granted, the theories that people had in prescientific times (diseases being caused by imbalances of the four bodily humors; the material world being made of earth, air, fire, and water; etc.) were indeed totally wrong. But since the basics of the modern scientific method were established, there are not that many cases of a theory being firmly established, using modern scientific methods, and then later being overthrown. That's why the examples people give are always the same examples, in theoretical physics.

Granted, the theoretical physics examples are very interesting, and the skeptic may well be right that we do not know the underlying truth of theoretical physics. But that doesn't stop us from knowing plenty of useful and interesting stuff about the real, mind-independent world.

14.5. Why Isn't Everyone a Bayesian?

We've seen the usefulness of probability theory, especially Bayes' Theorem, for analyzing issues about scientific reasoning, from the paradoxes of confirmation theory, to the virtue of falsifiability, to the virtue of parsimony. Nearly every issue about justification has a Bayesian analysis. From the way I've talked about it, you might be wondering, "Is everyone a Bayesian?"

Sadly, no. Most epistemologists are not Bayesians. Most are neither Bayesian nor anti-Bayesian; they just choose not to work on that, perhaps because all the mathematical stuff isn't that fun.

Some philosophers, however, are serious critics of Bayesianism. I should probably tell you something about that, lest people accuse me of undue bias.

14.5.1. The Problem of Old Evidence

One objection claims that Bayesians can't account for how a theory is supported by "old evidence", i.e., evidence that was known before the theory was devised. According to Bayes' Theorem,

$$P(h|e) = \frac{P(h) \times P(e|h)}{P(e)},$$

you get confirmation if and only if $P(e|h) > P(e)$. But since the evidence is already known, you have $P(e) = 1$. $P(e|h)$ cannot be greater than that, so you can't have confirmation.

In response, Bayesians typically say that to assess $P(e)$, you're supposed to look at the probability of e before it was discovered, or imagine a hypothetical state in which you didn't know e but the rest of your knowledge was otherwise as similar as possible to the actual state, or something like that.

14.5.2. The Probability of the Laws

Sir Karl (Popper) really didn't like Bayesianism for some reason (maybe because it undercuts the foundation of his entire philosophy). So he made some criticisms that try to use probability theory against the Bayesians; i.e., he tried to show that probability theory doesn't lead to the results that Bayesians want.

One of his claims (mentioned in §14.2.2) was that you should assign a prior probability of zero to any proposed law that applies to infinitely many things. This would include the Law of Gravity, the Conservation of Momentum, etc. The reason is basically that he thinks you can calculate the probability of the generalization as

$$P(A_1) \times P(A_2) \times P(A_3) \times \ldots$$

where A_1 is the proposition that the first thing the law applies to satisfies the law, A_2 is the proposition that the second thing satisfies the law, and so on. He thinks all of the A_i should have the same, nonzero probability, so the infinite product comes to 0. And note that if $P(h) = 0$, then $P(h|e)$ also $= 0$ by Bayes' Theorem.

Reply: Popper is wrong to assume that A_1, A_2, and so on are probabilistically *independent* of each other. Rather, A_1 probabilistically supports A_2, A_1 & A_2 supports A_3, and so on. The correct formula is:

$$P(A_1) \times P(A_2|A_1) \times P(A_3|A_1\&A_2) \times \ldots$$

(recall Axiom IV, §12.3.2). In that product, each factor is greater than the previous one. When you take that into account, you can get a nonzero product. (This is correct.)

Second reply: Some people think that laws of nature hold in virtue of *relationships between universals*. Now, if you reject universals, so you think that a law can only consist in an infinite conjunction of particular facts, *then* you would calculate the probability of the law as

$$P(A_1 \& A_2 \& A_3 \& \ldots) = P(A_1) \times P(A_2|A_1) \times P(A_3|A_1\&A_2) \times \ldots$$

But if you posit relations between universals, then to determine the probability of a law, say, "All A's are B", you would start with the possible ways that the two *universals* might be related to each other, e.g.: A necessitates B, A precludes B, A is irrelevant to B, A raises the probability of B (where this last possibility divides into infinitely many sub-possibilities). Each of those would then get a nonzero initial probability (perhaps each would get probability ¼?).

14.5.3. The Problem of Priors

The one serious objection to Bayesianism is the problem of prior probabilities. On the Bayesian view, to determine how justified any theory is in the light of any evidence, you need to first know the probability of the theory *prior* to the evidence, $P(h)$. And what the heck is that? What, for example, is the initial probability that humans evolved by natural selection, as assessed prior to collecting any evidence relevant to that? Any answer seems arbitrary.

It's no use saying, "Apply the Principle of Indifference." To do that, you would first need to list all the possible accounts of the origin of human beings. To avoid inconsistencies (per §12.6.3), you'd also need to identify the uniquely natural, or the most natural, way of describing that set of possibilities. Of course, no one can do these things.

The problem is pervasive. What, for example, is the a priori prior probability of the Earth orbiting the Sun? Of the Theory of Relativity being true? Of water being a compound of hydrogen and oxygen? Nobody knows these things.

Bayesians can make two related observations that might make you feel better about all this. The first is that the importance of the priors tends to diminish as you collect more evidence. I.e., people who start from different priors will tend to move closer together in their posterior probabilities as the evidence accumulates. The second observation is that to deploy Bayesian thinking, we need not have *precise* prior probabilities; we could instead start with a *range* of prior probabilities that we deem reasonable (but this range cannot just be the whole range from 0 to 1; see §12.5.6). Application of Bayes' Theorem would then get you a range of reasonable posterior probabilities, and that would typically be a *smaller* range than the range of priors you started with.

So, when you first hear "Maybe humans evolved by natural selection", no exact number suggests itself to you as the probability of that being true. But perhaps you have a pretty clear sense that you shouldn't say that's over 90% probable in the absence of any evidence, nor should you say it's less than 0.000000001% probable. If you can at least say that much, then the Bayesian machinery gets some purchase.

If you don't like this, *you* try giving a general account of justification that tells us the degree of justification any theory has in the light of any evidence. What's the alternative whereby you get to assess this without relying on any sense of the initial plausibility of the theory?

14.6. Conclusion

Scientific reasoning is non-deductive, but this isn't a problem. There are good reasons for why scientific method works the way it does—in particular, there are good, probabilistic explanations for why it makes sense to prefer falsifiable theories over unfalsifiable ones and simple theories over complex ones. Falsifiability matters due to the theorem of probability that, if nothing would be evidence against *h*, then nothing is evidence *for h* either. Simplicity matters because simpler theories typically make more specific predictions, and therefore receive greater confirmation if their predictions come true, than complex theories. This is because more complex theories have more parameters that could be adjusted to accommodate different possible data.

Science tells us a lot about objective reality, but not everything. E.g., we know that the Earth orbits the Sun, that humans evolved by natural selection, that salt is sodium chloride, that earthquakes are caused by tectonic shifts. Some big questions in fundamental physics remain up for debate and *perhaps* will never be resolved (it's too early to say now).

15. Moral Knowledge

In this chapter, we discuss whether and how we know what is good, bad, right, and wrong.

15.1. Background

15.1.1. Evaluation vs. Description

Philosophers like to distinguish *evaluative* propositions from *descriptive* propositions. **Evaluative propositions** are propositions that give a positive or negative evaluation of something, i.e., they say something is good or bad in some way. **Descriptive propositions** are propositions that are not evaluative. (We deliberately define things in this way so that we are sure our taxonomy covers all possibilities.) People sometimes also use "factual" in place of "descriptive", though "factual" is perhaps even more misleading than "descriptive" (it suggests that there aren't *facts* about what is good or bad, but that is a controversial assumption that should not be built into our terminology). We can similarly speak of evaluative truths, facts, statements, beliefs, and intuitions, though again, whether there are evaluative facts is up for debate.

People also sometimes refer to descriptive statements as "is" statements and evaluative statements as "ought" statements, as in "You can't derive an 'ought' from an 'is'." (This is slightly misleading because not all evaluative statements actually imply that anyone *ought* to do anything.)

15.1.2. Species of Evaluation

There are multiple species of evaluation. One type of is **epistemic evaluation**. That's the kind of evaluation we've been doing in this book when we talked about what beliefs are "justified", "reasonable", or "rational". These are evaluative because to say a belief is justified is to say something good about it; to call it unjustified is to criticize it. Epistemic evaluations are the kind of evaluation that distinctively applies to beliefs (i.e., nothing other than beliefs can be epistemically justified). Epistemic evaluation is commonly thought of as evaluation based on epistemic reasons, which are the kind of reasons that make something likely to be true.

Another type of evaluation is **aesthetic evaluation**. These are evaluations in terms of how beautiful something is, whether something is artistically good or bad, whether something is in good or bad taste, and stuff like that.

A third kind of evaluation is evaluation in terms of **practical rationality** (or, **practical evaluation**). This is where you evaluate an action in terms of the strength of reasons for and against it. To call an action irrational is to criticize it, to say something bad about it—that the agent had overall decisive and obvious reason against it, or something like that.

Within the realm of practical evaluation, there are at least two or three species, because there are at least two or three different *kinds* of reason for action. To begin with, there are **prudential reasons** for action, which are reasons from the standpoint of self-interest. An action or event is prudentially good or prudentially justified (for you) if it makes you better off.

Then there are **instrumental reasons** for action, which are reasons from the standpoint of an agent's actual goals. If you want something, then you have an instrumental reason for taking actions that increase the chances of bringing about what you want. This isn't the same as prudential reasons, because you can want things other than your own wellbeing. But prudential reasons might be parasitic on instrumental reasons, i.e., maybe you only have prudential reasons in virtue of *desiring* your own well-being.

Lastly, there is **moral evaluation**. "Meat-eating is wrong", "Slavery is unjust", and "Albert Schweitzer was saintly" are all morally evaluative statements, because each implies that something is morally good or bad; or, you might say, each morally criticizes or praises something. Moral evaluations are often understood as (at least) practical evaluations that are not based on self-interest or desire. Immanuel Kant made a big deal about how moral obligations are **categorical imperatives**, meaning that you have to satisfy them independent of what you *want*.

Some other philosophers, though, have claimed that there are no categorical imperatives and therefore that moral reasons must really be a species of instrumental reasons.

15.1.3. Questions About Moral Knowledge

We're going to focus mainly on moral knowledge, because that's the thing that a lot of people are most interested in. But it's worth noticing that the other kinds of evaluation are very similar—if you find *moral* evaluation puzzling, you should probably also be puzzled by epistemic, aesthetic, and (other) practical evaluation. And whatever we say about one form of evaluation we should probably also say about the others.

On the face of it, it appears that a lot of people know things about morality. Perhaps small children don't yet know that it's wrong to hurt other people. A small number of people, known as psychopaths, never learn this. But a normal, non-psychopathic adult certainly knows that it's wrong to physically injure other people under normal circumstances (obviously, we aren't talking about self-defense situations, etc.—just assume that I mean what I obviously must mean given the context).

But that knowledge is also puzzling. You can't see moral wrongness with your eyes, hear it with your ears, etc. Nor can you measure it with scientific instruments. It does not appear that anything that we do observe about the world is observably affected by the existence of moral values. So how exactly is it that we know anything about morality?

15.2. Skepticism

Of course, there is always the skeptical cop out: "What knowledge? Nobody knows anything about that!" There are three versions of this, which we should say something about before we discuss positive accounts of knowledge. This isn't a book on meta-ethics, so I'll discuss these only very briefly.[145]

15.2.1. *Expressivism*

The first way you might deny the existence of moral knowledge is to deny that there are any moral *propositions*, i.e., to claim that moral statements aren't genuine assertions. When you say "Abortion is wrong," you're not purporting to describe any fact about the world; instead, you're expressing your feelings about abortion, or telling people not to have abortions, or something like that. It's like if you said, "Boo on abortion!" or "Stop aborting!" On this view, moral "statements" are neither true nor false and thus cannot be expressions of knowledge at all. This view used to be called "**non-cognitivism**" ("cognitive" means "pertaining to knowledge"), but for some reason philosophers have shifted to calling it "**expressivism**".

The main objection to this view is the **Frege-Geach problem** (named after philosophers Gottlob Frege and Peter Geach). There are various sentences that contain other sentences as parts, where the part has to be an assertive sentence. For example, in "If A then B", A has to be replaced with an assertive sentence. E.g., you can say, "If it's raining, then take an umbrella", but you can't say, "If shut the door, then take an umbrella" or "If hurray, then

---

[145] For more on metaethics, see my book *Ethical Intuitionism*.

take an umbrella". There are many more examples: "I wonder whether ___"; "It's not the case that ___"; "It's possible that ___"; "Probably, ___"; "I doubt that ___"; "It's true that ___"; and so on. In all of those, the blank has to be filled in with a proposition-expressing sentence; otherwise, the whole thing doesn't make sense. And notice that in every single context like that, it's okay to stick in a phrase such as "abortion is wrong", and the result makes sense. This shows that "abortion is wrong" is a proposition-expressing sentence.

15.2.2. Nihilism

The second way of rejecting moral knowledge is to hold that all positive moral assertions are *false*. (Positive assertions are assertions that something has some property. I phrase the **nihilist** view this way because presumably they would accept certain *negative* moral statements as being true, statements that *deny* that something has a moral property.)

This is a surprisingly popular absurd idea. The main problem with nihilism is that it entails things like "there's nothing wrong with raping your friends". That's a literal consequence of the view, since nihilism says that nothing is wrong. Since this claim seems obviously false on its face, the nihilist would have to have some impressive argument for nihilism. As we discussed earlier (§4.4.3), the premises of a skeptical argument must each be *more initially plausible* than the common sense belief that the skeptic is denying. It's hard to see how you're going to find philosophical premises more obvious than "rape is wrong"; certainly no nihilist has done so. They tend to rely on such premises as "moral properties are weird", "intuition isn't a legitimate knowledge source", or "it's impossible for there to be categorical imperatives", all of which are *way, way* less obvious than "rape is wrong".

Another common approach for criticizing nihilism is to point to other kinds of evaluations. The arguments against moral facts typically also apply to other kinds of evaluative facts. E.g., if you think moral values are weird, then epistemic values, aesthetic values, and non-moral practical values are also weird. But it's even more implausible to deny all of these. In the case of epistemic values, the nihilist might wind up in a self-defeating position: If he says that it's rational to believe nihilism, that implies that there is at least one evaluative truth, since "rational" is an (epistemically) evaluative term.

15.2.3. Mere Skepticism

The last way of rejecting moral knowledge is to be a mere skeptic, that is, to hold that although there may well be things that have moral properties—some actions may be right, wrong, good, bad, etc.—we simply do not know which things have which moral properties.

The main motivation for this view would be dissatisfaction with the positive accounts of moral knowledge that non-skeptics have offered. So the most satisfying way to deal with this would be to go through those accounts and find one that works. We'll try that below.

But we can still make some general remarks here. Again, in order to justify a skeptical conclusion, the skeptic has to present an argument whose premises are more initially plausible than the denial of the conclusion. The skeptic's conclusion implies that no one knows whether child rape is wrong or not; it's hard to see how the skeptic is going to find premises that are certain enough to support that. For instance, surely it's more absurd to claim that *no one knows whether it's wrong to rape children* than it is to claim that *intuition is a legitimate knowledge source*. Indeed, I would say that literally *any* of the accounts of moral knowledge that have been given is more plausible than the nihilist view.

15.3. The Is/Ought Gap

15.3.1. The Traditional Doctrine

Here is the first thing to consider: Can we know moral truths based solely on descriptive truths?

There is a widely accepted doctrine known as the **is/ought gap** or "Hume's Law", which says that it is impossible to validly deduce an evaluative conclusion solely from descriptive premises. If you want to prove an evaluative statement, you always need at least one evaluative premise. People who try to deduce evaluations from descriptive premises are sometimes said to be committing the **naturalistic fallacy**.

Example: Suppose someone says that we know democracy is good because people in democracies are generally happier, wealthier, and live longer than people in undemocratic states. You could cite a lot of empirical evidence to that effect. So it looks like we have empirical evidence for the moral claim, "Democracy is good."

But wait. In addition to the empirical evidence, the argument *also* depends on the assumption that happiness, wealth, and longevity *are good*. If you don't assume that, then there's no reason to conclude that democracy is good. If you thought those things were bad, you would infer that democracy is *bad*.

And basically, all normal examples of arguing for a moral conclusion (i.e., all arguments that normal people might actually give) are like that. They always have at least one moral premise, whether implicit or explicit. Given that we can't complete an infinite series, then, we must have some moral premises that aren't deduced from other things.[146]

15.3.2. The Open Question Argument

Sometimes, people try to *define* certain evaluative statements to be true. This is also sometimes called "the naturalistic fallacy".[147] For instance, I might say that I just define the "morally good" to be that which promotes happiness and pleasure for sentient beings.

G.E. Moore refuted this type of definition using an argument called "the Open Question Argument". Basically, he asks you to consider the question, "Is pleasure good?" He invites you to notice that that is a meaningful question, and that it obviously does not mean the same as, "Does pleasure promote pleasure?" Therefore, "is good" does not mean the same as "promotes pleasure". You can give a similar argument for any other attempt to define "good" using non-evaluative terms.

I take it that the argument *doesn't* work when used on expressions that really are synonymous. For instance, suppose I say that "good" means "desirable" (which is true). We then consider the question, "Are desirable things good?" Well, that sounds to me the same as "Are good things good?"

Some philosophers complain that Moore's argument assumes that we can tell what our sentences mean just by reflection, and that maybe this is not always true. Maybe we're mistaken in thinking that "Is pleasure good?" has a different meaning from "Does pleasure promote pleasure?"

In reply, Moore's argument need not make any unreasonably strong assumptions. It need not assume that we always immediately know with certainty what our words mean. Moore can rest content with a much weaker assumption, such as that, once an analysis has been stated, and experts have reflected carefully on that analysis, then their linguistic intuitions provide at least a prima facie guide to the facts about meaning. That's enough to get Moore's argument to work. And if you don't accept even that much, then it's hard to see how you would think that we *ever* know anything about our own meanings. I would add that I think it's super-duper implausible to deny that we have any access to facts about the meanings of our own sentences.

15.3.3. Cute Philosopher Tricks

Sometimes, philosophers come up with clever linguistic tricks to make it look

---

[146] For a general proof of (a version of) the is-ought gap, see Toomas Karmo's "Some Valid (but no Sound) Arguments Trivially Span the 'Is'-'Ought' Gap" in *Mind* (1988).
[147] For examples of the naturalistic fallacy in action, see Sam Harris' popular philosophy book, *The Moral Landscape* (2010).

like you can derive an "ought" from an "is". I don't want to spend much time on this because these tricks generally do not connect to any general account of how people gain moral knowledge, so thinking about them isn't really illuminating about the underlying problem. But let me give you an example.[148]

Consider the disjunctive proposition,

P   Abortion is wrong *or* it's raining.

Is that evaluative or descriptive? Either answer enables you to construct a deduction that spans the is-ought gap. If you say P is evaluative, then consider the inference:

It's raining.
Therefore, abortion is wrong or it's raining.

That derives an evaluative conclusion from a descriptive premise. Alternately, suppose P is descriptive. Then consider this inference:

Abortion is wrong or it's raining.
It isn't raining.
Therefore, abortion is wrong.

Now that derives an evaluative conclusion from two descriptive premises.

In reply, the right answer is that the status of P depends on what else is true in the world.[149] *If it is in fact raining*, then "Abortion is wrong or it's raining" is descriptive. The intuitive idea here is that, if it's actually raining, then the truth of the disjunction doesn't depend on the moral status of abortion; both pro-lifers and pro-choicers should agree on the overall truth of the sentence.

On the other hand, if it *isn't* raining, then "Abortion is wrong or it's raining" is evaluative, because if it isn't raining, then the truth-value of P depends on the moral status of abortion.

With this understood, the first inference—

It's raining.
Therefore, abortion is wrong or it's raining.

—fails to span the is-ought gap in a useful way, because, if the premise is true, then the conclusion is descriptive, not evaluative. And if the premise is false, then the inference can't generate knowledge, so who cares?

In the second inference—

Abortion is wrong or it's raining.

---

[148] Based on A.N. Prior's "The Autonomy of Ethics" (*Australasian Journal of Philosophy*, 1960).
[149] Based on Karmo, *op. cit.*

It isn't raining.
Therefore, abortion is wrong.

—if the second premise is true, then the first premise is evaluative (we can't tell whether it's true unless we know the moral status of abortion). And if the second premise *isn't* true, then the argument is unsound and so can't generate knowledge. Since our central question is how we gain moral knowledge, the above cute arguments don't help us.

15.4. Moral Explanations

15.4.1. The Basic Explanationist Idea

Okay, so you can't gain moral knowledge by *deducing* it from descriptive facts. What about *non-deductively* inferring moral conclusions from descriptive premises?

Well, induction obviously isn't going to work, because induction just generalizes from particular cases, so it could only take you from *particular* evaluative truths to some evaluative *generalization*, or from particular descriptive truths to a descriptive generalization. It's not going to take you from descriptive to evaluative content.

What about inference to the best explanation? Perhaps moral facts sometimes help to *explain* descriptive facts, and perhaps this has something to do with how we know moral facts.[150]

At first glance, it seems that moral truths sometimes help to explain things. For instance, it seems that the best explanation for why Adolf Hitler ordered the Holocaust is that he was evil. You could think of alternative explanations—e.g., maybe he was delusional and he thought he was ordering a pizza, or maybe he actually had excellent evidence that the Jews were going to destroy the world unless he ordered the Holocaust, etc. But none of these explanations is as plausible as the theory that he was just a terrible person.

Since we know empirically that he ordered the Holocaust, and the best explanation for this is that he was evil, we're justified in believing that he was evil.

---

[150] See the debate between Gilbert Harman and Nicholas Sturgeon on moral explanations, on which I draw for some of the explanation below. (Harman, *The Nature of Morality*, 1977; Sturgeon, "Moral Explanations" in *Morality, Reason, and Truth*, 1985; Harman, "Moral Explanations of Natural Facts—Can Moral Claims Be Tested Against Moral Reality?", *Southern Journal of Philosophy*, 1986; Sturgeon, "Harman on Moral Explanations of Natural Facts", *Southern Journal of Philosophy*, 1986).

15.4.2. Objection #1: Presupposing Values

The first obvious objection is that the moral explanations only work if you assume certain values. Sure, if you assume that human life is valuable and that irrational hatred is wrong, *then* it's plausible that Hitler ordered the Holocaust because he was evil. But that just pushes the question back to how you know those starting values.

Defenders of moral explanation might say that you shouldn't really be bothered by this feature of the moral explanations, because something similar is true of scientific explanations. In science, a theory rarely if ever explains any observations *by itself*. Rather, a theory will explain some evidence only when combined with a host of background beliefs.

For instance, it is sometimes said that Newton's Theory of Gravity explains why the planets move in elliptical orbits with the sun at one focus. But the Theory of Gravity *by itself* doesn't explain anything like this. You also have to assume the laws of motion, assume some things about the masses of the sun and planets, assume some things about the initial conditions of the solar system, and assume the absence of any *other* significant forces that would observably affect the planetary orbits. These other assumptions are not direct observations; they're theories too. Nevertheless, people don't seem to have a problem with saying that the Theory of Gravity is supported by the facts about planetary motion. Similarly, you shouldn't have a problem with saying that moral theories are supported by the observations that they explain, even though these explanations depend on background theoretical (moral) beliefs.

In response, however, it seems that there must be some story about how we justify the *first* moral belief; otherwise, we have an infinite regress or a circularity problem. If moral explanations only work given a moral background, then the *first* moral beliefs must come from somewhere else. But if that's the case, then maybe we don't need inference to the best explanation at all—whatever the source is of our starting moral beliefs, maybe we can use that to explain all of them.

15.4.3. Objection #2: Redundancy

The second obvious objection (the objections are all connected) is that the moral explanations are redundant, in the sense that we already have complete explanations, which are not in dispute, based on descriptive facts. In the Hitler case, we already know that Hitler ordered the Holocaust due to certain descriptive, psychological facts about him—that he intensely hated Jews, that he lacked the scruples against killing that most people have, and things like that. It's not as though a person who doesn't believe in moral facts will be completely at a loss to understand what happened; he'll just describe what happened in psychological terms, without moral evaluations. Adding that extreme hatred combined with a lack of regard for human life *is evil* does not add anything to your predictive or explanatory abilities.

It's important that, in this objection, the contrast with the moral explanation is a nihilistic, or completely morally skeptical view, not a view that accepts conventional morality in general but then just doesn't accept that Hitler was evil. Note that, in the putatively analogous case of scientific reasoning, there is no question that a person who rejects science wholesale would be unable to explain lots of things that a modern scientist can explain. Similarly, it's reasonable to ask whether a person who rejects morality wholesale would be unable to explain things that modern ethicists can explain.

Perhaps the best thing for the moral explanationist to say here is that moral concepts can add some *unifying* power to our explanations.[151] To see what I mean by that, suppose someone wants to know why a certain peg won't fit into a certain hole. You have two explanatory strategies available. You could plot the trajectories of all the elementary particles in the peg and the perforated object while someone tries to push the peg into the hole. Or you could just cite the fact that you can't put a round peg in a square hole (where the side is smaller than the diameter of the peg).

The elementary-particle explanation is undoubtedly correct. But there's a way in which the "square peg/round hole" explanation is better: It helps you know what to expect when someone tries to put *another* square peg, with a different configuration of elementary particles, into another round hole. In that sense, the "square peg/round hole" explanation unifies cases that intuitively seem relevantly alike. The elementary particle explanation would treat each new peg as a different case.

So maybe there is something like that with moral explanations. E.g., maybe there are certain regularities that we can see in evil people, which apply across types of evil that are realized in different particular combinations of psychological traits. This, however, is pretty speculative; it's far from obvious that there are any observable behavioral similarities across different kinds of evil that are based on different psychological traits.

15.4.4. Objection #3: Alternative Value Systems

The third obvious objection to the explanationist approach is that people with alternative values can explain the same empirical facts.

Let me start with a scientific example—which, by the way, is totally fair, because these explanationist people appeal to science all the time, trying to convince you that there's an analogy between moral and scientific explanation.

---

[151] See Michael S. Moore's "Moral Reality Revisited", *Michigan Law Review* (1992).

So take the theory that water is H₂O. Here is how we know that: If you apply an electric potential difference to a sample of water, you can actually decompose the water. The quantity of water decreases, and some gas is produced, which turns out to be a combination of hydrogen and oxygen, in a 2:1 ratio by volume. Also, if you prepare a container full of hydrogen and oxygen gas and you introduce a spark into it, a fire occurs. After the fire, there is less gas, and some water has appeared on the sides of the container.

Notice how the theory that water is H₂O explains these results. Notice also that alternative theories could *not* explain them. If you think water is an element, or you think that water is NaCl, you have no natural way of explaining the results of those experiments.

Now turn to the moral theory which says that Hitler was evil. This theory, we have said, helps to explain why Hitler ordered the Holocaust, given the background assumption that racial hatred plus lack of regard for human life is evil. But a person with an opposing moral theory could explain exactly the same events in parallel ways. If, for example, you think that racial hatred is good or that human life is bad and should be destroyed, then you can explain why Hitler ordered the Holocaust by citing the theory that Hitler was *good*.

Above, we suggested that moral explanations have an advantage in *unifying* phenomena, compared with explanations that only cite psychological traits non-morally described. But even if this is true, *alternative* moral theories would gain that same advantage. A person with the reverse of your values would unify all the same phenomena using the category "good" that you unify using the category "evil".

It therefore does not seem that we know moral truths by inference to the best explanation.

15.5. Testimony

If you ask students how they know moral truths, some of them are going to say that they know moral truths because adults *taught* them moral truths when they were children.

Fair enough. This is a legitimate way of learning moral truths, provided that the person who is teaching you actually knows moral truths and you're justified in trusting their statements.

Aside: Some philosophers doubt that moral testimony confers knowledge; they think that you have to see the wrongness of an action for yourself in order to genuinely know that it's wrong. I disagree. Granted, in some cases, taking testimony would be *weird*. If you believe purely on testimony that it's wrong to torture children, then there's something wrong with you. But what is wrong is that you *shouldn't need* testimony for that, not that testimony isn't a valid source of moral knowledge. (Also, by the way, if you can't immediately see the wrongness of torture, then you probably don't understand what "wrong" means, in which case you wouldn't even understand other people's testimony about it.)

It would also be weird to accept someone's testimony on a point that is controversial even among experts, such as that abortion is wrong. In this case, the problem is that there's no strong reason to believe a particular person's opinion over all the experts who disagree.

But there are other cases where accepting moral testimony is fine and not weird. For instance, if homosexuality seems wrong to you, but you learn that most people, including nearly 100% of ethicists, consider it to be perfectly okay, there's nothing wrong with deferring to the consensus view.

Be all that as it may, here's the main point I want to make: Testimonial knowledge presupposes non-testimonial knowledge. If you learned that homosexuality is permissible from someone else, that just pushes the question back to: How did *they* know it? There can't be an infinite regress, so someone must have figured it out on their own. And the philosophically interesting cases are going to be the cases of original acquisition, where you acquire moral knowledge without being told by someone else.

15.6. Emotion and Desire

Our emotions have something to do with our moral values. People are frequently emotional about the things that they judge morally significant. But what exactly is the connection? There are at least five main answers to that. These are not necessarily conflicting, so two or more of these may be correct.

15.6.1. Evaluative Statements Express Emotions

We ran into this idea above (§15.2.1): Maybe moral statements serve to express our emotions, e.g., "Abortion is wrong" expresses a sentiment of disapproval toward abortion.

We noted above that there is excellent reason to doubt that evaluative statements are *simply* expressions of emotion; they act like assertions in all known respects. However, it may be that evaluative statements express emotions *in addition* to asserting evaluative propositions. This would make sense of why you can say things like "If abortion is wrong, then God is angry" while also explaining why it is incongruous to say, "Abortion is horrible, but that's not important to me." The latter is odd, perhaps, because the first half of the sentence expresses a strong negative attitude that the second half disavows.

Note, however, that the emotional attitudes commonly expressed by evaluative statements might be only *implied* rather than literally part of the *meanings* of those statements. Philosophers like to distinguish between what a person literally says (including what is logically entailed by one's statement) from what a person *suggests* or *implies* by their statements. E.g., if I say, "Have you stopped kissing squirrels?", I have *implied* that you were kissing squirrels, though I did not actually say this. Similarly, it may be that if I say "Abortion is horrible," I am merely *implying* that I feel strong disapproval about it.

This thought draws support from cases in which it is very natural to affirm a moral judgment while disavowing an associated emotion. E.g., when I heard that the ancient Roman Emperor Nero murdered both his wife and his mother, I of course saw that that was extremely wrong. At the same time, though, I did not care. I'm a lot more upset about someone cutting in front of me in line at the supermarket than I am about Nero's murders, even though obviously I know that the murders were vastly more wrong. This shows that emotion and moral judgment are distinct mental states that are not *necessarily* correlated.

15.6.2. Emotions Make Evaluative Statements True

Some people think that moral statements are made true by facts about our attitudes. For instance, perhaps "Murder is wrong" is true *in virtue of* the fact that people in our society disapprove of murder. The wrongness just is the property of being socially disapproved. Note that in this account, "disapprove" cannot be taken to mean "believe to be wrong" (else we have a circularity problem); disapproval is to be construed as a particular negative emotional state, rather than a belief. On this account, wrongness is relative to a culture—what is wrong in one society may be right in another.

Alternately, perhaps "Murder is wrong" means "I disapprove of murder", in which case wrongness is relative to an *individual* and what is wrong for me may be right for you.

The main objection to this account is that it implies that statements such as the following are true: "If society approved of torturing children, then it would be right to torture children", "If I approved of torturing children, then it would be right to torture children", "Abortion is wrong if and only if society disapproves of it".

Take the case of Oscar Schindler, the German businessman who saved hundreds of Jews from the concentration camps during World War II by employing them in his factories. He did this at great personal risk and had to expend his fortune in the process. This is dramatized in the excellent movie *Schindler's List*. Now, if you're a cultural relativist, when you watch that movie, you would have to say that Oscar Schindler was the villain of the story, since society approved of sending Jews to concentration camps. Or, if you're an individualist relativist, maybe you'd say that Schindler's actions were good *relative to you*, but they were bad *relative to the Nazis*, and that's all there is to say; there's no fact about who was right or wrong really. It's hard to think of a worse understanding of morality.

In brief, it doesn't seem that actions are made right or wrong by our approving or disapproving of them.

15.6.3. *Evaluative Judgments Cause Emotions*

The above theory held that right actions are right because we approve of them. But it's more plausible to hold that, at least in normal cases, we approve of certain actions *because* they are right (or, perhaps more precisely, because we take them to be right), and we disapprove of actions because we consider them to be wrong.

The point applies to many emotions. Suppose someone steps on your foot. If you think that they did it intentionally, and you take such foot-stepping to be wrong, then you are likely to be angry. If you find out that the act was unintentional, your anger will typically subside (though not immediately and completely; due to our imperfect rationality, you may retain some residual irritation). Alternately, suppose you have some odd belief system in which you consider it to be a sign of goodwill to step on another person's foot. In that case, when your foot is trampled, you will judge that this is good, and then you will probably be glad, rather than angry.

So the emotion of anger seems to be connected to judgments about wrongdoing on the part of others. Similarly, the emotion of fear is connected to danger; you normally fear that which you consider dangerous. Gratitude is connected to the judgment that someone else's action has been beneficial to you and supererogatory. Sadness is connected to the judgment that something valuable has been lost. And so on.

But note that in many cases, a person will feel an emotion without genuinely *believing* the evaluative proposition that would seem to match that emotion. For instance, some people fear flying in airplanes despite *knowing* that airplanes are very safe. In such a case, we might say that the person incorrectly *perceives* flying as dangerous (or flying *seems* dangerous or *feels* dangerous to them), despite *judging* that it is safe.

So we can only say that evaluative judgments often but not always cause emotions, and sometimes non-rational perceptions also cause emotions.

15.6.4. Emotions Represent Evaluative Facts

Cases like the fear-of-flying case admit of more than one interpretation. Perhaps emotions just *are* evaluative appearances. So when you have a fear of flying, it's not that the perception of danger causes your fear, nor does the fear cause the perception of danger; the fear *is* the perception of danger. Likewise, perhaps, to feel anger is to experience someone as having done wrong (or something like that), to feel gratitude is to have the appearance of someone's action as supererogatory, etc.

This view also suggests an account of the source of moral knowledge: Maybe we know moral truths through our emotions. Earlier (§5.2), we suggested that we have foundational justification for believing that things are the way they appear, unless and until we have specific grounds for doubting this. If you seem to see a table in front of you, it's rational to presume that there's a table in front of you. Likewise, if some event *seems* morally good to you, it's rational to presume that the event is morally good. If emotions are just appearances of value, then they can justify evaluative beliefs, prima facie.

What one can say about emotion one can also say, with comparable plausibility, about desire. (This applies to the earlier views about the emotion/value connection too.) Perhaps to *desire* something is to perceive it as good, and thus we know about what is good and bad through our desires.[152] It is also plausible to draw a link between emotions and desires. Perhaps emotions, at least the ones that involve value appearances, contain desires as constituents. E.g., maybe fear contains a desire for safety, anger contains a desire for justice, gratitude contains a desire to benefit one's benefactor.

However plausible all this may be, it does not seem to account for *all* basic moral judgments—not all (non-inferential) moral judgments are based on emotions or desires. This is particularly true when you consider very abstract evaluative judgments, such as the following:

> One ought not to treat others in a way that one would not wish to be treated.
>
> If A is better than B and B is better than C, then A is better than C.
>
> If it's wrong to do A, then it is wrong to pay someone else to do A.

I think those are too abstract for you to feel any particular emotions or desires when you think about them. Nevertheless, I bet you are able to judge those statements as correct.

---

[152] See Graham Oddie's *Value, Reality, and Desire* (2005).

15.6.5. Emotions Bias Evaluative Judgments

Another way that emotions and desires relate to moral knowledge is that they may *interfere* with moral knowledge by biasing our judgments. For example, it used to be common for people to believe that homosexuality is morally wrong. (Some people still believe that, but it is an increasingly rare opinion.) Why did people think that? Sometimes, they would give arguments about "naturalness" or they would appeal to religion, but come on. Those were pretexts. The reason people thought homosexuality was wrong was that they *felt* that it was wrong. That is, when thinking about homosexuality, straight people would commonly feel a certain negative emotional reaction, including a strong desire to avoid homosexual activities.

There are many cases like this, in which people make a moral judgment by consulting how they feel about something. A common heuristic is what I call the **attraction/aversion heuristic**: If you feel attracted to something, you judge that it is good; if you feel aversion, you judge that it is bad, with the degree of goodness or badness proportional to the strength of your attraction/aversion.

Fortunately, it is possible for people to overcome their biases, as the majority of people have done in the case of homosexuality. This may involve thinking about explanations for why some action might be right or wrong; often, one then realizes that there is no plausible explanation for a certain alleged moral fact. One can also reflect on explanations for one's own emotions, e.g., one might have a certain emotional reaction only because of the culture one happened to be raised in.

What can we conclude about the role of emotion and desire? They may contribute to moral knowledge, but they aren't the sole source of it, and sometimes they interfere with it.

15.7. Ethical Intuition

15.7.1. The Intuitionist View

Some smart and wise people endorse a theory known as **ethical intuitionism**, which holds (*i*) that there are objective evaluative truths, (*ii*) that these truths are irreducible (cannot be explained in non-evaluative terms, per §15.3.2), and (*iii*) that our evaluative knowledge originates in ethical intuitions. Let's focus on thesis (*iii*), the intuitionist account of moral knowledge.

15.7.2. What Is an Intuition?

No doubt you recall from §5.2.1 that there is a type of experience known as an "appearance" or "seeming", which is what you report when you say "It seems to me that *p*". This is a mental state that represents something as being the case (it "has propositional content", as philosophers say), it is distinct from a belief, but it normally *causes* beliefs—under normal circumstances, you believe what seems true to you, because it seems true.

There are several species of appearance, including sensory experiences, memory experiences, introspective awareness, and (of most interest to us here) **intellectual appearances**. Intellectual appearances are appearances that result from exercising the faculty of reason, i.e., thinking about things, as opposed to looking with your eyes, hearing with your ears, etc. Among intellectual appearances, there are two species: *inferential appearances* and *intuitions*. Inferential appearances are experiences in which some proposition seems true to you *in the light of* some other propositions that you already believe (or that already seem true to you) that (seemingly) support that proposition. These are key to explaining how reasoning justifies conclusions, according to the theory of Phenomenal Conservatism. Intuitions, on the other hand, are intellectual appearances that are not inferential, that is, they are experiences in which some proposition seems true to you on its own, rather than in the light of something else.

An *ethical* intuition is simply an intuition that has an ethical subject matter, that is, it is about what is morally good, bad, right, or wrong. To sum up: An ethical intuition is an immediate, intellectual appearance about an ethical proposition.

The above is my account of intuitions. Some philosophers give different accounts. Another view is that an intuition is a type of *belief* (or perhaps an inclination to believe), specifically, a belief that is directly justified by one's *understanding* of the proposition believed. For instance, if you understand the proposition [nothing can be completely red and completely blue], that understanding is enough to make you justified in believing that nothing can be completely red and completely blue.

A third view is that an intuition is a type of direct acquaintance with certain abstract facts. For instance, maybe you are directly acquainted with the incompatibility between red and blue; thus you "intuit" that nothing can be completely red and blue.

These are all reasonable views; however, I regard the appearance-based account as preferable to the others, mostly because the appearance account accommodates the fact that a person can be skeptical about their own intuitions, as well as the fact that you can have false intuitions, which (I take it) justify beliefs in the same way that true intuitions do.

15.7.3. Some Ethical Intuitions

Here are two famous hypothetical examples from ethics:

> *Trolley:* There is a runaway trolley that is shortly going to collide with and kill five people. You cannot get the people out of the way, nor can you stop the trolley. The only thing you can do is to switch the trolley onto another track, where it would collide with and kill only one person. Should you switch the trolley?

In this case, most people answer *yes*, switch the trolley.

> *Organ Harvesting:* You are a doctor with five patients who need organ transplants (for five different organs), without which they will die. You also have one healthy patient who happens to be compatible with the five. You can kill the healthy patient, make it look like an accident, and then transplant five of his organs into the patients who need transplants, thus saving five lives. Should you kill the healthy patient?

In this case, nearly everyone answers *no*, do not harvest the organs (and they give this answer even after being primed with the Trolley problem).

You might notice an interesting parallel between the two hypotheticals: Both envision an opportunity to sacrifice one person to save five others. You can probably see both why someone would think such sacrifice justified, and why someone would think it unjustified. What is interesting is that the great majority of people give *opposite* answers in the two cases: Sacrificing one to save five is *right* in the first case, they say, but *wrong* in the second.

People have spent a lot of time trying to figure out why this might be. Most things that people come up with on first hearing about this puzzle totally don't work. E.g., people say that the trolley was already headed for the 5 people before you showed up. But it's also true that the transplant patients were already sick and going to die before you showed up. People say that a doctor has special obligations to his patients. But you can suppose that the one healthy person isn't your patient but is just some rando off the street, or even that you're not a real doctor (though you have enough knowledge to be able to save the five anyway). Etc. It's interesting and educational to spend a few minutes thinking about what the difference between the two cases might be.

But since this isn't an ethics book, we aren't going to answer that.[153] My purpose in mentioning those examples is to illustrate the concept of ethical intuition. Importantly, nobody (I assume) *taught* you the answers to those cases.

---

[153] I discuss this in *Justice Before the Law*, 29-32.

When I describe the cases to students, most have never heard or thought about them before. They also cannot infer the answers from any ethical theory that they held before hearing those cases. If you had any view about this sort of thing before hearing those cases, your view was almost certainly either (a) that it's wrong to sacrifice one innocent person to save several others, or (b) that it's okay to sacrifice one innocent person to save several others. If you held theory (a), that would give you the wrong answer to Trolley; if you held (b), that would give you the wrong answer to Organ Harvesting. Most people, try as they might, cannot even think of a credible theory that answers "yes" to Trolley and "no" to Organ Harvesting. Nevertheless, almost everyone is able to answer these questions, and the great majority answer "yes" to Trolley and "no" to Organ Harvesting.

That shows that you have a capacity for ethical intuition. When you consider an ethical question, sometimes, a certain answer seems correct to you, where this is not just remembering something you were taught or making an inference from a pre-existing belief.

15.7.4. How Intuitions Justify

According to the principle of Phenomenal Conservatism (§5.2), it is rational to assume that things are the way they seem, unless and until one has specific grounds for doubting this. Ethical intuitions are a species of appearances; hence, they justify ethical beliefs as long as we lack specific grounds for doubting them. On this account, ethical intuitions justify in the same basic way that sensory experiences, memory experiences, inferential appearances, and non-ethical intuitions justify beliefs.

Some philosophers remain skeptical about ethical intuitions. To justify such skepticism, they would need to identify a *relevant difference* between ethical intuition and all those other things. For example, what is the epistemological difference between the intuition that *it's wrong to kill the patient in Organ Harvesting*, and the intuition that *no object can be completely red and completely blue*? Both propositions seem obvious when you think about them. I assume that we're justified in believing the one about the colors (see ch. 10 on a priori knowledge). If we're *not* justified in believing the ethical proposition, this must be because there is some special reason for doubting the ethical proposition, or some reason for doubting the reliability of our ethical intuitions, that doesn't apply in general to non-ethical intuitions. What might that be?

15.7.5. "Intuitions Cannot Be Checked"

Upon first hearing about ethical intuitionism, some people object that there is never any way of *checking* our ethical intuitions to make sure that they're reliable.

If only we could do that in *some* cases, then perhaps we could rely on intuitions in other cases. Alas, we cannot.

What's wrong with this objection? Well, it does not actually cite any difference between ethical intuition and any other very general source of knowledge. For instance, there is no way to check whether memory is reliable without using your memory (see §11.2.1). There is no way to check whether the five senses are reliable without using the five senses. There is no way to check whether reasoning is reliable without using reasoning. And there is no way to check whether non-ethical intuitions are reliable without using non-ethical intuitions.

One might say (as the coherentists do, §4.3) that it's okay to check on these faculties using those very faculties. More precisely, you can check on whether your cognitive faculties give you results that *fit together*. If the beliefs that you form using sensory perception generally cohere, that's a reason to think sensory perception is reliable. And similarly for the other faculties.

Suppose we buy that. In that case, there's no problem for ethical intuition, because of course you can check on the reliability of ethical intuition, as long as you're allowed to use ethical intuition. You can check on whether your intuitions cohere with each other and whether they cohere with the intuitions of other people. If you're a basically normal person, you're going to find a pretty substantial degree of coherence there. This, however, brings us to the next objection.

15.7.6. Disagreement, Part 1: Hypothetical Disagreements

Traditionally, the most popular objection to ethical intuitionism, which takes most people under ten seconds to think of, is that people can have conflicting intuitions. Somehow, I guess this is supposed to show that something about intuitionism isn't true. Let's think more about what the problem might be.

Sometimes, people raise purely *hypothetical* disagreements. E.g., someone will ask you to imagine a person who has the intuition that torturing babies is the greatest thing in the world. If the rest of his intuitions were equally haywire, it might be impossible for us to convince him that he was mistaken.

It's hard to see how this is supposed to pose a problem for intuitionism, though. You can imagine similar hypotheticals for any of our knowledge sources. E.g., I could ask you to imagine a person who has bizarre but internally coherent hallucinations all the time, and we can't convince him that his hallucinations aren't veridical. Or imagine someone who seemingly remembers a completely different (but internally coherent) past from what the rest of us remember. Again, we can't convince this person that he's mistaken. Presumably, these hypotheticals don't show that sensory perception and memory aren't legitimate sources of knowledge. (Perhaps the lesson is that merely possible grounds for doubt aren't actual grounds for doubt.) So the analogous hypothetical doesn't refute the legitimacy of intuition either.

15.7.7. Disagreement, Part 2: The Fallibility of Intuition

A more promising version of the disagreement objection would cite *actual* people who have conflicting intuitions. Say, one person reports the intuition that abortion is comparable to murder, while another person intuits that abortion is perfectly fine.

Cases like this are usually misdescribed—normal people don't have intuitions like that. Almost all anti-abortion people in fact rely on an *argument* (albeit a simple one) against abortion—roughly, the argument is that fetuses are people, and it's wrong to kill people. Pro-abortion people disagree that fetuses are people, which on the surface looks like it's a descriptive, rather than an ethical disagreement. That being said, there surely are *some* genuine clashes of intuition. So let's just stipulate that we have two people with clashing intuitions about some issue. How does this pose a problem?

Perhaps the problem is that, since intuitions at least sometimes conflict, we know that not all intuitions are true. This would be a problem if we thought that intuitions were infallible.

But of course, no one thinks that, and no one ever thought that. Most epistemologists (including ~100% of non-skeptics) are **fallibilists**, meaning they think that you can count as "knowing" things even though your justification is fallible. Our justification for nearly all beliefs, including all beliefs about the external world, is fallible. As skeptics have been annoyingly insisting since the days of ancient Greek philosophy, we periodically suffer from illusions, hallucinations, and other mistakes. Most of us normal (non-skeptic) people think that's compatible with our knowing lots of stuff about the world around us. If you disagree with that, you're using the word "know" in a stronger sense than I use it, and one that, I would say, makes the word a lot less useful and interesting. Be that as it may, my main point here is that no interesting difference between ethical intuition and other belief sources has so far been cited.

15.7.8. Disagreement, Part 3: The Unreliability of Intuition

Maybe you're getting impatient with my slapping down lame versions of the objection. Fine, let's get to the best version of the objection from disagreement: Sure, just about any source of knowledge is going to have *some* error rate. Sensory perception, memory, and non-ethical reasoning all sometimes go wrong. But their error rate is *much less* than that of ethical intuition. We know this because there is a lot more disagreement about ethical questions than there is about most non-ethical subjects. Knowledge may be compatible with having some chance of being wrong, but it isn't compatible with having a *very high* chance of being wrong. Thus, intuition can't give us ethical knowledge.

The best response to this is a two-pronged approach: First, minimize the amount of ethical disagreement; second, separate areas of disagreement from areas of agreement.

Regarding the first point, notice that when we talk about ethics, we tend to focus our attention on the areas of disagreement, rather than areas of agreement. E.g., we don't spend time talking about the morality of murder, precisely because everyone agrees about that. Instead, we spend time talking about the morality of abortion, because that is controversial. This is understandable, but it winds up giving people an exaggerated impression of how much disagreement there is.

Another reason why the amount of ethical disagreement is overestimated is that we often fail to examine the underlying causes of a disagreement. Often, a superficially ethical disagreement has roots in an underlying descriptive disagreement. On the subject of abortion, for example, most of the disagreement concerns whether fetuses are people, rather than whether it's okay to kill people. On the subject of gun control, most of the debate concerns whether gun control laws are effective in reducing crime, rather than whether reducing crime is good. On the subject of socialism versus capitalism, much of the debate concerns the actual effects of socialist policies. And so on.

This is not to deny that there are any fundamental ethical disagreements. But when you look at hot button controversial issues, it really is far from obvious that there are more ethical disagreements than there are descriptive disagreements.

Now to the second point: We can separate controversial ethical questions from uncontroversial ones. Granted, we should not hold confident opinions about highly controversial issues (this goes for non-ethical as well as ethical controversies, by the way). But that hardly shows that we can't have knowledge about *any* issues. The existence of ethical controversies doesn't undermine our beliefs about *non*-controversial ethical questions. For instance, the existence of disagreement about whether it's wrong to kill a fetus might show that we don't know whether killing fetuses is wrong. But it obviously does not show that we don't know whether killing normal adults is wrong, since there is no controversy about *that*.

No one claims that we know *all* ethical truths. Intuitionists and other non-skeptics claim merely that we know *some* ethical truths. So it suffices that there are some non-controversial ethical questions.

15.7.9. Cultural Biases

One potential problem with ethical intuitions is that they can be easily influenced by the culture you happened to grow up in. People who grow up in a society that practices polygamy are much more likely to intuit that polygamy is fine than people who grow up in a society with enforced monogamy. People who grow up in a traditional Muslim society are much more likely to intuit that homosexuality is wrong than people who grew up in ancient Greece. And so on.

This is an important point, though it does not pose a *general* problem for moral knowledge. It shows that, if you hold some ethical view that is widely rejected in other cultures (say, that polygamy is wrong), then you have good reason to doubt that that particular view is correct, especially if you have no argument for it.

On the other hand, if you hold an ethical view that is widely *accepted* across cultures (say, that it's wrong to kill babies for fun), then you have no reason to doubt *that* view.

It happens, as a matter of fact, that human societies have been converging toward a particular kind of value system, what we might broadly call "liberal values", over the course of history. Two thousand years ago, nearly every society was (by modern standards) extremely illiberal—people endorsed such practices as slavery, dictatorship, oppression of women, wars of conquest, judicial torture, dueling, and other forms of cruelty and oppression. Over the last two thousand years, more and more societies have become more and more liberal. For instance, during the last two centuries, slavery came to be outlawed in every country in the world.

Now, if you were initially inclined to say that cultural *disagreement* was evidence that our moral beliefs are *unreliable*, you should, on hearing the above facts, agree that the cultural *convergence* is evidence that our moral beliefs are *reliable*. (Recall from §14.2.3 that e is evidence for h iff $\sim e$ is evidence against h.)

15.8. The Relevance of Evolution

15.8.1. Background: Evolutionary Psychology

The Theory of Evolution tells us (correctly) that human beings evolved by natural selection from other animals. As a result, the traits we should expect to see in human beings—at least for things that are subject to genetic influence—are the traits that would have helped one to reproduce in the environment of our ancestors. The reason is that individuals who had such traits, by definition, tended to reproduce more than those who did not, with the result that they left more copies of their genes in the gene pool.

Evolutionary psychologists try to apply this thinking to help us understand human psychology. Often, their explanations are controversial, but there are at least some cases where evolutionary psychological explanations are very plausible and hardly controversial. For instance, why do most human beings care a lot more for their immediate family members than they do for strangers? Because in the past, this concern would cause one to help those family members, which would result in their surviving and reproducing more. Since your immediate family members share a lot of your genes, this would result in more copies of your genes making it into the next generation. Notice that it isn't necessary that the genes get into the next generation directly *from you*; all that matters is that some behavior of yours increases the number of copies of your genes, from whatever source, that make it into the next generation. The tendency to cause more copies of your genes to exist in the next generation is sometimes referred to as **inclusive fitness**.

Not everything has this kind of explanation. Human beings evolved, so in one sense, everything about us is "the product of evolution". But not everything about us is an **adaptation**. An adaptation, in evolutionary psych talk, is a trait that has a genetic basis and was selected for because it contributed to inclusive fitness in the past. Love of one's family is (very probably) an adaptation. On the other hand, love of chess presumably is not: It's not true that the reason some people love chess today is that in our evolutionary past, people who loved chess reproduced more and therefore left behind chess-loving genes in the next generation. It's more likely that love of chess is a *by-product* ("unintended" by evolution, so to speak) of other intellectual traits that have functions other than causing you to play chess.

So it's interesting to ask how evolutionary psychology bears on our sense of morality. Is our capacity for moral intuition an adaptation? If it is, how does that bear on our prospects for gaining moral knowledge?

15.8.2. The Skeptical View

Some people apply evolution to our moral sense and thence derive a skeptical lesson. They think that our sense of morality evolved by natural selection, and that this means we can't trust that sense to reliably indicate the actual moral truth; hence, we can't have moral knowledge.

To illustrate the thinking, take my example of an adaptation above: People care more about their family members than about strangers. Let's assume that emotional tendency is an adaptation: We're genetically programmed to feel that way because this feeling increased inclusive fitness in our ancestors. It's extremely plausible that this is also the explanation for certain *moral beliefs* that most people have: Most people believe that they have special duties to their family members that go far beyond their duties to strangers. Thus, if your child and a neighbor's child are both drowning, and you can only save one, most people think that you *should* save your own child. This isn't merely what you'd want to do, but the morally correct thing to do. Indeed, even if the choice was between saving *two* strangers or *one* of your own children, I would bet that most people would say you should save your own child.

It's hard to explain why this would be morally right. But it's super-easy to explain why evolution would have favored people who *thought* that it was. Here, it doesn't matter whether we have genes that directly influence moral beliefs, or whether we merely have genes for certain emotional attitudes, which in turn bias our moral thinking.

Now, so what? Why would this realization make us skeptical? Evolution designed *all* of our cognitive faculties. Evolution designed our eyes, but no one says that means we shouldn't trust our eyes. Evolution designed our faculty of memory, but no one says this means we shouldn't trust our memory. Evolution gave us the faculty of reason itself, but this is no reason to distrust reason.

But here is the key difference. In *most* cases, when you explain why it's adaptive to have a particular cognitive faculty, the explanation implies the reliability of the faculty. Thus, vision is adaptive only because it tells you about things that are really there. If you see a lion approaching you, that is adaptive if and only if there actually is a lion approaching. If you frequently "see" stuff that isn't there or fail to see what is there, that's going to tend to interfere with your survival and reproduction. That's why evolution gave us reliable vision.

But that's *not* true when it comes to morality. When you explain why our moral beliefs might be adaptive, that explanation does *not* need to cite the actual moral facts. For instance, the intuition that *you're obligated to care for your children* would be adaptive *whether or not* there actually exists such a moral obligation. And the same seems to be true across the board: If there are real moral facts, they don't seem to *do* anything to the physical world; the descriptive properties of an action fully account for the action's physical effects. Thus, moral facts have no independent impact on our inclusive fitness. And thus, we have no reason to expect evolution to have endowed us with accurate moral intuitions, if indeed moral facts exist at all.

15.8.3. *The Byproduct View*

The evolutionary argument for skepticism works best against **moral sense theorists**, people who think that we have a separate faculty specifically for detecting moral facts. They would have a hard time explaining why that faculty should be reliable.

However, very few people today, even among intuitionists, are moral sense theorists. Most intuitionists hold that ethical intuition is just the application to ethics of the general faculty of reason or intellect; there isn't a separate faculty for having moral intuitions, any more than there is a separate faculty for having intuitions about chess.

You may not like that view, but you should accept that that is in fact the dominant intuitionist view, and therefore that is a view that the moral skeptics need to address. The evolutionary argument doesn't really address it. Presumably, the moral skeptic doesn't want to reject reason as such (which would be self-defeating, among other things), so she'll admit that reason in general is reliable. If reason in general is reliable, then there's no obvious reason (certainly none we've seen thus far) why it can't be reliably applied to ethics, even if this is not what it evolved for, just as it can be applied to chess even though that is not what it evolved for.

The best response for the skeptic is to say that the particular content of our moral beliefs does not look like something produced by pure reason; it bears too many of the marks of natural selection. There are many widespread moral beliefs that make this point: the belief that one has special duties to one's family, that one has much lesser obligations (if any) to foreigners, that homosexuality is wrong, that sexual promiscuity is bad if you're female but good if you're male, that adultery is a horrible offense, and even that one is obligated to follow the conventions of one's society. Without going into detail (I'm sure you can fill in the details yourself), let's just say that each of those has a very plausible evolutionary explanation.

The most reasonable response for the non-skeptic is probably to agree that *sometimes*, our moral beliefs go awry because we are *biased* by our emotions, our upbringing, or other non-rational factors. Those are cases in which we lack moral knowledge. But the non-skeptic can maintain (reasonably) that this is not *always* true. There are some cases in which we have moral beliefs that look more like impartial dictates of reason, rather than adaptations designed to maximize our reproductive success.

For example, if all moral beliefs were the product of natural selection, then you'd expect all or nearly all people to be something close to ethical egoists (with some modifications to allow for helping one's immediate family). In fact, however, almost no one finds ethical egoism at all plausible, nor does anyone think that you only have obligations to your family. Granted, an evolutionary psychologist could probably come up with *some* story about how believing an altruistic morality could somehow promote your own inclusive fitness, but only because they can come up with such a story for pretty much everything. The important point is that, if we don't start out as skeptics, we haven't been given any specific *reason* for doubting that our belief in (somewhat) altruistic morality is correct.

As noted earlier (§15.7.9), human values have changed a lot over human history. Perhaps the values that we had 2000 years ago were adaptive (back when people thought it was cool to attack other societies, enslave them, and stuff like that). But then the evolutionary skeptic has no explanation for our *current* moral beliefs, which are very different from the adaptive beliefs of the past. The change in values has occurred too quickly to reflect genetic changes. What it looks like is that we've increasingly overcome our natural biases through rational reflection.[154]

15.9. The Role of Empathy

Some wise and brilliant people think that empathy plays a key role in moral knowledge, such that without it, we would be unable to reason morally.[155] This is supported by the case of psychopathy.

Psychopaths, who make up about 1%-3% of the population, are incapable of empathizing with others. They also appear to be incapable of understanding morality. There is some dispute about this, as psychopaths sometimes use moral terms and have at least some sense of what things are commonly called "right", "wrong", and so on. But they also make striking errors that suggest that they fundamentally do not understand moral concepts. For instance, when asked to give examples of the worst wrongs, psychopaths listed breaking bottles in the street, turning around one-way street signs, and pulling gates off posts.[156]

A plausible explanation is that psychopaths are unable to reason morally *because* they are unable to empathize with others. Empathy is a kind of perspective-taking, a matter of seeing things from another's point of view, particularly seeing the affective significance of events for others. Because psychopaths lack this capacity, they are locked in their own perspectives; they only see the significance of events to themselves. But morality requires impartially taking into account the perspectives of all individuals who are affected by a given situation. Thus, psychopaths are unable to think morally.

You might wonder how this account bears on the intuitionist account of moral knowledge. This account need not reject the importance of intuition in moral knowledge, but it denies that intuition is *sufficient*. One must also at least

---

[154] For more on this, see my article "A Liberal Realist Answer to Debunking Skeptics: The Empirical Case for Realism" from *Philosophical Studies* (2016).
[155] See Iskra Fileva, "The Curse of Psychopathy" (unpublished ms.), from which the ideas of this section derive.
[156] See Jonathan Glover, *Responsibility* (1970), 138.

possess empathy in order to learn moral reasoning, and this is distinct from the capacity for intuition. This is consistent with the fact that most psychopaths have normal intelligence, despite their moral blindness.

You might also wonder how the empathy account relates to the challenge from evolutionary psychology. The capacity for empathy may be an adaptation. It may have evolved to aid in social cooperation, roughly because one can more easily cooperate with others if one is able to understand their perspectives. If this crucial necessary condition on moral reasoning is an adaptation, you might then wonder whether this revives the evolutionary challenge to moral knowledge (§15.8). I think it does not, because the most natural explanations for the evolutionary value of empathy depend upon empathy being veridical—that is, empathy helps you cooperate with others only if it helps you *correctly* understand their perspectives. Thus, empathy is similar to vision, reason, or memory, in that its evolutionary origin gives us no reason to doubt its reliability. And presumably, if moral judgment is shown to depend on some cognitive capacity that is generally reliable, that fact doesn't cast doubt on our moral judgments.

15.10. Conclusion

How do we know what is good, bad, right, and wrong? Some people say we have no such knowledge, either because moral statements fail to express propositions, or because they express false propositions, or because we simply don't know when they are true.

The first view is rebutted by the fact that moral statements can be inserted in any context that requires a proposition-expressing sentence (e.g., "I wonder whether ____") and the result makes sense. The second view is rebutted by the fact that it's wrong to rape your friends. The third is rebutted by the fact that most people know that it's wrong to rape your friends. The G.E. Moore shift applies in the last two cases.

Turning to positive accounts of moral knowledge: It is widely accepted that one cannot deduce evaluative truths from descriptive truths, nor can one simply define evaluative terms using descriptive terms. The attempt to do such things is called "the naturalistic fallacy". Such attempted definitions are refuted by the Open Question Argument, in which we see that such questions as "Is *D* good?" (where *D* is any descriptive property) do not have the same meaning as "Is good good?"

Some have argued that moral facts help *explain* empirical facts; e.g., Hitler's evil helps explain the Holocaust. However, this can't be used to derive moral knowledge, because the same empirical facts could be explained by someone with an opposite value system; e.g., a Nazi could explain the same events by citing Hitler's "virtue". To identify correct moral explanations, one needs pre-existing moral knowledge.

Many people gain most of their moral knowledge from other people. However, this depends on some other people's gaining moral knowledge on their own, which still needs to be explained.

Some people appeal to emotions and desires as sources of moral knowledge. Though this is plausible in some cases, it doesn't explain very abstract moral knowledge, and there are other cases in which emotions and desires instead bias our moral judgment.

The best account of moral knowledge appeals to ethical intuitions, which are non-inferential, intellectual appearances about good, bad, right, and wrong. These justify beliefs in accord with the principle of Phenomenal Conservatism. Some object that intuitions can't be checked without using intuition and that intuitions can sometimes go wrong. However, these things are equally true of *all* our cognitive faculties. Others say that ethical intuitions seem to be less reliable than other kinds of cognitions, since there is more disagreement about them. However, there are substantial areas of ethical agreement, which are not undermined by the existence of *other* ethical issues where there is disagreement.

Some say that evolution shaped our ethical intuitions to promote inclusive fitness and that this means there is no reason to think our intuitions are objectively true. This objection applies more to the theory that we have a special moral sense, rather than to the view that ethical intuition is just the result of applying the faculty of reason to an ethical subject matter. Anyway, though there are some ways our instincts bias our moral judgment, the evolutionary account can't explain cases in which we've overcome those biases over the course of recent history.

Finally, there is evidence that empathy is needed to develop moral reasoning capacities, as psychopaths (who lack empathy) are unable to reason morally. This is probably because morality requires impartially taking account of everyone's perspective, which begins with the ability to *see* others' perspectives.

16. Religious Knowledge

In this chapter, we talk about whether and how we know religious truths.

16.1. Faith vs. Evidence

There are two main views about how we should form beliefs about religion: one, that we should rely exclusively on rational, evidence-based arguments (evidentialism); two, that we should rely on faith (fideism).

16.1.1. Epistemic Evidentialism

There are two variants of evidentialism, which I will call "epistemic evidentialism" and "moral evidentialism". I'll talk about moral evidentialism later.

Epistemic evidentialism holds that the epistemic justification for a belief (or other attitude) is entirely determined by the evidence. The more evidence there is for p, the more justification one has to believe p; if there is no evidence for p, then belief in p is completely unjustified and suspense of judgment would be justified instead. This is taking "justified" in the epistemological sense that we've been using throughout this book.

Okay, but what is "evidence"? Generally speaking, evidentialists are going to include facts that you observe using the five senses, such as that there is a capybara in front of you (when you are seeing one there); facts that you are introspectively aware of, such as that you're feeling hungry (when you are); and facts that are self-evident, such as that $17+1=18$. All your justified beliefs must be inferable from these kinds of facts.

What if you have a religious experience in which God seemingly appears to you? Most evidentialists would say that the fact *that you had that experience* (i.e., that it *seemed to you* that God was present) counts as part of your evidence, but the alleged fact that *God actually appeared to you* does not. (But this is up for debate; see below.)

So that's a pretty good list of what most evidentialists would count as evidence. It's hard to find a satisfying *definition* of "evidence", though. Sometimes, it seems as though epistemologists are just using "evidence" to mean "that which confers justification". Evidentialism would then amount to the view that epistemic justification is entirely a function of ... whatever confers it. That's not very informative, is it?

Another way of defining evidence would be this: *Evidence for h* consists of propositions that have some foundational justification and that raise the probability of *h*. Evidentialism would then amount to something very close to, if not indistinguishable from, foundationalism: the view that epistemic justification is entirely a function of foundational justification and probabilistic support by foundational propositions (where entailment counts as a special case of probabilistic support, namely, the case where the probability of *h* given *e* is 100%).

Well, what is it that the evidentialists are trying to rule out? Who disagrees with evidentialism?

Basically, they're trying to rule out that non-epistemic reasons, like *prudential* or *moral* reasons, could affect your epistemic justification. So, suppose that it's morally virtuous to have faith in God (I don't believe this, but just pretend that for the sake of argument). That would constitute a *moral* reason to believe in God. Also, believing in God might increase your chances of getting into Heaven after you die. So that gives you a *prudential* reason to believe in God. According to evidentialists, those reasons are *completely irrelevant* to what you are epistemically justified in believing. (But not irrelevant to what you are morally or prudentially justified in believing!) Thus, e.g., they would be irrelevant to your knowledge; you could not *know* that there's a God on the basis of such reasons.

Thus explained, evidentialism seems very plausible. Maybe you think it's obvious at this point. I'm just going to briefly mention two reasons why it might be false.

First objection: If you buy into an objective Bayesian epistemology (as you should; see §12.6, ch. 14), then you should accept that some propositions are going to just start out with high a priori prior probabilities. Given a sufficiently complex set of propositions, there is no coherent probability distribution that doesn't assign *some* things a high prior probability. E.g., say you apply the Principle of Indifference to a set of 100 alternatives, $\{A_1, A_2, ..., A_{100}\}$. Then $\sim A_1$ gets an a priori prior probability of 99%. Note that $\sim A_1$ would not be "self-evident" in the traditional sense, since it is a contingent, empirical proposition. It looks like one can be justified in having a high credence in such propositions, prior to collecting any evidence for them. That looks like a counter-example to epistemic evidentialism.

Second objection: Note that there is a distinction between merely *having a high credence* in something and *outright believing* it. Outright belief (which we normally just call "belief") is a qualitative attitude—roughly, it's a matter of deciding that it's time to close the inquiry into whether p is true and just proceed on the assumption that it is. You then use p itself, rather than some estimate of the probability of p, as a premise in future reasoning. Or something like that. There are practical reasons why it's good that we can form outright beliefs. But note that the attitude itself is a cognitive attitude (not, e.g., a conative or affective attitude) and therefore subject to *epistemic* evaluation.

When we form outright beliefs, we almost never have 100% conclusive evidence. So there is almost always a nontrivial question of what is the threshold level of evidence one needs to justify moving from *high credence* to *belief*. This question can't itself be settled solely by looking at the evidence. (The evidence for p doesn't tell you how much evidence you *need* for p.) Plausibly, it has something to do with practical considerations, such as how important it is to avoid error about p, how valuable it is to have a definite conclusion, how difficult it is to collect further evidence, and how likely further evidence is to make a big difference to your credence. Thus, even if the justified *credence* in p is solely determined by the evidence for p, there can still be non-evidential, practical reasons that influence whether *belief* is justified.[157]

I'm pretty sympathetic to both of these objections to evidentialism. But they leave room for an adjacent position, which would hold that (*i*) non-epistemic factors never influence the probability of a proposition, and (*ii*) there is some threshold level of probability that is necessary for any belief to be justified, regardless of what non-epistemic reasons there are (e.g., it can never be rational to believe something that is less than 50% probable). This is enough to oppose fideism (which we'll get to below).

16.1.2. Moral Evidentialism

Moral evidentialism holds that it is *morally wrong* to hold a belief that isn't evidentially justified. This includes believing things for which there is no evidence, as well as believing something more strongly than the evidence warrants. As W.K. Clifford famously put it, "It is wrong, always, everywhere, and for anyone, to believe anything upon insufficient evidence."[158]

Why would someone think this? The argument turns on imagining cases in which an unjustified belief causes harm to others. Say you're the President of country U, and you're deciding whether to invade country Q.[159] You're going to decide on the basis of whether Q is building Weapons of Mass Destruction

---

[157] For discussion, see David Owens' very interesting *Reason Without Freedom* (2000).
[158] See his "The Ethics of Belief" (1877), which is widely reprinted in philosophy anthologies.
[159] This example is purely fictional. Any resemblance to U.S. President George W. Bush is entirely coincidental.

(WMD's) or not: If they are, you plan to invade; if not, then not. Assume also that this would be a good reason for invasion—avoiding nuclear proliferation is so important that it justifies preemptive war.

Now, say you conduct a shoddy investigation in which you just look at a few pieces of circumstantial evidence. Without bothering to look for alternative explanations of the evidence, you jump to the conclusion that Q *is* producing WMD's. So you order an invasion, which winds up killing hundreds of thousands of civilians and toppling the government of Q. After years of chaos and struggle, Q winds up being taken over by terrorists. Oh, and it turns out that Q never had any WMD program in the first place. Question: Did you do something wrong?

Surely you did. But by stipulation, your action was justified *given* the belief that Q had a WMD program. Thus, the locus of your immorality must be in *forming the belief* that Q had a WMD program. That was immoral because it was epistemically unjustified.

If you buy that, it's plausible to argue that, even when things turn out okay, it's still immoral to form an unjustified belief, because the morality of your choice should be a matter of what information was available to you at the time, not a matter of luck in how things turn out. So even if Q had turned out, by chance, to *have* a WMD program, you would still have acted immorally by believing without enough evidence.

Now, you might think this only applies to beliefs that have practical consequences for others. But, W.K. Clifford claims, beliefs always have potential practical consequences. Once you form a belief, you wind up inferring other beliefs from it, then other beliefs from those beliefs, then planning hitherto-unforeseen actions based on those beliefs, etc. You can't trace out in advance all the potential consequences. So the only way to avoid the risk of causing harm through your unjustified beliefs is to not have any unjustified beliefs.

A couple of potential objections: First, the argument apparently assumes **doxastic voluntarism**, the view that people can choose their beliefs. Many philosophers hold that we have no direct control over our beliefs (see §17.3.5 below). However, you can at least choose whether to gather more evidence about a question, whether to look for counter-arguments, and so on. So the evidentialist can say you're obligated to do things like that, *until* your belief is adequately justified. Most evidentialists would be happy with that.

Second, the claim that unjustified beliefs *always* carry potential risks to others seems overdrawn. In some cases, perhaps, the risks are so small as to be morally negligible. But, be that as it may, religious beliefs are particularly likely to have practical consequences. So it remains reasonable to apply evidentialism in the realm of religious belief, which is really what the evidentialists most care about (plus maybe political and moral beliefs).

16.1.3. Fideism

Some people say that religion is properly a matter of *faith*. What does this mean?

Let's start by setting aside some irrelevant uses of the word "faith": Some people just use "faith" to mean a religion (as in "many faiths are represented at this school"), or belief in a religion (as in "he lost his faith"). These uses of the word are not relevant for us, because they do not name a possible explanation of why someone believes; they just denote the belief itself.

Some theists like this verse from the Christian Bible: "[F]aith is the substance of things hoped for, the evidence of things not seen."[160] This doesn't make much sense, though. Faith is presumably an attitude that you have; in what sense could that be the "substance" or "evidence" of something? A more accurate translation renders the verse as: "Now faith is the assurance of things hoped for, the conviction of things not seen."[161] That sounds to me like: Faith is belief in something that you hope is true but do not have decisive evidence for.

This more or less matches how many people use the term in discussions of theism. "Faith" is commonly understood as a kind of belief that is either not supported by evidence at all, or at least not supported by decisive evidence, and yet the belief is held with great confidence, disproportionate to the evidence. This is exactly what the evidentialists are against.

Aside: Of course, not just *any* belief that is disproportionate to the evidence counts as "faith". If a hypochondriac is convinced that he has Ebola because he recently met an African and now he has a headache, that is not an example of "faith". That's just garden-variety irrationality. One difference is that Ebola is something bad, whereas faith must be in something "hoped for". But let's not worry about this aspect of the definition of "faith".

Fideists are people who support religion based on faith and thus reject evidentialism. The 2nd-century Christian thinker Tertullian is often (mis)quoted as saying, of the Resurrection, "I believe it because it is absurd" or "It is certain because it is impossible", thus apparently rejecting rationality. (*Note:* This is not totally fair to Tertullian.[162]) So, what are the main reasons for this view?

---

[160] *Hebrews* 11:1 (King James Version).
[161] From the English Standard Version, which is a particularly literal translation of the Bible.
[162] The first version is a misquotation. The second one may have been in reference to the argument that the story of the resurrection was so seemingly unbelievable that no

On the face of it, you might think that fideists could not have any reasons for their view, since they're rejecting the reliance on reason and evidence. If they gave good *reasons* in favor of having faith, that would make the faith rationally justified and hence no longer faith, right? This makes their position sound crazy, like saying that you should believe *p* because there is no reason to. Obviously, the mere fact that there's no reason to do something does not mean you should do it. Thus, just citing "faith" by itself can't explain why one should believe religion.

Fortunately, serious philosophical fideists are usually not that crazy; they don't just say you should believe religion for no reason. They try to give *non-epistemic* reasons for having faith. The most common argument for fideism, which you often hear from amateur-philosopher theists, is that all belief systems are inevitably based on faith. If you're thinking of basing your beliefs on science, well, that's just placing faith in science. That's just as arbitrary as any other faith. If you say you have *arguments* that science is reliable, they'll just say you're placing faith in your own reason, assuming that reason is reliable. So, you might as well pick a faith that you like. And hey, I've got this nice religion here that makes a lot of people happy, it might (if true) help get you into heaven, and it creates a sense of meaning and purpose in life. Might as well go for that.

Problem: This argument turns on confusing foundational beliefs with faith. It portrays any belief that is not based on *reasons* as an *article of faith*. But this isn't correct. For instance, suppose I have a headache. I know that I'm in pain because I'm immediately, introspectively aware of the pain. I don't know it by constructing an *argument* that I'm in pain. In this case, it would not be correct, in any normal use of the words, to say that I "take it on faith" that I'm in pain. The Bible tells us that faith is confidence in things *not seen*. The obvious corollary is that if you *do* see something, then you cannot have faith in that thing. I take this to extend to the more general lesson that if you're directly aware of something, then you can't believe it on faith. E.g., God and the angels presumably do not themselves take God's existence on faith. It is only we humans who can do so, since we have not observed God.

Another argument for faith: If there is a God, then religious belief might help you get into heaven and avoid hell. Blaise Pascal argued that, since heaven is an infinite reward, any nonzero chance of getting into heaven has infinite expected value.[163] Thus, if there is even a *chance* that God exists, becoming a believer is worth it. So the prudentially *rational* thing to do is to try to convince

---

one would make up such a story; thus, the originators of the story must have actually witnessed it.
[163] This argument, from his *Pensées* (1670), is known as "Pascal's Wager".

yourself that there's a God. (And then, of course, do all the other things that might be needed to get into heaven—go to church, avoid mortal sins, etc.) If there isn't enough evidence to make belief in God epistemically justified, you should try to believe it anyway.

It's hard to say what, if anything, is wrong with Pascal's argument. One response is to say that it's equally possible that you'll be sent to heaven for *not* believing in God. In fact, maybe this is *more* likely than the idea that you'd go to heaven for believing. After all, if there is a God, he's studiously avoided showing himself to (most of) us, so he probably *doesn't* want us to believe in him. Another response is to say that Pascal's whole theory, wherein Christianity is true and we receive infinite rewards for being Christian but infinite punishment for being atheists, has probability zero. This might be true because there is a contradiction in the idea of a perfect being who punishes people infinitely for being epistemically rational. Or it might be true because Pascal's theory is one of infinitely many, equally-credible alternatives. Or it might be because Pascal's theory involves a metaphysically impossible kind of infinity (note that there are many paradoxes that result from postulating actual infinities).[164]

Fortunately, most theistic philosophers, and most sophisticated theists in general, are not fideists. Most of them argue that belief in God is epistemically rational. So for the rest of this chapter, we'll look at ideas about how religious belief can be epistemically justified.

16.2. Religious Testimony

The main reason most religious people are religious is that they were taught their current religion from a young age—when, again, people are naturally credulous. Perhaps this is okay. Testimony is a source of a great deal of knowledge, including some extremely secure and important knowledge. E.g., the sole way that I know that Japan is in Asia, that the Earth orbits the sun, or that there are more than a million people in the world, is by testimony. Yet all those things are *very* secure; I definitely know those things. So … maybe we know religious truths by testimony?

Some atheists and agnostics, in their eagerness to reject this, take overly skeptical positions about testimony. E.g., an atheist might claim that the fact that a billion people say *p* is no evidence for *p*. If you're very skeptical about testimony—e.g., you think testimony always requires inductive evidence of the reliability of a particular testifier about a particular subject matter—then you're

---

[164] For more on the paradoxes of the infinite, see my *Approaching Infinity* (2016), the only place where you will find plausible solutions to most of the paradoxes.

going to talk yourself out of almost all your knowledge, including your knowledge of science, history, etc. (see ch. 13).

So let's not be silly. *Of course* if someone tells you that *p*, that is *some* evidence for *p*, other things being equal. And of course if *more* people say that *p*, that is *better* evidence for *p*, other things being equal, than if few people say that *p*. But now, having acknowledged those fairly trivial truths, I want to say that the religious testimony that you've probably received in your life is only *weak* evidence for the truth of any religion. There are four reasons for this.

i. *Conflicting religions:* There have been many conflicting religions throughout human history. If you had been born in another society, you would have heard different religious claims during your childhood and thus, if you are like most people, would have adopted a different religion from your current religion (if any). Since religious testimony by a given person or group regularly contradicts other religious testimony by other people (especially people in other societies), religious testimony as a class must be highly unreliable.

ii. *Non-independence:* As I say, if many people say that *p*, this is generally *better* evidence for *p* than if only a few people say that *p*. This is because it is easy for one person or a few people to make a mistake, but the more people say that *p*, the less likely it is for all those people to have coincidentally made the same mistake. Example: Ten different people are not all going to have a hallucination of the same thing at the same time. But note that this reasoning depends upon these different people exercising some degree of *independence*. If a billion people all believe *p*, but they all got that belief from one original source, then it's no longer so improbable that the billion could all be wrong, since you only need one error at the beginning. And that's kind of the situation with religion: Almost everyone gets their religious beliefs from other people. So massive error isn't so improbable.

iii. *Shortage of source reliability information:* In the case of scientific beliefs, we have pretty great information about how currently accepted doctrines came about. At least, the information is available if you want it: You can look up the experiments or observations that people made (according to their own testimony) and follow along with the reasoning. For central theoretical tenets, the observations and experiments have typically been done by many different people and there's no debate about whether they come out the way the textbooks say. If you try following the reasoning from those data to the conventional theories, it makes sense. So there's a great account of how the people who originated current scientific doctrines knew that those doctrines were true. By contrast, what we know of the sources of current religious doctrines is less impressive. In many cases, there is a specific person or a small group of people who testified to specific, unrepeatable events a long time ago. Often, they claim some form of supernatural revelation that normal people don't have access to and can't check. As a result, you can seriously doubt the reliability of the religious sources much more easily than that of the scientific sources (i.e., creating much less tension with the rest of your belief system).

iv. *Practical demonstrations of knowledge:* You probably have little or no direct access to the results of scientific experiments. But you have access to many things that are *symptoms* of the reliability of science. For instance, if you use a car, or a cellular phone, or a camera, those things were designed using modern scientific theories. If scientists didn't know what they were talking about, those things wouldn't work. And by the way, you should realize that those things are *extremely* sophisticated; if you try to make one of those things without having *a lot* of *very precise and detailed* knowledge, you are absolutely going to fail. That is why stuff like that didn't exist for the first 200,000 years of human existence. But religious people can't give any similar demonstrations that they know what they're talking about. There's no incredibly sophisticated thing that they can reliably do that wouldn't work if their religion wasn't true. Today's theists cannot, in virtue of their religion, do anything that people 100,000 years ago couldn't do.

Here's a way of summing that up: Scientific testimony usually coheres extremely well with other beliefs; religious testimony coheres a lot less. Since I think coherence explains most of the justification of testimonial beliefs, I think religious testimony provides weak justification at best for religious beliefs.

16.3. Foundational Theism

16.3.1. The Sensus Divinitatis

Some people say that theism, or even Christianity, is foundational.[165] How might this be so?

Some believe that human beings are endowed with a special faculty for sensing God, the *sensus divinitatis*.[166] God gave us this faculty so that we could know him. The way it works is that when we encounter something that is related to God in some way, we (sometimes) spontaneously form a belief, or at least feel inclined to form a belief, about God. E.g., when you see a beautiful

---

[165] See Alvin Plantinga's "Is Belief in God Properly Basic?" (*Noûs*, 1981). He uses "properly basic" for "foundational". His whole philosophy basically revolves around rationalizing Christianity.

[166] In *Warranted Christian Belief* (2000, 171–2), Plantinga approvingly quotes John Calvin to this effect.

sunset, you spontaneously find yourself thinking that it shows the glory of God; when you read the Bible, you spontaneously feel that God is speaking to you; when you commit a sin, you spontaneously sense that God disapproves of it. The beliefs that you thereby form count as knowledge because they are produced by a reliable faculty that is properly functioning and that was designed (by God) for getting you true beliefs (cf. §2.5.3). Of course, the way we know all that is partly by using our *sensus divinitatis*. But that's pretty much how things go with all basic sources of knowledge—you can't check the reliability of sense perception without using sense perception, etc. (see ch. 6).

Thus, John Calvin, one of the biggest founders of Protestant Christianity, thought that everyone had a natural sense of God, regardless of the culture they grew up in. Professed atheists, he thought, had to perversely struggle to deny God and couldn't quite manage it:

> Indeed, the perversity of the impious, who though they struggle furiously are unable to extricate themselves from the fear of God, is abundant testimony that this conviction, namely that there is some God, is naturally inborn in all....[167]

16.3.2. A Non-theistic Interpretation

Philosophers discussing the *sensus divinitatis* theory tend to focus on the account of knowledge that it uses and/or the epistemic circularity in the account of why we should trust this putative sense. No doubt you can see how there would be questions about these things.

But the most trenchant problems with the theory are empirical. *Pace* John Calvin, everyone does not have this sense of the divine that he talks about. Calvin's view of atheism as stemming from a perverse, self-deceptive resistance against one's natural tendency to believe in God is wildly kooky. Most atheists are atheists because they have no sense of the divine; indeed, many atheists intuitively find traditional religious doctrines ridiculous. That is why they make up things like the Flying Spaghetti Monster (the deity of the jocular Pastafarian religion) to express how they see traditional religious ideas. Some go so far as to doubt whether most *religious* people really believe their professed religions.[168]

It's common for people to reason from their own experiences and attitudes to conclusions about other people's mental states. Probably John Calvin thought that everyone had a sense of the divine in part because *he* had such a strong sense of it. But, needless to say, Calvin wasn't a typical human

---

[167] Calvin, quoted in Plantinga, *Warranted Christian Belief*, 172.
[168] See my post, "Do Religious People Believe Religion?", https://fakenous.substack.com/p/do-religious-people-believe-religion.

being. He was *a lot* more religious than all but a tiny fraction of people. (For starters, consider that most people don't found a new branch of a religion.) Most people do not constantly have spontaneous inclinations to refer their experiences to God, and what inclinations they have are usually pretty weak.

Also relevant is the experience of people in different cultures, in which children are raised without being taught Christianity or any other monotheistic (believing in a single God) doctrine. These people do not find themselves spontaneously forming the sort of beliefs about God that Calvin talks about. The vast majority of human societies have had some sort of religion and/or mythology, but few have been monotheistic (it's just that a couple of monotheistic religions—Christianity and Islam—have spread very widely). Most believed in many supernatural entities—gods and other spirits—none of which resembled the Christian God. E.g., they weren't supposed to be anything close to all-powerful or all-knowing or all-good, they weren't triune, they weren't said to have done the stuff attributed to God in the Bible, etc. In some Eastern traditions, notably Taoism, Confucianism, and Buddhism, gods play very little role or no role at all.

So if the Christian God actually gave everyone a *sensus divinitatis* for the purpose of granting us knowledge of Him, it's very surprising how badly that sense fails *almost all the time*, unless someone expressly teaches you Christian doctrines first. None of the other cognitive faculties that God gave us is this bad at its function.

What is the best explanation of all this? It seems to me that the best explanation of (what some people call) the *sensus divinitatis* is not that God gave it to us to let us know him. The best explanation is that it is an artifact of already believing in a monotheistic religion, usually because one was taught that religion by adults when one was a child (recall the natural instinct of credulity discussed in ch. 13). If you have a strong standing belief, then you are going to spontaneously interpret things you experience in terms of that belief when given the chance. Hence, you'll find yourself "spontaneously" having thoughts that entail that belief. (Spontaneously in the sense that you don't *decide* to have these thoughts, they just naturally occur to you, and you may not know why.)

This happens not just with religion but with any belief that you feel strongly about. For example, if you are strongly, emotionally committed to a certain contemporary social justice ideology, then you are going to find yourself periodically "seeing" "obvious" discrimination in the world that people who don't share your beliefs don't see. If you're strongly committed to Marxist ideology, you'll "see" exploitation in your society that other people don't see. If you're a committed libertarian, you'll "see" tyranny and abuse of power that other people don't see. (I had to include that last one to show that I'm not just picking on leftists.) In all of these cases, you'll find yourself spontaneously inclined to form other beliefs that entail your main ideological or religious view.

So if you're one of the people who spontaneously interprets events in your life in terms of God, that's probably because you already believe in God, and if you had some other belief system, then you would probably be forming different spontaneous interpretations in terms of that other belief system. And if that's all so, then I think you can see that these belief inclinations don't provide very good evidence that God exists.

By the way, notice that I haven't claimed to give any evidence that God *doesn't* exist, nor do I assume atheism in the above discussion. Everything that I said above is stuff that you can appreciate without having made up your mind about theism.

16.4. Religious Experience

16.4.1. Prima Facie Justification by Religious Experience

Some people have religious experiences that they claim put them in touch with great spiritual truths. Some lame quasi-examples were mentioned above (§16.3.1), such as feeling an inclination to believe that God is speaking to you when you read the Bible. But many religious experiences are on their face more impressive than that. Many people have had experiences in which they felt they were in direct contact with God, sometimes literally seeing or hearing Him, sometimes "perceiving" Him in some non-sensory way.

This sounds on its face like some reason to believe in God. This follows the general principle that it's reasonable to assume that things are the way they seem unless given a specific reason for doubt (see §5.2).

Maybe you don't like that general principle (Phenomenal Conservatism). Be that as it may, you probably accept that it's rational to trust ordinary, non-religious sensory perception: When you have a visual experience of a penguin, you should believe a penguin is present unless you have specific grounds for doubt. So the theist is within his rights to demand an explanation of why religious experience should be treated any differently. If it's just because you're inclined to reject religion, that's question-begging.

In case you're going to complain that we lack independent verification of the reliability of religious experiences, notice that this is also true of ordinary sensory perception, memory, introspection, intuition, and reasoning. We can't verify the reliability of any of those faculties without using them, yet we don't therefore reject all of them.

Furthermore, at least the more robust religious experiences are not as easily explained as the lame "experiences" discussed in §16.3, which I said could be explained simply as effects of already believing some religion. While it is true that having a strong belief tends to cause one to spontaneously form other beliefs that presuppose the first belief, what does *not* normally happen is that you have robust hallucinations caused solely by a pre-existing belief. E.g., if you believe that the weather is going to be sunny, but then it rains, your pre-existing belief will not cause you to hallucinate a cloudless sky. So it won't do to *just* say, e.g., that people seem to hear God's voice because they already believed in God.

So it seems that we should accept religious experience as providing at least some *prima facie* justification for religious belief. The next question is whether we have defeaters, i.e., grounds for doubt that might neutralize or outweigh this prima facie justification.

16.4.2. Freud & Marx

Sigmund Freud and Karl Marx both offered debunking explanations of religion.[169] I mention these here, not because they are such great theories, but because they are often talked about, so I suppose you should know something about them.

Freud thought that religion derived, in essence, from wishful thinking. Human beings have a deep-seated psychological need for protection and love from a parental figure. This leads us, in adulthood, to postulate a more powerful and permanent parental figure than our parents, namely, God. Of course, postulating such a being doesn't *actually* protect us from the dangers of life, but it somewhat allays the pain and fear of life. At the same time, the story of heaven and hell caters to our psychological need for justice. Telling this story doesn't actually produce any justice, but it reduces the unhappiness we experience from all the injustice we see in the world.

Marx famously described religion as "the opium of the people". It serves to comfort people whose lives are full of suffering due to the exploitation and alienation produced by capitalism. It convinces the oppressed to be content with their lot in life since everything supposedly happens according to God's plan and since the injustices of this world will supposedly be remedied in the next world. The dominant class has deliberately used religion to support the status quo and avoid revolution: The wealthy and powerful traditionally fund the church, while the church traditionally preaches obedience to traditions and established authorities.

These are certainly entertaining theories. The question of interest to us now is whether they constitute grounds for doubt about the truth of religion

---

[169] See Freud's *The Future of an Illusion* (1927) and Marx's "Contribution to the Critique of Hegel's Philosophy of Right, Introduction" (1844).

or the reliability of religious experience. If there were powerful evidence for these theories, then they would. But neither Freud nor Marx gives more than token evidence for their views; they simply announce their speculations as if they were fact. In general, the mere possibility of imagining an unsavory cause for some set of cognitions does not constitute a defeater for the whole set; one needs specific evidence of the story's truth. Otherwise, the brain-in-a-vat story (§8.2.2) would be a defeater for all of your sensory experiences.

Young people, by the way, are often emotionally attracted to theories like the above due to their naturally rebellious spirit. It is important not to succumb to the **Argument from Cynicism**, so to speak—I mean the tendency to confuse the enjoyable feeling one gets from cynical theories with evidence. If my presentation of Freud's or Marx's theory above sounded persuasive to you, then you probably fell prey to that tendency.

It's of course true that the truth of traditional religious doctrines would satisfy some strong human desires. So that could bias our judgment in favor of those doctrines, and we should be on guard against such bias. But this doesn't suffice to explain religious experiences and certainly isn't evidence that the experiences are delusory. Similarly for the Marxian view.

16.4.3. Neurological Explanations

Some people have done scientific studies of religious experiences. They've found brain states that are typical of religious experience, which are similar to those that occur during certain kinds of seizures or with certain mental disorders.[170] Some people think that the Prophet Muhammad was an epileptic who experienced his putative revelations during seizures. Similar brain states and experiences can be artificially induced using drugs, as is done in some Native American rituals.

Atheists tend to think that this sort of finding undermines the argument from religious experience: We don't have to postulate God, since we can explain the experiences as just due to unusual brain activity.

However, this is a pretty weak argument, since all experiences whatsoever, whether religious or not, are correlated with brain states. Seeing a penguin is correlated with a particular brain state. No one thinks that means that penguins aren't real or that penguin experiences are unreliable.

You might say the difference is that religious experiences are produced by *abnormal* brain states. But in what sense would this be true? You might say the brain states causing religious experiences are abnormal in the sense that they rarely happen. But so are the brain states underlying penguin experiences;

---

[170] See d'Aquili and Newberg's *The Mystical Mind* (1999).

indeed, probably more people have had a religious experience than have seen a penguin with their own eyes.

You might hypothesize that religious experiences are abnormal in the sense that they're caused by a *disorder* of the brain. But most people who have religious experiences appear normal in all other ways. So there's only a disorder involved if *having a religious experience* is itself a disorder. But it would be question-begging to assume that.

I conclude that, interesting as they may be, neurological accounts of religious experience don't undermine the credibility of those experiences.

16.4.4. The Problem of Conflicting Experiences

Now I'm going to tell you the real problem with the argument from religious experience. The real problem is that people around the world have very different religious experiences, and these experiences tend to (according to the experiencers) support religious beliefs typical of the culture that the experiencer happens to be in or the religion that the experiencer antecedently was exposed to. As one scholar describes it, mystical experiences commonly purport to give the subject a more direct awareness of things that other members of the community only know indirectly through scriptures: "[S]uch experiences are highly specific, more often than not reinforcing the structures of established religion even down to its most technical doctrinal detail."[171]

In monotheistic cultures, particularly those influenced by Judaism, Christianity, and Islam, religious experiences tend to be perceptions of God. Some people have literally heard God speaking to them; others just feel God's presence in a particularly compelling way. In tribal societies, on the other hand, shamans have the experience of traveling into the spirit world and communicating with various spirits (who do not resemble the Christian God). Sometimes an animal spirit leads them on a journey. In Eastern religious traditions, people have experiences, not of communicating with particular beings, but of directly perceiving some great spiritual principle. Thus, one might have the experience of seeing the emptiness of all things, or the illusoriness of the self, or the essential oneness of everything.

There are two closely-related problems here for the argument from religious experience. One is that religious experience on the whole appears to be an unreliable source of religious information, since it has led people to support many conflicting religions. The other is that the contents of religious experiences, or the interpretations that people place on their religious experiences, appear to be rooted in their pre-existing religious beliefs or the beliefs of their culture. This means that a troubling kind of circularity is

---

[171] Steven Katz, *Mysticism and Religious Traditions* (1983), 21.

involved in using those experiences to support those beliefs. It also directly suggests that the particular content of one's religious experiences is not caused by God (or other spiritual realities) but by culture, which is an undercutting defeater for the religious beliefs those experiences seem to support.

16.4.5. Agent-Relative Justification

How could one address the above problem? Some religious thinkers, acknowledging that religious experiences have been used to support different religions, conclude that each individual is justified in believing the religious claims supported by his own experience.[172] There is no contradiction here, since justification is agent-relative (a proposition can be justified for one person but not another). Of course, *truth* is not relative; truth is absolute. So only one of a set of conflicting religions can be true. "And the true one," says the religious apologist, "is mine. Other people are perfectly *reasonable* in thinking that theirs is the true one, but, however reasonable, they are mistaken. And the way I know this is by my own religious experiences." This is epistemically circular, but epistemologists have long known that epistemic circularity is pretty much inevitable.

Apologists who mention the problem of divergent religious experiences tend not to even attempt any explanation for why such divergent experiences would occur. They instead tend to focus on a priori argumentation in defense of the epistemic circularity involved in relying on one's own tradition to justify the belief that one's own tradition has the only reliable religious experiences.

I don't see how one could find such a stance a satisfying solution. I agree with the main theoretical claims in the above explanation: Justification is indeed agent-relative and produced by one's own personal experiences. And *perhaps* a person who just came into the world, knowing nothing about other people, learning for the first time that other people have radically different perceptions from himself, would simply conclude that other people are sadly cognitively deficient.

But I don't see how a person with all the background knowledge of a normal human being in the actual world, and a modicum of curiosity about philosophical truth, could rest content with that. Given the similarities among humans in other respects; given the reliability of other human beings' sensory perception, memory, reasoning, and other cognitive abilities; and given that other human beings also have religious experiences; surely it cries out for explanation why people in only one religious tradition would have veridical religious experiences.

---

[172] See Plantinga's *Warranted Christian Belief* and William Alston's *Perceiving God* (1991).

We should ask the believer: What explains why it is only people who were taught your religion whose faculty of religious perception works? If God gives people religious experiences to enable them to know him, is it not strange that most people who have religious experiences have false ones? If you think that God causes the religious experiences of all the different traditions, why do they conflict with each other? If you think God only causes the religious experiences of your own tradition, is it not strange that people in other traditions have religious experiences that are parallel to those in your tradition, except that they support different religious doctrines? *Aren't you a bit curious about that?*

That pattern is not what I would expect to see if indeed there were some underlying spiritual reality that could be known through some kind of religious experience. But it is what I would expect to see if religious experiences were hallucinatory. If every other religious tradition spawns hallucinatory religious experiences, then your tradition probably does likewise. Whether or not the main tenets of your religion were true, there would probably be people who had religious experiences seemingly supporting those tenets.

Fans of religious experience like to draw analogies to sensory experience. Here is a disanalogy. I believe (reasonably and correctly) that *if* the physical objects presently in front of me were not there, I would not be having perceptual experiences as of those objects. I don't have any psychological faculty that would generate such experiences. By contrast, *if* the Christian God did not exist (but people were still taught that he exists), you should predict that people *would* still have religious experiences as of the Christian God, because that is what happens in all religious traditions.

16.4.6. *Reconciling Religious Traditions*

The other major approach to the problem of divergent religious experiences is to look for some common ground among different religious traditions and declare that common ground to be the lesson justified by religious experience.

Unfortunately, I think this just doesn't work. Basically, you wind up having to do one of two things:

i. You can give religious experiences some non-literal or non-factual interpretation. E.g., one can claim that the "truth" of religious ideas consists in their effectiveness at bringing about spiritual transformations in human life.[173]

ii. You can find some incredibly vague lesson, such as "there is a spiritual reality beyond the physical world" or "compassion is good". In some cases, by the way, even very vague lessons that people try to draw just are not in

---

[173] See John Hick's *An Interpretation of Religion* (2004), 373–5.

fact universal—e.g., I don't think the value of compassion is at all universal among human religions; there is quite a lot of support for cruelty (particularly against unbelievers and foreigners) in traditional religions.

My problem with approach (*i*) is that it abandons the claims that everyone was interested in. People who have religious experiences think the experiences are literally revealing objective facts to them. That is what is in dispute. If you're going to interpret them metaphorically or non-factually, then you're really rejecting religious experience.

My problem with approach (*ii*) is that in order to make the common ground universal, you have to make it so vague and general that you are hardly saying anything (e.g., "there's a spiritual reality"). It is not at all impressive that *that much* common ground can be found, since it could be expected in advance that, however unreliable religious experience might be as a source of information, at least *some* super-vague, super-general lesson could be attributed to all such experiences. Indeed, this might be guaranteed merely by semantics, since experiences that don't have *anything* in common with the other religious experiences just won't be *called* "religious experiences". For instance, depressed people sometimes have experiences of seeing the meaninglessness of life, but we don't call those "religious experiences". If we did, then there might be nothing at all in common among all "religious experiences".[174]

Think how impressive it would be if all, or even a great many, religious experiences really had substantial commonalities. What if people in multiple different cultures that had no contact with each other all had visions of speaking to a divine being who had four arms, an elephant head, and called himself "Ganesha". Okay, if that happened, I'd really start to think maybe Ganesha is real. That's the sort of thing that I would expect if religious experiences were really caused by supernatural beings. But of course, we don't see anything like that. Instead, we have only the minimal possible commonalities, like that all religious experiences are in some sense experiences of "spiritual realities". Super-lame.

16.5. Philosophical Arguments

We come to one final way that we might know religious truths: By

---

[174] Aside: It's interesting to compare the case of ethics. If there were as little commonalities among ethical intuitions as there are among religious experiences, then we should be moral skeptics. In fact, ethical beliefs show convergence over time across cultures, toward a broadly liberal value system, as discussed in my article, "A Liberal Realist Answer to Debunking Skeptics: The Empirical Case for Realism" (*Philosophical Studies*, 2016).

philosophical arguments. There are traditional arguments that are supposed to prove the existence of God, such as the Ontological Argument, the Cosmological Argument, and the Argument from Design.

The most interesting argument for the existence of God is the Fine Tuning Argument, which appeals to the fact that certain parameters of the universe (e.g., the gravitational constant, the mass of the proton, or the ratio of the gravitational to electromagnetic force) had to take on extremely specific values in order for life to be possible. Some people say that the best explanation for why the universe permits life at all, given how demanding the conditions for life are, is that God designed the universe to have life in it.

Of course, there are also philosophical arguments against theism. The most important of these is the Argument from Evil, which says that the existence of bad things in our world is evidence that there is no God. If a perfect being created this world, then this should be the best of all possible worlds; but clearly it isn't.

I'm going to be very brief here, because the issues about these arguments are really not interestingly *epistemological*. They're just metaphysical, scientific, or sometimes (in the case of the Ontological Argument) logical. The epistemology is pretty straightforward: Belief in God is justified if we have a good argument for it which isn't defeated by any objections or arguments for the opposite conclusion.

I'm not going to try to answer whether there is any such good argument here, because that would require a long, non-epistemological discussion.[175]

16.6. Conclusion

How should we form beliefs about religion? We should believe the things that are epistemically justified, which are the things most likely to be true. This is close to, though perhaps not the same as, the evidentialist view that we should base beliefs solely on "evidence". It stands in contrast to the view that one should choose beliefs for moral or prudential reasons. There's a plausible argument that it's immoral to adopt epistemically unjustified beliefs about religion, since religious beliefs are likely to have unforeseen practical consequences, which may, if one's beliefs are false, be harmful to others. You will be to blame for any harm caused by unjustified beliefs, so don't form any such beliefs.

Pascal famously argued that it is prudentially rational to believe in God, since doing so may help one get infinite rewards in heaven. This is questionable since it is equally possible that one would get an infinite reward by withholding

---

[175] For some discussion, see my *Knowledge, Reality, and Value* (2021), chs. 9–10.

belief and being epistemically rational. It's also not obvious that the heaven/hell theory Pascal uses has a nonzero probability.

Most people believe religion based on testimony. Though testimony in general is a valid source of knowledge, *religious* testimony is not very trustworthy, since (*i*) religious testimonies from different cultures contradict each other; (*ii*) when different religious people's claims agree with each other, it is not because they independently arrived at the same idea but because they all got their ideas from the same source; (*iii*) religious beliefs usually originate in experiences that can't be verified by other people and aren't supported by a large network of other beliefs; and (*iv*) unlike people who know science, people who "know" religion can't thereby do any impressive things that non-believers can't do. Thus, religious testimony provides weak reason at best for believing religious claims.

Some people think that God gave us a sense of the divine, which explains why we spontaneously form beliefs about God in the course of life, as when you see a sunset and it makes you think "God must be great to have created this." Unfortunately, atheists have no such sense and often experience the opposite, i.e., a sense of the absurdity of traditional religious claims. People from other cultures instead have spontaneous beliefs supporting the religions of their societies, which often contradict monotheistic religions. The best explanation of what's going on is that having *any* strong belief (whether religious, ideological, or other) causes you to spontaneously interpret other events in terms of that belief.

Some people have more striking religious experiences, in which they appear to be directly perceiving God. This is prima facie evidence for God. However, people from different traditions have different religious experiences that seem to them to support whatever religious beliefs are embraced in their culture. This includes animistic beliefs and non-theistic beliefs. The most reasonable thing to believe is not that God gives reliable religious experiences only to people from your culture, but that every culture generates religious experiences that match it. So if your religion were false, there would still be religious experiences that seemed to support it. Some try to find common ground among religious experiences, but this generally involves either rejecting the literal, factual claims of religious experiencers, or relying on some incredibly vague and almost empty statements.

The best hope for justifying religious claims, therefore, would seem to be to find sound philosophical arguments. Several arguments have been given both for and against theism, the most interesting (to me) being the Fine Tuning Argument for theism, and the Argument from Evil for atheism. But evaluating the arguments regarding theism is beyond the scope of this book.

Part IV: Applied Epistemology

17. Irrationality

In this part of the book, we address some less abstract and more applied issues, mainly about how you should form beliefs in controversial cases. We start, in this chapter, by thinking about why people are so often irrational.[176]

17.1. The Disagreement Puzzle

People have disagreements about nearly every subject. But some topics call forth a lot *more* disagreement than others. Thus, we disagree especially about politics, religion, morality, and philosophy in general. Let's call those "controversial topics". We disagree much *less* about mathematics, natural science, and history.

I note three common characteristics of disagreements about controversial topics: (a) They are *widespread*, meaning that many people disagree about many questions within the controversial subject matters. (b) They are *strong*, meaning that the disagreeing parties tend to hold their views with high confidence. (c) They are *persistent*, meaning that it is extremely difficult to resolve them. Lengthy discussion, presentation of evidence, and so on barely moves people's positions.

The abortion issue is an excellent example. For many years, Americans have been about evenly split between "pro-life" and "pro-choice" (roughly, anti- and pro-abortion) positions.[177] One can find many people who appear utterly convinced that abortion (in most cases?) is *obviously* murder, and many others who seem equally certain that abortion is (in most cases?) *obviously* not problematic in the least. Lengthy debates, in which each side presents their

---

[176] Most of this chapter's ideas come from my essay, "Why People Are Irrational About Politics", http://www.owl232.net/papers/irrationality.htm.
[177] I get that from polls, e.g., Gallup's "Abortion Trends by Gender", https://news.gallup.com/poll/245618/abortion-trends-by-gender.aspx. Caveats: It's unclear how respondents interpreted the question, i.e., how strictly they read the "pro-life" position and how permissive the "pro-choice" position. Also, as of this writing, the latest polls show a sharp increase in "pro-choice" sentiment in the wake of the Supreme Court decision in *Dobbs v. Jackson Women's Health Organization* (2022).

supposedly decisive proofs, fail to produce any softening of positions. This is on its face puzzling.

Disagreement poses a practical problem for a few reasons. It directly causes social tension; it causes partisans of different views to waste resources trying to defeat each other; and, perhaps most importantly, it likely results in our making bad decisions since we do not know what the right decisions are. Or perhaps more precisely, the *unreliability* of our ways of forming beliefs causes disagreement and also causes bad decisions. Unfortunately, it is precisely on certain kinds of practical questions (politics and morality) that we are most likely to disagree.

So it seems important to ask why we have such widespread, strong, and persistent disagreements about certain questions. Why, for example, is politics so different from science?

17.2. The Case for Irrationality

Here are some possible explanations: (*i*) The controversial issues are very difficult, which leads reasonable people to make frequent mistakes; (*ii*) we haven't yet gathered enough evidence to resolve the controversial questions; (*iii*) the disagreements concern value questions, which perhaps lack objective answers; (*iv*) most people are irrational when they think about controversial topics.

I intend theories (*i*)-(*iii*) to be compatible with people being perfectly reasonable. In this section, I explain why (*i*)-(*iii*) on their own are inadequate, and thus why a large part of the explanation has to lie in our irrationality.

17.2.1. Difficulty of Issues

First, we should acknowledge that controversial issues are typically much more complex than it appears at first glance. For instance, there are several subtle issues related to the morality of abortion (issues about personal identity, about the foundation for rights, about the status of potential persons, about positive versus negative rights, etc.).[178] And part of the reason for ongoing disagreement is that people tend to oversimplify the issues.

That being said, most controversial issues are really not anywhere near as difficult as some issues in advanced science or mathematics on which people have made much more progress. It's a lot easier to understand the question "Is abortion wrong?", and to follow the discussion surrounding that question, than it is to understand the General Theory of Relativity and the discussion

---

[178] See my post, "Abortion Is Difficult", https://fakenous.substack.com/p/abortion-is-difficult.

surrounding it. Yet humans have managed to think through General Relativity a lot more successfully and with a lot more agreement than the morality of abortion.

You might say that only very smart people talk about General Relativity, whereas everyone feels qualified to weigh in on abortion. But note that even *among very smart people*, there is no agreement on the morality of abortion.

Furthermore, if disagreement about abortion were really just due to the intrinsic difficulty of the issue, and not to human irrationality, we could not explain why partisans hold such confident opinions. The more difficult an issue is, the less confident you would expect people to be about their answers. If in this area, people are going ahead and forming extremely confident opinions *even though* the issue is very difficult for them, that would seem to be a form of irrationality.

17.2.2. Ignorance

A similar objection applies to the theory that we simply lack sufficient evidence to resolve controversial issues: If there is a shortage of information, then again you would expect people to form only weak, tentative opinions at most. If we are forming extremely confident beliefs in the absence of necessary evidence, that's irrational.

The "difficulty" and "insufficient evidence" explanations also fail to explain why people's opinions about political issues are significantly correlated with cognitively irrelevant personal characteristics, such as a person's race, gender, age, occupation, aesthetic preferences, and general personality traits. For example, why is it that people who like dreadlocks also tend to like socialism?

Another puzzle is why beliefs that are logically unrelated tend to go together. For instance, if you know someone's opinion about gun control, you can, with greater than chance success, predict their opinion about health care, despite the lack of connection between the two issues. In some cases, two issues *are* logically connected, yet the correlation between people's beliefs on the issues is the opposite of what you would expect. For instance, the issue of animal rights is obviously logically connected to that of fetus rights. Roughly speaking, more expansive conceptions of rights would tend to support rights for both fetuses and animals; more restrictive conceptions would tend to support rights for neither. So opinions on those two issues should be correlated. Yet the correlation we actually see is the opposite of the one that makes sense: Belief in animal rights predicts *dis*belief in fetus rights, and vice versa.

None of this is explained by saying that political issues are difficult or that we lack sufficient data to resolve them; only irrationality seems to explain it.

17.2.3. Divergent Values

Perhaps most controversial issues relate to values, and people tend to have divergent values. But why do we have divergent values? Perhaps because evaluative questions lack objective or knowable answers, and our values just reflect our interests, emotions, and desires.

There are four problems with this explanation. First, evaluative questions *do* have objective, knowable answers (see ch. 15).[179] So we still need an explanation of why people disagree about values.

Second, if value questions *didn't* have objective, knowable answers, this wouldn't really explain the disagreements. People don't, for example, have ongoing debates about food preferences, because there aren't any objective facts about what foods are tastiest. If there weren't any objective or knowable answers to value questions, you would expect people to treat these questions like questions about tastiness of food. Unless, of course, people were widely deluded and *thought* that these questions had objective, knowable answers. But then we need an explanation of that widespread delusion.

Third, the value divergence theory still does not explain the correlations among logically unrelated beliefs (e.g., beliefs about gun control and health care policy), nor the perverse correlations that are the opposite of what would make sense (e.g., beliefs about animal and fetus rights).

Fourth and most importantly, the divergent values theory doesn't explain the many disagreements about non-value questions. Take, e.g., the gun control issue. Granted, you can find some potential value disagreements, such as disagreements about the relative importance of freedom and security. But as a matter of fact, almost all the debate centers on *descriptive facts*. Gun control proponents claim that gun control laws make us safer by keeping guns out of the hands of criminals. Opponents claim that gun control laws put us in danger by stopping law-abiding citizens from defending themselves, while having little effect on criminals.

Or consider the question of health care policy. Again, you can find some value disputes in this area, but most of the expressed disagreement is about matters of descriptive fact. E.g., some people think that government-run health care would save money and increase availability of health care, without diminishing quality. Others think that government-run health care would increase costs, lower quality, and lower availability of health care.

---

[179] See my *Ethical Intuitionism* (2005).

I won't multiply examples. Suffice it to say that there are *many* cases like this. Indeed, probably *most* controversial issues are primarily about descriptive questions.

I conclude that disagreement about controversial topics can't be explained without appealing human irrationality. Next, we'll try to understand why people are irrational about certain topics.

17.3. The Theory of Rational Irrationality

17.3.1. Rational Ignorance

Before I get to irrationality, let me first mention ignorance. Ignorance is just a lack of information about some question. People tend to remain ignorant about a great many questions that might seem important to you and me. Surveys regularly show ordinary people having shockingly little knowledge of the world outside their personal lives. For instance, most Americans can't name their representative in Congress, most cannot name the *form of government* they live under (from the choices "direct democracy", "republic", "oligarchy", and "confederacy"), and most cannot even name the three branches of their government.[180]

Why is this? They have no incentive to gather that kind of information. Granted, the costs of learning those particular bits of information are small—just a little time and effort. But the expected benefits are approximately zero. Most people are selfish, so they won't do things for which the costs obviously exceed the benefits.[181]

Granted, in a democracy, it is important for the populace, especially those who vote, to be well-informed. But that is irrelevant to you, since you don't have any choice about whether *the populace as a whole* is informed. You only have a choice about whether *you personally* will be informed or not. If you decide to become better informed, the rest of the country will remain just as ignorant as it currently is. If you're not delusional, I assume you know that you're not ever going to actually alter the outcome of a national election with your vote—more precisely, that the probability of that happening is extremely small in a society of millions of people. So if you decide to become well-informed, you take the

---

[180] In case you're wondering, the government is a republic, and the branches are the executive, legislative, and judicial branches. Which really is about the least you could possibly know about the American political system, so I hope you knew that. For some hilarious, presumably cherry-picked examples of ignorance, see https://youtu.be/g2oMv93EUpY.

[181] For more on the theory of rational ignorance, see Anthony Downs, *An Economic Theory of Democracy* (1957).

costs of that on yourself, which will be substantial since there are many issues you have to learn about, and you have almost no chance of ever seeing any benefit from that decision. It's kind of a no-brainer: Of course you don't gather the information.

So that's why most people are extremely politically ignorant. (They also tend to be historically, scientifically, and philosophically ignorant too, though we elites don't worry as much about that.) The exceptions are people who positively *enjoy* gathering political information. In that case, it doesn't matter that you're never going to affect the outcome of an election, since the entertainment value of political information outweighs the costs of gathering it.

17.3.2. From Ignorance to Irrationality

A similar logic applies to *irrationality* as applies to ignorance.[182] Where ignorance is a matter of lacking information, irrationality is a matter of *incorrectly processing* the information that you have—drawing unsupported conclusions, refusing to draw supported conclusions, ignoring defeaters, and so on. More precisely, that is what we call *epistemic* irrationality.

To understand how there can be "rational irrationality", we have to distinguish two kinds of rationality (per §§2.3.2, 15.1.2). *Epistemic* rationality is the kind of rationality needed for acquiring knowledge. It is a matter of forming beliefs that are likely to be true, avoiding unjustified assumptions, logical fallacies, contradictions, and stuff like that. *Instrumental* rationality, on the other hand, is the kind of rationality that applies to action. It is a matter of taking the actions that are likely to satisfy your goals, according to your beliefs.

So the way in which you could be rationally irrational is that it could be *instrumentally* rational to form beliefs that are *epistemically* irrational. In other words: Sometimes, you're more likely to get what you want by believing stuff that isn't likely to be true.

The logic of rational ignorance applies also to rational irrationality: In any large democracy, each voter pretty well knows that his vote is never actually going to alter the outcome of any election. Therefore, the personal cost of having false political beliefs is essentially zero. So if there is any nontrivial cost involved in ensuring that your political beliefs are likely to be true, selfish people will not take that cost.

What's the cost of having epistemically rational, or likely-to-be-true, political beliefs? For one thing, it requires some effort—you have to think things through, question your assumptions, and so on. More importantly, if

---

[182] The theory of rational irrationality is due to Bryan Caplan; see *The Myth of the Rational Voter* (2007).

you're epistemically rational, *you don't get to believe whatever you want to believe*. The beliefs that you're emotionally attached to might turn out to be contradicted by the weight of evidence. You then have to experience the pain of giving up those beliefs. There can be ancillary costs too, such as alienating your friends who have false political beliefs. So all in all, it doesn't seem worth it. That's the core reason why most people think irrationally about politics.

17.3.3. What Are We Irrational About?

Let's understand how other subjects differ from politics. When you think about issues in your personal life—say, where you want to live or what job you want to do—the situation is different, because if you form a wise and well-justified opinion, you then *actually get* the thing that you decided was best. Hence, rational beliefs are personally beneficial. In the political realm, by contrast, if you form a justified opinion, you do *not* thereby get the thing you decided was best; you still get what the majority of other people voted for. So we tend to be more rational about our personal lives than about politics.

In the case of mathematics and science, there is usually little to no personal incentive to get things right (if you form correct beliefs about the Big Bang, you don't thereby get some big personal benefit). But there also is no significant incentive to get things *wrong*. That is because most people do not have strong emotional attachments to scientific beliefs, in the way they do with political beliefs. Hence, we are more rational about science than about politics.

What about moral beliefs? In this case, incorrect beliefs can have serious negative consequences: They may cause you to behave immorally. However, that isn't really a *personal cost*. Most people are primarily selfish and have very little moral motivation. Hence, they have little incentive to get things right about morality. Meanwhile, they tend to have emotional attachments to particular moral beliefs. Hence, we tend to think irrationally about morality.

What about philosophy in general? Again, the personal costs to having false philosophical beliefs are usually negligible (though it really depends on the issue), while the costs of being rational are significant, since we are often emotionally attached to philosophical beliefs. Hence, there is a lot of irrationality about philosophy.

Finally, what about religion? In this case, the costs to being wrong *could* be enormous, even infinite (if, say, people with the wrong religion get sent to hell). But that is only if some religion is in fact *true*. If all religions are false, then the costs to mistakenly believing one of them are much smaller. Sure, it could cause you to give up some fun sins in this life, but there are also big benefits to belonging to a religion. You get a community, you get a sense of meaning in life, and you generally feel better about the world. So we should predict that selfish people who think that religion is false will think irrationally about religion. This might extend to trying to talk themselves into believing a religion (ala Pascal's wager), or simply pretending to believe a religion.

17.3.4. Non-Epistemic Belief Preferences

Let's examine the assumptions behind the theory of rational irrationality. To begin with, the theory assumes that people have what I call **non-epistemic belief preferences**; that is, there are things we want to believe, for reasons unrelated to the truth or epistemic justification of those beliefs. Is this true?

Come on, of course it is. I bet if you introspect, you can notice that sometimes, political information that you hear makes you feel good, and other times, it makes you uncomfortable or annoyed. And I bet the kind that makes you feel satisfied is the kind that supports your existing beliefs, while the kind that makes you uncomfortable or that you find irritating is information that conflicts with your existing beliefs. Why would that be? Because your existing beliefs are the ones that you want to maintain.

By the way, it's not as though we just don't like getting bad news. For instance, if someone is deeply concerned about global warming, you might assume that this person would be relieved to hear information suggesting that global warming is less bad than he thought it was. But anyone who has been around political partisans knows that the truth is the exact opposite. The person will be annoyed and will try everything possible to avoid accepting that information. This shows that we don't simply want to hear that the world is the way we *want the world to be*; we want to hear that the world is the way we *currently think it is*. That is because our current political beliefs are, by and large, the things that we most wanted to believe.

Why would people prefer some beliefs over others? Here are a few reasons:

i. *Self-image:* We want to build a sense of the kind of people we are, and political beliefs help us do that. E.g., you can portray yourself (to yourself and others) as compassionate by supporting social welfare programs, just as you can portray yourself as strong and not-to-be-trifled-with by supporting greater military spending.
ii. *Social bonding:* We want to associate with certain other people or groups. Holding the beliefs of those people helps us do that. One must profess certain religious beliefs to belong to a certain church, just as one must hold certain political beliefs to be accepted in certain social circles.
iii. *Emotional biases:* Adopting particular political beliefs can help us to rationalize certain emotional reactions that we are already inclined toward. For instance, most people are instinctively suspicious of foreigners, which

leads them to adopt the belief that foreign trade and immigration harm the economy. Relatedly, our political beliefs may simply serve to *express* our feelings.

iv. *Drama:* I've come to increasingly appreciate this one over the years. Ordinary life is boring. We turn to politics, religion, and philosophy for entertainment. Ideologies, religions, and philosophies tell us a *story*, and that story needs to be dramatic. Thus, if your ideology says, "Things are going pretty well and will probably continue that way, with incremental improvements. There's not much we need to do," that ideology is a loser. Too boring. That, I'm convinced, is why almost every ideology is constantly saying that some disaster is impending, even while by all objective measures, life keeps getting better, generation after generation.

17.3.5. Doxastic Control

Another key assumption of the theory of rational irrationality is that people have some degree of *control* over their beliefs. Is this true?

Doxastic voluntarists think that you can directly choose your beliefs. Most philosophers reject doxastic voluntarism, though. They usually give examples like this:

> *Giraffe Prize:* I offer to pay you $1 million to believe that you are a giraffe for the next hour. I have a 100% reliable brain scanner so I can see if you *really* believe it. Do you think you could get the money?

Most people answer "no", which shows that we can't control what we believe. Or at least, we don't always have complete control.

Fortunately, we don't have to resolve the truth of doxastic voluntarism, because everyone at least agrees that you can make choices that *indirectly influence* your own beliefs, even if you can't *directly choose* to believe something. And that is enough for the theory of rational irrationality to work.

Say you want to believe *p*. Here's what you could do:

i. Only gather information from sources that you already know agree with *p*. This is pretty easy, since many news outlets have a well-known, consistent political orientation. This all but guarantees that you won't get any evidence that undermines your belief in *p*.
ii. Try not to think of any objections to *p*, and if you accidentally think of one, avert your attention from it. Instead, spend your time thinking about the arguments *for p*.
iii. Embrace speculative, subjective, and anecdotal reasoning. These are the kinds of reasoning that are most susceptible to bias, which means they are good for maintaining your existing beliefs.

What do I mean by these? *Speculative* arguments are essentially ones that turn on guesses that we don't have enough data to verify (e.g., "if we hadn't done the economic stimulus, the recession would have been worse"). *Subjective* arguments turn on judgment calls (e.g., "Louis CK is offensive"). And *anecdotal* arguments draw generalizations from just one or a few cases (e.g., "Drug prohibition is bad, because here's a story of someone whose life was ruined by it").

Do people do those things? You know they do. All the time. So that is how we get ourselves to believe what we want to believe.

17.3.6. Automatic Bias

My description of why people form irrational beliefs might have sounded too cynical. Do people really say to themselves, "I know my political beliefs won't make a difference, so I think I'll just adopt some irrational beliefs"?

No, not just like that. If you introspect, you probably won't ever notice yourself thinking that. But the theory of rational irrationality doesn't require people to be explicitly, consciously choosing irrationality like that. What is more likely is that our desires and emotions act as *biases* of which we are rarely fully aware. You don't have to choose to be biased; you're *automatically* biased, unless you somehow actively suppress the tendency. The way biases work is that if there is ever more than one way of interpreting some piece of information, your brain selects whichever interpretation is more in line with your emotions and desires. That interpretation then just strikes you as obvious; more often than not, you don't even notice that there is any other interpretation.

For example, suppose person A is generally anti-abortion. Person B says, "I am pro-choice." The way this strikes A is that B just said that he supports killing any fetus at any time, for any reason. That's obviously what it means to be pro-choice, right? A proceeds to attack that position.

B, for his part, assumes that A thinks it is always wrong to kill any fetus at any time, for any reason. So B proceeds to attack *that* position. Both ignore more moderate positions. The reason is that it is *easier* to attack extreme positions; therefore, it would be more convenient for each person if the other were asserting a super-extreme position; therefore, that's how each person perceives the other's position. Neither party is *consciously trying* to straw man the other; they just do it unthinkingly, by default, because that's how the human mind works.

Now, that's a simple and dramatic example. Most real life examples are a little more subtle than that. But that's to illustrate the tendency. And it works not only with interpreting other people's *words*, but also with interpreting *evidence*. Let's say *A* is a gun rights advocate, while *B* is a gun control advocate. Both learn that cities that have stricter gun laws also tend to have higher homicide rates (as mentioned in §14.4.1). To *A*, this obviously proves that gun control laws cause homicide. No other interpretation even occurs to her. To *B*, however, *A*'s interpretation intuitively seems absurd. To *B*, the evidence obviously just means that cities with high crime tend to wisely adopt stricter laws to combat that crime. Guns are probably coming in from neighboring areas with laxer laws, so this just shows that we need nationwide gun control.

Neither party is consciously trying to dogmatically cling to their position by interpreting everything in line with their initial assumptions. That's just what human minds *automatically* do unless something stops them. Or more precisely, incorporating the theory of rational irrationality, that is what human minds automatically do *when there is no incentive to get things right* and the person does not take deliberate, conscious steps to avoid the bias.

17.4. Becoming Rational

17.4.1. Turning the Magnifying Glass on Ourselves

Most people who hear this theory seem to agree with it. That is, they agree that other people are irrational. Those other people are so benighted! We should probably just ignore everyone who disagrees with us from now on, since they're so irrational. Whew.

Well, I didn't tell you all this so you could have an excuse to dismiss people who disagree with you. But I know (sadly) how people think, so I know many of you would take it that way, if I didn't expressly disavow that. The reason I told you all this stuff about irrationality is so that you could be on guard against *your own* irrationality. If you don't do that, you've learned nothing. And if you can't think of any potential biases you might have, that probably just means you're too biased to even know you're biased.

"But wait," you might protest. "Why should we combat irrationality? Didn't you just explain how it is *rational* to be irrational?"

Well yes, it is rational from the standpoint of most people's current goals. But it is also immoral, because irrationality is harmful to society (cf. §16.1.2). It causes societies to waste resources, have much worse policies than they could have, etc. This is the worst social problem. It is worse than world poverty, or global warming, or war, because this is the problem that *prevents us from solving the other problems*. We can't solve global poverty until we form rational beliefs about what causes it, what the effects of proposed policies are, and so on.

You should avoid being a part of this problem, at least if you can do so at little cost. And although being epistemically rational will deprive you of the "benefit" of believing whatever you want to believe, that really isn't much of a benefit. Having unjustified beliefs might feel good, but it deprives you of the more genuine good, which is true knowledge and understanding.

Let's assume you're convinced and you want to be more rational. How can you do this? Let's look for some practical steps toward that end …

17.4.2. Identify Your Biases

The first thing is to be aware of cases in which you might be biased. I hypothesize that being aware of bias might reduce its effect. To that end, here are some tips about where you might be biased:

i. If you feel emotional when discussing a particular topic, e.g., thinking about abortion is upsetting to you, then you're likely to be more biased and less rational than usual about that topic. That's true, by the way, regardless of whether your emotional reaction is appropriate (so don't say, "I'm not biased, because this topic is objectively upsetting!").

ii. If your beliefs pretty much follow the standard "left-wing" or "right-wing" orthodoxy down the line, for many unrelated issues, then you're likely biased. If your beliefs imply that one side reliably gets everything wrong, it's more likely that you're biased than that that is really true.

iii. If you have strong beliefs about empirical questions before gathering empirical evidence, or your beliefs do not change (or simply become stronger) when you gather empirical evidence, then you're probably biased.

iv. If your beliefs are pretty much what one would expect, given your race, gender, occupation, personality traits, and other cognitively irrelevant characteristics, that's probably the effect of bias.

v. If you know what beliefs are generally approved of by the people you like and want to associate with, or what beliefs are generally held by people you dislike, that is probably biasing you.

vi. Finally, you almost certainly suffer from biases toward overconfidence and dogmatism. That is, you almost certainly tend to form credences that are *more extreme* (closer to 1 or 0) than the evidence warrants (that's **overconfidence**), and you almost certainly tend to adjust your credences *too little* when confronted with counter-evidence (that's **dogmatism**). Nearly every human being in the world has those failings. The opposite traits are possible but so rare that we don't even have a word for the trait of *over*-adjusting one's credences in the face of counter-evidence.

If you are highly confident that you know the answers to many highly controversial issues, and if you never or almost never change your mind about such issues, then you are probably suffering from these biases.

17.4.3. Diversify Your Sources

I mentioned earlier that one of the ways we indirectly control our beliefs is by selecting information sources that we already know agree with us (§17.3.5). Conservatives listen to conservative news and opinion sources; progressives listen to progressive sources.

To combat this, you should diversify your information sources: Listen to people with a variety of viewpoints. If you have an opinion on a matter of controversy, and you don't know what the other side's argument is or what their objections to your argument would be, then your opinion is unjustified. Needless to say, if you can't stand listening to "the other side", that's a sign of a bias that you need to overcome.

Note that not all sources are equally good. I do not recommend listening to the *most popular* sources with a given point of view. I recommend listening to the *most sophisticated* sources who also tend to have views that you haven't heard before. This usually means academic sources. Thus, if you wanted to learn about abortion, you should not listen to speeches by politicians or popular entertainers, nor rely on the website of an abortion advocacy group. Those sources are likely to be unsophisticated or propagandistic and deliberately misleading. You'd do much better to look at articles on the ethics of abortion published in academic philosophy journals.[183]

Again, if you wanted to form an opinion about gun control, I don't recommend looking at popular discourse or the web site of a gun control or gun rights advocacy group. I suggest instead looking at articles in criminology or philosophy journals.[184]

If this sounds like too much work and you don't have time for all this, that's okay. Then you should just conclude that you don't have time to have an opinion about these issues.

17.4.4. Consider Objections

Another way that we indirectly control our beliefs is through directing our attention. We tend to direct our attention toward arguments whose conclusions we like, and away from arguments whose conclusions we don't like. Most people suffer from **confirmation bias**, which is a bias toward only looking for evidence in favor of a view. This is very widespread and even applies to views that you have no stake in—when asked to assess whether some hypothesis that

---

[183] See, e.g., Don Marquis' "Why Abortion Is Immoral" (*Journal of Philosophy*, 1989), Judith Thomson's "A Defense of Abortion" (*Philosophy and Public Affairs*, 1971), and Michael Tooley's "Abortion and Infanticide" (*Philosophy and Public Affairs*, 1972).

[184] See, e.g., my article, "Is There a Right to Own a Gun?" (*Social Theory and Practice*, 2003), http://www.owl232.net/papers/guncontrol.htm.

they don't even care about is true, most people immediately start to look for evidence *for* the hypothesis, while ignoring evidence *against* it.[185]

To combat this, you should make a special effort to think of objections to your views. When an idea occurs to you, always try to think of reasons why it might be *wrong*. When you make an argument, stop for a moment and ask yourself, "What would an opponent say to this?" When you do this, try imagining the smartest, best-informed opponent, not the dumbest opponent you can think of. If you have a controversial view, and you can't think of any worthwhile objections, that probably just means that you don't know enough. You may need to do more reading, or talk to some people who have different views.

One of the reasons for polarization (people forming very strong, mutually opposed opinions) is that when we hear a piece of evidence supporting our beliefs, we tend to accept it at face value, but when we hear a piece of evidence against our beliefs, we tend to scrutinize that evidence very carefully for any possible reasons for discounting it, e.g., looking for any possible shortcoming in the design of a study. Pretty much all evidence in this world is imperfect, so you can almost always think of reasons to discount the evidence that you don't like. To counteract this, you should try scrutinizing even the evidence that you like for possible reasons why it might not be as strong as it initially appears.

17.4.5. Avoid Speculative, Subjective, and Anecdotal Arguments

If you're like most people, when you try to justify your beliefs, you'll naturally reach for speculative, subjective, and anecdotal arguments. You should make a point of trying to notice this and avoid it.

When you're about to tell someone a story about a particular case that supports some general view of yours, ask yourself whether that is really a typical case, or whether you've cherry picked it. Are there other cases that could be given to illustrate an opposite lesson?

By the way, apropos of anecdotal evidence: It's worth noting the distinction between using an example to *explain* an idea, and using an example as *inductive evidence* for a generalization. In the case of citing inductive evidence, it is important how typical the example is, how many cases we have examined, and the variety of circumstances we have looked at. So if I say drug prohibition is overall bad, and I support this by citing someone whose life was ruined by it, this is anecdotal evidence, and we have to ask how typical the case is, etc.

Of course that's not true for a mere explanatory example. E.g., take the example of someone getting emotional about abortion (§17.4.2), where I say

---

[185] See, e.g., Peter Wason's classic "On the Failure to Eliminate Hypotheses in a Conceptual Task" in the *Quarterly Journal of Experimental Psychology* (1960).

this person is probably going to be biased on that topic. That is not supposed to be evidence for an inductive generalization; it is just an example to explain the idea of an emotional bias.

17.4.6. Have Productive Discourse

It's hard to combat biases on your own. One of the most important tools is *discussion* among people with *differing perspectives*. Because these people will have different biases, they can correct each other. But for this to work, the discussion has to be conducted in a productive manner. There is a strong tendency among human beings for discussions of controversial issues to degenerate into personal contests, and thence into strings of bitter recriminations.

To avoid this, first, it is important to refrain from insulting other parties to the discussion. Don't mention how ridiculous, stupid, or evil the thing they just said is (even if you find it such), and don't express surprise that anyone would think such a thing. The reason for this is not simply that insulting people is mean. The reason is that personal attacks tend to divert discussion away from the matters of import. Most people tend to be overly sensitive to potential slights directed against themselves, and relatively insensitive to slights they might be directing outward. So a little bit of personal attacking tends to escalate. Then, once a discussion has become a personal contest, people direct less attention to the original subject matter and more to the putative flaws of the other people in the discussion. This prevents us from learning from each other.

Some qualifications: This is not meant to preclude people from stating arguments that are actually relevant to the topic under discussion. For instance, suppose the topic under discussion is whom one should vote for in the next election. Then arguments that one or more of the candidates are morally corrupt are apt, despite that they might be insulting to those candidates. (But arguments about the moral character of *the people you're talking to* are still inapt.) Or suppose the topic of debate is why there are fewer female than male mathematicians. Then arguments that women tend to be worse at math than men are fair game, regardless of whether some participants find this idea insulting. Again, the point of discussion is for us to learn things from each other and correct each other's biases. This works by people saying what they actually think about the topic of discourse, while refraining from diverting into irrelevant matters.

A second important guideline is to be a cooperative listener. Thus, if the other party says something ambiguous, try to interpret it in the way that makes the most sense, not the way that makes the least sense. If you aren't sure, ask for clarification. If the other person seems to be saying something ridiculous, there's a good chance you're misunderstanding them. If the person gives a hypothetical example, and (as is always true) they don't fill in all the details, assume that the details are to be filled in in the way that makes sense given the other person's point.

Example: You're talking to a utilitarian, who thinks that the morally right action is always the action that produces the most total wellbeing for all parties affected. The utilitarian gives you an example in which you have to choose between letting a trolley run over five people, and diverting it so that it only runs over one person (as discussed in §15.7.3). Do not say, "What if the one person is just about to discover the cure for cancer?" or "What if the five people are all mass murderers?" You don't have to ask those things, because you already know that those things aren't true in the story, because (besides that these are highly unusual conditions) they would obviously defeat the point of the example. In other words, don't add complications to an example that only serve to distract or change the subject; just accept the example as it was obviously intended.

When you give examples to make a point, choose the examples to be as uncontroversial as possible, given the point you're trying to make. Do not try to pack your ideology into the example, don't use the example to inject jibes at the other side, and don't design the example to presuppose controversial assumptions that the other person obviously wouldn't agree with. For instance, if you're trying to give an example of an unforgivable crime, use something like serial murder, not something like "being a greedy capitalist".

In talking with people who disagree with you, it helps to have realistic expectations. If you think you're going to just say your brilliant point and then the other person will have a "road to Damascus" style conversion to your ideology, then you're in for a lot of frustration. A more realistic goal is for both parties to gain a better understanding of exactly where and why they disagree. What is the fundamental divergence of intuitions or experience that gives rise to the disagreement that you started with? Occasionally, people change their views on controversial topics, but it almost never happens during one conversation. If another person has deeply misguided ideas, the best you can usually do is to plant some seeds of doubt that may gradually grow in their mind over a period of weeks or years.

17.5. Conclusion

There are widespread, strong, persistent disagreements about things like politics, religion, and philosophy. These are not adequately explained by saying that the issues are difficult, or we don't have enough data, or we have differing values. The best explanation is that most people are irrational about these subjects. On political, religious, and philosophical issues, people *want* to believe particular claims, for reasons unrelated to the truth or justification of those claims. E.g., we prefer to believe things that fit with our self-image, that fit the beliefs of other people we want to associate with, that rationalize or express our emotions, and that are dramatic and entertaining. Because we know, in certain cases, that our beliefs won't actually affect the world (e.g., we're not actually going to change public policy), we indulge our preferences and fail to exert effort to think rationally and form accurate beliefs. It's not that we explicitly decide to deceive ourselves; it is more that our desires create *biases* that make it easy to believe what we want, and we fail to take steps to counteract our biases.

We can maintain and strengthen our desired beliefs by selecting information sources that agree with us; directing our attention to arguments for our preferred beliefs and away from objections; and relying on speculative, subjective, and anecdotal arguments.

Though all of this is instrumentally rational given most people's actual goals, it is immoral and harmful to society, since widespread epistemic irrationality prevents us from solving other social problems. Individuals should therefore work to reduce their biases and irrational tendencies. We can do this by taking care to collect information from smart people with different perspectives; to think about objections to our views; and to avoid speculative, subjective, and anecdotal reasoning.

Discussions with other people can help counteract our biases, provided that we interact in a cooperative way, genuinely trying to understand each other's perspectives, and avoid turning discussions into personal contests. The realistic goal for discussions of controversial issues is for all parties to come to better understand each other, and perhaps for some participants to plant seeds of doubt that may gradually influence others' beliefs over time.

18. Critical Thinking and Trust in Experts

In this chapter, we discuss to what extent you should try to figure out controversial issues for yourself, and to what extent you should defer to experts.

18.1. The Issue of Critical Thinking vs. Trust

Across America, and I assume most of the world, colleges and universities have courses in "critical thinking". These are largely informal logic courses, which teach students how to recognize standard fallacies, such as argument ad hominem, affirming the consequent, and appeals to emotion. And that's all cool, of course. (Well, I have some problems with the usual treatments, but nevermind that.[186])

But there is another aspect of the idea of "critical thinking" that I want to scrutinize. It is that individuals should *think issues through for themselves*, rather than taking conclusions on trust. Thus, one reads remarks like these in critical thinking books:

> [T]he aim of this book is not to offer solutions to a set of ethical dilemmas, but to encourage readers to do the thinking for themselves about these issues.[187]

> In this conversation, all sides of an issue should receive a fair hearing, and then you, the reader, should make up your own minds on the issue.[188]

This is of course not to say that one should completely disregard the opinions of experts. But, according to the standard view, it is appropriate to receive pronouncements from others with some skepticism, to scrutinize their

---

[186] For discussion, see my *Knowledge, Reality, and Value*, ch. 4.
[187] Anne Thomson, *Critical Reasoning in Ethics* (1999), 2.
[188] Louis Pojman, *Introduction to Philosophy: Classical and Contemporary Readings* (1991), 5.

reasoning for mistakes, and to exercise one's own judgment, even when listening to the most intelligent and educated experts. This, at any rate, is how one is supposed to treat issues that are controversial in one's society. So that is what I take as the **Critical Thinking Philosophy**.

I think the critical thinking philosophy used to be widely taken for granted, at least in American universities. Today, it might be slightly more controversial, due to some recent social developments. It actually turns out that, if people try to think issues through for themselves, they don't all come to the "right" conclusions. (Who knew?) E.g., many ordinary people, when thinking for themselves, will come to the conclusion that global warming either isn't happening, or isn't man-made, or isn't so bad. This conflicts with the views of mainstream climate experts. You could try getting into the weeds with the climate skeptics, taking up their arguments point by point, and some people do that. But many people today prefer a much briefer approach: Many simply appeal to the opinions of the majority of experts. They say that, if you aren't a climate scientist, you have no business trying to evaluate climate issues yourself; you should just accept the word of the experts.

There are many other issues that are like this, that is, where if an ordinary person tries to think the issue through for herself, it is by no means certain that she will arrive at the same conclusion as the majority of experts. This typically happens when an issue is either political or *politicized* (i.e., it isn't inherently political, but people have managed to associate views about it with different political factions).[189]

So I hope that makes clear that there's an interesting issue here. To what extent should one evaluate controversial issues for oneself, and to what extent should one simply trust the testimony of the smarter, better-informed people?

18.2. The Case for Deference

The dominance of the critical thinking philosophy (at least for most of the last several decades) is something of a mystery, because there are very simple, obvious arguments against it. To wit:

18.2.1. The Reliability Argument

Let's start with a simple example:

> *Unequal Tests:* You're trying to diagnose an illness that you have. The doctors have two tests they can run, but you may only take one of them. Test A is

---

[189] Other examples: creationism vs. evolution, group IQ differences, biological bases for behavior, vaccine effectiveness.

about 90% reliable. Test *B* is only 70% reliable, and it's also more expensive and time-consuming. Assume all other things are equal. Which test should you take?

I hope you answered "*A*". This illustrates a general point: You should prefer more reliable over less reliable belief-forming methods. Granted, in some cases, it makes sense pragmatically to use a less reliable method, if doing so is cheaper or easier. But obviously you wouldn't use the less reliable method if it is also more difficult and costly and there are no other benefits.

That's like the choice between thinking things through for yourself (where you are not an expert) and deferring to experts. The experts tend to be highly intelligent, to be well-informed, and to have spent a great deal of time thinking about the issue on which they are experts. That, after all, is why we call them "experts" in the first place. All those things—intelligence, knowledge, and time investment—are positively correlated with reliability in figuring out the correct answer to a question. If you're just an ordinary non-expert, you're going to be less informed, to have spent less time on the issue, and typically also to be less intelligent than the experts (sorry). So it seems obvious that the experts are going to be more reliable than you.

Furthermore, thinking things through for yourself is also more difficult and time-consuming than deferring to experts. So it seems like a no-brainer: Of course you should prefer the easier, more reliable belief-forming method over the harder, more time-consuming, and less reliable method.

18.2.2. The Coherence Argument

Suppose I am interested in a controversial issue, but I haven't had time to think it through for myself. Say, I wonder whether the soul is immortal. I run into a former student who took a critical thinking class at my university and got an "A". This student tells me that he has recently investigated the issue of the immortality of the soul, applying all the lessons that he learned in his critical thinking class. Assume that I believe all this. The student next tells me that, after thinking the issue through for himself and weighing all the arguments on both sides just like we taught him, he has come to the conclusion that the soul indeed persists after death. Question: At this point, should I now believe that the soul is immortal?

No. Obviously not. For one thing, if I did that, then I myself would not be thinking critically. Moreover, everyone knows that the opinion of a college student about a controversial philosophical issue is not reliable, regardless of whether the student took a critical thinking class and regardless of whether the student applied the lessons he learned there. One way we know this is that different students who think the issue through will come to different conclusions, just as professional philosophers do. Indeed, I venture to say that learning this student's opinion should have *no discernible impact* on my credence that the soul is immortal.

But now we come to the incoherence in the critical thinking philosophy. If *I* wouldn't trust this student's judgment, then why would I advise *the student* to trust the student's judgment? By stipulation, the student applied the critical thinking lessons that I and my colleagues in the philosophy department taught him. If I don't accept his conclusion as true upon learning that, I am implicitly admitting that critical thinking, as taught in the philosophy department, *is not reliable*, that is, it isn't highly likely to lead to a true conclusion. Which means I'm implicitly admitting that we gave him bad advice. Assuming he wants to form true beliefs and avoid false ones, we should have told him that he should *not* trust his own judgment about issues like this.

18.2.3. Objections

Here are some objections to the preceding arguments.

Objection 1: Are there really such things as *experts* in philosophy, religion, or politics? Sure, there are professors who have studied these things for a long time, but as they haven't reached any consensus, perhaps it's too much to call them "experts".

Reply: It doesn't matter whether you call them "experts" are not. What matters is that they have cognitive advantages over you (again, they have greater intelligence, knowledge, and time devoted to the issues). If that isn't enough to enable them to figure out the truth, then it's even less likely that *you* could figure out the truth.

Objection 2: How do we know who the experts are? Don't we have to use critical thinking to figure that out?

Reply: When X is a controversial issue, the question of who the experts about X are is typically *much* easier and less controversial than X itself is. E.g., people who have PhD's in climate science are experts on climate science; random political partisans on the internet aren't. You don't need to consult experts to figure that out, because that's an easy question. But you *do* need to consult experts to know whether climate change is man-made, because that is a much more difficult question, requiring much more extensive, specialized knowledge.

Objection 3: The case against critical thinking turns on its lower reliability in arriving at the truth. But what if we have other goals besides truth? E.g., maybe we value having a coherent belief system, or a practically useful belief system.

Reply: Experts are going to be better at those other things too. They're more likely to have a rich, coherent system of beliefs about the topic of their expertise, and more likely to have practically useful beliefs too, than a lay person who forms beliefs independently. So again, it makes more sense to adopt the experts' beliefs.

Objection 4: Society needs to train the next generation of experts, and to do this, we need to train students to think for themselves.

Reply: As a defense of teaching critical thinking, this is pretty weak, because only a minuscule fraction of students will or should ever become academics. It doesn't make sense to gear our teaching toward the 0.1% of our audience who will need to become experts like us, rather than the other 99.9%.

Moreover, the issue wasn't what is useful for society; the issue was what is epistemically rational. Objection 4 doesn't touch the argument that it is *epistemically irrational* to rely on your own judgment about controversial issues, in that doing so is unlikely to result in true beliefs.

18.3. The Case Against Science

In spite of what I have said above, there are some strong reasons for distrusting experts. Experts have often been wrong, and indeed perhaps are *usually* wrong—though it matters a great deal what the subject matter is, as some subjects are much more error-prone than others. I'm going to start with some scientific errors. In order to understand how science is often wrong, we need to first review some stuff about how a wide class of scientific studies work.

18.3.1. A Common Scientific Method

Let's say you want to know whether cellphones cause cancer. You get a large group of people, about half of whom have cellphones (the **experimental group**) and half of whom don't (the **control group**). In the ideal case, you would randomly assign which people get the cellphones (thus performing a **randomized, controlled trial**), but sometimes this isn't feasible (e.g., because people refuse to give up their phones!), so you just have to look at people who already have cellphones versus people who don't (thus conducting a mere **observational study**). You then look at how common cancer is in both groups.

If you have a large group (which you should), the frequency of cancer is going to differ between the cellphone group and the no-phone group. So now you need to assess whether that difference is just due to chance, or whether cellphones actually have some connection to cancer. You do this using a "significance test". Basically, you look at the *difference* in the frequency of cancer between the two groups, and you calculate the probability of getting a difference that large purely by chance (i.e., conditional on the assumption that there is no meaningful connection between cellphones and cancer). That probability is referred to as the ***p*-value**. If the *p*-value is sufficiently low, you get to say that the difference is "**statistically significant**", and you "reject the **null hypothesis**" (namely, the hypothesis that there is no real connection between cellphones and cancer).

How low does the probability have to be? People commonly use thresholds of 5% or 1%. This will commonly be indicated in a scientific study by the authors writing, in parentheses, "$p < 0.05$" or "$p < 0.01$". Where did these thresholds come from? Well, they're just numbers that seem pretty small, which is what we want if we're testing a theory—we want the theory to successfully predict something that is unlikely if the theory is false. If you use larger thresholds for p, then you have a greater risk of letting through false hypotheses. If you use smaller thresholds for p, then you have a greater risk of missing true hypotheses.

It's easy to get confused about what p measures. In particular, sometimes people think p indicates the probability of the hypothesis being false given the evidence. That's not right. Rather, p essentially measures the probability of the *evidence* given the negation of the hypothesis (i.e., assuming that there is no connection between factors A and B, how likely is it that we would observe a difference as large as the one we observed?).

An enormous number of studies—probably millions—have been done using essentially this method, and more are being done every day. These are often reported in popular media, where they tell you, e.g., that cellphones cause brain cancer, that red wine reduces heart attack risk, or that religion makes people happier. When you hear a headline like that, it is generally based on the methodology described above. This type of study is especially common in medicine, social science, and psychology.

18.3.2. The Replication Crisis

Recently, people found out that most of the "discoveries" made using the above methodology are wrong—that is, the hypotheses that pass the significance tests are nevertheless *false*. The way we know this is that when someone tries to *replicate* one of these studies, they usually fail—they don't get the same result as the original study. In medical research, studies are frequently refuted by later studies. This happens to about 80% of non-randomized trials (the most common type) and 25% of randomized trials.[190]

---

[190] David H. Freedman, "Lies, Damned Lies, and Medical Science", *The Atlantic* (Nov.

In psychology, a group of 270 psychologists got together between 2011 and 2015 to try to replicate 100 studies in psychology, all of which had been published in leading journals in 2008.[191] Of the 100 studies, 97 had reported statistically significant results. Yet in the replication experiments, only 35 had statistically significant results, and the effects observed were on average about half the size reported in the original studies.

In 2021, the Center for Open Science published the results of 50 replication experiments on cancer biology. They found that 46% of effects replicated successfully on more criteria than they failed, and effects observed in the replication studies were, on average, 85% smaller than the effects reported in the original studies.

It is generally agreed that this is a widespread problem across many fields, not just medicine and psychology. In 2016, *Nature* published the results of a survey of 1,576 scientists in a variety of fields. 70% reported having tried and failed to reproduce another scientist's results. Half agreed that there is a replication crisis, though, bizarrely, under a third think that the failure to replicate a published result means that the result is probably wrong.[192]

18.3.3. Why Science Goes Wrong

What? How can this be? I thought science was the source of all truth!

There are a number of reasons why science goes wrong. Say you have two properties, *A* and *B* (e.g., "being a cellphone user" and "having cancer"). Even if there is no connection at all between *A* and *B*, if you do a study of their correlation, 5% of the time (1 in 20 times), just by chance, you'll find a statistically significant correlation between them (significant at the 0.05 level). That's what the 5% significance level *means*. Note also that there are thousands of teams of scientists around the world who are constantly doing research into various questions, trying to find associations between variables. So if 20 different scientists study the same *A* and *B*, on average, one of them is going to find a "significant" correlation between them, even if *A* and *B* are completely unrelated.

The next thing you have to understand is **publication bias**. Publishers of academic journals like to publish *interesting* findings. E.g., if you have a finding that says some familiar thing that we thought was innocuous actually causes cancer, that is interesting. People will want to read that, cite it, etc. Which

---

2010), 80.
[191] Brian Nosek, et al., "Estimating the Reproducibility of Psychological Science", *Science* (2015): aac4716.
[192] Monya Baker, "1,500 Scientists Lift the Lid on Reproducibility", *Nature* (2016): 452–4.

means the journal wants to publish things like that. On the other hand, if you have a study that only reports null results, so it doesn't find any connection between anything, that's a lot less interesting. So if several teams of scientists found no connection between *A* and *B*, but *one* team found a causal connection, the literature is probably going to reflect what that one team found.

Of course, scientists know this, and they really want to get publications so that they can gain prestige, earn tenure, and so on. So they try to fudge things in order to get significant results. One way you can do this is by collecting data for a lot of different variables, testing many different hypotheses, then reporting whatever correlation passes the statistical significance test and saying that that was your hypothesis. This is known as ***p*-hacking**. If you test more than 20 different pairs of variables, again, probably one pair will pass the test of statistical significance (at the 0.05 level) just by luck. By the way, one way to get more hypotheses to test is by combining variables. E.g., if cellphones by themselves don't cause cancer, maybe cellphones combined with being an older female cause cancer. This is why you often hear study results that mention multiple variables.

People who are good at getting "interesting" results get publications, tenure, and prestige. They find it easier to get grants, which means they will now be directing more research in the future, compared to the poor sods who couldn't get significant results.

But here is the most important reason why so many research findings are false: Because *almost all hypotheses that we would be testing in the first place are false*. The "base rate" for a hypothesis being true, as we say, is very low. The standard scientific methodology described above (§18.3.1) does not take that into account. It tries to assess hypotheses solely by looking at *p*-values. Recall Bayes' Theorem from §12.3.2:

$$P(h|e) = \frac{P(h) \times P(e|h)}{P(h) \times P(e|h) + P(\sim h) \times P(e|\sim h)}$$

The standard methodology basically just looks at $P(e|h)$ and $P(e|\sim h)$ and accepts a hypothesis if the former is much higher than the latter. The methodology doesn't look at $P(h)$ at all. This is a particularly serious oversight if $P(h)$ is extremely low, because that can lead to the whole right-hand side of the equation being very low. Which is in fact usually the case.

Here is an illustration.[193] Let's say you're testing 100,000 genes to find out if any of them cause an increased risk for schizophrenia. Let's say that 10 of them actually have that effect. (All of this is realistic.) You use a 0.05

---

[193] Adapted from John Ioannidis' famous paper, "Why Most Published Research Findings Are False", *PLOS Medicine* (2005).

significance level for detecting the causal connection. Now, let's be optimistic and assume that all 10 of the schizophrenia-causing genes are going to pass the statistical significance test. In addition, 5% of the genes that *don't* cause schizophrenia will also pass that test. How do I know that? Because *that is what the 5% significance level means.*

So you get 10 true positives (things that pass the test and really do cause schizophrenia), and you get $(100{,}000 - 10)(0.05) = 5{,}000$ false negatives (things that pass the test but do not actually cause schizophrenia). So, of all the genes that pass the significance test, $10/5{,}010 = 0.2\%$ actually have a causal connection to schizophrenia. In other words, our methodology is wrong 99.8% of the time when it "finds" a causal connection.

That's an extreme example, of course. But that explains how it can wind up that most published research findings are false. You just need a lot of people testing hypotheses, in an area where false hypotheses vastly outnumber true ones.

People are now working on how to reduce the rate of error in research findings. They've come up with some good ideas, such as pre-registering studies (this is where you declare in advance what your hypothesis is and how you're going to test it, so you can't *p*-hack) and having journals that commit to publishing any result, positive or negative. Some people also suggest lowering the *p*-values used for statistical significance, but this of course has the drawback of excluding more *true* hypotheses. Unfortunately, however, few people are looking at the core, philosophical error at the heart of the traditional methodology, probably because most scientists don't like philosophy.

The fundamental, philosophical error is that of ignoring *prior probabilities* and hence disregarding Bayes' Theorem. (The prior probability of a hypothesis can be thought of as an estimate of what percentage of similar hypotheses would be true. Hence, ignoring prior probabilities is pretty much the same as ignoring the base rate for hypotheses being true.) Why do scientists do this? Basically because there is no very satisfying, general theory of how to assign prior probabilities (see §§12.6.3, 14.5.3). It seems to require a lot of guesswork or judgment calls, which don't feel scientific. Thus, the people who came up with the now-standard methodology decided they needed a method that doesn't require anyone at any point to assess the prior probability of a hypothesis. They got a method that works fine as long as the prior probabilities of hypotheses are not too extreme, but it gives lots of false positives for low-probability hypotheses.

18.4. The Case Against Political Experts

After what we just heard about science, you'll be unsurprised to learn that political experts aren't terribly reliable either. The political psychologist Philip Tetlock conducted a now-famous, 20-year study of political forecasting.[194] Basically, he found experts on a variety of different politics-related areas and asked them to make predictions in their areas of expertise. E.g., an expert on the Middle East might be asked to predict whether war would break out between Israel and Syria in the next two years, or an expert on the U.S. economy might be asked to predict whether the economy would go into recession during the next three years. All of these were predictions that would be definitely proved true or false within a specified time period.

The participants were asked to express their confidence in these predictions by giving probability estimates. Tetlock waited to see which predictions came true, then calculated how well **calibrated** the predictions were. Basically, what this means is that when people say they are 70% confident of something, they should turn out to be right about 70% of the time; when they are 100% confident, they should be right all the time; etc. That's called being well calibrated.

It turned out that the political experts were very poorly calibrated. The best experts did only a little bit better than ordinary people, while ordinary people were basically equivalent to random guessers. The experts tended to be highly *overconfident* (assigning overly extreme probabilities to things). They would have been better calibrated if they had just assigned an equal probability to every possible outcome. For instance, on average, events that they predicted with 65–70% confidence actually happened only about 12–15% of the time.

On further questioning, it turned out that the political experts, though not very good at correctly predicting real events, *were* quite skilled at explaining away their errors. Tetlock observed the following kinds of excuses:

a. Some would explain a failed prediction as due to some minor error that doesn't reflect on the accuracy of their underlying theories.
b. Some would say that, though their prediction didn't technically come true, it *almost* came true, so that really shows that their understanding of the subject is basically sound.
c. Some would say that the prediction failed because some external force that they couldn't be expected to anticipate came in and interfered with the system.

---

[194] Tetlock, *Expert Political Judgment: How Good Is It? How Can We Know?* (2005). Later, Tetlock did a study of how some people can become extremely good at making political predictions; see his *Superforecasting* (2016). However, it's not clear that the lessons from the latter study can be extended to contested philosophical or ideological questions.

d. Some would say that though they made an error, it was a prudent error to make—e.g., they'd justify overestimating the probability of a terrorist attack by saying that this is prudentially better than underestimating it.
e. Some would say that they were just off on the timing, and that the thing they predicted was still going to happen, but at a later date.
f. Some would say that they simply got unlucky.

Notice, by the way, that each of these things has a surface plausibility to it. Each of these could well be true in any given case. But no one ever made parallel remarks to explain away a *correct* prediction. E.g., when they get something right, no one ever says that the prediction *almost* turned out wrong, or that it only came out right due to the interference of some external factor, or that they just got lucky.

By the way, the forecasters with the biggest media presence tended to be especially inaccurate. This makes sense, since media pundits are selected for entertainment value, not accuracy. The way to be entertaining is usually to be extreme, ideological, and overconfident. This results in being wrong a lot, but when pundits get stuff wrong, typically no one calls them to account for it or even remembers what they said.

Tetlock's study only looked at certain kinds of political questions, ones for which there was going to be a very definite answer at a known time in the not-too-distant future. Many political questions are not like that. E.g., if you ask an "expert" whether abortion should be legal, that question is never going to be decisively resolved. You might think that the *important* questions are typically of the kind that won't be decisively resolved, particularly normative questions, rather than straightforward empirical predictions. So we don't know how well calibrated political experts are on the kinds of questions that really matter.

However, it is reasonable to assume that the experts are no better with respect to the latter kind of questions. If someone is no good at answering questions of objective fact, they're probably going to be even worse at answering questions that require more difficult and complicated judgment calls. When it comes to the straightforward factual questions, the expert at least has had a chance to be corrected by experience in the past and to adjust his belief-forming methods accordingly. When it comes to contested judgment calls, the expert never gets decisively corrected, so his judgment is probably going to be even less well calibrated.

18.5. The Case Against Philosophy

You knew this was coming: How reliable are professional *philosophers* when it comes to correctly answering questions in our area of expertise? How often do we get to the philosophical truth?

There are no empirical studies of philosophers' reliability (as far as I know), partly because no one has a technique of decisively verifying whether a philosopher got anything right.[195] But we hardly need studies; you already know that philosophers are the worst. Philosophical theories are practically always wrong. This is true even when the philosopher insists that he has an absolutely conclusive, irresistible proof that could not possibly be mistaken. Like when Descartes "proved" the existence of God, or Kant "proved" that we can never know things in themselves. (Most philosophers reject those "proofs".) One way we know that philosophers are usually wrong is that on any given question, philosophers usually advance a variety of incompatible positions, where no single position has majority support—that guarantees that most of them are wrong, even if we don't know what the true position is.

Occasionally, philosophers will reach a consensus on something. But even then, you shouldn't be too sure that they're on to anything. The consensus often evaporates, with later philosophers forming an opposing consensus. In the Middle Ages, philosophers were strongly agreed on the existence of God and the truth of Christianity. Today, most reject both. In the nineteenth century, most philosophers were agreed on the truth of *idealism*, of all things (as defined in §9.1). Today, practically no one takes idealism seriously. In the early 20th century, most analytic philosophers agreed that logical positivism was the truth. Today, almost no one does.

So if a philosopher tells you that he's figured out something of philosophical interest, you should probably pretty much assume that thing is false. Present company excepted, of course.

18.6. Conclusions

18.6.1. In Praise of Withholding

So we've seen some reasons for trusting experts over your own judgment (§18.2), followed by some reasons for distrusting experts (§§18.3–18.5). What can we conclude from all this?

Actually, the arguments of those sections are consistent with each other. The argument of section 18.2 was not that experts are generally *reliable*, full stop; it was that experts are probably *more* reliable *than you*. This is completely consistent with the fact that experts are highly unreliable on a wide variety of important questions. To reconcile this, we need only add that *you*, as a non-expert, are probably *even worse*. And this, as a matter of fact, is pretty clearly true. You may not be able to trust scientists, political pundits, or philosophers,

---

[195] There *are* surveys of the opinions of philosophers (see https://philpapers.org/surveys/); they just don't tell us who is *right*.

even in their areas of expertise, but you sure as hell can't trust some random person off the street. And if you yourself are not an expert, then you're pretty much a random person off the street. (Okay, if you're reading this book, you are probably smarter than the average person on the street. But still probably highly unreliable about difficult questions.)

What this means is that you are probably wrong about many of the controversial issues that you have opinions about. Since you can't really trust the experts either, you should probably just withhold judgment about all or most controversial issues. Of course, I know you're not actually going to do that, any more than I am.

18.6.2. When to Believe the Science

Talk about "trusting science" or "distrusting science" paints with too broad a brush. Most published research findings are false, yet this doesn't mean that you should distrust science as such. It means that you should distrust *certain kinds* of scientific claims. What kind?

a. You should be skeptical of claims based on statistical studies that have not been replicated, especially if the studies are only observational.
b. Theories that are of recent origin are more likely to be mistaken, compared to theories that have been around for several decades or more. Essentially, theories that have stood the test of time are more likely true.
c. Theories of more complicated things are more likely to be wrong. Thus, you can bet that the theories in physics and chemistry are going to be highly accurate when it comes to predicting observable events (though there can be disputes about their interpretation; see §14.4.1). Biology is a little more difficult, psychology is harder still, and social science is the hardest of all to get right.
d. Theories that fit with a particular political ideology are more likely to be mistaken. The reason for this is that scientists, as human beings, have political ideologies just like the rest of us. Plus, even if a scientist isn't himself ideological, he can feel pressure from ideologues. Thus, for example, scientific claims about race and gender issues typically cannot be trusted.
e. Claims appearing in popular media about scientific studies are usually unreliable. Journalists very frequently misreport what a study says, for several reasons: They're too dumb to understand it, they don't have time to be careful, they know readers aren't going to look up the study, and/or they know they'll get more readers if they make it sound more dramatic. If you want to know what was actually discovered, look up the original study.

f. If a research finding sounds amazing, it's probably false. Example: Until recently, students in college psychology classes were taught that, if you have people read a bunch of words having to do with old age, that makes them walk more slowly immediately afterwards. Amazing! Also false. That's one of the studies that didn't replicate.[196]
g. Incentives matter. If the people asserting *p* have an obvious incentive to assert *p* regardless of whether *p* is true, be suspicious. On the other hand, if the people asserting *p* stand to lose a lot if they are wrong, then be less suspicious. Example: If I tell you that subscribing to my blog will make you live longer, earn more money, and be more attractive to others, you should probably be skeptical.[197]

In recent times, there seems to be more suspicion of scientists than there used to be. The question of trusting scientists has, unfortunately, become politicized, and there is a risk that people will make foolish decisions (e.g., refusing vaccines for a deadly illness), possibly even getting themselves killed, because they refuse to listen to what the experts know. I would like to tell you that all the suspicion is just foolish ideology and we should all trust the scientists. But I can't tell you that, because I know that scientists have in fact often gotten things wrong, and they have on occasion been coopted by political interests. So the above list of observations is the best I can come up with now. Let's hope that science becomes de-politicized at some point in the near future.

18.6.3. Some Political Biases to Avoid

When thinking about political issues, most people are prone to certain stereotypical biases. We know these are biases in part because they tend to go away when people learn more (especially more about economics), regardless of their initial political orientation. Here are three common biases to watch out for:[198]

i. *Anti-foreign bias:* Most people are instinctively suspicious of foreigners, probably because in our evolutionary past, humans were frequently

---

[196] Original study: J.A. Bargh, M. Chen, & L. Burrows, "Automaticity of Social Behavior: Direct Effects of Trait Construct and Stereotype Activation on Action", *Journal of Personality and Social Psychology* (1996).

[197] It's worth a try, though: https://fakenous.substack.com.

[198] These are taken from Caplan's *The Myth of the Rational Voter*, which discusses them at greater length. Caplan also includes "make-work bias", a tendency to think of *jobs* rather than *labor* as a scarce resource that we need to preserve, thus implying that it is good to use inefficient production methods. For more common mistakes, see Hans Rosling's *Factfulness: Ten Reasons We're Wrong About the World—and Why Things Are Better Than You Think*.

attacked and killed by other tribes of humans. This makes us eager to believe, e.g., that foreign trade and immigration are harmful.

ii. *Anti-market bias:* People tend to underestimate the value of market-produced outcomes and overestimate the value of government interventions. It appears that most people assume that markets are controlled by greedy people, and that greed must produce bad outcomes; at the same time, they tend to overlook the possibility that governments are run by equally greedy or otherwise selfish people.

You might suspect, by the way, that the inclusion of this item is a bias on my part. I don't think it is, though. People who seriously study the effects of government programs and regulations normally wind up growing much more pessimistic about them.[199]

iii. *Pessimistic bias:* I once heard this aphorism: "Throughout human history, two things have always been true: Things have always gotten better, and people have always been convinced that things were getting worse." That's an exaggeration, but not by much. People in the developed world today are fabulously wealthier, safer, better educated, live much longer, and are just generally happier than almost everyone in human history. Yet prognosticating disaster of one kind or another seems to be one of the most popular pastimes for political ideologues. Remember that when you find yourself entertaining doom and gloom scenarios, which I'm sure you're going to be doing if you think about the future of society at all.

18.6.4. What to Believe About Philosophy

There's a strong prima facie case that almost everyone should withhold judgment about almost all disputed philosophical questions. But the idea that we should withhold judgment about controversial philosophical theses is itself a controversial philosophical thesis. So that suggests that we should withhold judgment about whether we should withhold judgment … but then we seem to descend into incoherence.

I'm not sure what to make of that problem. But surely one cannot, just by reflecting on that problem, thereby know that philosophers *are* actually (contrary to all appearances) reliable about philosophical beliefs. Nor can one thereby know that one is more reliable than the professional philosophers, nor

---

[199] For discussion, see *Reason's* interview with Ronald Coase ("Looking for Results", Jan. 1, 1997, https://reason.com/archives/1997/01/01/looking-for-results/); Robert Hahn and John Hird's "The Costs and Benefits of Regulation: Review and Synthesis", *Yale Journal on Regulation* (1991); and John Dawson and John Seater's "Federal Regulation and Aggregate Economic Growth", *Journal of Economic Growth* (2013).

that it's okay to form beliefs about a topic despite being obviously unreliable about it. And I can't see how one could defend any of those ideas.

But I also somehow don't think that people can be convinced to withhold judgment about all disputed philosophical questions just by reflecting on how philosophers are unreliable. At least, I doubt that people who are interested in philosophy in the first place could be convinced.

So the best advice I can come up with is: Don't be too certain about your philosophical beliefs. Acknowledge that you may well be wrong, and remain open to hearing objections.

19. Peer Disagreement

The previous chapter was about how we should regard our epistemic superiors. This chapter is about how we should regard our epistemic peers. Specifically, what should we think about issues on which equally qualified people disagree with us?

19.1. Peer Disagreement Scenarios

Let's say you're an expert on some topic. You know another expert on the same topic who, before you hear his opinion, appears to be equally qualified as yourself—he is as intelligent, is as well-informed, has spent as much time thinking about the issue, and in all other ways you can think of (other than actually having the right opinion on the issue) appears to be as well positioned to know the truth about the issue as you. Yet this other expert disagrees with you about the issue. What should you make of this? Should you suspend judgment about the issue? Should you just stick to your guns? Should you do something in between?

This is the issue of "**peer disagreement**".[200] **Epistemic peers** (with respect to some issue) are people who are equally well-positioned to determine the truth about an issue. So we can rephrase the question as: How should you react when you learn that an epistemic peer disagrees with you?

By the way, it's common to define epistemic peers as being exactly equally qualified in all respects. I think that's too strong (it results in there not being any epistemic peers); I think we should just define epistemic peers as being approximately equally qualified overall. So I'll assume that understanding from here on.

Here is a real-life example: David Lewis disagrees with Peter van Inwagen about free will.[201] Lewis endorses compatibilism, while van Inwagen supports

---

[200] I have imagined a disagreement between *experts* because this makes things more interesting; however, epistemic peers as defined need not be experts.
[201] See Lewis' "Are We Free to Break the Laws?" (*Theoria*, 1981) and van Inwagen's *An Essay on Free Will* (1983). Van Inwagen discusses the disagreement in "'It Is Wrong,

libertarian freedom. Both are extremely intelligent, well-respected experts on the topic. Each has heard all the arguments of the other and remains unconvinced. On the face of it, this poses a puzzle: Since each philosopher is about equally well-qualified to judge the free will issue, it seems that each would be about equally likely to be correct. Both philosophers should be able to figure that out. Therefore, on learning of the other's view, each philosopher should now withhold judgment about who is correct. Of course, neither of them did that. In the face of the disagreement, both continued to believe they were right.[202]

That is far from an unusual case. Expert philosophers are constantly disagreeing with each other, and constantly remaining unmoved by learning of each other's views and arguments. Hardly any philosopher ever suspends his beliefs upon learning of peer disagreement.

The phenomenon extends beyond philosophers. Scientists sometimes disagree with each other (not as often as philosophers, of course), and these disagreements commonly persist even though all sides know of the others' views and arguments. Granted, scientific disputes get resolved more often than philosophical disputes do. But the relevant point here is that the mere fact that another scientist disagrees with one rarely changes a given scientist's views. (The change generally comes when new empirical evidence arrives.)

There are at least four main views people have about this sort of situation. One view is that, upon learning of a peer disagreement, the epistemic peers should each take up a credence in the disputed proposition about halfway between the credences the two initially had. So if you were 90% confident of A and I was 20% confident of A, we should both move to 55% credence in A. This is called the **Equal Weight View** (you should give about equal weight to the other party's judgment as your own); it's also a **conciliatory** view (one that recommends significantly changing your position in the direction of the peer who disagrees with you).[203] People hardly ever actually do this, but that could just be because we are irrational and dogmatic.

Everywhere, Always, for Anyone, to Believe Anything upon Insufficient Evidence'" in *Faith, Freedom, and Rationality* (1996).
[202] Lewis passed away in 2001. As far as I know, van Inwagen still holds the same views.
[203] By the way, splitting the difference evenly only makes sense when the other person's credence and yours are equally distant from 50%. If one of you initially arrives at a *more extreme* (farther from 50%) credence than the other, then the two parties should compromise to a position that is closer to that more extreme credence. The intuitive reason is that the person who comes up with something closer to 50% is closer to *having no opinion* on the topic; hence, his assessment is weaker evidence than that of the person with a stronger opinion.

The second view is that you should, or at least *may*, stick to your original view. This is sometimes called the **Steadfast View**.

The third view is the **Right Reasons View**. It says that whichever party *in fact* correctly assessed the evidence to begin with should stick to her view, while the other party should change (even though it might be extremely hard to tell which party is which).

The fourth view is the **Total Evidence View**. It holds that the rational response to disagreement is the outcome of weighing both the **first-order evidence** and the **second-order evidence**. Here, "first-order evidence" refers to evidence directly about the issue, e.g., the arguments for and against libertarian freedom; "second-order evidence" refers to evidence about what is the correct assessment of the first-order evidence, and/or about the reliability of the people assessing the evidence. (More on how to weigh these below.)

Let's discuss the arguments bearing on each of these views.

19.2. The Case for Equal Weight

19.2.1. *The Obvious Motivation*

The basic motivation for the equal weight view is obvious and was indicated above: On the face of it, epistemic peers should be about equally likely to correctly answer the question with respect to which they are peers.[204] That's almost true by definition, since peerhood *means* that they are about equal, overall, in respect of the reliability-relevant factors (knowledge, intelligence, time investment, and whatever else you want to add in).

To illustrate the idea:

> *Equal Tests:* You're trying to determine whether you have Covid-23 (a little-known respiratory disease that escaped from a lab in New Jersey in 2023, which affects about half the population). The doctors have two tests that they can do, test *C* and test *D*. Both are 80% reliable.[205] First you take test *C*, and it says that you have Covid-23. Then you take test *D*, and it says that you do *not* have Covid-23. At this point, what should you believe?

This seems pretty straightforward. You should withhold judgment about whether you have Covid-23 or not, and your credence that you have it should be about 50% (assuming you have no other evidence). This illustrates the

---

[204] See David Christensen's "Epistemology of Disagreement: The Good News" in the *Philosophical Review* (2007).
[205] Assume 80% is both the specificity and the sensitivity.

general principle that if equally reliable belief-forming methods support two incompatible propositions, you should withhold belief.[206]

There's no obvious reason why it should matter if one of the "belief-forming methods" involves the exercise of your own intuition, reasoning, and judgment. Nor should it matter if one of the methods is taking testimony from another person. Therefore, if your own intuition, reasoning, and judgment lead you to a conclusion that conflicts with another person's statements, and the other person is about equally reliable as you, then you should suspend judgment.

19.2.2. More Examples

The Equal Weight View is also supported by ordinary-life examples in which we behave as the view recommends. For instance:

> *Restaurant Check:* You are out with your philosophy buddies one night, eating and getting smashed, as philosophers are wont to do. At the end of the meal, you do some quick calculations to figure out each person's share of the bill (after agreeing to divide it up evenly). You come up with $43. Then your buddy, Plado, tells you that he just calculated everyone's share, and it comes to $45. Plado is about equally good at arithmetic as you are, equally smashed, and in general equally reliable. What do you now think about the correct shares?[207]

Stipulate that there is no misunderstanding of the problem (e.g., you didn't use different tip amounts). One of you just made an error in calculation. It seems obvious that you should withhold judgment about which of you made the error, and that is what most people would in fact do, pending a recalculation. Thus, you would decrease your credence in the "$43" answer to around 0.5 or lower.

Here's a less likely but still interesting sort of case:

> *Somebody's Hallucination:* You and Plado are looking out the window of your office. You see your colleague Arisdodle hanging out in the quad outside, in plain view, as he sometimes does. You comment on this, whereupon

---

[206] But note that if the prevalence of Covid-23 in the population were either greater or less than 50%, then there would be a different answer, per the reasoning discussed in §18.3.3.

[207] Adapted (with a little color added) from Christensen's "Epistemology of Disagreement: The Good News".

> Plado sincerely informs you that he doesn't see anyone there. What do you now think about Arisdodle's presence?[208]

Assume again that there is no misunderstanding or insincerity (Plado is looking in the right place, he's not lying or playing a joke, etc.); one of you is just hallucinating. It seems again that you should withhold judgment about which of you is hallucinating, and that is what most people would in fact do, pending further evidence.

You can give a similar example involving memory, where again most people would withhold judgment about who was misremembering something (I'll let you fill in the details yourself). These cases show that we accept the Equal Weight View in disputes about normal things outside of philosophy, politics, and other typically controversial areas. It's hard to see why the epistemological principle should change when you're disagreeing about typically controversial issues. More likely, people just get more emotionally attached to their views when they're dealing with a controversial philosophical or political issue and therefore feel more reluctant to modify their views.

19.2.3. Don't Use First-Order Evidence to Assess Reliability

One way of reacting to a disagreement would be to downgrade your assessment of the other person's reliability, based specifically on their disagreement with you about a particular issue. You might then conclude that the other person isn't your epistemic peer after all, and thus that you don't have to revise your own opinion (or at least, don't have to change it nearly as much as you would if they were really your peer).

Friends of the Equal Weight View reject this; they think there is something question-begging about it. You have to assess the other person's reliability *independently* of their view on the current issue; if you would judge them equally reliable on independent grounds, then you have to give equal weight to their opinion on the particular issue that you're now disagreeing about.

This seems right in the above examples. E.g., in Restaurant Check, suppose you declare that your calculation is probably correct since you are better at calculating than Plado is. Prior to tonight, you *thought* that Plado was equally good at arithmetic as you, but now that you know that he's incorrectly calculated the shares of tonight's bill (getting $45 when the right answer, per your calculations, is $43), you conclude that he's less good at arithmetic. Therefore, he's not your epistemic peer.

---

[208] Adapted from Richard Feldman's "Reasonable Religious Disagreements" in *Philosophers Without Gods* (2010).

Or suppose that, in Somebody's Hallucination, you declare that your vision is better than Plado's, since Plado is unable to see the person in the quad whom you can see; therefore, Plado isn't your epistemic peer.

In either of these cases, your reaction seems dogmatic and pathetically circular.

19.2.4. The Self-Defeat Objection to Equal Weight

Here is a cute objection to the Equal Weight View: The epistemology of disagreement is itself a locus of peer disagreement. The proponents of the Steadfast View are about equally well-qualified to assess the issue as the proponents of the Equal Weight View (they're about equally smart, well-informed, etc.). Therefore, on the Equal Weight View, proponents of the Equal Weight View should give up the Equal Weight View. Hence, the Equal Weight View is self-defeating and cannot be rationally maintained. The Steadfast View, on the other hand, is perfectly coherent: On the Steadfast View, it's fine to stick to the Steadfast View when you learn of the disagreement with the Equal Weight people.

How could one respond to this cute objection? Equal Weighters could claim that the Equal Weight View contains an exception clause: We ought to give equal weight to views of our epistemic peers *except* with respect to the truth of this very proposition. That enables them to consistently remain steadfast about the truth of the Equal Weight View.

This response, however, looks pretty blatantly ad hoc and hypocritical. Whatever considerations you think support the Equal Weight View in other cases, why wouldn't those considerations also apply in the dispute about the epistemology of peer disagreement?

It's sort of like if I embrace the principle, "Nobody *but me* should ever steal." I could not evade charges of hypocrisy merely by pointing out that, whenever I steal, I'm acting in accordance with my explicitly stated principle.

Equal Weight advocates might say that this isn't really ad hoc because it is part of a *general* principle about epistemological theories: *All* epistemological theories, to be consistent, have to dogmatically endorse themselves. Imagine that the magazine *Consumer Reports*, in addition to rating ordinary consumer products, also rated consumer ratings magazines. To be consistent, it would have to rate its own rating system as the best. That's like how an epistemological theory has to "dogmatically" endorse itself.[209]

I leave it to you to judge whether that sufficiently addresses the ad hocness concern.

---

[209] See Adam Elga's "How to Disagree About how to Disagree" in *Disagreement* (2010).

19.3. The Case for Steadfastness

19.3.1. Non-Dogmatic Steadfastness

On to the Steadfast View. To clarify, this view doesn't endorse irrational dogmatism; the view to be discussed is *not* that everyone may always stick to their original view when confronted with disagreement. *Of course* you should first listen to the other side's evidence and arguments with an open mind.

But now we're assuming that, after hearing all the evidence and arguments, your initial view still seems correct to you. The other side's reasons didn't seem very good and, after weighing them carefully and open-mindedly, it appears to you that the reasons in favor of your initial view strongly outweigh the reasons given by the other side. This often happens. And it is in this sort of case that (according to the Steadfast View) you're entitled to stick to your guns.

Of course, the other person might be in a symmetrical, opposed position: After carefully and open-mindedly listening to *your* arguments, it seems to him that *his* reasons strongly outweigh the ones that you cited. And so he might be justified in sticking to his guns as well. So the two people can rationally just "agree to disagree", as we say.

This is okay, because justification is agent-relative: A proposition isn't simply justified *in general*; it is justified or unjustified *for* a particular person, and it might be justified for one person but unjustified for another. In such a case, we can say the two people have a **rational disagreement** (a disagreement in which both parties are rational in holding on to their views).

This is not to say that all or most disagreements are in fact rational—often, people have *irrational* disagreements—e.g., because one or both parties are refusing to listen to the other's reasons, because one or both is unduly biased, etc. The point is just that rational disagreement is possible and would occur in the sort of case described above.

19.3.2. Examples of Steadfastness

In §19.2.2, we saw examples in which the Equal Weight View gives intuitively correct results. But there are other examples in which steadfastness seems more appropriate …

Brillo Pads: You go to your doctor, complaining of a stomach ache. The doctor has a medical degree from a reputable school and years of clinical experience. You, on the other hand, have no degree, no clinical experience, and approximately zero medical knowledge. After examining you, the doctor tells you that you need to eat two Brillo pads, then jump up and

> down for 15 minutes, and this will cure your condition. What should you think?[210]

Despite the doctor's advice, and despite that the doctor *antecedently* appeared more qualified than you to judge medical matters, I hope you agree that you should *not* proceed to eat two Brillo pads and jump up and down. The prior probability of that being a good treatment is so low that, even after conditionalizing on the doctor's testimony, it is still highly unlikely that that is a good treatment. This shows that you may sometimes use your own judgment as a basis for rejecting the judgment of someone who initially appeared to be better positioned to make a judgment than you. And of course, if that is so, then you can also sometimes use your own judgment to reject that of an epistemic peer.

I said "initially" because, once the doctor tells you his prescription, you might want to revise your opinion of his medical qualifications. You might conclude that he is a quack just on the basis of this one prescription. Nor does this seem question-begging in any objectionable sense (contra the argument of §19.2.3).

Many similar examples could be given, in which someone disagrees with you about something you are extremely certain of. E.g., a colleague disagrees that 2+2=4, or that the Earth is round, or that China is a country. In these cases, it seems that you should not withhold judgment. You should just conclude that the other party is crazy, or incredibly ignorant, or something like that. (Admittedly, it is unclear how these cases differ from the case of Somebody's Hallucination [§19.2.2], in which you also began with very strong justification for your initial belief, yet it was defeated by the other person's testimony.)

19.3.3. Ineffable Evidence

Defenses of the Steadfast View usually wind up saying that the parties to a rational disagreement actually have different evidence, even after each party has listened to all of the arguments the other party has to give.

One reason for this might be that not all of one's justification for a given view is capable of being articulated. Perhaps you just have a philosophical insight into the nature of free will that can't be fully put into words. Based on your understanding of freedom, you can see that it rules out being predetermined. You can't get David Lewis to see this, but that shouldn't undermine your knowledge of the libertarian conception of freedom; it just

---

[210] I got this example from an undergraduate student many years ago. I think the student was using it to illustrate how one should not always trust experts.

means that you haven't been able to convey to Lewis your real evidence for the view. Since you couldn't adequately convey your evidence, it's understandable that Lewis isn't convinced and indeed may not even realize that you have extremely good evidence.[211]

Problem: If you have inarticulable evidence for your philosophical view, it seems likely that the other person also has inarticulable evidence for *his* view. Why should you assume that your ineffable evidence for *p* is stronger or less misleading than the other party's ineffable evidence against *p*?

19.3.4. Agent-Centered Evidence

A variation on this theme is suggested by the theory of Phenomenal Conservatism (§5.2). If all our justification derives from appearances, then in one sense, you can only convey your evidence to someone else if you can *induce the same appearances* in that other person. It is not enough to merely inform the person that *you* have an appearance that *p*. Even if they know that you have this appearance, *they* do not, merely in virtue of knowing that, thereby gain any justification to believe that *p*. They only gain some justification for *p* if *they* start to have the appearance that *p*. The purpose of presenting arguments, on this view, is to modify how things seem to the other person. When you succeed in modifying those appearances, the argument convinces them; when you don't, it doesn't.

How does this view explain the epistemic value of testimony? The fact that another person believes that *p* or has an appearance that *p* is *by itself* no reason at all for you to believe that *p*. However, all normal people in fact have certain background knowledge (derived from their own appearances) that, when *combined* with the knowledge that another person has an appearance that *p*, supports *p*. Namely, all normal people have extensive evidence that other people tend to have reliable cognitive faculties (ch. 13).

This explains cases like Restaurant Check and Somebody's Hallucination: You have excellent background evidence that other people are reliable about arithmetic and directly observable physical facts. Thus, when you learn that another person has done a calculation that conflicts with yours, or is having sensory experiences that conflict with yours, that defeats your justification for your own arithmetical or sensory belief.

The difference in cases of disputes about philosophy, politics, and similar controversial topics is that you *don't* have excellent evidence that other people are reliable about *those* topics. Indeed, quite a lot of evidence points to the

---

[211] This is something like what van Inwagen said of his dispute with Lewis.

opposite. So when you hear about another person's conflicting philosophical, etc., views, that fails to defeat your own view.[212]

19.3.5. *The Importance of Self-Trust*

There is an asymmetry between self-trust and trust in others.[213] Self-trust is *fundamental:* You have to start out with an attitude of trust in your own cognitive faculties. If you don't have that, then obviously you're not going to get anywhere (recall §6.2). You couldn't use an argument to establish your own reliability, because that argument would rely on your own faculty of reason and thus be circular. The same isn't true of your trust in other people. Other people's faculties are not among your faculties and thus, from *your* point of view, they need to be vindicated with evidence of reliability. Other people are just like any external measuring device that purports to indicate some feature of the world beyond itself: You should use the device if and only if it has proven reliable in the past.

Again, in *some* areas other people have, from your point of view, proved reliable, but in others they may have proved unreliable. That explains how in some areas it can be rational to stick to your guns in the face of disagreement. The other parties can also be rational in sticking to *their* guns since *they* also lack adequate evidence to show that *you* are reliable about the disputed topics.

19.3.6. *The Common Humanity Objection*

It's pretty tenuous to draw a sharp disanalogy between judgments about controversial topics and all other judgments in the manner just suggested (§§19.3.4–19.3.5). Granted, at first glance, it might seem reasonable to hold that other people are reliable in their perception, calculation, etc., but unreliable in their philosophical (and political, religious, etc.) judgments. But surely one can't just stop there. One should reflect on why other people seem to be so unreliable about certain topics.

Maybe it is because, say, they have certain biases derived from their emotions and desires (see ch. 17). These emotions and desires might come from evolution, from their culture, and from personal experiences, all of which are insensitive to the objective truth about the philosophical issues. That is a plausible (if vague) story about how people get to be unreliable about certain topics.

But now, *you're* a human being too. Might you have some emotions and desires that also influence your beliefs in ways that are insensitive to the actual

---

[212] For discussion, see my "Epistemological Egoism and Agent-Centered Norms" in *Evidentialism and its Discontents* (2011).
[213] For discussion, see Richard Foley's *Intellectual Trust in Oneself and Others* (2001).

truth of the believed propositions? In light of everything that a mature human being knows, it is extra-crazy implausible to hold that you're the only one who doesn't have emotional or conative biases, or that you're the only one who luckily almost always gets the truth in spite of those biases. That is to say, once you realize how widespread bias is among human beings with regard to certain topics, that acts as a *defeater* for your beliefs about those topics.

Furthermore, the general conclusion doesn't depend on that specific account of why other people are unreliable. *Any* plausible account of what makes the vast majority of human beings unreliable about philosophy is going to cite factors that also apply to *you*. That is to say, it's super-implausible to hold that you are special in being much more reliable about those topics than all or nearly all other human beings who ever lived. For example, say you claim that people are unreliable about philosophy because they haven't acquired enough data to resolve most philosophical questions. Well, it's super-implausible to claim that you have more philosophically relevant data than all or nearly all human beings who ever lived. So you should be unreliable in the same way as other human beings.

Why did I say "all or nearly all human beings who ever lived"? Well, I assume that partisans of the Steadfast View would hold onto some of their philosophical convictions in the face of disagreement with any human being, or nearly any human being, in history. E.g., if you learn that Aristotle (possibly the greatest philosopher ever) disagreed with your current view about free will, and you hold the Steadfast View of peer disagreement, you probably wouldn't renounce your view of free will. Nor would you defer to whomever you consider the smartest contemporary philosopher who also has expertise in the subject. Maybe you'd defer to *some* people about *some* topics (especially topics you haven't studied well). But I take it that for Steadfast people, there are at least *some* philosophical topics on which they would not conciliate with anyone. This appears to be the attitude of most philosophers about their core views in their area of specialization. This requires placing more trust in your own judgment about those topics than in that of anyone else in history. It's hard to see how any reflections on agent-centered evidence, or the fundamentality of self-trust, or whatever, can make it rational to view yourself as *the most reliable person in the history of the world* with respect to certain philosophical questions.

A possible reply: "No, I'm almost certainly not the most reliable person in the history of the world. But I'm more reliable than the great majority of other people, and I don't know who the more reliable people are. One can know that there are almost certainly *some* people who are more reliable without being able to identify any specific such person. Hence, when confronted with disagreement from a specific person, it can be rational to refuse to defer to that individual."

The above seems like something that some smart people could reasonably believe. Bear in mind that reliability about (e.g.) philosophical questions is not simply a matter of IQ and information. (If it were, we could resolve philosophical disputes a lot more easily.) To be good at correctly answering philosophical questions, one must not only be smart and informed but also possess *good judgment*. Many people who are very smart (in the sense that they could correctly answer a lot of questions on an IQ test) also possess terrible judgment. This could be revealed in practical contexts (e.g., they would invest a lot of money in doomed business ventures) or purely intellectual contexts (e.g., they would endorse absurdly skeptical philosophical theories). Unfortunately, diagnosing "good judgment" is extremely difficult and itself requires good judgment; there is no algorithmic test for it. So you can see how it might be difficult for an individual to know who really possesses better judgment than oneself in philosophical matters.

19.4. The Case for Right Reasons

19.4.1. *The Right Reasons View*

According to the Right Reasons View, the proper response to a disagreement is determined by the objectively correct assessment of the first-order evidence.[214] If the two parties have different first-order evidence, then they should share their evidence with each other. In most cases of interest, this can be done (bracketing the issue of ineffable evidence). If they still disagree after this, then at least one of them is incorrectly evaluating that evidence. That person should change her mind. In the event that *both* are incorrectly evaluating the evidence, both should change their minds (in the latter case, both might need to suspend judgment or switch to some third view that neither of them initially held). The person, if any, who correctly assessed the first-order evidence should stick to that assessment.

And by the way, this view is *not* assuming that we can easily tell who is incorrectly evaluating the evidence! Some people have difficulty grasping this point. Each person might of course *think*, and it might *seem* to them, that the other is incorrectly evaluating the evidence, and there is no algorithm for answering who is really correct. But that's not an objection to the Right Reasons View. The difficulty of telling who is making a mistake does not prevent it from being true *in fact* that one of them is making a mistake. So the view is that that person, whoever it is, ought to change her position, even though she does not know this.

---

[214] See Michael Titelbaum's "Rationality's Fixed Point (or: In Defense of Right Reason)" in *Oxford Studies in Epistemology* (2015).

(Aside: The reason some people have difficulty grasping this is that they assume an internalist conception of epistemic norms (see §3.3) with some strong access requirement. I.e., they assume that what an individual "should" or "should not" believe may only depend on conditions that the individual is aware of or can easily become aware of, or something like that. The facts about who is actually correctly evaluating the evidence are outside the awareness at least of the person who is incorrectly evaluating it. This is not to say that they are in principle inaccessible, though. They are merely difficult, perhaps extremely difficult, for that person to access.)

19.4.2. Is the Right Reasons View Analytic?

Why would someone hold the Right Reasons View? One reason is that the view appears to be tautological (given the assumption that *there is* a single correct evaluation of the evidence). By definition, you should reason correctly and not incorrectly. So if you arrived at your current view by making some error in reasoning (including an error of overall judgment), then you have an unjustified view that you ought to give up. That's why the Steadfast View is wrong. The Equal Weight View is wrong because the person (if any) who *didn't* make any mistakes doesn't have anything to correct and thus doesn't need to give up his view.

But why think that there is a unique correct evaluation of the total evidence? What if there are two interpretations of the evidence that are equally reasonable? (Cf. the underdetermination problem, §14.4.1.) Well, if there really are two equally reasonable, incompatible interpretations of the evidence, then it is irrational to believe either of them, knowing that the other one is equally good. What you should do is assign equal credence to each of them.

Note that this is not the Equal Weight View, because the Equal Weight View holds that it is *the other person's opinion* that gives you reason to change your own view. The Right Reasons View would say, in the case of two equally good interpretations of some evidence, that you have to assign equal credence to both *regardless* of what anyone else thinks, and hence, regardless of whether anyone actually endorses either of the interpretations.

19.4.3. Examples

The Right Reasons View is also supported by examples such as this:

> *Flat Earth:* You meet a Flat Earther, who maintains that the Earth is flat. (There are actually people like this!) You disagree, claiming that the Earth is round. The two of you have a long exchange during which you explain all the evidence you know of that supports a round Earth, while the Flat Earther explains all of her evidence for a flat Earth. When confronted with

> arguments for the other side, each of you comes up with responses that seem convincing to you but not to the other person. Your sense is that the Flat Earther is resorting to implausible rationalizations to dogmatically cling to her absurd belief. She thinks the same about you.

Anyone who has talked to human beings about controversial issues has had experiences like the above, though perhaps not with beliefs as crazy as the Flat Earth theory. The situation where the other person is making up ridiculous rationalizations so they can dogmatically cling to their absurd assumptions happens all the time.

In this case, how should you react to the disagreement? Assume the Flat Earther is, as far as you know, of comparable intelligence to yourself (e.g., she scored the same as you on an IQ test), and, after talking with each other, the two of you now appear to have all the same evidence available. You have no reason for regarding her as unreliable about questions regarding the shape of the Earth, *other than* the fact that she erroneously thinks it is flat. (Note: All this is in fact realistic.) Should you therefore split the difference, and adopt about a 50% credence that the Earth is flat?

Surely not. You know the Earth is round, whether or not you can convince the Flat Earther. (In this example, I assume, obviously, that the evidence for a round Earth is decisive, as in fact it is.) The Flat Earther is incorrectly evaluating the evidence for some reason. Whatever the reason, it is the Flat Earther who needs to stop being irrational and accept that the Earth is round.

If you buy that example, then it's hard to see why a similar principle wouldn't apply to disagreements about things that are less certain. Granted, the correct answer to the free will issue in metaphysics is more difficult to discern than the correct answer to the shape of the Earth. But there is still going to be something that is the best overall evaluation of the evidence, and there are going to be some people who are in fact mistakenly assessing that evidence.

19.4.4. *The Restaurant Check Objection*

Despite what I've just said above, the Right Reasons View does not seem so good when applied to other cases, such as the Restaurant Check case from §19.2.2. When you and Plado disagree about the correct division of the restaurant check, at least one of you has made an objective mathematical error. Yet it is surely wrong to say that that person, whoever it was, would be rational to immediately drop his belief and accept the other person's calculation as correct; nor would it be rational for the person who *didn't* in fact make the error to just hold on to his answer and ignore the fact that the other person got a different answer. Rather, both parties, if rational, would move to about a 50% credence in each answer.

Let's say that you, Plado, and the other philosophers all repeat the calculation. This time, everybody comes up with $45. So now you know that it was you who made the mistake. Nevertheless, everyone at the table, looking back, will agree that it *was* reasonable for you and Plado to each be about 50% confident in the $45 answer and about 50% confident in the $43 answer, before the re-calculation was done. No one will say that you were being irrational to think there was a good chance that your answer was correct. So the Right Reasons View seems wrong.

19.5. The Case for Total Evidence

19.5.1. The Total Evidence View

According to the Total Evidence View, in a case of peer disagreement, you should believe whatever is best supported by your total evidence.[215] Wait; that's trivial. All views agree that you should believe what your total evidence supports; they just disagree about what exactly that is. So let's add some more to the view to make it interesting.

The Total Evidence View (let's stipulate) also holds that the correct response to peer disagreement depends on a *weighing of both first- and second-order evidence*. Again, the first-order evidence is the evidence directly about the issue that is under controversy. For instance, if the issue is free will, first-order evidence could include evidence from brain science about the causes of decisions, evidence from physics about the truth of determinism, and philosophical intuitions about how freedom is presupposed in rational deliberation. The second-order evidence, on the other hand, is evidence about the reliability of the two parties to the dispute (not including the first-order evidence just mentioned)—for instance, evidence about the IQ of each party, how much reading each person has done on the issue of free will, how much time each has spent thinking about the issue, and any biases either party might have. On the Total Evidence View, you have to weigh up both of these kinds of evidence, in order to decide whether and how much you should adjust your own view in light of a peer disagreement.

This disagrees with the Equal Weight View, which would have us focus on second-order evidence only. Of course, you use first-order evidence in forming your initial view, but then, in deciding how to *adjust* it in the light of the disagreement, on the Equal Weight View, you are supposed to only look at the evidence regarding your and the other person's reliability. In assessing the other

---

[215] See Thomas Kelly's "Disagreement and the Burdens of Judgment" in *The Epistemology of Disagreement* (2013).

person's reliability, you are not supposed to use your evaluation of the first-order evidence about the issue in dispute.

The Total Evidence View also disagrees with the Right Reasons View, which would have us focus solely on *first*-order evidence. On the Right Reasons View, you should simply correctly evaluate the evidence directly about the issue in dispute. If you do that, you then don't have to adjust your view in the light of second-order evidence at all.

A strong version of the Steadfast View, wherein you *always* stick to your own view in light of peer disagreement, would also counsel ignoring second-order evidence. (I doubt if anyone holds such a strong position, though.)

19.5.2. Accommodating the Examples

Before elaborating the Total Evidence View further, let's look at the biggest motivation for the view. The view does better than any of the preceding theories at accounting for the examples we've been discussing. This is simply because the Total Evidence View doesn't give a blanket answer wherein you *always* trust your assessment of the first-order evidence or *always* defer to the second-order evidence; it enables you to respond differently in different cases. It's implicit in the notion of *weighing* that sometimes you'll find the first-order evidence to be more important, but other times you'll find the second-order evidence more important. Thus, we can make sense of conciliating (giving significant credence to the other party's belief) in the cases of the Restaurant Check and Somebody's Hallucination, yet also refusing to budge in the Flat Earth and Brillo Pad cases. We just have to say that the weighing comes out differently in those cases.

19.5.3. Weighing Evidence, Part 1: Downgrading Reliability

Let's fill in more about how one weighs first- and second-order evidence so as to get the intuitively right results in the above-mentioned cases, namely, Restaurant Check, Somebody's Hallucination, Flat Earth, and Brillo Pads.

In a case of peer disagreement, by definition, the other party initially appears about as reliable as you (within the relevant area). So if the two of you were to make judgments about 1,000 questions in that area, you and she would be right about equally often. That means that, among the cases in which you would disagree with each other, you would be wrong about equally often as the other person would be wrong. Knowing this, in any particular case of disagreement, you must on average consider it equally likely that you are wrong as that the other person is wrong. That's just a requirement for you to be probabilistically coherent. (You can't, e.g., think in each case that you're 80%

likely to be right, but also think that overall, you're only right 50% of the time.) This is another way of phrasing the basis for the Equal Weight View.

That reasoning is more or less correct. But there are two important caveats. The first caveat is that the reasoning assumes that hearing the other person's answers to particular questions does not itself change your estimation of that person's reliability. But sometimes, it *should*. That's what happens in Brillo Pads and Flat Earth. If a doctor tells you that eating Brillo pads and jumping up and down is a good idea, that is surely evidence that she is not a good doctor. You don't need to be a doctor yourself to know that. Likewise, if someone tells you that the Earth is flat, that is pretty solid evidence of the person's being kooky (and hence unreliable about certain kinds of questions). Since you drastically downgrade the other party's reliability upon hearing her view, there is no inconsistency in your refusing to conciliate with her position.

Why isn't this an objectionable form of question-begging? Whether (e.g.) the Earth is flat is precisely the point in dispute between you and the flat Earther, so why isn't it circular to claim that the other person is unreliable due to having the wrong view about the flat Earth theory?

Well, it would be question-begging if you presented this as an *argument addressed to the Flat Earther*. You could not expect to *persuade her* by telling her that your judgment is obviously more reliable than hers because she holds the kooky Flat Earth theory. But that is really irrelevant, because the question we were trying to answer was not "How can we persuade the other person?" The question of interest was "What should *you* think about the disagreement, given all the information available to you?" To that question, it doesn't matter that the point about the insanity of the Flat Earth theory couldn't persuade *the Flat Earther*. It's enough that the Flat Earth theory is one that *you* initially assign extremely low credence in, such that, given your existing belief system, anyone who holds that belief is likely to be a bit crazy.

And of course, there need not be (and usually is not) any circularity in how you arrived at your beliefs about the shape of the Earth—they were based on compelling first-order evidence (e.g., pictures of the Earth taken from space, the possibility of flying around the world in airplanes, the possibility of seeing ships at sea disappear over the horizon, etc.) If that evidence is very compelling, then when you encounter someone who disagrees with the Round Earth Theory, the most reasonable thing for you to think is that that individual is a nut. That is a much simpler explanation than that all that other stuff you seem to know about the Earth is somehow wrong.

Now, why can't you reason similarly in all other cases, in order to dogmatically dismiss anyone who disagrees with you about anything? Briefly, because in most cases, the other person's disagreement simply is not significant evidence of their unreliability. In the Restaurant Check case, either you or

Plado is wrong about the correct division of the check. But whoever is wrong in this case, that should not make any significant difference to your estimate of that person's reliability at arithmetic. Everyone already knows that everyone sometimes makes arithmetical mistakes, and this case is just the sort of case in which a person of normal mathematical ability might well make an error. Notice that things would be different if Plado suddenly declared that 2+2 is 5. *Then* you would have serious reason to question his mathematical competence. But you have no reason to question his mathematical competence based on his possibly having made an error in dividing this particular restaurant check. So your general estimate of Plado's reliability as being about equal to your own stands, and thus, you should regard him to be about equally likely to be right about the correct shares of the restaurant check.

The case of Somebody's Hallucination is a little more complex. There are three cases to consider:

i. Assume that, like most people, you have never (to your knowledge) hallucinated anything in your life. You are now just meeting Plado for the first time and have no prior knowledge about his perceptual reliability. You find him not seeing something in plain view that you see. In this case, I think you should believe that Plado is probably hallucinating (or whatever you call it when someone fails to see what is there in plain view). Perhaps Plado has a mental disorder, or has some serious optical defect, or is a user of psychoactive drugs.

ii. You have never had a hallucination, but also, you know Plado well and have never known him to have anything other than normal perception, just like you and everyone else. In this case, whichever one of you is hallucinating, this hallucination is an extremely unusual event in that person's life, and thus it does not indicate that either of you is much less reliable about perceptual matters than previously thought. So there is no basis for concluding that Plado is unreliable, so there is no good reason to dismiss his perceptual evidence in this case, and so you must withhold judgment about whether Arisdodle is really in the quad.

iii. You know that you periodically have hallucinations, but Plado, as far as you know, is perfectly normal. In this case, you should conclude that you are probably hallucinating, and you should defer to Plado's perception.

19.5.4. Weighing Evidence, Part 2: Varying Confidence

The second caveat about the argument for the Equal Weight View (as described in §19.5.3) is this: The argument establishes only that, if person A is equally reliable as you in general, then *on average*, in any case of disagreement, A's probability of being correct is equal to yours. However, one cannot infer *in any particular case* that *A*'s probability of being correct is equal to yours. There could be some cases in which you are more likely to be correct, and others in which *A* is more likely to be correct, such that the likelihood of being correct averages out the same overall.

This matters if there are particular cases in which you think you are especially likely to be correct. (Which of course means that there are other cases in which you are especially likely to be incorrect.) This is part of what is going on in Brillo Pads and Flat Earth. In most cases in which you disagree with a doctor about a medical treatment, you would be wrong, as you should recognize (if you're not a doctor). However, in the particular case where you are disagreeing with a doctor's opinion that eating Brillo pads is an appropriate treatment for a stomach ache, there you are unusually likely to be right. That's because this is a particularly obvious judgment, which does not seem to require a lot of expertise to make (according to your current belief system, if you're a normal person). So it's perfectly coherent to stick to your guns in the Brillo pad disagreement, despite thinking that doctors are usually more reliable than you.

The same applies to the Flat Earth disagreement. Perhaps the Flat Earther would be right more often than you about some other questions. But on the question of the shape of the Earth, it makes sense to be unusually confident that you are right, since the evidence in this case seems particularly compelling, compared to other things that people disagree about.

Again, it's reasonable to think that you are more reliable than the Flat Earther *in general* (per §19.5.3), but now I'm making the additional point that, among things that you would disagree with the Flat Earther about, this is one where it makes sense to be particularly confident that you're correct.

19.5.5. Identifying Peers

Lastly, I want to reiterate a point from §19.3.6. Identifying epistemic peers is not as straightforward as is sometimes assumed. *Some* of the requirements are reasonably easy to assess, such that we can expect general agreement that two people satisfy them. For instance, if David Lewis and Peter van Inwagen are about equally intelligent, in the sense that they'd score comparably on an IQ test, this is relatively straightforward to know. Thus, I expect that most observers, including Lewis and van Inwagen themselves, would agree on it. Similarly, most observers, including Lewis and van Inwagen, could agree that Lewis and van Inwagen are about equally well-informed about the free will issue.

But part of what goes into being reliable about philosophical questions is the much vaguer condition of "having good judgment". This is proficiency at making correct judgments, in the sense discussed in §7.4. This is probably positively correlated with, but not the same thing as, and not *perfectly* correlated with, proficiency in noticing and calculation (again, see §7.4). Thus, it is not terribly unusual for someone to be much better, say, at calculation than at judgment. This is difficult to decisively verify, and thus it is understandable for two people to disagree about who has better judgment. IQ tests, by the way, generally include a lot of tests of calculation, memory, and similarly straightforward cognitive skills; they do not typically include questions to assess one's judgment.

Furthermore, to some extent one's assessment of the quality of a philosopher's judgment will be intertwined with one's substantive philosophical views. E.g., I find Thomas Reid's philosophical judgment more reliable than David Hume's, in part because my own epistemological views are much closer to Reid's than to Hume's.[216]

You might wonder: Is there something objectionably circular about refusing to defer to Hume on the grounds that Hume has poor judgment, while finding Hume's judgment flawed on the grounds that he is wrong about many philosophical issues? As in the case of the Flat Earth dispute, the answer is no. If I were trying to *convince a Humean*, I of course could not appeal to Hume's poor judgment. But that is not the question; the question is what is reasonable for *me* to believe. From my point of view, given all of my philosophical beliefs and intuitions before I start reading Hume, the simplest and most reasonable conclusion to draw once I learn of Hume's views is that Hume has terrible judgment.

Again, David Hume or one of his followers *might* think that Hume has great judgment and that *I* have terrible judgment.[217] Should this give me pause? Not really. It would of course force me to revise my views *if* I started out with the assumption that Hume and his followers were epistemic peers. But I don't start out assuming that; they have to prove themselves reliable in order for *me* to have reason to credit their testimony (see ch. 13, §19.3.5). From my point of view, Humeans are unreliable about philosophy, so their judgment that they *are* reliable is not to be relied upon.

---

[216] I switched the example away from van Inwagen/Lewis to Reid/Hume because I realized that I don't consider *either* Lewis or van Inwagen to have good judgment. Lewis believes in an infinity of parallel universes wherein anything that's logically possible happens (see his *On the Plurality of Worlds*), while van Inwagen thinks that rocks don't exist (see his *Material Beings*).

[217] I say they *might* think this, but I actually doubt it. More likely, they would claim not to know what I meant by "good judgment" and to be skeptical that such a thing exists. Which would reinforce my view that they lack it.

That being said, there are more difficult cases in which we disagree with others who appear to have equally good judgment as ourselves—these will generally be people who agree with us about most philosophical matters, but may disagree about a few things here and there. In these cases, it is plausible that you really should withhold judgment about the matter in controversy.

19.6. Why Is There So Much Disagreement Anyway?

19.6.1. The Disagreement Puzzle

The phenomenon of expert disagreement is super-puzzling. It's not weird that uninformed people often disagree with experts, or that uninformed people disagree with each other. But it is very weird that experts who are equally qualified often strongly disagree with each other while seemingly having access to the same evidence and arguments. Thus far, we've focused on how one should respond to this situation. But an equally interesting question is how this situation could possibly have come about in the first place. I don't mean "Why don't the experts split the difference, as per the Equal Weight View?" What I mean to ask is: "Why is there a difference to split in the first place?"

In chapter 17, I gave an explanation for why disagreement is pervasive with political issues (and, to a lesser extent, philosophical and religious issues). The explanation basically appeals to motivated reasoning: People have other goals that they're trying to serve with their political beliefs besides truth.

But disagreement is also very common in non-political philosophical matters, and the theory of rational irrationality is less satisfying here, though maybe it still plays some role. One reason why it is less satisfying is that people are usually less emotional about abstract (non-political) philosophical issues than they are about politics. Most of these abstract issues are also further removed from our interests than political issues are. (Consider, e.g., the epistemological internalism/externalism debate, or the empiricism/rationalism debate.) Thus, we should expect far less influence of bias on abstract, non-political philosophical thinking than on ordinary political thinking. And indeed, if you see two expert philosophers discussing a non-political, philosophical issue, you will usually be hard pressed to detect any emotional or other non-truth-seeking biases. As far as one can tell, the philosophers are both trying to understand the truth, and they simply see the issue differently. At least, that's how it (usually) looks to me.

19.6.2. Gestalt Perceptions

So here is a different explanation of what is going on in at least some philosophical disputes. I start with an analogy. Recall the duck-rabbit image from §7.3.2 (fig. 10):

Figure 10: The duck-rabbit again

You either see it as a duck *or* see it as a rabbit at any given time. When you see it as a duck, that is a matter of your brain automatically interpreting all the various lines on the page as fitting together in a certain way, under a certain general schema so to speak. You aren't aware of the processing leading to this; what you're aware of is just the overall "conclusion": The image just strikes you as a duck. This kind of perception, wherein you see the overall pattern rather than a set of individual details, is sometimes called "**gestalt perception**", and it was the focus of an influential school of 20th-century cognitive psychology, Gestalt psychology.

Now, in this particular case, most people can see both aspects of the image. Most can even switch between the two gestalt perceptions at will. But this need not always be the case. If no one points it out to you, or if you don't have a concept of a rabbit to begin with, you might be unaware of the "rabbit interpretation" of the image. There are some other ambiguous images in which people often have trouble seeing one or the other interpretation.

I think there is something similar to this in the realm of *intellectual* perception. In ordinary (sensory) perception, your brain automatically, non-consciously fits together many sensory details (bits of color, shapes) into an overall interpretation. So also, in intellectual perception, your brain fits together many bits of evidence into an overall interpretation. You aren't aware of this process; what you're aware of is just the output: A certain abstract, philosophical idea just strikes you as true. In your intellectual perception, various details all fit together in a way consistent with that idea. You may initially be unaware of any alternative interpretations. But in fact, for most philosophical issues, there are other possible gestalts; there are other ways of fitting everything together consistent with some overall philosophical theory.

Typically, you are unaware of these alternative interpretations at first. Then someone tells you about the alternative philosophical views. But they just strike you as false, perhaps even as nonsensical, like someone suggesting that something you can clearly see as a beak is instead an ear. Even after you encounter other philosophers who see one of the alternative interpretations, you may be unable to *see* those interpretations yourself. Imagine someone who can only see the duck aspect of the duck-rabbit image. Someone tells him that it can also be seen as a rabbit, and perhaps he even *believes* that this is true, but he just can't *see* the rabbit in that image. That is how it often is with philosophical disagreements.

19.6.3. Finding the Right Gestalt

The above might seem to suggest a relativistic view of philosophy—maybe there are just many different ways of viewing things that are all equally valid. But if you know me at all, you know that I hate relativism. Yes, there are many ways of viewing things, but there is only one way that *things in fact are*. If the duck-rabbit were a real object, it could not *be* both a duck and a rabbit; it must be one or the other (or neither), regardless of how we can or can't *perceive* it.

One thing that we do with philosophical discussion is to try to enable others to see the way we see things. But we often fail, in part because we do not ourselves even know all of why we see things the way we do—again, much of the brain's processing is non-conscious. So philosophy requires a certain amount of skill at cognitive introspection.

Enabling everyone to see the way everyone else sees things is the first step to figuring out the truth. Often, it's hard enough to even make that step. But there is more we need to do: We need to figure out which perception is an illusion. Metaphorically speaking, we need to examine the duck-rabbit more closely, searching for details that don't fit with the object's duckhood, or don't fit with its rabbithood. Perhaps we'd find, say, that the texture of the "duck bill" is too similar to the texture of the rest of the object and so doesn't fit with that of a normal duck bill; thus, the "rabbit" interpretation is better.

So that's the other thing we try to do in philosophical discussion. We try to draw each other's attention to details that might have been overlooked in forming a particular gestalt and that don't fit well with that overall picture. Of course, these details are not as concrete as the lines in the duck-rabbit image or the colors and shapes of a real, visible object. They are instead things that we intuit (or that *some* of us intuit); thus, they are themselves often open to dispute. It is as though we were arguing over whether we had a duck or a rabbit picture, and some people were seeing some of the lines in different places on the page, and furthermore, your overall perception of the image as a duck or a rabbit could sometimes *alter* your perception of the lines on the page. That would make the debate pretty annoying and extremely hard to resolve. That's like philosophical debate.

19.7. Conclusion

Peer disagreement is the phenomenon wherein people who are equally well qualified to address a question arrive at incompatible answers. This is especially common in philosophy. Philosophers wonder how one rationally ought to respond to such disagreement. We discussed four views:

i. The Equal Weight View says that when an epistemic peer disagrees with you about an issue, you should attach equal weight to her opinion and thus withhold judgment about the issue henceforth. You're also not allowed to use your opinion about the issue to justify denying that the other party is reliable about that issue.

   This view is motivated by the general idea that you should attach equal weight to equally reliable information sources. The view works well in cases like Restaurant Check, wherein two people get different answers to an arithmetic problem. However, the view has trouble accounting for cases such as Flat Earth, in which someone whom you thought was an epistemic peer declares that they think the Earth is flat. The view also runs into a self-defeat problem wherein its defenders are forced to give up their view in light of the experts who disagree with the Equal Weight View itself.

ii. The Steadfast View holds that it is rational to stick to your own assessment in the face of peer disagreement, provided that you have done your best to take into account the other person's reasons and that after doing so, your initial assessment still seems correct in light of all the reasons available to you. This might be justified because you have private evidence (such as your own appearances, or your own grasp of the concepts involved) that the other person lacks and that you can't adequately convey to them. You might also have a standing entitlement to trust your own cognitive faculties by default, but no such entitlement to trust other people.

   This view can be challenged by pointing to the likelihood that other parties also have private evidence for their own views, and the implausibility of holding that one's own private evidence is better and less misleading than anyone else's, including the leading other experts in the field.

iii. The Right Reasons View holds that whoever *in fact* correctly assessed the first-order evidence to begin with should keep their view, and the person who made a mistake should change theirs. One could argue that this is analytic.

   This view, however, has trouble accounting for the Restaurant Check case, in which it really seems that both parties should withhold judgment, pending a recalculation to determine who made the error.

iv. The Total Evidence View holds that the right response to a peer disagreement is determined by a weighing of both first- and second-order evidence. In some cases, such as Flat Earth, one may use one's assessment of the first-order evidence to justify concluding that the other party is unreliable (especially if they are saying something crazy on its face). In other cases, such as the Restaurant Check, no such inference is warranted, and thus one should rest with the conclusion that the other party is equally likely to be right. It is also permissible in some cases, if one finds the first-order evidence particularly compelling, to conclude that the other party is probably wrong *about this specific case*, even without downgrading one's assessment of their reliability in that field.

In philosophy, one way in which an expert might be less reliable than another is through possessing generally worse judgment, despite having a comparable IQ and comparable knowledge of the subject. It's okay to use your first-order philosophical beliefs in assessing someone else's judgment and thus, perhaps, downgrading one's estimate of their reliability.

Of the four views discussed, I find the Total Evidence View, as elaborated above, most satisfactory. A remaining puzzle that we should all ponder is why there is so much peer disagreement in philosophy in the first place. This appears to be not mainly due (as in politics) to emotional biases, but rather to a kind of gestalt perception in the intellectual realm, wherein one's brain fits together all the information one is aware of into an overall pattern fitting some coherent philosophy. Similar to the duck-rabbit image, it may be possible to parse the same pattern of information in different ways, and thus different people may intellectually "see" different philosophical views as true.

The best known approach to these differences is for the parties to patiently explain how they see things in an effort to enable others to perceive the same things, and then for each to scrutinize the different world pictures to find ways in which one philosophy fits the pattern of facts and intuitions available to us better or worse than another.

Afterword

This concludes my introduction to epistemology. I hope you enjoyed some of it, that you gained a better understanding of knowledge and rational belief, and that you have not become a crazed skeptic or anything like that. If you liked this book, consider looking up my other books, including:

Knowledge, Reality, and Value (2021)
> A general introduction to philosophy, including major issues in epistemology, metaphysics, and ethics, such as philosophical skepticism, free will, the existence of God, the nature of morality, etc.

Skepticism and the Veil of Perception (2001)
> A defense of a direct realist account of perception, with responses to four arguments for external-world skepticism.

Ethical Intuitionism (2005)
> A defense of ethical intuitionism. Argues that there are objective values, that they are irreducible, that they are known through rational intuition, and that they provide reasons for action independent of desires.

The Problem of Political Authority (2013)
> Argues that no state has genuine authority. Explains how a non-governmental social order could work.

Approaching Infinity (2016)
> Defends a novel theory of infinity that helps resolve seventeen paradoxes.

Paradox Lost (2018)
> Explains and resolves ten other paradoxes, including the Liar Paradox, the Sorites Paradox, Newcomb's Problem, etc.

Dialogues on Ethical Vegetarianism (2019)
> A philosophical dialogue between a vegetarian and a meat eater about the ethics of our food choices. Highlights the reasons for being vegetarian.

Justice Before the Law (2021)
> Identifies several serious, systematic injustices in the U.S. legal system. Argues that agents in the system have a moral duty to place justice ahead of the law.

Is Political Authority an Illusion? A Debate. (2022; co-authored with Daniel Layman)

A debate about whether any state has genuine authority. I argue no; Layman argues yes.

Can We Know Anything? A Debate. (Forthcoming; co-authored with Bryan Frances)

A debate about external world skepticism and also partly about skepticism about controversial beliefs. I defend knowledge; Frances is skeptical.

Consider also checking out my blog (fakenous.substack.com) and my website (owl232.net).

Glossary

Here are definitions of all the important vocabulary words that appear in boldface throughout the text. In parentheses, I include the section of the book where they were introduced.

A priori knowledge: Knowledge whose justification does not depend on observations. (§7.1.2) Contrasted with empirical knowledge.
Access internalism: The view that knowledge requires justification, and justification is entirely determined by factors that one can be introspectively aware of. (§3.3.1)
Adaptation: A feature of an organism that has a genetic basis and that exists because it promoted inclusive fitness in the organism's evolutionary ancestors. (§15.8.1)
Adjustable parameters: In a theory: Quantities whose hypothesized values can be adjusted (without giving up the basic theory) to accommodate the available data. (§14.3.3)
Aesthetic evaluation: The evaluation of things in terms of their beauty, artistic merit, or other aesthetic qualities. (§15.1.2) Contrasted with epistemic and practical (including moral) evaluation.
Agrippa's Trilemma: The trilemma among three possible structures for a series of reasons: It must stretch back infinitely, or go in a circle, or end in something that one has no reason for. Used by the ancient philosopher Agrippa to argue for global skepticism. (§4.1)
Analytic philosophy: A style of philosophy that arose in English-speaking countries in the 20th century, emphasizing clarity of logical argumentation. (§2.1) Contrasted with continental philosophy.
Analytic: Of a sentence: True by definition; the negation of an analytic sentence is a contradiction. (§10.1.2) Contrasted with synthetic statements.
Antecedent: The first clause in a conditional; in [If A then B], the antecedent is A. (§1.3.2)
Appearance: The mental state one is in when it seems to one that something is the case. Also called a "seeming". (§5.2.1)

Argument from cynicism: A fallacious tendency to accept certain kinds of theory due to the pleasure one derives from being cynical. (§16.4.2)
Argument: A series of statements in which one is supposed to be supported by the others. (§1.3.3)
Attraction/aversion heuristic: A method of making judgments that relies on one's feelings of attraction or aversion to something to judge how good, bad, right or wrong the thing is. (§15.6.5)
Attributor factors: In the theory of contextualism: Features of a speaker's situation that might affect whether the speaker is correct to say that S "knows" something, e.g., how important it is to the speaker that S be right, what alternative possibilities have been mentioned in the conversation, etc. (§3.1.2) Contrasted with subject factors.
Awareness: A mental state that non-accidentally roughly-correctly represents something. (§9.2.1)

Basing condition: The principle that a belief counts as knowledge only if the belief is based on the factors that provide justification for it. (§9.4.4)
Bayes' Theorem: The theorem that, for any h and e, $P(h|e) = P(h) \times P(e|h) / P(e)$. (§12.3.2)
Bayesian account of confirmation: The view that e confirms h if and only if $P(h|e) > P(h)$. (§14.1.4)
Bayesianism: An approach to epistemology that seeks to explain all cogent non-deductive reasoning in terms of the principles of probability theory, especially Bayes' Theorem. (§12.5.1)
Beg the question: To give a circular argument. (§1.3.3)
BIV: Abbreviation for "brain in a vat". (§2.5.4)
Bleen: The property of being blue if observed before 2100 A.D. and green otherwise. (§12.8.1)
Brain in a vat: A brain that is being kept alive in a vat of nutrients and artificially fed electrical stimulation to simulate life in the real world. The brain-in-a-vat hypothesis is the hypothesis that you are a brain in a vat. (§2.5.4)
Burden of proof principle: The thesis that those who make positive claims have the burden of providing evidence, and that there is a presumption in favor of negative claims. (§14.3.1)

Calibrated: Said of a set of credences wherein, when one has a credence of about $x\%$ in a proposition, that proposition tends to be true about $x\%$ of the time. (§18.4)

Categorical imperative: A proposition stating that some action is right or wrong independent of one's goals or desires; an obligation that one must follow regardless of what one wants. (§15.1.2)

Causal theory of reference: The view that one can only have an intentional state referring to x if one has had some causal interaction with x, or with things in terms of which x could be described. (§8.3.3)

Certainty skepticism: A form of skepticism that says we lack knowledge because our beliefs are not absolutely certain. (§8.2.4) Contrasted with justification skepticism.

Circular: Of an argument: Having premises that contain the conclusion or depend for their justification on the conclusion. (§1.3.3)

Classical interpretation of probability: An interpretation according to which the probability of an event is the ratio of the number of possible situations in which the event occurs to the total number of possible situations. (§12.3.3)

Closure principle: (a) Closure for knowledge: The principle that if one knows p, and p entails q, then one is in a position to know q (or something like that). (b) Closure for justification: The principle that if one has justification for p, and p entails q, then one has justification for q (or something like that). (§2.4, n10; §3.2.1)

Cognitive faculties: Faculties by which we acquire (what we usually take to be) knowledge, e.g., sensory observation, memory, reason, introspection, and intuition. (§6.2.1)

Coherence theory of justification: The view that justified beliefs are justified because they are supported by a system of beliefs that fits together well, where this is a matter of the beliefs in the system supporting each other, not contradicting each other, explaining each other, etc. (§4.3.1)

Coherentism: See coherence theory of justification.

Compositionality of meaning: The principle that the meaning of a sentence is determined by the meanings of the component parts and the structure of the sentence. (§10.3.3)

Conceptual scheme: A system for mentally grouping things into categories and distinguishing them from other things. (§2.1)

Conciliatory view: Any view according to which, when epistemic peers disagree, each should significantly adjust his credence in the direction of the other person's credence. (§19.1)

Conclusion: The proposition that an argument is supposed to support. (§1.3.3)

Conditional: A sentence/proposition of the form "If A then B". (§1.3.2)

Conditionalization: A way of updating beliefs upon acquiring new evidence, e, in which, for each proposition h, you set your new credence in h to what was previously your conditional credence in h given e, i.e., you set $P_{new}(h) = P_{old}(h|e)$. (§12.5.3)

Confirm: To provide some support for; to render (a proposition) more likely. (§14.1.1)

Confirmation bias: The common tendency to look only for evidence supporting a theory rather than looking for evidence against it. (§17.4.4)

Confirmation holism: The view (associated with W.V.O. Quine) that a statement cannot be confirmed or disconfirmed in isolation; one can only test a belief system as a whole (or: one can only test a statement *given* a background belief system). (§10.4.1)

Conjunct: One of the clauses in a conjunction; in [*A* & *B*], *A* and *B* are conjuncts. (§1.3.2)

Conjunction: A sentence/proposition of the form "*A* and *B*". (§1.3.2)

Consequent: The last clause in a conditional; in [If *A* then *B*], the consequent is *B*. (§1.3.2)

Content (of a belief): The proposition that one believes. (§1.3.1)

Contextualism: A theory according to which the standards for someone to count as "knowing" a proposition shift depending on the conversational context; i.e., the correctness of knowledge attributions depends not only on subject factors but also on attributor factors. (§3.1.1)

Continental philosophy: A style of philosophy that became popular on the European continent, especially France and Germany, in the 19th-20th centuries. Often less clear and logical than analytic philosophy, with which it is contrasted. (§2.1)

Contingent: Said of a proposition that could have been true and could have been false; that is, it is neither necessary nor impossible. (§8.1)

Control group: In an experiment: The group of things, people, etc., that did not receive the intervention whose effect one is trying to test. (§18.3.1) Contrasted with the experimental group.

Credence: A person's degree of confidence in a proposition; subjective probability. (§12.3.3)

Critical thinking philosophy: The view that one should attempt to think through controversial issues for oneself, rather than trusting experts. (§18.1)

Deduction: A form of reasoning in which the premises are supposed to entail the conclusion, such that the premises could not all be true *and* the conclusion fail to be true. (§12.1.1)

Deductivism: The thesis that only deductive reasoning is cogent; entails inductive skepticism. (§14.4.3)

Defeasibility theory: The theory that knowledge is justified, true belief with no (genuine) defeaters. (§2.5.7)

Defeasible: (a) Of a belief: Having only defeasible justification. (b) Of a (source of) justification: In principle subject to defeaters, i.e., capable of being outweighed or neutralized by further information. (§5.2.1)

Defeater (for a proposition, p): (a) In the defeasibility theory of knowledge: A true proposition that, if added to one's beliefs, would result in one's no longer being justified in believing p. (§2.5.7) (b) A proposition that one believes or has justification for believing that gives one reason to doubt p, where p would otherwise be justified. (§4.5.1) *See also* rebutting defeaters; undercutting defeaters.

Descriptive proposition: A proposition that is not evaluative. (§15.1.1)

Direct realism: The view that perception gives us direct awareness and non-inferential knowledge of the external world. (§8.3.5) Contrasted with indirect realism.

Direct awareness: A state of awareness of something that does not depend upon awareness of anything else. (§9.2.2) Contrasted with indirect awareness.

Disjunct: One of the clauses in a disjunction; in [*A* or *B*], *A* and *B* are disjuncts. (§1.3.2)

Disjunction: A sentence/proposition of the form "*A* or *B*". (§1.3.2)

Disjunctive conception of experience: The view that there is no mental state in common between normal perceptual experiences and hallucinations, hence "sensory experience" is a disjunctive kind. (§9.2.4)

Disjunctive syllogism: A form of argument in which one takes a disjunction as a premise, rejects all but one disjunct, then concludes that the remaining disjunct must be true. (§4.4.1)

Disjunctivism: See disjunctive conception of experience.

Dogmatism: The common tendency to under-adjust one's credences in response to evidence that undermines one's initial beliefs. (§17.4.2)

Doxastic justification: The justification of an actual belief in virtue of its actually being based on something that provides propositional justification. (§2.3.3)

Doxastic voluntarism: The view that we can voluntarily control our beliefs. (§16.1.2)

Empirical knowledge: Knowledge whose justification depends on observations. (§7.1.2) Also called a posteriori knowledge. Contrasted with a priori knowledge.

Empiricism: The view that there is no synthetic, a priori knowledge; the view that all substantive knowledge of the world depends on observation. (§10.2.1) Contrasted with rationalism and Kantianism.

Entrenched: Of a predicate: Frequently used in actual people's inductive reasoning. (§12.8.3)

Epicycle: In Ptolemaic astronomy: A smaller circle that planets were held to be moving in, where the small circle itself moves in the main orbit around the Earth. Often used as a metaphor for ad hoc complications added to a theory. (§14.3.2)

Epistemic circularity: The alleged mistake of using a belief-forming method in coming to the conclusion that that method is good. (§6.3.2)

Epistemic evaluation: The evaluation of beliefs (or similar things) in terms of their epistemic justification. (§15.1.2) Contrasted with practical (including moral) and aesthetic evaluation.

Epistemic evidentialism: The view that the epistemically justified attitude about any proposition at any given time is solely determined by one's evidence. (§16.1.1)

Epistemic peers: People who are about equally well-positioned to evaluate a given issue, in terms, e.g., of their intelligence, relevant knowledge, and time spent thinking about the issue. (§19.1)

Epistemic probability: A type of probability that indicates the degree of justification that one has for a given proposition. (§12.3.3)

Epistemic reason: A reason for believing or not believing something of the sort that shows the would-be belief to be probable or improbable. (§2.3.2)

Epistemically justified: Rational in the sense of being supported by sufficient epistemic reasons, or being sufficiently likely to be correct. (§2.3.2)

Epistemology: The study of philosophical questions about knowledge, justified belief, and things like that. (Preface)

Equal Weight View: The view that, when epistemic peers disagree, each peer should give about equal weight to the other person's opinion as to his own. (§19.1, §19.2.1)

Equivalence Condition: The thesis that if *p* and *q* are logically equivalent, then whatever confirms *p* confirms *q*. (§14.1.3)

Ethical intuitionism: The view that there are objective, evaluative facts which are irreducible and knowable on the basis of ethical intuitions. (§15.7.1)

Evaluative proposition: A proposition that positively or negatively evaluates something; a proposition that entails that something is good or bad in some respect. (§15.1.1)

Evidentialism: See epistemic evidentialism; moral evidentialism.

Experimental group: In an experiment: The group of things, people, etc., that received the intervention whose effects one is trying to test. (§18.3.1) Contrasted with the control group.

Expressivism: The view that moral statements fail to express propositions and instead serve to give commands, express emotions, or express some other type of non-cognitive attitude. Also called "non-cognitivism". (§15.2.1)

Externalism: The negation of internalism. *See* access internalism; internal state internalism; semantic internalism.

External world: The world outside one's own mind. (§4.4.1)

External world skepticism: The view that we don't know, or aren't justified in believing, any contingent propositions about the external world. (§4.4.1, 8.2)

Fallibilism: The view that knowledge can be uncertain; i.e., one's knowing p is compatible with $\sim p$'s having a non-zero probability. (§15.7.7)

Falsifiable: Of a theory: Testable; capable of being proven false, or at least shown to be likely to be false, *if* it were false. (§8.3.4, §14.2.1)

Fideism: The view that we ought to believe religion based on blind faith, as opposed to evidence. (§16.1.3)

First-order evidence: Discussed especially in cases of disagreement: Evidence directly about the matter in controversy. (§19.1) Contrasted with second-order evidence.

Foundational belief: A belief whose justification does not depend upon reasons, i.e., does not depend upon being supported by other beliefs. (§4.5.1)

Foundational justification: Epistemic justification that does not depend upon reasons. (§4.5.1)

Foundational knowledge: Non-inferential knowledge. (§7.1.1)

Foundationalism: The view that some items of knowledge or justified belief do not require reasons, and that all other knowledge or justified belief is based upon those things. (§4.5.1)

Foundherentism: The view that our belief systems are justified by virtue of a small amount of foundational justification for certain beliefs, combined with coherence relations among the beliefs. (§5.4)

Frege-Geach problem: The problem for expressivists of explaining what moral statements mean when they are embedded within larger statements, in contexts where a proposition-expressing clause is normally required. (§15.2.1)

Fully grounded: Having no false beliefs in its evidential ancestry. Also known as having "no false lemmas". (§2.5.1)

Generality problem: The problem for reliabilists of specifying what counts as "the method" by which a belief was formed, esp. deciding how specific one's description of the method should be. (§2.5.2)

Genuine defeaters: In the defeasibility theory of knowledge: The sort of defeaters that prevent you from having knowledge; defeaters that aren't misleading. E.g., the fact that Tom has an identical twin genuinely defeats your belief that you saw Tom steal a book from the library. (§2.5.7)

G.E. Moore shift: See Moorean response.

Gestalt perception: A perception in which one perceives a complex scene or object as a unified whole, rather than a set of individual details. (§19.6.2)

Global skepticism: The view that we don't know, or aren't justified in believing, anything whatsoever. (§4.4.1)

Grue: The property of being green if observed before 2100 A.D. and blue otherwise. (§12.8.1)

Hallucination: A sensory experience that fails to represent any real object. (§9.3.2)

Hume's Law: See is/ought gap.

Idealism: The view that there are no material things existing independent of the mind; there are only minds and "ideas" in the mind. (§9.1) Contrasted with realism.

Illusion: A sensory experience that represents a real object but misrepresents one or more of its characteristics. (§9.3.2)

Inclusive fitness: In evolutionary biology: An organism's tendency to cause more copies of its genes to exist in the next generation. Includes both its tendency to directly reproduce and its tendency to promote the survival and reproduction of kin who are likely to carry the same genes. (§15.8.1)

Indirect awareness: A state of awareness of something that depends upon awareness of something else. (§9.2.2) Contrasted with direct awareness.

Indirect realism: The view that perception gives us direct awareness and non-inferential knowledge only of something dependent on our own minds (such as mental images), but that it also enables us to have *indirect* awareness and *inferential* knowledge of external objects. (§8.3.5) Contrasted with direct realism.

Induction: A type of non-deductive reasoning in which one generalizes from particular cases, i.e., the premises say something about certain objects, and the conclusion extends what was true of those objects to a wider class of objects. (§12.1.1)

Inductive skepticism: The view that inductive reasoning never provides any justification at all for its conclusions. (§12.1.2)

Inference to the best explanation: A type of non-deductive inference in which one infers that some theory is likely true because it provides the best explanation for some evidence that would be improbable if there were no explanation. (§12.7.1)

Inferential knowledge: Knowledge that is justified on the basis of other beliefs. (§7.1.1)

Infinitism: The view that justified beliefs are justified because they have an infinite series of supporting reasons available. (§4.2.1)

Initial plausibility: The degree to which a proposition seems correct, prior to argument. (§4.4.3)

Instrumental reasons: A species of practical reasons (reasons for action) that are based on the agent's actual desires or goals. (§15.1.2)

Intellectual appearances: Mental states in which something seems true to one on the basis of intellectual reflection, as opposed to observation. (§15.7.2)

Intentionality: The property of representing something; being *of* or *about* something. (§8.3.3)

Internalism: See access internalism; internal-state internalism; semantic internalism.

Internal-state internalism: The view that knowledge requires justification, and justification is entirely determined by one's internal mental states. (§3.3.1)

Intuition: A mental state in which something seems correct upon direct, intellectual reflection, as opposed to observation or reasoning. (§7.1.3)

Intuitionism: (a) In epistemology: The view that our synthetic, a priori knowledge is not innate but is acquired by a non-observational faculty which gives us intellectual insights. (§10.5.1) (b) In metaethics: ethical intuitionism.

Is/ought gap: The thesis that one cannot validly infer an evaluative conclusion from descriptive premises. (§15.3.1)

JTB: Short for "justified, true belief", which is the traditional definition of knowledge. (§2.4)

Justification skepticism: A form of skepticism that says we lack knowledge because our beliefs are not even justified. (§8.2.4) Contrasted with certainty skepticism.

Kantianism: The philosophical views of Immanuel Kant, which prominently include that there is synthetic, a priori knowledge; that this knowledge is explained by the fact that our mind imposes a certain structure on everything that we are aware of; and that as a result, we can only know things as they appear, not things in themselves. (§10.6.1) Contrasted with rationalism and empiricism.

KK Thesis: The thesis that if one knows that p, then one knows that one knows that p. (§6.1)

Knowledge by acquaintance: Being in a position to refer to something in virtue of having direct awareness of that thing. (§5.1.1) Contrasted with knowledge by description.

Knowledge by description: Being in a position to refer to something in virtue of understanding a description that uniquely applies to that thing. (§5.1.1) Contrasted with knowledge by acquaintance.

Kolmogorov axioms: The four basic axioms of probability theory, namely, (i) that the probability of anything is greater than or equal to 0, (ii) that the probability of any tautology is 1, (iii) that the probability of $(a \vee b) = P(a) + P(b)$ if a and b are mutually exclusive, and (iv) that the probability of $(a \& b) =$ the probability of a times the probability of b given a. (§12.3.2)

Law of large numbers: The principle of probability theory that if an outcome O has a probability p of occurring in circumstance C, then if C is repeated many times, the frequency with which O happens will tend to approximate p (with increasing accuracy and certainty as the number of trials increases). (§12.3.2)

Level confusion: A confusion between knowing p and knowing that one knows p, or between justifiedly believing p and justifiedly believing that one justifiedly believes p, or something like that. (§4.5.4)

Likelihood (of a hypothesis, h): The probability of e given h, $P(e|h)$. (Yes, this is a weird name for it.) (§12.5.4)

Likelihood ratio (of a hypothesis, h): The ratio of the likelihood of h to that of $\sim h$, i.e., $P(e|h)/P(e|\sim h)$. (§12.5.4)

Logical positivism: The view that there is no synthetic, a priori knowledge *and* that the meaning of a sentence is given by its verification conditions; the conjunction of empiricism and verificationism. (§10.3.1)

Logical probability: Probability construed as a logical property of a proposition or a logical relation between propositions; often glossed as the proportion of possible worlds in which a given proposition is true. (§12.3.3)

Matters of fact: In David Hume's philosophy: Propositions that are made true by mind-independent facts and therefore can only be known empirically; propositions whose expression is synthetic and that can be known only empirically. (§12.1.2) Contrasted with relations of ideas.

Meta-belief: A belief that is about one or more beliefs. (§4.5.4)

Meta-justification (for a belief): An argument that shows that the characteristic that (allegedly) makes a given belief justified is one that in general renders beliefs highly likely to be true. (§4.5.4)

Meta-knowledge: Knowledge about one's own knowledge. (Ch. 6)

Misleading defeaters: In the defeasibility theory of knowledge: The sort of defeaters that don't prevent you from having knowledge. E.g., in the case where Tom does not actually have a twin, the fact that Tom's mother *says* that Tom has an identical twin is a misleading defeater for your belief that you saw Tom steal a book from the library. There is no consensus on exactly what differentiates genuine and misleading defeaters. (§2.5.7)

Moorean response: A type of response to skepticism in which one argues that one of the skeptic's premises must be false since the skeptic's conclusion is so implausible. (§4.4.3)

Moral evaluation: Evaluation of an action in terms of whether it is morally right or wrong. (§15.1.2) Contrasted with epistemic and aesthetic evaluation.

Moral evidentialism: The view that it is morally wrong to hold epistemically unjustified attitudes. (§16.1.2)

Moral sense theory: The view that we have a faculty specifically designed for apprehending moral truths. (§15.8.3)

Naïve Comprehension Axiom: In set theory, the principle that for any meaningful predicate, there is a set containing all and only the things satisfying that predicate. Now known to be false since it generates Russell's Paradox. (§5.1.3)

Naïve realism: See direct realism.

Nativism: A form of rationalism that holds that some synthetic, a priori knowledge is innate. (§10.5.1) Contrasted with intuitionism.

Naturalistic Fallacy: (a) The mistake of trying to deduce an evaluative conclusion from purely descriptive premises. (b) The mistake of trying to define an evaluative term using only descriptive terms. (§§15.3.1-2)

Nearby possible worlds: Possible worlds (or ways that the world could have been) that are similar to the actual world (the way the world in fact is). (§2.5.4)

Necessary: Said of a proposition that could not have been false; the negation of it is impossible. (§8.1)

Negation: A sentence/proposition of the form "It's not the case that A". (§1.3.2)

Negative claim: A claim that something does not exist or does not have some property. (§14.3.1) Contrasted with positive claims.

Nicod's Criterion: The three-part thesis that (*i*) observation of an A that is B confirms [All A's are B], (*ii*) observation of an A that is non-B disconfirms [All A's are B], and (*iii*) observation of a non-A is irrelevant to [All A's are B]. (§14.1.3)

Nihilism: In metaethics: The view that nothing has any moral properties and thus all (positive) moral statements are false. (§15.2.2)

Non-cognitivism: See expressivism.

Non-deductive reasoning: A form of reasoning in which the premises are supposed to render the conclusion more likely but not to entail the conclusion. (§12.1.1)

Non-epistemic belief preferences: Desires to believe or not believe certain propositions for reasons independent of their truth or degree of epistemic justification. (§17.3.4)

Non-inferential knowledge: Knowledge that does not depend on other beliefs for its justification. (§7.1.1)

Null hypothesis: In a statistical study: The hypothesis that the variables being studied have no causal connection, and thus that any observed correlations are due to chance. (§18.3.1)

Objective Bayesianism: A form of Bayesianism that holds that there are significant constraints on rational initial credences beyond the Kolmogorov Axioms. (§12.5.1) Contrasted with subjective Bayesianism.

Observational study: A type of study in which the scientists do not have control over who does and does not receive the treatment whose effects are being evaluated. (§18.3.1)

Occam's Razor: The thesis that, other things being equal, the simplest explanation of some evidence is most likely to be correct. (§14.3.1)

Overconfidence: The common tendency to hold credences that are more extreme (closer to 0 or 1) than the evidence justifies. (§17.4.2)

Peer disagreement: Disagreement between epistemic peers. (§19.1)

Perceptual experience: See sensory experience.

Perspectival variation: The phenomenon whereby sensory appearances vary depending on the observer's relationship (esp. spatial relationship) to the object, as opposed to the object's intrinsic properties. (§9.3.1)

p-hacking: The practice of performing multiple statistical tests using different pairs of variables in order to find one that passes a test for statistical significance. (§18.3.3)

Phenomenal Conservatism: The theory that if it seems to one that *p*, and one has no reason for doubting that appearance, then one thereby has at least some justification for believing *p*. (§5.2.1)

Platonism: The view that universals exist necessarily. (§10.5.4)

Positive claim: A claim that something exists or has some property. (§14.3.1) Contrasted with negative claims.

Practical evaluation: Evaluation based on reasons for and against actions. (§15.1.2) Contrasted with epistemic and aesthetic evaluation.

Practical rationality: The property of being best supported by an agent's reasons for action. (§15.1.2)

Practical reason: A reason for performing or not performing an action. Includes prudential, instrumental, and moral reasons. (§2.3.2) Contrasted with epistemic reasons.

Predicate (of a proposition): The thing that a proposition attributes to its subject. E.g., in the proposition [John is bald], the predicate is baldness. Also used for a linguistic expression that is used to ascribe a predicate, e.g., the phrase "is bald". (§1.3.2)

Premise circularity: The fallacy that one commits when one infers a conclusion from itself. (§6.3.2)

Premises: The starting points of an argument; the statements that are used to support the rest. (§1.3.3)

Prima facie justification: Justification that is foundational and defeasible. (§5.2.1)

Primary qualities: Qualities of external objects, such as shape, size, mass, and number, that, according to some philosophers, are objective, in contrast to the "secondary qualities". (§10.6.3)

Principle of Charity: The idea that one should generally try to interpret other people as having mostly true, or at least reasonable, beliefs. (§13.3.3)

Principle of Indifference: The thesis that if there are no reasons for favoring either of two alternatives over the other, then they have equal epistemic probabilities. (§12.6.1)

Prior probability ("prior" for short): The probability that a proposition has prior to gathering evidence about it. (§12.5.4)

Propensity: A type of probability that indicates the strength of a causal tendency of some circumstance to produce some outcome. Used in indeterministic interpretations of quantum mechanics. (§12.3.3)

Proper function analysis: The theory that knowledge is true belief formed by a properly functioning, reliable, truth-directed faculty operating in the conditions it was designed for. (§2.5.3)

Proportional syllogism: A type of non-deductive reasoning in which one reasons from the fact that some event occurs in $x\%$ of cases to the conclusion that the event will occur in a given case (with $x\%$ confidence). E.g., if 90% of A's are B, and you know only that y is an A, you might infer (with 90% confidence) that y is B. (§12.4.1)

Propositional content: The proposition that a belief or other mental state is about. (§5.1.2)

Propositional justification: Epistemic justification that one has available for a given proposition. (§2.3.3)

Propositions: The sort of things that can be true or false, that can be asserted, believed, doubted, etc. (§1.3.1)

Prudential reasons: A species of practical reasons (reasons for action) that are based on self-interest. (§15.1.2)

Publication bias: The phenomenon whereby scientific studies are more likely to be published if they report statistically significant results. (§18.3.3)

p-value: In a statistical study: The probability of obtaining a result of the size observed, given the null hypothesis. (§18.3.1)

Randomized, controlled trial: A kind of experiment in which there is a control group and an experimental group, and the people/things being tested are randomly assigned to either the control or the experimental group. (§18.3.1)

Rational disagreement: A disagreement in which both parties are rational in sticking to their views. (§19.3.1)

Rationalism: The view that there is synthetic, a priori knowledge, or: that there is substantive knowledge of the world that does not depend on observation for its justification. (§10.5.1) Contrasted with empiricism and Kantianism.

Real World Hypothesis: The "hypothesis" that one is perceiving the world normally. (§8.3.4) Contrasted with the brain-in-a-vat hypothesis.

Realism: (a) In general: The view that some class of phenomena of philosophical interest exists objectively and is knowable. (b) In philosophy of perception: The view that external objects exist objectively and can be known through perception. (§8.3.5) *See also:* direct realism, indirect realism.

Rebutting defeater: A defeater for a proposition, *p*, which works by supporting ~*p*. (§4.5.1)

Regress argument: (a) For skepticism: The argument that we can't know (or have justification for believing) anything because we cannot base knowledge/justified belief on something that we have no reason for, nor on circular reasoning, nor on an infinite regress of reasons. *See also:* Agrippa's trilemma. (§4.4.1) (b) For foundationalism: The argument that our knowledge (or justified beliefs) must be based on things that are self-evident, or that we do not need reasons for, since we can't have an infinite regress and we can't rely on circular reasoning. (§4.5.2)

Relations of ideas: In David Hume's philosophy: Propositions that are made true by the meanings of words or the relationships of concepts and therefore can be known a priori, e.g., [All squares have four sides]; propositions whose expression is analytic and that can be known a priori. (§12.1.2) Contrasted with matters of fact.

Relevant alternatives (to a proposition): Alternatives that need to be ruled out in order for one to know a given proposition; commonly understood to be the alternatives that could fairly easily have been realized. The Relevant Alternatives Analysis holds that knowledge is true belief supported by evidence that rules out all the relevant alternatives, where this is a proper subset of the logically possible alternatives. (§2.5.6)

Reliabilism: Roughly, the view that knowledge is true belief formed by a reliable method, i.e., a method that if used many times would tend to generate true beliefs a great majority of the time. (§2.5.2)

Representationalism: See indirect realism.

Right Reasons View: The view that the rational response to a case of peer disagreement is for the party who *in fact* made a mistake to change his view and the party with the correct view to remain steadfast. (§19.1, §19.4.1)

Rule circularity: The alleged mistake of using a form of inference in reasoning to the conclusion that that form of inference is good. (§6.3.2)

Russell's Paradox: The paradox that results from the notion of the set of all sets that don't contain themselves: This set must contain itself if and only if it doesn't contain itself. (§5.1.3)

Safety: Where S believes that p, this belief is "safe" if and only if p is true in all the nearby worlds in which S believes p; that is, S would not easily have been wrong in believing p. The safety condition on knowledge says that S knows p only if S's belief that p is safe. (§2.5.5)

Scientific realism: The view that science reveals to us important truths about mind-independent reality. (§14.4)

Secondary qualities: Observable qualities of external objects (such as color, taste, smell, sound, and temperature) that, according to some philosophers, are not entirely objective but in some way depend upon our sensory faculties; sometimes thought to be illusory, or to be dispositions to produce certain sensations in us, or to be constituted by collections of primary qualities that give rise to said dispositions. (§10.6.3) Contrasted with primary qualities.

Second-order evidence: Discussed especially in cases of disagreement: Evidence about who is more reliable, which assessment of the evidence is more likely to be correct, and the like, as opposed to evidence directly about the matter in controversy. (§19.1) Contrasted with first-order evidence.

Second-order knowledge: See meta-knowledge.

Seeming: The mental state one is in when it seems to one that something is the case. Also called an "appearance". (§5.2.1)

Semantic externalism: The view that what one's mental states represent depends in part on factors external to one's mind. (§8.3.3) Contrasted with semantic internalism.

Semantic internalism: The view that what one's mental states represent depends only on purely internal features of one's mental states. (§8.3.3) Contrasted with semantic externalism.

Sensitivity: Where S believes that p, this belief is "sensitive" if and only if, if p were false, S would not believe p. The sensitivity condition on knowledge says that you know p only if your belief that p is sensitive. (§2.5.4)

Sensory experience: The purely internal mental state that one has during perception or hallucination; a state of seemingly perceiving something. (§9.2.1)

Skeptical scenario: A scenario in which everything would appear to you as it presently does but most of your beliefs would be mistaken. (§8.2)

Skepticism: A philosophical theory according to which we don't know many of the things we normally think we know. (§4.4.1, §9.1) *See also* external world skepticism, global skepticism, certainty skepticism, justification skepticism.

Sound: Of an argument: Valid *and* having all true premises. (§1.3.3)

Statistically significant: Of an experimental result: Having a low p-value, typically either <0.05 or <0.01. (§18.3.1)

Steadfast View: The view that it is epistemically permissible to stick with your original view when you learn that an epistemic peer disagrees with you. (§19.1, §19.3.1)

Subject (of a mental state): The being who has a given mental state. (§1.4)

Subject (of a proposition): The thing that a proposition is about. E.g., in the proposition [John is bald], the subject is John. (§1.3.2)

Subject factors: In the contextualist view of knowledge: Features of a potential knower's situation that might affect whether that person counts as "knowing", including the truth of their belief, their justification, etc. (§3.1.2) Contrasted with attributor factors.

Subjective Bayesianism: A form of Bayesianism that holds that any set of initial credences that satisfies the Kolmogorov Axioms (with at most minor additions) is rational. (§12.5.1) Contrasted with objective Bayesianism.

Subjective probability: A type of probability that indicates a person's degree of confidence in a proposition; credence. (§12.3.3)

Synthetic: Of a sentence: Not true by definition; the negation of a synthetic sentence is consistent. (§10.1.2) Contrasted with analytic statements.

Testimony: The act of one person's telling someone else something. (Ch. 13)

Total Evidence View: The view that the rational response to peer disagreement is the outcome of a weighing of both first-order and second-order evidence. (§19.1, §19.5.1)

Tracking analysis: The theory that knowledge is true belief formed in such a way that if the proposition were false, one would not have believed it, and if it were true, one would have believed it. (§2.5.4)

Track-record argument: A type of epistemic circularity in which one forms a number of beliefs using some method M, introspectively observes the content of those beliefs, then concludes that method M has gotten one true beliefs on all these occasions and therefore is likely reliable. (§6.3.3)

Undercutting defeater: A defeater for a proposition, p, which works by casting doubt on the reliability of one's method of forming the belief that p. (§4.5.1)

Underdetermination: In science: The phenomenon whereby the empirical data can be explained by more than one theory. (§14.4.1)

Uniformity Principle: The principle that unobserved things tend to resemble observed things. (§12.1.2)

Valid: Of an argument: Such that the premises could not all be true while the conclusion was false. (§1.3.3)

Verification criterion of meaning: See verificationism.

Verificationism: The view that the meaning of a sentence is given by its verification conditions; hence, if there cannot be evidence for or against a particular statement, then that statement is meaningless. (§10.3.1)

Weak foundationalism: See foundherentism.

Printed in Great Britain
by Amazon